Project-Based
Software Engineering

Project-Based Software Engineering
An Object-Oriented Approach

Evelyn Stiller
Plymouth State College
Plymouth, New Hampshire

Cathie LeBlanc
Plymouth State College
Plymouth, New Hampshire

Addison Wesley

Boston San Francisco New York
London Toronto Sydney Tokyo Singapore Madrid
Mexico City Munich Paris Cape Town Hong Kong Montreal

Senior Acquisitions Editor: Maite Suarez-Rivas
Project Editor: Katherine Harutunian
Executive Marketing Manager: Michael Hirsch
Production Services: P.M. Gordon Associates, Inc.
Copyeditor: Peter Reinhart
Technical Art: John Sanderson/Horizon Design
Composition: Windfall Software
Text Design: Glenna Collett
Cover Design: Gina Hagen
Cover Illustration: Susan Cyr
Prepress and Manufacturing: Caroline Fell

Access the latest information about Addison-Wesley titles from our World Wide Web site: http://www.aw.com/cs

The programs and applications presented in this book have been included for their instructional value. They have been tested with care, but are not guaranteed for any particular purpose. The publisher does not offer any warranties or representations, nor does it accept any liabilities with respect to the programs or applications.

Library of Congress Cataloging-in-Publication Data

Stiller, Evelyn.
    Project-based software engineering: an object-oriented approach / Evelyn Stiller, Cathie LeBlanc.
    p. cm.
    ISBN 0-201-74225-X (alk. paper)
    1. Software engineering. 2. Object-oriented methods (Computer science) I. LeBlanc, Cathie. II. Title.
QA76.758.S75 2001
005.1'17–dc21
                                                2001034333

2 3 4 5 6 7 8 9 10—CRS—04 03 02 01

Contents

CHAPTER **4**   **Product Design**   **111**

CHAPTER 5   Class Design   163

CHAPTER **8**   **Testing**   **263**

Preface

In teaching software engineering, experience has shown us that students are not convinced of the benefits of using software engineering techniques until they experience the benefits themselves. Completing a semester-long project is the most effective way of convincing students that software engineering is critical to their professional development. The software engineering course offered at Plymouth State College is therefore a very practical, hands-on course focused on the development of object-oriented software. Through the years, however, we became frustrated with the lack of textbooks appropriate for such a course. The majority of the available texts focus on the theoretical aspects of software engineering at the expense of its practical aspects. The texts that are project-based do not focus on the object-oriented paradigm. We wrote this textbook to fill this market gap.

This textbook focuses on actually performing software engineering. Theoretical concepts and terminology are introduced when they are necessary for successful software development. Although we recognize that there are a very large number of ways to develop software, we focus on a particular object-oriented software development methodology applied to a class project.

Having students engage in this semester-long team project also allows them to experience professional collaboration, which they seem to enjoy. Selecting an appropriate project is the most critical and most difficult aspect of teaching a project-based software engineering course. The project must be complex enough to engage a software development team of three to five students and yet be readily completed in fifteen weeks. More challenging than achieving proper scope is finding a project that interests and excites the students. To this end, we have provided a class project in the text. This project has been tested by Plymouth State College students and was successfully and enthusiastically implemented by a team of four students with varying programming and analytical skills.

This text is targeted to undergraduate computer science majors with little or no theoretical computer science in their background. The text is also written in a manner that is as programming language independent as possible. When language details are unavoidable, we have chosen Java as the programming language. We do not mean this text to be a reference manual of software engineering techniques and procedures. Instead, we provide a particular development methodology that will allow the completion of a significant software project over the course of a fifteen-week semester.

Since we assume the students will complete a project over the course of the semester, we have included the semester schedule for our course in Chapter 2. This schedule allows the project to begin swiftly at the start of the semester. Because we want students to experience as much of the software development methodology as possible, certain topics receive a less than comprehensive treatment. In particular, eliciting functional requirements from discussions with nontechnical users is a difficult task that requires much experience to accomplish successfully. Thus, we have presumed that the requirements will have been nearly completed by the instructor prior to the beginning of the semester.

To reinforce the practicality of the text, we also provide two running case studies. These are presented in a manner that models the development of the semester-long project. Sample deliverables are presented as part of the case studies to give students examples of the types of materials they are expected to deliver during the life cycle of their project.

Another important characteristic of this text is that it focuses on the object-oriented software development paradigm almost exclusively. Although we see the object-oriented approach as a logical extension of previous industry-adopted paradigms, this text is structured for an object-oriented project conceptualization, analysis, design, and implementation. A historical overview of software engineering techniques is presented to introduce students to the precursors to the object-oriented paradigm.

Although the long-enduring software crisis is not presented as the exclusive motivation for using software engineering techniques, a series of software development horror stories is included in the text so that students can see the results of ignoring various aspects of software engineering. Rather than addressing these stories as introductory material, they are included later in the text, so that there is less delay in getting to chapters needed to start the software engineering project.

In introducing the techniques that comprise the object-oriented paradigm, the Unified Modeling Language (UML) is used to model the software. Since UML is extremely large and intimidating, a subset of the notation is introduced on an "as-needed" basis. This book is not intended to serve as a comprehensive reference on UML. Many such references exist. Instead, UML is used as a tool in this text, much as it is used as a tool in the development of "real-world" software.

Pedagogical Features

- Each chapter begins with a list of important concepts that will be covered in the chapter.
- A class project that has been tested on our students runs throughout the text. The project is large enough for three to five students to complete over the course of a semester. Each chapter includes a set of activities that must be carried out in order to complete the class project. A specification of the deliverables for each part of the project is also included with the activities.
- Although the text includes a class project, the text is written so that an instructor can simply ignore the class project sections. If the instructor chooses to ignore the class project, a different project (or set of projects) can be substituted.
- Review questions are included at the end of each chapter. These exercises allow students additional practice with each of the topics covered in the book. They vary in complexity and difficulty.
- Exercises are included throughout each chapter. These exercises are most often presented as thought experiments and in most cases can be completed in class or out of class as deemed appropriate by the instructor.
- Unified Modeling Language is presented only when needed. When a particular modeling technique is needed for a particular step in the development methodology, the technique is described and examples are given. Through this approach, a subset of UML is presented.
- Two case studies run through the text. The first case study begins early in the text and is developed as the various steps in the methodology are presented. The second case study begins in Chapter 6, which acts as a review of the analysis and design phases of the development methodology. This second case study is then carried through the remainder of the text.
- Summary boxes are presented to allow a review of the development methodology at a quick glance.
- The chapters are organized so that students can realistically complete the class project in a single semester. For example, during the last four weeks of the class, while the students are engaged in coding and testing their projects and the topics of implementation and testing have already been covered, the text addresses topics such as project management, risk management, design patterns, and software development horror stories.
- Projects and schedules that have actually been tested in the classroom are included in the text.
- The last chapter of the text turns the tables on the students, requiring them to reflect on their experiences with the class project. It is entirely possible that the experience of some project development teams may be less successful than

others, so the discussion allows the students to review their course of action and suggest improvements. The final chapter guides students through a formal and professional presentation of their projects to the instructor and other classmates.

Supplements and Instructor Materials

Support materials are available to instructors adopting this textbook for classroom use and include the following:

- PowerPoint slides for each figure in the book
- PowerPoint lecture slides for each chapter
- Solutions for the *Questions for Review* sections
- Sample solutions or hints to spark discussion for the exercises embedded in each chapter
- A sample set of deliverables for the embedded class project
- Materials for two alternate class projects
- Source code for the Game2D case study.

Please check online information for this book at www.aw.com/cssupport for more information on obtaining these supplements.

In addition to these resources, we anticipate publishing a student supplement every two years that contains materials and exercises relevant for two different class projects.

Class Project

Instructors are encouraged to substitute their own projects, or an alternate project that has been provided as supplemental instructor material, for the specific class project included in the text. Each chapter that pertains to the development of the class project contains a section specifying class project-related goals and objectives. These sections have been written in a generic manner and should pertain to an alternate project as well as the project provided in the textbook.

There are a few sections of the book that address the included class project specifically. These sections have been included because the sample project serves as a particularly good example to illustrate a few of the design objectives discussed in the text. In order to understand these sections, students do not need to be familiar with the details of the included project, but rather simply need understand the idea of playing a multi-player game over the Internet. The examples address the sequence events comprising initiating such a multi-player game or making a board game-type move.

The following sections contain specific references to the class project:

- Section 1.10 contains the requirements specification. You may substitute an alternate project description here. This section should be skipped if an alternate project is being used.
- Section 2.2.2 illustrates a sample informal scenario, which can be easily understood by anyone familiar with common board games. We recommend using this example even if another class project is being used.
- Section 4.9 illustrates modeling the interprocess communication in the sample class project. This illustration can be easily understood by someone who is familiar with any multi-player, Internet-based game, so we recommend its use by those using an alternate class project.

Acknowledgments

Thanks to Maite Suarez-Rivas and Katherine Haruntunian from Addison Wesley for the incredibly positive support in the writing of this text. Jody Girouard was instrumental in the development of materials for instructors adopting the textbook as well as in providing feedback about the book from a student's perspective. John Girouard, Mark Henwood, Nick Rago, and David Sleeper were students in the first software engineering course that used the Use Case Centered Development methodology. They implemented *Galaxy Sleuth* and provided tremendous feedback about the methodology. Liz Johnson from Xavier University used an early version of the text in her software engineering class and helped us understand where our writing was unclear. Finally, numerous reviewers provided us with valuable feedback on the manuscript as it progressed. Some of these reviewers remain anonymous and we thank them for their work. The following reviewers examined later versions of the manuscript and helped us to tighten up our prose to provide better explanations:

Michael Beeson, San Jose State University
Jorge L. Diaz-Herrera, Southern Polytechnic State University
Jozo Dujmovic, San Francisco State University
Mohamed Fayad, University of Nebraska, Lincoln
J. W. Fendrich, Illinois State University
J. A. "Drew" Hamilton, Naval Postgraduate School
Alex Iskold, New York University
Jonathan Maletic, University of Memphis
Michael McCracken, Georgia Institute of Technology
Fatma Mili, Oakland University
Robert Noonan, College of William and Mary

Srini Ramaswamy, Tennessee Technological University
Steve Roach, University of Texas, El Paso
Don Shafer, Athens Group, Inc.
Bill Shay, University of Wisconsin, Green Bay
James E. Tomayko, Carnegie Mellon University
David Umphress, Auburn University
Shon Vick, University of Maryland, Baltimore County
Linda Werner, University of California, Santa Cruz
Janusz Zalewski, University of Central Florida

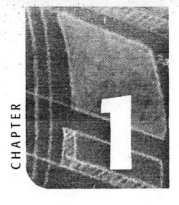

Introduction to Software Engineering

 Key Concepts

The following is a list of key concepts and skills for this chapter.

- Sources of complexity in developing software
- Why and how software development projects fail
- Why interpersonal communication is difficult
- Why maintenance requires so many human resources
- Problem conceptualization
- Problem characterization
- Structured programming

- Functional decomposition
- Levels of abstraction
- Structured analysis and design
- Abstract data types
- Inheritance
- Data modeling
- Elements of a software development paradigm
- Objectives of a software development paradigm

 Why Engineer Software?

Imagine that you have graduated from college and are working for an international software development company. You are on an airplane, bound for a customer site across the country. The lights are low in the cabin, and most of your fellow passengers are napping. It is dark outside, and the visibility is very poor because of the dense clouds. Suddenly, the plane veers to the left, and out of nowhere you see the wing of another aircraft as it passes perilously close to the wing of your plane.

The sudden movement of the plane wakes most of the passengers, and suddenly the cabin is loud with talk. The airline personnel either do not know or will not say what happened. When you finally land an hour and a half later, you feel lucky and wonder if you'll ever feel safe enough to fly again.

As far as we know, nothing like the preceding scenario has happened recently. We feel that it is really luck rather than good planning that has prevented such incidents. In fact, during one week in early December 1998, three separate incidents in which computer outages caused planes to fly too close to each other were reported [17]. The system that currently controls air traffic in much of the airspace over the United States is more than 25 years old. The software is horrendously outdated, able to handle only a fraction of the traffic expected by the year 2003 [72]. The software also runs on hardware that is 25 years old, for which replacement parts are increasingly difficult to find. Incidents of this system going down are becoming increasingly common [33]. The system needs to be replaced.

Replacing the air traffic control system has been a high priority for the Federal Aviation Administration (FAA) since the early 1980s. The contract for replacing the system was awarded to IBM Federal Systems in 1989, had a deadline of 2001, and bore an estimated price tag of $2.5 billion [21]. This software project represented one of the most complex undertaken, with highly stringent requirements. For example, the air traffic control system must have total integrity and has to be available seven days a week, 24 hours a day with no downtime even for upgrades or regular maintenance. Any corruption of data could cause huge loss of life, and any downtime would cause worldwide travel delays and potential danger. The response time of the system can be no more than 2 or 3 seconds. In addition, the system must be designed in such a way as to allow private pilots and owners of small planes to continue to use their old equipment and to allow the software to be ported to new hardware as advances are made [30].

The air traffic control system upgrade is included in this textbook as a horror story, an example of software development that is out of control. When IBM was awarded the contract, the majority of the cost of the system came from software with only about $80,000 for hardware [78]. IBM Federal Systems, the IBM subsidiary responsible for the contract, was sold to Loral Corporation in 1993 [7], and by 1994, $2.3 billion had already been spent on the system, without a single piece of the system having been delivered. By 1994, the estimate for a completed system had risen to $5 billion [21]. In late 1994, FAA Administrator David Hinson undertook a major investigation of the fiasco. During the investigation, Hinson explained that the problems with the system were the result of an overly ambitious development and implementation plan (including cost and schedule estimates), especially given the complexity of the software system, inadequate oversight of IBM's performance, especially in the early stages of development, and finally, the fact that the FAA was indecisive about some of the basic requirements of the system [3]. In addition, the FAA and contractor representatives said that technology had evolved faster than their ability to use it [3]. As a result of this investigation, the FAA canceled or modified four major portions of the system [63]. Realizing that many travelers were in danger because of the computer dinosaur that is the current air traffic control system, the FAA ordered a stopgap system to be developed by Formation, a software developer located in Moorestown, New Jersey [33]. Loral was bought by Lockheed Martin in January 1996 [71]. Lockheed Martin then lost a major portion of the contract to Raytheon in September 1996 [72].

This story has not played out. We do not yet know whether a reliable air traffic control system will result from the mess we have described. Solving complex problems is difficult, but it is not impossible. Software engineering, the subject of this textbook, is one way to reduce the chance that the software development process will turn into a labyrinth of wrong turns and wasted resources.

The state of software development over the last three decades has been described as a societal affliction [88]. Large-scale systems development has been compared to dinosaurs being pulled into a tar pit [18]. Such descriptions suggest that large-scale software development, despite some successes, has a long history of painful failure. Some of the successes include the impressive sophistication of today's office applications. For every successful software development project, however, there are many failed initiatives that pass unnoticed into oblivion. Such failures are rarely brought to the attention of the general public because the companies that own the failures want to avoid negative publicity. In general, the development of large-scale software is risky business [9].

The central question is, Why do so many software development projects fail? The single-word answer is **complexity**. Many of these software projects are extraordinarily complex on a number of planes. For example, the application domain, which is the area of expertise in which the software will operate, is frequently complex. In addition, the people who understand the application domain are probably not the people who will actually be creating the software. These domain experts must, therefore, communicate their needs to the technical staff. After the complexity of understanding the problem and the needs of the future users of the software has been dealt with, the software must be created. Anyone who has ever written a program knows that creating software that actually accomplishes a particular task is a complicated process. Finally, many of the software development projects that are undertaken are very large, too large, in fact, to be completed by a single person. The technical staff, therefore, must divide the development task into manageable modules, and once these pieces have been created, the staff must assemble the pieces so that they work as a coordinated whole. This process of breaking a large project into pieces to be created by a variety of individuals and then ensuring that the pieces work together is another source of complexity in the software development process.

Consider for a moment the task of creating a genetic information repository. You, as a technical person creating the software to manage this repository, are likely to be at most superficially familiar with all the possible forms of and uses for genetic information. Where do you begin in your information-gathering process? Can you simply store genetic sequences associated with an organism? Does it matter what sort of molecule is being sequenced? How do you represent a three-dimensional molecule? Will the scientists want to manipulate genetic information in three dimensions? There are probably a thousand other questions that arise as you think about the task with which you are faced.

In order for your software to be successful, you must speak to someone who knows more about such questions, someone who is an expert in the domain of genetics. You begin your information-gathering process by talking to the lead geneticist, and you soon realize that the geneticist has a vocabulary very different from your own. When she attempts to explain the relevant characterizations of tertiary molecular structure, you are unfamiliar with much of the vocabulary. When you encourage her to characterize the specific system she has in mind, she is unable to articulate the system in terms that are meaningful to you. This incompatibility between distinct vocabularies in different areas of expertise is called **impedance mismatch** [14]. One does not have to work in a scientific field to experience impedance mismatch. Many industries have developed their own vocabularies.

The ambiguity inherent in spoken and written language adds another level of complexity to the communication problem between the domain expert and the technical person creating the software. For example, perhaps the lead geneticist expressed the following system need: "Render the tertiary structure on the computer screen in such a way that the scientists can maneuver around the graphic representation." You may believe you understand this request, and therefore you create the software so that if the molecule does not fit on a single screen, the user can scroll around to look at parts of the molecule that are off the edges of the screen. The geneticist, however, has used a piece of software in the past that allows the user to generate a three-dimensional view from within the internal folds in the molecule. She would like this new software to have that same capability. The real issue complicating interpersonal communication is that we all possess different **background knowledge**, which leads us to interpret the same phrase in different ways based on our past experiences.

Future users, who may or may not be domain experts, should be involved at every stage of the development of the system. plan of A software development plan that allows the end users to evaluate the system as it is being developed is essential. Unfortunately, many in the software industry believe that the users should be solicited for knowledge only in the early stages of the development of a system and then at system completion. Such an attitude has very likely led to the failure of many software development projects.

When creating software, complexity is also inherent in the application itself. Most software development projects require the efforts of several developers to bring the project to completion on time. These concerns mean that in order to conceptualize a system of moderate size consistently and efficiently, we will need a mechanism for writing down the structure and communicating that structure among several people. This representation of the system should reduce the system's complexity in our minds and facilitate communication between collaborating individuals, including the domain experts and end users. See Summary Points box 1.1.

For much of this chapter, we have been talking about software development projects that fail. The phrase **software failure** itself merits clarification. Software can fail in a number of ways.

- The software development process can result in no functioning software.
- If functioning software results from the software development process, it may not adequately address the requirements of the domain experts or the needs of the users. The software may simply not do what it is expected to do.
- The resulting software may seem to meet the requirements, but the underlying computations may be incorrect. The results of the software may be wrong.
- The software may meet user requirements and the calculations may be correct, but the software may malfunction as a result of user error. Correct usage of the software may not be intuitive or make sense to the users.
- The software may do everything the users require but be unusable because response time is too slow.

Another major concern for the software industry is the amount of human effort dedicated to **maintenance**. A software system that is successfully developed will be in use for a long period of time. The system must be periodically modified to accommodate the changing needs of the organization using the system, to enhance its functionality, and to repair defects. The amount of human effort dedicated to maintaining software as compared to creating new software is rather large [9].

SUMMARY POINTS 1.1

Why Software Can Be Difficult to Create

1. Complex application domain.
2. Difficulty for people with different background knowledge and vocabularies to communicate effectively.
3. Ambiguity of natural language.
4. Difficulty of mentally grasping the details of large development projects.

Since maintaining software systems is inevitable and, in fact, desirable, one of the main goals of software engineering is to reduce the amount of effort such maintenance requires. Well-structured systems that are built using modular components require less effort to maintain because an individual module or group of modules can be modified without affecting other functions of the system. As modifications are made, the source for new errors is then localized to at most a few modules. In addition, if software is written in a modular manner, then even if a certain type of task is required to be performed in many places in the software, there will be only one piece of code, called from many places, for that task. When that one module is modified, then the same change occurs throughout the system. This utilization of the same code from many places in system is called **code reuse**. The idea behind code reuse is to create general-purpose modules that can play multiple roles in the system.

Figure 1.1 shows a scenario typical in industry in which too many technical personnel are involved in maintaining poorly structured systems, leaving insufficient numbers of people engaged in developing new systems.

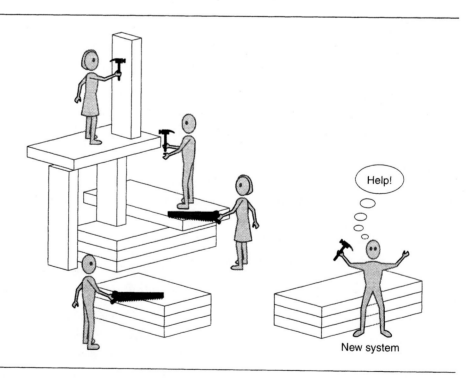

FIGURE 1.1 Maintenance Out of Control

So, the software industry is faced with a very complex task when new software is to be developed. Multimillion-dollar software development initiatives far too frequently produce nothing of value. What can we do about it? The simple single-word response is **organization**. We can conquer the complexity of the software development process by being organized. The basic objective of software engineering is to control the development process and produce a well-structured, accurate software solution. The techniques we use in developing software and getting organized define our software development **paradigm**.

Contemplate the process of building a toolshed with a group of four friends. What would happen if you simply asked your friends to pick up tools and lumber and start hammering and sawing until a toolshed emerges? How would you go about ensuring that a reliable, well-built, and sturdy shed results from the process?

EXERCISE 1.1

Elements of a Software Development Paradigm

A software development paradigm is a set of techniques used to guide the software development process. On a grand scale, one may view software development processes as having the following three components:

- Conceptualization
- Representation
- Implementation

Ideally, the three components will be compatible, resulting in a smooth development process. It is possible, however, to create successful, useful software if you use a representation from one paradigm for the project and an implementation of the project from another paradigm. Such paradigm shifting adds an additional layer of complexity to a process that, as we have already seen, is complex enough. To eliminate this unnecessary level of complexity, all three components should be compatible. We will now examine each of the components in detail.

1.3.1 Project Conceptualization

The **conceptualization** of the project addresses how the software developer thinks about the problem to be solved. The kinds of elements used to think about

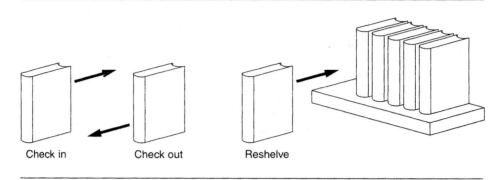

Check in   Check out   Reshelve

FIGURE 1.2 Process-Oriented Conceptualization of a Book-Tracking System

and discuss the system to be programmed determine its conceptualization. For example, processes (functions, procedures, and subprograms) are used to characterize systems under a process-oriented paradigm. A process-oriented characterization of a book-tracking system for a library is illustrated in Figure 1.2. The processes of the system are expressed in terms like *check out*, *check in*, and *reshelve*. These elements represent the activities of the system and correspond to the real-world activities to be undertaken by users of the system.

In contrast, an object-oriented conceptualization for the same system must identify the objects (or things) and ideas that make up the system. In this conceptualization, we are concerned with books, shelves, patrons, and librarians and the relationships among these things. Figure 1.3 illustrates this conceptualization. For example, patrons check books out and in. In this conceptualization, *check out* and *check in* are relationships that exist between the book objects and the patron objects. Each object is related to other objects in the conceptualization through some relationship.

The conceptualization of a system describes the mental constructs that the developers use to organize their thoughts and discussions of the project. When discussing software systems, objects tend to be more intuitive than processes for most people, whether they are technical personnel or domain experts [57]. Because an efficient software development paradigm seeks a smooth progression from one stage of development to the next, using a conceptualization that translates to a form that domain experts can readily understand and assist in evaluating is desirable. This easy translation allows the future users of the system to be more readily involved in the creation of the system.

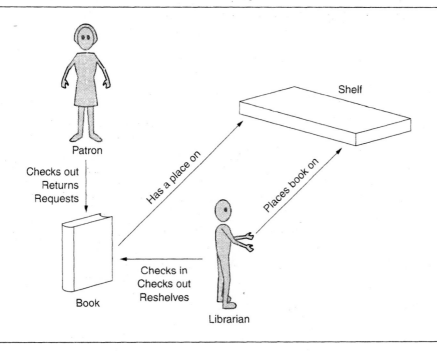

FIGURE 1.3 Object-Oriented Conceptualization of a Book-Tracking System

How would you conceptualize the process of building a toolshed in object-oriented **EXERCISE 1.2**
terms versus process-oriented terms? Is there a difference? Why or why not? Is a
software system that manages the building of toolsheds any different? Why or why
not?

1.3.2 Project Representation

The project conceptualization must be written down in some manner in order to
be communicated from one person to another. The writing down of the project
conceptualization is the **representation** of the project that will be used in the software development paradigm. The representation must convey what the project is
all about in an efficient, unambiguous manner. When creating such a representation, we agree on a set of rules for how to represent various pieces of the project.
These rules are called the **notation** that we are using for our representation. All
major software development paradigms have several notations for representing
software systems. The notations specify a view of the software to be developed.

Software development paradigms popular in industry use graphic representations to communicate the project conceptualization. For example, a notation for the process-oriented paradigm may use ovals to represent processes and directed edges (arrows) to represent data flow among the processes. A notation for the object-oriented paradigm, in contrast, may use rectangles to represent objects and directed edges to represent the relationships among the objects.

Why is notation so important to software development? One fundamental objective of a notation is to represent the system in a manner that is unambiguous and unaffected by the background knowledge of the person viewing the characterization. The notation should ideally result in a representation of the system that means the same thing to the domain expert as it does to the technical personnel. The topic of notation will be discussed in further detail in the next chapter.

EXERCISE 1.3   In order to ensure an orderly process of toolshed construction, what form would the instructions given to the builders take? How would you ensure that everyone interprets the instructions in the same manner?

1.3.3 Project Implementation

Project **implementation** addresses how the source code that will make up the software is structured. All programming languages support some mechanism for creating units of programming language instructions. These units are the modules that will work together in the final software system to meet the needs of the users. Recall from the previous section that modularity is a desirable feature in well-structured software systems. Before the object-oriented paradigm became popular, most industrial systems were structured around the process-oriented paradigm. In contrast to process-oriented systems, an object-oriented system uses classes (object skeletons) as its mechanism for modularity. Ideally, the mechanisms for modularity in the project implementation are the same as the elements that comprised the project conceptualization and representation. If the conceptualization and representation of the project are expressed in terms of objects, it makes sense to use an object-oriented language to implement the project.

 ## A Brief History of Software Engineering Techniques

Historically, the process-oriented paradigm was the paradigm of choice in industry. Recently, more projects have been developed in an object-oriented manner.

Although many regard the adoption of the object-oriented paradigm as a radical departure from previous techniques, we view this adoption as a logical continuation of the software engineering techniques that precede it. Thus, we feel that understanding software engineering techniques that came before the advent of the object-oriented paradigm is important.

Figure 1.4 places software engineering techniques in the context of other developments in the computer industry. We can divide the costs of software development into two parts: the costs of the hardware on which the software will run and the costs of the software developer salaries. As the development costs devoted to hardware decreased, the costs devoted to salaries increased. As the relationship between these costs inverted, tools were developed to make the human effort in software development more efficient. These tools became increasingly complex as efforts were made to automate some of the tedious tasks in software development. As the tools became more complex, the applications created by these tools became more sophisticated and took on more and more of the tasks of everyday life. As these applications proliferated, society became more dependent on these applications. The current state of affairs is that society depends on complex software applications

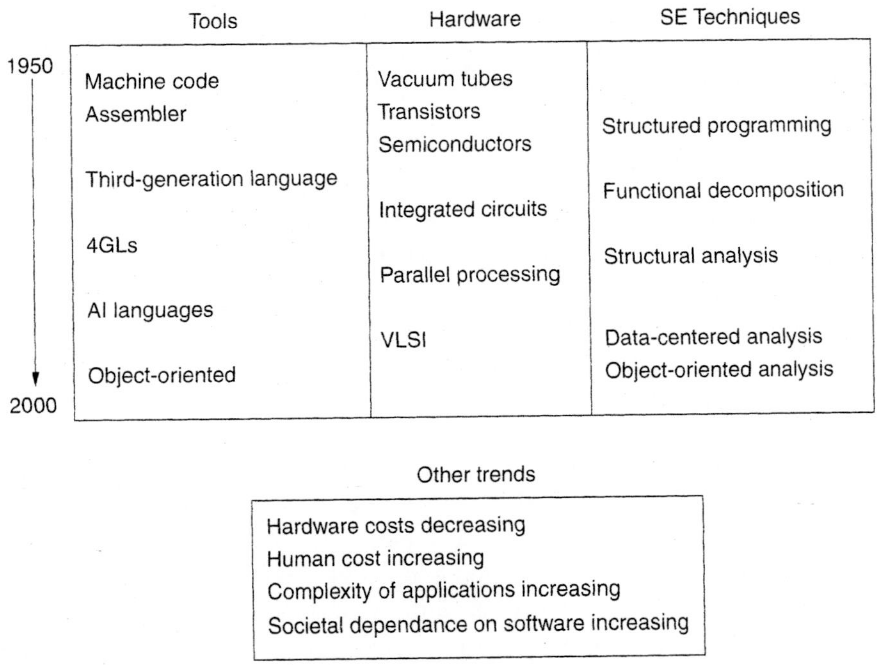

	Tools	Hardware	SE Techniques
1950	Machine code Assembler	Vacuum tubes Transistors Semiconductors	Structured programming
	Third-generation language	Integrated circuits	Functional decomposition
	4GLs	Parallel processing	Structural analysis
	AI languages	VLSI	Data-centered analysis
2000	Object-oriented		Object-oriented analysis

Other trends

Hardware costs decreasing
Human cost increasing
Complexity of applications increasing
Societal dependance on software increasing

FIGURE 1.4 General Trends in the Computer Industry

to function properly. The development of these complex applications, however, is prone to failure, for reasons discussed earlier in this chapter. For society to function properly, the development of new software applications must proceed in a manner that is most likely to result in successful, useful software.

1.4.1 Structured Programming

With the advent of **structured programming** in the late 1960s, the *goto* statement was officially banished from software [32]. The motivation for this banishment was to improve source-code structure and to improve the robustness and reliability of the resulting system. The use of the *goto* statement leads to poorly structured programs. When *goto* statements are used in a program, the flow of control, or the order in which instructions are executed, can be difficult to understand and, therefore, difficult to control. In structured programming, the *goto* statement is replaced with function calls, and therefore program structure is simplified. When a function is invoked, the flow of control is not strictly linear, but control will (probably) eventually return from the function to the line of code following the function call.

As the systems to be implemented grew more complex, it became apparent that structured programming alone was not sufficient to ensure the delivery of quality software. Even if structured programming techniques are used, the resulting software can be difficult to understand and use. This realization lead to the development of the technique of functional decomposition.

1.4.2 Functional Decomposition

Functional decomposition is the process of decomposing the system to be implemented into a series of increasingly detailed conceptualizations. These conceptualizations can then be communicated using a representation called a **structure chart**, which uses rectangles to represent each process created and then arrows to subprocesses. Figure 1.5 shows an example of a structure chart that will be discussed in greater detail later. The iterative decomposition of the system leads to a highly modular result because each successive decomposition can be represented and implemented as a module. Because the primary role of each of these modules will be to perform a function or an activity in the final system, functional decomposition is used within the process-oriented paradigm. Such a conceptualization of the system to be developed is by definition process oriented.

To understand how modularity can result from increasingly detailed conceptualizations, let us explore what is meant by these conceptualizations. We will use the example of the book-tracking system shown in Figure 1.2. When we say "book-tracking system," we are describing, in the most abstract terms possible, the system

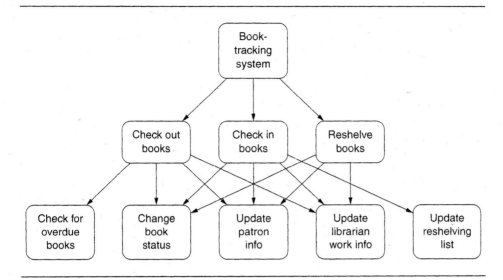

FIGURE 1.5 Book-Tracking-System Structure Chart

to be implemented. This system can then be **decomposed** into its constituent, more detailed modules (from a process-oriented perspective). The functions that need to occur in a book-tracking system are *check out*, *check in*, and *reshelve*. This set of modules is a second **level of abstraction** because it describes the book-tracking system in more detail than the term "book-tracking system."

Each element in the second level of abstraction can be further decomposed, creating yet a third level of abstraction. For example, the *check-out* process may be further decomposed into the following modules: *check-for-overdue-books*, *change-book-status*, *update-patron-info*, and *update-librarian-work-info*. The *check-in* process may be decomposed into the following modules: *change-book-status*, *update-patron-info*, *update-reshelving-list*, and *update-librarian-work-info*. Finally, the *reshelve* process may be decomposed into its constituent functions: *change-book-status*, *update-reshelving-list*, and *update-librarian-work-info*. The combined result of decomposing each element from the second level of abstraction forms the third level of abstraction. Figure 1.5 shows the structure chart for a functional decomposition of the book-tracking system, where common modules are shared among modules in a higher level of abstraction. Notice that this is not a complete functional decomposition because some of the processes are still too abstract. For example, all three modules at the second level of abstraction share the *change-book-status* process. The details of how the book status is to be changed in each situation have not yet been defined but must be defined in a later decomposition of the individual processes.

This example illustrates one of the most important concepts in all software development paradigms: **abstraction**. As a software development team begins their work, their first and most critical task is to study the system to be developed. Their initial understanding of this system will be imprecise and vague, and can only be conceptualized very abstractly. For example, the software development team's knowledge may be limited to knowing the system is to be used by a library to track books. As a result, the team uses a notation to represent the system as a *book-tracking system*. As the team studies the problem at hand, additional details will emerge, and these details can be incorporated into representations of later system conceptualizations.

The objectives of functional decomposition are to provide an orderly mechanism for understanding the system to be developed through abstraction and to produce a well-structured software system as a result. We can translate the modules at the various levels of abstraction into functions, procedures, or subprograms in the actual system implementation. Thus the conceptualization and representation of the system are compatible with its actual source-code structure. The technique of starting with an abstract conceptualization of the system and moving to progressively more detailed levels of abstraction is **stepwise refinement**. The technique of stepwise refinement continues to be used today, but the structure charts that resulted from early functional decomposition tasks typically did not provide enough information to ensure a well-structured, accurate solution. To begin to add some of that necessary information, structured analysis and design techniques have been developed.

EXERCISE 1.4 How would you functionally decompose the process of building a toolshed? How can you use the results of the functional decomposition to assign work tasks to those people helping to build the toolshed?

1.4.3 Structured Analysis and Design

The next major development in software engineering is **structured analysis and design** [31, 39]. The advent of structured analysis and design marks the introduction of the first software engineering **methodology**. A methodology is a set of techniques that together describe the entire software development process. Structured analysis is built from its predecessor techniques—structured programming and functional decomposition—and therefore uses techniques of abstraction to produce a modular outcome.

With the introduction of structured analysis and design, the delivery of the final implemented system became one of several milestones in the software development process rather than the only milestone. The analysis of the problem to be solved and the well-thought-out design of software to solve that problem began to be recognized as important steps in the software development process. With the advent of structured analysis and design, we also see the introduction of notations to communicate more of the results of the analysis and design steps.

Recall that the results of functionally decomposing a software system can be communicated using a structure chart. Structure charts provide only a very limited amount and type of information. A structure chart will tell you that several modules share a submodule, but it will not tell you what data are shared among the modules or how the modules interact with each other, even if such information was discovered during the conceptualization process. Many representations exist to communicate the variety of information that might be discovered while thinking about the system to be developed.

In software engineering, the representation of the system to be developed is often called a **model** of the system. Modeling the system involves using geometric symbols, labels, and other notational extensions to represent elements of the system in a clear and unambiguous manner. Different software development paradigms will model different aspects of the system. For example, in the object-oriented paradigm, models are focused on objects and their interrelationships, while in the process-oriented paradigm, the models are focused on processes and data transmission between them. The importance of modeling and the notations used in those models will be discussed in greater detail in the next chapter.

In the process-oriented paradigm, we use **data-flow diagrams** as a means to express the results of the analysis and design phase. These diagrams represent the manner in which data will move among the various processes in the final software implementation. Functional decomposition is one of the primary techniques used in the process-oriented paradigm. The results of the functional decompositions are represented in data-flow diagrams, where each set of diagrams expresses a level of abstraction.

Figure 1.6 is a data-flow diagram for a portion of the *check-out* process in the book-tracking system. The diagram represents the manner in which the *check-out* process is completed. In particular, the diagram shows which subprocesses are invoked and what information is transmitted between the processes. For example, the connections between the *check-out* process and the *check-for-overdue-books* process indicates that the patron ID is passed from the *check-out* process to the *check-for-overdue-books* process. The *check-for-overdue-books* process returns a boolean value, *true* or *false*, to the *check-out* process. The *check-for-overdue-books* process also invokes another process, *read-patron-record*, by passing it the patron ID. The *read-patron-record* process returns either a patron record or null if no patron record was found.

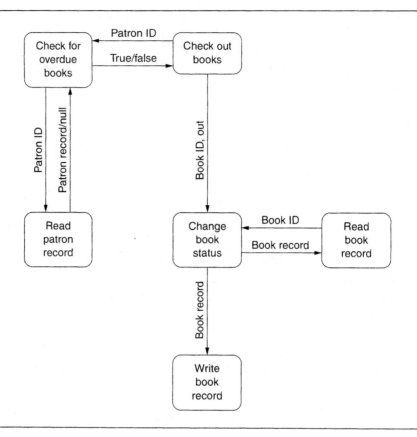

FIGURE 1.6 A Piece of the Book-Tracking-System Data-Flow Diagram

1.4.4 Data-Centered Paradigm

As organizations used computers over a longer period of time and computerized applications became more numerous, it became apparent that modeling individual applications was no longer sufficient if the desired result was an efficient software configuration. The primary problem was that different applications within the same organization frequently required common data elements and these data elements were typically duplicated within each application. As multiple applications were used on a daily basis by an organization, these duplicated data elements soon contained conflicting and erroneous values. These erroneous values occurred because as values changed during application use, not all duplicated versions of each data element were updated. For example, an employee working for a company moves and files a change of address form. This form invariably results in the update of the file for the payroll application, while the original, now erroneous, address may remain in the benefits or retirement application.

The contribution of the data-centered methodology is to extend structured analysis with an additional technique called **data modeling**. Data modeling occurs before individual applications are developed. The objective of data modeling is to determine the data needs for the entire organization and then create a centralized, integrated data repository, like a relational database. Individual applications can then be developed and take their data from this centralized database. The data model will be represented using a graphical technique called **entity relationship (ER) diagrams** [24]. The original purpose for ER diagrams was in relational database design. After the initial stage of data modeling, individual applications can be developed using structured analysis and design focusing on data from the central data repository.

In ER diagrams, we seek to show how entities, or the things that comprise the system, are related to each other. In the diagram, the various entities are represented by rectangles labeled with the name of the entity. The relationships between the entities are represented by arrows and diamond-shaped boxes between rectangles representing the two related entities. The diamond-shaped boxes are labeled with the name of the relationship. In addition, the ER diagram can represent the **cardinality** of the relationships. The cardinality of a relationship describes how many instances of each kind of entity may join in a relationship. For example, a library patron may have a single address, so the cardinality between a patron and an address is *one-to-one*. In contrast, a library patron may check out many books, but a book can only be checked out by a single patron, so the cardinality on the relationship between a book and a patron is *one-to-many*. Figure 1.7 illustrates an entity-relationship diagram, where the entities are depicted as rectangles, relationships are depicted as diamonds with an in arrow and an out arrow, and the cardinalities are represented as labels on the relationship arrows.

The data-centered paradigm should not be confused with the **data-structure-oriented design method** [40, 53, 80, 99]. In the data-structure-oriented design method, the software is structured around the data structures of the proposed system. The **Warnier-Orr** design method includes a diagramming technique that facilitates a hierarchical breakdown of the data structures. The **Jackson System of Programming** [53] is another approach that begins with data structures and derives program structure. Few details of these data-structure-oriented design methods will be given here because none of these methods address the important issue of data-structure design. Because they fail to address this issue, these methods do not address the full software development process and, therefore, do not qualify as full-fledged paradigms.

Unfortunately, the data-centered paradigm is not widely known or used in industry. Before the data-centered approach could gain a foothold in industry, the object-oriented paradigm was developed. The object-oriented paradigm synthesizes the analysis of data with the analysis of the application to be developed into the construct of an object, which contains both data and processes.

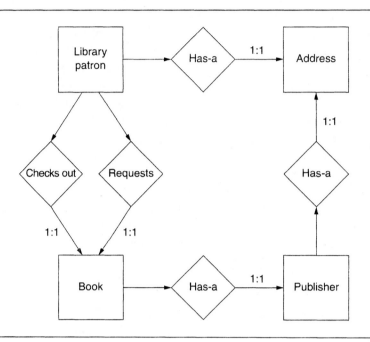

FIGURE 1.7 An ER Diagram for the Book-Tracking System

1.4.5 Object-Oriented Paradigm

The object-oriented paradigm shares many features with the approaches described earlier in this chapter. Abstraction, as introduced through functional decomposition, is fundamental to the object-oriented paradigm as a means for controlling the complexity of the system to be developed. Using diagrams to model various aspects of the software system is also central to the object-oriented paradigm. Of course, the diagrams in the object-oriented paradigm differ in nature from those used in the process-oriented paradigm because the two paradigms focus on different aspects of the software. In fact, the ER diagrams used in the data-centered paradigm are closely related to an important aspect of object-oriented modeling.

Because objects are the coupling of data and operations performed on the data, objects are closely related to **abstract data types** (ADTs). A data type is an aggregation (or grouping) of potentially heterogeneous pieces of data. An abstract data type aggregates not only the data but also the operations that act upon those data [45]. The process of creating abstract data types is **data abstraction**.

The use of data abstraction as a software engineering approach involves developing software out of abstract data types by specifying the data types and how they will relate to each other through their operations. Through data abstraction, we protect the data inside the abstract data type so that manipulation of the data can occur only through the operations defined in the data type. The ADT's operations, therefore, serve as an interface between the data and any software that wishes to interact with those data. This principle of protection via an interface is known as **encapsulation**. Through encapsulation, the implementation details for an ADT can be hidden from the user of the ADT. A programmer need only be aware of the interface of an ADT to be able to use the ADT effectively. The software, therefore, can be divided into a specification section, which defines the interfaces, and an implementation section, which is the actual source code for the operations on the data.

Figure 1.8 shows a **stack** abstract data type that has three operations: *push*, *pop*, and *isempty*. The user of the stack has access to these operations only, which in turn have access to the underlying data in the stack ADT. The actual implementation of the stack, whether as an array, as shown in implementation option 1, or as a linked list, as shown in implementation option 2, does not affect how the user interacts with the ADT. The user of the ADT, therefore, need only be concerned with its interface as defined through its operations.

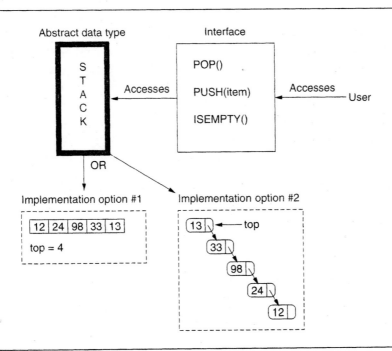

FIGURE 1.8 A Stack Abstract Data Type

Abstract data types are similar to objects in the object-oriented paradigm, but objects have an additional possibility not available in ADTs. In particular, **inheritance** is an important concept in the object-oriented paradigm. Objects may be defined in an **inheritance hierarchy**, where a more detailed class of objects inherits the data and operations of its more general ancestor class of objects. The idea of inheritance arose first in the field of artificial intelligence.

Advances in knowledge representation in the field of artificial intelligence have had an influence on techniques for modeling software systems. Artificial intelligence practitioners, seeking to model human thought and memory, made several knowledge representation advances during the early to mid-1970s [69, 89]. In the context of semantic networks [26], cognitive psychologists postulated the internal structures of human memory by building data structures in computer programs. To test how closely these data structures modeled the hypothesized knowledge structures in the human mind, the psychologists set up empirical tests comparing human performance to the performance of the program. One human memory structure tested in this context was an inheritance hierarchy. The researchers were trying to determine if human memory organized concepts into a hierarchy with the most general concepts at the top of the hierarchy and the most detailed concepts at the bottom. A more specific concept then inherits all the characteristics of all of its ancestor concepts.

Figure 1.9 shows a portion of a bird inheritance hierarchy. The *sparrow* node at the bottom left of the hierarchy is at the most specific level, and is, therefore, more detailed than its ancestor nodes, *song bird*, *flighted*, and *bird*. The *sparrow* inherits all the characteristics of these ancestor nodes; therefore, the *sparrow* must *have a call*, *can fly*, and must have *two wings*, *feathers*, *two legs*, and a *bill or beak*. The *sparrow* also possesses its own attribute, the *color brown*, which none of its ancestors possesses. The *penguin*, shown in the bottom right of the hierarchy in Figure 1.9, shares, with the sparrow, the four attributes from the *bird* node but then inherits from its other ancestor nodes the attributes that it *cannot fly* and has *flipper wings*. In addition, the *penguin* possesses its own attribute, that its *home is Antarctica*. The notion of inheritance is extremely important in the object-oriented software engineering paradigm.

In summary, the three major software engineering paradigms are the process-oriented paradigm, the data-centered paradigm, and the object-oriented paradigm (see Summary Points box 1.2). Although the rest of this text will focus exclusively on the object-oriented paradigm, it is interesting to note the following three unifying concepts of the three major paradigms:

1. Modularity
2. Modeling
3. Abstraction

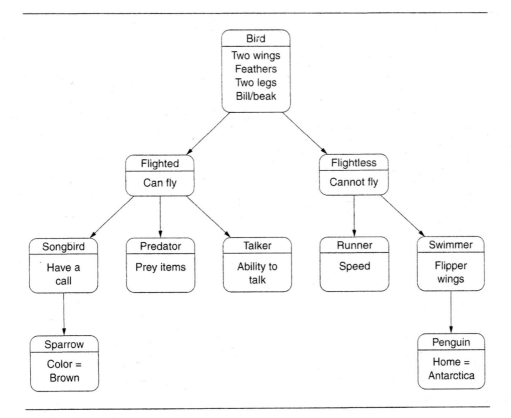

FIGURE 1.9 A Partial Bird Inheritance Hierarchy

SUMMARY POINTS 1.2

Chronology of Software Engineering Techniques

1. Structured programming
2. Functional decomposition
3. Structured analysis
4. Data-centered analysis
5. Object-oriented analysis

The Costs of Not Engineering Software

If one views project development as simply the production of source code, the application of software engineering techniques may appear to simply add overhead to the process. Because many of the activities of software engineering do not directly result in lines of code, those who are unfamiliar with the benefits that can be gained by practicing software engineering may be tempted to skip many of the software engineering steps discussed in this textbook. The reality is, however, that neglecting the initial phases in the software engineering process often leads to such costly consequences as

- Having to restructure code
- High maintenance costs due to poorly structured code
- Producing a product unacceptable to end users
- Producing buggy or unreliable code
- Having to rewrite code due to misunderstandings
- Having difficulty integrating separate pieces of the system
- Difficult project management
- Budget and time overruns

 ## Why Software Engineering Is Not Universal

If society has been plagued by a software crisis over the last three decades, and if techniques exist to improve the quality, reliability, structure, and success rate of software, why hasn't everyone eagerly adopted software engineering techniques? A number of factors work against the adoption of software engineering techniques. First, software engineering has recently gone through a paradigm shift. The process-oriented paradigm has been replaced by the object-oriented paradigm. Many believe that the object-oriented paradigm is not yet sufficiently mature to be used in industry. We believe that we will show throughout the rest of the text that the object-oriented paradigm is indeed mature enough to be used. Second, nontechnical management personnel most often understand software to be a set of computer instructions. From this point of view, the only tasks that count in software development are those that add to the number of computer instructions that have been written. Technical staff often compound this problem by measuring progress in terms of lines of code. Since software engineering techniques add to the quality of code rather than to the quantity of code, these techniques are often viewed as adding little to the software development process.

All too frequently when a project deadline looms, corners are cut to speed "development," that is, production of lines of code. These corners typically involve the initial phases of software engineering such as analysis and design. Unfortunately, ignoring good software engineering practices is costly in terms of both time and money for the overall project because errors or misconceptions that are found after coding has begun are more expensive to fix than errors found during the analysis and design phases. By taking the time to ensure, before coding begins, that the software design meets the needs of the users and solves the problem at hand, time and money will be saved in the long run.

When practicing good software engineering techniques, software developers will sometimes be engaged in activities that do not immediately produce source code. The objective of these activities is to engineer a modular, robust, reliable solution. The risky nature of large-scale software development makes the initial software engineering investment well worthwhile. In addition, an efficient, modular software structure will make future debugging and maintenance easier.

Until more publicity is generated concerning costly, failed software development initiatives, many organizations will not be motivated to investigate and practice good software engineering techniques.

Compare the process of building a large structure, like a skyscraper, to the process of creating a complex piece of software, like a spreadsheet or database management system. It is conventionally understood that significant time and effort go into architecture and design for a skyscraper, but for many, it is not clear how important these efforts are to producing equally reliable software. Why do you suppose this point is not understood?   **EXERCISE 1.5**

The Role of the Project

Our motivation for structuring this software engineering textbook around an actual software project is that we feel students will learn software engineering techniques best when they have the chance to put them into practice. Therefore, the major goal of this text is to allow the completion of a software project during the course of a semester. Due dates for the various project deliverables must be strictly maintained because there are no possible extensions to the semester. In addition, one of the major goals of software engineering is to allow developers to be in control of a project and to deliver a completed, correct, well-structured, and robust project on time.

In our experience, students do not fully appreciate the importance of applying good software engineering principles to problem solving until they experience the benefits firsthand. As a result, we include in this textbook a semester-long project that was successfully implemented by students at Plymouth State College.

The project involves the analysis, design, and implementation of an Internet-based version of a murder mystery board game, in which players compete against one another over the Internet. The project is fully described in section 1.10.

An important element of successfully completing the class project is working effectively with your software engineering team. The early chapters of this text provide various pointers for successful team interaction.

 ## Working in Teams

One of the most challenging aspects of carrying out a software engineering project is working in a team. Effective human collaboration is always challenging no matter the context. Some elements of collaboration to keep in mind are the following.

After each software engineering team member has studied the initial problem statement, the problem is divided up into smaller pieces and given to members of the team. Unless an SE team is particularly large, there is no redundancy of effort. Therefore, the entire team depends on the punctual delivery of each team member's contribution to the project. So, it is critical to be conscientious about due dates for the sake of your teammates.

Another issue to keep in mind is that human beings vary dramatically in their interests, skills, and work ethics. One team member may be passionate about engaging in the project, while another may be much less interested in software engineering. Such differences may cause friction within a team, and the instructor may have to intervene to resolve problems equitably. Ideally, each teammate takes on and completes an equal share of the project. If you find yourself struggling to complete your project deliverables in a timely fashion, be willing to take a reduced project grade in return for scaling down your portion of the project. The teammate who takes on additional work needs to be rewarded in some fashion, perhaps through extra credit, exemption from exams, or fewer written assignments.

An additional challenge is interpersonal communication. It is vital to meet regularly with your team to share deliverables, make collaborative decisions on the project, and develop effective interobject communication. To respect each teammate's time, it is essential to conduct effective team meetings. Section 1.9 provides suggestions for conducting such meetings.

 ## Creating the Project Team

Although the first two chapters of this textbook present introductory information rather than discussing the phases of software development, the creation of the project teams should begin immediately. Teams should be selected and should begin meeting during the first week of the semester. Each development team should establish a weekly meeting time, which may be during the class period if the instructor allows.

The composition of the software team is extremely important to the success of the project (see Summary Points box 1.3). If possible, each team should have at least four students. The students should be assigned to the teams according to their strengths in such a way that each team has a variety of skills. Some key skills to look for when establishing teams are

- Good programming skills
- Multimedia skills (creating graphics and sounds)
- Graphical User Interface (GUI) design and programming
- Algorithm creation skills (ablility to derive complex algorithms)
- Network programming skills (ability to conceptualize and structure program to program communication over sockets)
- Multithreading skills (ability to effectively structure multithreaded applications)

If multimedia facilities or skills are scarce or if fewer than four students are on a project team, a text-based, nongraphic version of the project may be created.

In the first team meeting, the structure of subsequent meetings should be established. Since students tend to have full, busy schedules during the semester, well-focused, effective meetings are essential. In order to accomplish this purpose, an agenda should be created prior to each meeting, and this agenda should be strictly adhered to. During the first meeting, the method for creating the agenda should be established. Some of the questions that need to be answered are the following: When is the deadline for placing items on the agenda? Who is responsible for distributing the agenda? Who is allowed to place items on the agenda?

One successful model for teamwork is to have a rotating chair, where each team member takes a turn. The responsibility for creating and disseminating the agenda could fall on the chair for that meeting. This model prevents a single person from dominating the activity of the team and involves students who may not be adequately heard from otherwise.

Objectives of your first team meeting:

- Establish a common meeting time.
- Assign the responsibility of creating the first agenda and chairing the meeting.
- Establish the sequence of team members for chair rotation.
- Assign responsibility for recording team meetings.
- Discuss tool preferences and areas of expertise.
- Discuss how to share work products.

Working Effectively in Teams

1. Be conscientious about due dates for each deliverable for the sake of your entire team.

2. If you are less able or willing to work on the project, address this issue immediately with your team.

3. Meet regularly with your team.

4. Always create an agenda for every team meeting.

5. Rotate responsibility for chairing team meetings.

1.10   *Class Project:* Functional Requirements

CLASS PROJECT

The **functional requirements** of the class project will be laid out here. The functional requirements of a proposed software system describe, in a complete and unambiguous form, what the system is supposed to do. Functional requirements may take a narrative form, frequently called the **functional specifications** or **requirements statement**. The goal of software engineering is to transform the narrative requirements statement into a set of diagrams that serve as a blueprint for programming. Under normal circumstances, the acquisition of a formal requirements statement is a challenging software engineering objective. The source and completeness of such a document vary from situation to situation, and the topic of dealing with users to obtain the requirements statement will be addressed more fully in subsequent chapters. We include the functional requirements of the class project in this chapter before the topic is formally introduced in order to allow the software development teams to begin the class project as soon as possible.

Each team member should read the following project requirements statement and create a list of questions and ambiguities that arise from it. The statement should be read multiple times until its basic functionality can be discussed without excessive referral to the written statement. After all team members have had the opportunity to familiarize themselves with the requirements, the team should meet to discuss the statement and address the following items:

• Identify and address questions and ambiguities.
• Identify project elements requiring network programming (since this particular project is Internet-based).
• Identify project elements requiring graphic image manipulation.
• Identify project elements that lend themselves to audio.

- Identify project elements requiring special algorithm creation.
- Create a preliminary project conceptualization.
- List three to six key classes comprising the system.
- Establish areas of interest on which individual team members would like to work.

1.10.1 Project Overview

The goal of the class project is to implement an Internet-based; whodunit-style game, called Galaxy Sleuth, which is closely modeled after the board game Clue. The game is Internet based; that is, players will be able to play each other from remote sites on the Internet. This application will, therefore, take on a client/server structure, where each client supports one player's view of the game while the server coordinates communication between players and orchestrates the sequence of events of the game.

The game is an intergalactic murder mystery that emulates a board-game scenario in which players spin a wheel to determine a randomly selected number of moves by which they travel through space to various planets. The objective of the game is to gather a series of clues while traveling about the universe. Each player receives information concerning the murder, and no players receive the same piece of information. As the players travel through the universe, they are permitted to ask questions of their fellow players. The questions take the form of hypotheses about the circumstances and perpetrator of the murder, which the remaining players are invited to disprove with their evidence. The murder hypothesis is communicated to all players. If a player can disprove the hypothesis, that piece of information is communicated only to the inquiring player. The other players are informed that the hypothesis was refuted, but are not shown the piece of evidence that refuted the hypothesis. If the hypothesis cannot be refuted, all players are informed of that fact. After gathering a certain set of clues and applying deductive reasoning, players may deduce the perpetrator and circumstances of the murder. The first player to accomplish this goal wins the game. If a player draws an incorrect conclusion, he or she loses the game.

The game involves elements of both luck and strategy. The objective of player movement throughout the universe is to investigate specific planets to determine whether each was the murder site. Part of the game, therefore, involves reaching suspicious locations quickly to investigate them. This element is dictated largely by luck, since the spin of the wheel determines the speed at which a player reaches a destination. Players may also travel through a few strategically placed wormholes. The wormholes connect certain planets to each other. The strategy of the game is embodied in selecting questions to ask other players, selecting planet destinations, and efficiently deducing the correct murder scenario.

1.10.2 Game Elements

The intergalactic context for the game consists of nine planets, *Cathitar*, *Earth*, *Evilon*, *Linuta*, *Neudel*, *Pheadrun*, *Ping*, *Psu*, and *Verlute*. Three to six players may participate in this game. Each player has a graphic representation of the galaxy on his or her remote computer. Each player is represented by a token of a different color in the game window. Each token represents a character in the murder mystery. Each player is, therefore, both trying to solve the murder mystery and taking on the identity of one of the six murder suspects. The murder suspects are *Tina Time Traveler* (red token), *Sam Space Voyager* (blue token), *Mona Moon Walker* (yellow token), George Galaxy Wanderer (green token), *Uhura Universalist* (purple token), and *Steve Stargazer* (white token).

Each token occupies a physical location in the galaxy at any given time. When a player (as represented by the token) is not residing on a planet, his or her token must reside on one of the locations in space. Space is segmented into squares as shown in Figure 1.10, the graphic representation of the galaxy. To move between planets, a player may either spin the spinner in the center of the game by clicking on it or select a wormhole. The spinner will land on a randomly selected number between one and six. In order to move through a wormhole, the player must be residing on one of the four planets which has access to one.

The game environment also contains six lethal instruments: a *phaser*, a *hyper rope*, a *laser sword*, *biological agents*, a *flamethrower*, and *radioactive chemicals*. One of these items is the murder weapon. The final element of the game is a window that may be used by players to record the results of the questions posed to the other players. This window serves as an aid in deducing the circumstance and perpetrator of the murder.

1.10.3 The Game Sequence of Events

Players of Galaxy Sleuth point their web browsers to the home page containing the client applet code or invoke a local version of the client. Which action the players take depends on the language used to implement the class project. The player selects either a *start game* or *join game* button depending whether a game has already begun or not. The first player to initiate a game decides on the parameters for waiting for additional players to join the game and may select a suspect and associated token to move during the game. The player either selects a time limit for when to begin the game or chooses to wait for a specified number of additional players. As players join the game, each selects a game token from those remaining. Once sufficient players join the game or the time limit elapses with at least three players, the game begins.

First, the game server selects a random murder scenario, consisting of a perpetrator, a murder weapon, and a planet where the murder takes place. The remaining

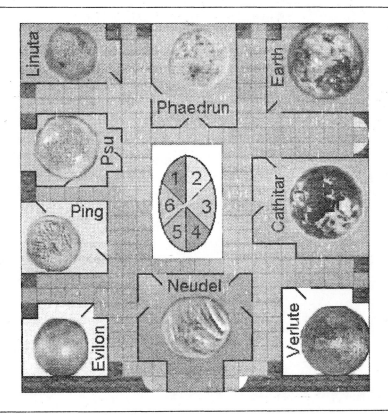

FIGURE 1.10 A Depiction of the Game Board

evidence consists of the suspects, excluding the actual murderer, the possible murder weapons, excluding the actual murder weapons, and the planets, excluding the site of the murder. This evidence is then distributed to the players one piece at a time, starting with the first player who joined the game and continuing in order of player sign-on until the evidence is exhausted. If a player has a piece of evidence, for example the planet *Earth*, that player knows the murder did not take place on Earth. Therefore, all the evidence held by a player serves to refute a part of a murder hypothesis.

Each suspect and associated token has a fixed starting point in the game represented by a specific cell in the game representation. The game-board representation places each token in its respective starting location. The predetermined playing order starts with Tina Time Traveler, and thus the player who selected the associated token moves first. The remainder of the order is Sam Space Voyager, Mona Moon Walker, George Galaxy Wanderer, Uhura Universalist, and Steve Stargazer.

A player turn consists either of a spin of the spinner followed by the movement of the player's token the appropriate number of cells or the movement of the player's token through a wormhole (if the player's token is on one of four special planets with a wormhole connection to another planet). If the player lands on another planet as a result of the move, he or she may pose a murder hypothesis to the following player. In other words, the first player poses his or her question to the second player joining the game, the second queries the third, and so on. The last person queries the first player. If the player to whom the hypothesis was posed cannot refute the murder hypothesis with a piece of evidence, then the next person in the starting sequence is asked, until all players are exhausted or someone successfully refutes the hypothesis. To refute a hypothesis, a player shows only a single piece of evidence even if the player holds more than one piece that refutes the hypothesis. Each player also has a special window to assist in keeping track of the evidence shown and hypothesis outcomes.

If a player attempts to respond erroneously to a murder hypothesis, for example, by responding that a hypothesis cannot be refuted when he or she has a refuting piece of evidence or by trying to show an irrelevant piece of evidence, the game should prohibit this attempt from succeeding. In other words, the game allows only correct responses to be given, but if there is more than one correct response, the responding player can choose which he or she would like to give.

1.10.4 Moving and Landing on Planets

In order to visit a planet, a player must enter the planet's atmosphere at one of the predefined entry points. Each planet has between one and three predefined atmospheric entry points. These entry points are graphically depicted on the game representation as a slanted line off a square on the board leading into the atmosphere of a planet. A player visits a planet by making legal moves on the board until a cell adjacent to an atmosphere entry point is reached. It costs the player a single move to enter the atmosphere from the adjacent cell, and the player is considered to be on the planet as soon as the planet's atmosphere has been entered. The player does not have to enter the planet's atmosphere in an exact number of moves. A player whose token resides on one of four planets having wormhole connections to other planets may choose not to spin the spinner and instead take the wormhole directly to the other planet. The planets Linuta and Verlute have a wormhole connecting each other, as do Earth and Evilon. A player may not revisit the same planet on a single turn.

A legal move consists of a player moving his or her token the number of moves determined by the spinner, either horizontally or vertically, but not diagonally. The player may change directions any number of times, but cannot enter the same cell twice during a single turn. Also, a player may not move into a cell occupied by the token of another player.

1.10.5 Winning the Game

A player wins the game by announcing his or her murder hypothesis (as a solution to the murder mystery) consisting of a planet, a perpetrator, and a murder weapon any time during his or her turn, and having the server determine that the hypothesis is correct. The solution is then broadcast to all players. If an announced hypothesis is not correct, the player loses the game and cannot pose hypotheses any longer or make moves on the board, but must continue to refute the hypotheses of other players. When the correct hypothesis is announced all players are informed of the circumstances of the murder.

1.10.6 Project Time Frame

Figure 1.11 shows the approximate time frame for developing the project. A listing of project deliverables is associated with a bar indicating one or more weeks during which it will be developed. In the final column several deliverables are grouped into a phase of development.

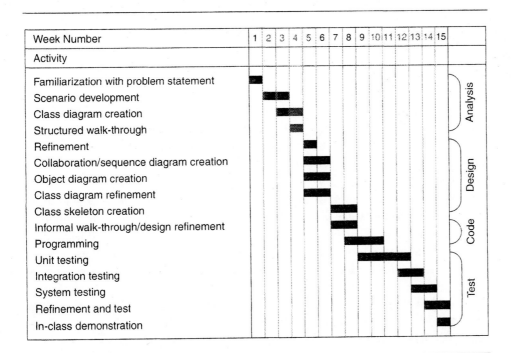

FIGURE 1.11 Timeline for Project Development

Questions for Review

1. Why are large-scale software systems complex? List at least three sources of complexity.
2. Why are narrative problem statements (description of the problem to be automated) error prone?
3. What are the objectives of software engineering?
4. What elements does a software engineering paradigm possess?
5. How has the object-oriented software engineering paradigm evolved?
6. What is abstraction and how is it used in software engineering?
7. What techniques do the object-oriented paradigm and the process-oriented paradigm share?
8. What modeling techniques does the process-oriented approach possess?
9. What are the dangers of not following a software engineering paradigm?
10. Why do some organizations choose not to apply software engineering techniques?
11. Given the following problem statement, try to sketch out a general object-oriented conceptualization. Answer the question by listing major classes and their interrelationships. A major class is one that plays a role in the system other than serving simply as an attribute for another object. For example, *customer* is likely to be a major object in a banking system, whereas *address* is likely to be a minor object, because its primary role is as an attribute for *customer.*

Banking Case Study

You have been asked to develop a banking system for Mom & Pop Banking (M&P). M&P Banking have conveniently already purchased the hardware and networking portion of the system. They need you to write the software to automate savings and checking account transactions as well as ATM services that they wish to offer their customers.

M&P has one kind of savings account and two different checking accounts. The savings account bears interest based on the prevailing rates, compounded monthly. Transactions carried out against the savings account are free as long as they are carried out at a branch and not at an ATM. Two checking account options exist. The Rich Club Account (RCA) bears interest at 1 percent less than the savings account, checks are free, and no monthly fee is applied as long as the total balance of all accounts is at least $5,000. The other checking account, the Poor Slob Club (PSC), has no minimum balance. PSC accounts are charged a monthly fee of $5.00, and each check costs the customer $.10.

Because you are familiar with other ATM functions, you can conveniently make the following assumptions:

- Customers of M&P can withdraw cash from either their checking or savings accounts. The customer profile determines which checking account is relevant for any given customer.
- Customers can inquire about the balance of any accounts that they hold with M&P.
- Customers will be charged a $.50 fee for all transactions after the third free transaction.
- Customers may also deposit money into either checking or savings.
- Customers need a receipt of all their ATM transactions including any service charges.
- Customers can initiate transactions from ATM machines owned by other banks and stores at an additional cost of $1.00.
- Customers with accounts from other banks can use M&P ATMs at a cost of $1.00 per transaction.

M&P is a member of the global EFT (electronic funds transfer) system and needs the account number, password, and transaction information to facilitate transactions belonging to other banks for which M&P receives $.50 from the member bank. In a similar manner other ATM machines can transmit M&P transactions at a cost to M&P of $.50.

12. Study the classes derived from the banking case study. Are there any classes in an inheritance hierarchy? Reassess the classes and construct an inheritance hierarchy.
13. What minor classes can you derive from the banking case study?
14. You want someone to write a program to automate your household finances. Write a narrative description of this problem, so that a second party can use this description to write a useful program.
15. Exchange your household finance narrative with a classmate's, and critique the description for ambiguities and omissions.

Object-Oriented Paradigm Overview

 Key Concepts

- Informal scenarios
- Object-oriented conceptualization
- Inheritance
- Software development life cycle
- Waterfall model
- Prototyping

- Incremental/iterative development
- Hybrid life cycles
- Module cohesion
- Module coupling
- Module reuse
- Unified Modeling Language (UML)

2.2 Getting Acquainted with the Class Project

Because the time frame for developing the class project is dictated by the length of the term for this course, it is essential that students begin familiarizing themselves with the class project immediately. The first step is to read the requirements specification provided in the previous chapter.

Most students taking an introductory software engineering course are well acquainted with programming and perhaps some program design issues. These activities comprise later stages of the software development process. Because much of their education has focused on implementation issues, students tend to struggle with the early stages of software engineering. In fact, these early stages are challenging even to seasoned professionals.

Once the requirements specification has been read, students should begin to create **informal scenarios** based on the specification. Through an informal scenario, we tell a "story" of how users will be using the system. The story should be concrete. For example, a poorly written informal scenario tells a story of "user A entering all necessary data in the dialogue window" whereas a well-written informal scenario specifies that "Andrea enters her name and password in the login screen."

2.2.1 Guidelines for Creating Informal Scenarios

Although we call this portion of the software development process **informal**, there are some guidelines for creating these informal scenarios to achieve the greatest benefit (see Summary Points box 2.1). The guidelines are as follows:

- A software system should consist of a number of small informal scenarios, rather than one large informal scenario.
- An informal scenario should address one coherent aspect of the system, such as *user logs onto system, server deals cards to users, user makes a move, user wins/loses the game*, and so on.
- Each informal scenario should specify concrete values whenever possible. Rather than writing that a user spins the spinner and moves the specified number of spaces, students should write that Andrea spins the spinner, which lands on the number 6. She then moves four spaces forward and two spaces left. The latter conveys the potential complexity of managing user moves on the game board, while the former does not.
- In the informal scenarios, you should address some types of user error that the system will handle, but you should not attempt to exhaustively cover all possible errors.
- Implementation details should be omitted in expressing each informal scenario. For example, an informal scenario should not mention linked lists or other data structures.
- Each scenario should describe the state of the system upon initiation of that scenario. For example, the *user makes a move* informal scenario should describe the example configuration of the game board prior to the user move.
- Each scenario should terminate by indicating which scenario is next.

The tendency is to make the informal scenarios too abstract rather than sufficiently concrete. The problem with characterizing the use of the system in abstract terms is that the complexities of the system are not as apparent when described abstractly as when a detailed situation is discussed. The point of creating informal scenarios is to allow the developers to gain increased understanding of the project to be developed.

Creating Informal Scenarios

1. Informal scenarios should be short.
2. Informal scenarios should address one activity.
3. Informal scenarios should specify concrete values.
4. Informal scenarios may address some type of user error.
5. Implementation details should be omitted.
6. The state of the system prior to initiation should be described.
7. The next scenario should be indicated.

2.2.2 Sample Informal Scenario: *User Makes a Move*

Current System State

The system state consists of each player at his or her starting location on the game board. The three players in the game, Andrea, Max, and Emma, have each been dealt six cards. Because the value of each card is irrelevant to this informal scenario, these values are omitted.

CLASS PROJECT

Informal Scenario

Andrea has the next move. She spins the spinner, which lands on the number 5. Andrea has the white playing piece. She moves this piece one space to the left, one space toward the top of the game board, two spaces to the right, and finally, one space to the top of the game board. Because of the final position of her game piece, Andrea has no additional options, and her turn ends.

Next Scenario

This scenario is repeated with the player to the left of Andrea. Therefore, Max has the next turn.

As a warm-up exercise to writing informal scenarios pertaining to the class project, create an informal scenario about using a dishwasher. Pick one of the following scenarios: *loading the dishwasher*, *starting the dishwasher*, or *unloading the dishwasher*.

EXERCISE 2.1

Break the playing of the game for the class project into as many different informal scenarios as you can think of. Divide these scenarios among your project development team members. Each of you should come up with informal scenario descriptions using the guidelines of the previous subsection. This task is useful for quickly engaging everyone on the team in the project development and should be undertaken as early in the semester as possible. The remainder of this chapter will address general issues concerning object-oriented software engineering.

Object-Oriented Conceptualization

As discussed in the previous chapter, software development works best when all aspects and stages of the development process are compatible with each other. Therefore, one should conceptualize an object-oriented software project in terms of objects.

Recall the simple object-oriented conceptualization of the book-tracking system from the previous chapter (see Figure 1.3). This figure illustrates our first pass at selecting important objects that might comprise the system. Figure 2.1 depicts another library scene that may aid our selection of important objects for our system. We should note that for any software development project, the initial conceptualization represents a starting point, and further analysis may eliminate one or more of these objects or add other objects. In addition, this initial object configuration is probably similar to the configuration with which most people would start because the elements making up the conceptualization are familiar and common.

We should also note that objects comprising a software system are not always tangible objects that can be pictured. Objects are named with words that are nouns. If a noun can be nontangible, so can an object. In designing software systems, however, many people think of tangible objects first [57]. Ideas and representations of abstract, nontangible elements of a system are frequently essential objects of a system and must be added to the system at some point. For example, the book-tracking system may contain **work unit** objects in an effort to assess the contribution of each librarian to the running of the library. A work unit object may assign varying work units to the tasks accomplished by the library staff. The work required to reshelve a book might be different from the work required to check a book in. The work unit object determines how much work each task requires. We do not have a concrete picture of a work unit, but a work unit is a legitimate object nonetheless.

FIGURE 2.1 A Library Scene for Object-Oriented Conceptualization

To conceptualize an object-oriented system, once we have selected the objects that comprise the system, we must characterize these objects in terms of their behavior. Characterizing object behavior requires thinking about objects of a particular class in relation to objects of other classes. Just as the initial selection of objects reflects a starting point and is expected to change during further analysis, the initial determination of interobject relationships can be expected to change after further analysis. There are three basic types of relationships that can exist between objects:

- Application specific
- Inheritance
- Aggregation/containment

Consider a garden management system that automates all physical chores associated with gardening. If you were to conceptualize the problem in object-oriented terms, what objects would you start with?   **EXERCISE 2.2**

2.3.1 Application-Specific Relationships

Figure 1.3 shows arrows between certain classes. The arrows are labeled to define the nature of the relationship. Each label represents a particular relationship. For

Book   Patron

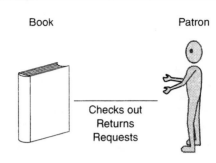

Checks out
Returns
Requests

FIGURE 2.2 Three Application-Specific Relationships

example, the arrow between the library patron and the book in Figure 2.2 has three labels: *Checks out*, *Returns*, and *Requests*. These three labels represent three relationships between library patrons and books and are examples of application-specific relationships. In particular, library patrons may check out, return, and request books. Similarly, the arrow between the librarian and the book in Figure 1.3 is labeled with *Checks in*, *Checks out*, and *Reshelves*, indicating the things a librarian can do with a book. These examples illustrate the fact that objects of two different classes can be related to each other through the message passing between them.

Another type of application-specific relationship is based on **use**. In this type of relationship, one object uses an object of another class. The used object frequently appears as a parameter in one of the user object's method definitions. For example, in the book-tracking system, perhaps a *Patron* object has a method for creating a list of *Book* objects that the *Patron* currently has checked out. The *Patron* object does not contain a list of these books but must create one by looking at all the checked-out books and who has the books checked out. The *Patron* object uses a *List* object that is not one of the attributes of the *Patron* object.

2.3.2 Inheritance

In an object-oriented system, classes can be related to each other through inheritance. Inheritance is a **primitive** interobject relationship. A primitive relationship is implemented through some aspect of the object-oriented programming language. Inheritance is a mechanism built into the programming language.

The inheritance relationship is important in many software systems. The book-tracking system thus far has no inheritance. If we extend the system slightly, however, we can begin to see the need for the inheritance relationship. For example, if the library owns items other than books, such as videos and compact discs, the

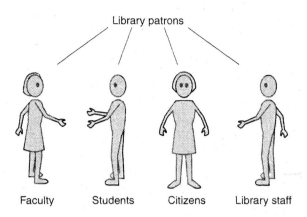

Library patrons

Faculty   Students   Citizens   Library staff

FIGURE 2.3 An Inheritance Relationship

book-tracking system must keep track of all these items. Therefore, we could define a *Resource* class, which then acts as a generic parent class to the more specific
Book, *Video*, and *Compact Disc* classes. The system must behave slightly differently when a patron checks out each of these items. For example, a book might be
able to be checked out for two weeks, whereas a video can only be checked out for
two days. The relationship between the *Resource* class and the three child classes
is hierarchical because, for example, a *Book* is a *Resource* and therefore inherits
all of the attributes and methods from the *Resource* class but has additional, more
specific behavior.

Figure 2.3 shows another inheritance relationship among classes that may act
as library patrons. This figure shows that there are four possible categories of library
patrons: faculty, students, citizens, and library staff.

2.3.3 Aggregation/Composition

The second primitive interobject relationship is called **aggregation/composition**.
This relationship occurs when one class contains another class. For example, the
Patron class has an address as an attribute. If we create an *Address* class, a *Patron*
object contains an *Address* object. A *Patron* object may be viewed as an aggregation
of its attributes. When some of those attributes are objects from other classes, these
classes are interrelated to each other by the aggregation/containment relationship.

Figure 2.4 depicts some of the building blocks that make up the *Patron* class.
Some of these building blocks are other classes, such as the patron address and list of
checked-out resources, while others are attributes, like the overdue fine and patron

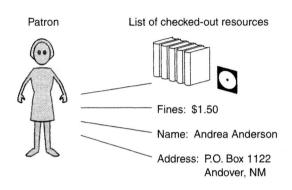

FIGURE 2.4 Aggregation Relationships with the Patron Class

name. When we address the aggregation/composition relationship, it is important to note that we are talking about relationships between classes and not attributes.

EXERCISE 2.3   Review the objects that you selected in the previous exercise for the garden management system. What application-specific relationships exist between these objects? Do any aggregation or inheritance relationships exist between the objects?

2.3.4 Other Categorizations of Relationships

Although other categorizations for interobject relationships exist, the relationships we have described tend to be the common denominator of other such characterizations [14, 16, 23, 47, 88]. Because the **Unified Modeling Language (UML)** will be the object-oriented modeling notation of choice for this text, the primary interobject relationships used in that notation are outlined here. The authors of UML specify the following four relationships [16]:

- **Dependency**: One class may affect the semantics (meaning) of another, because objects of one class *use* instances of another, for example, as arguments in a parameter list.
- **Association**: One class has a link to another class. This relationship includes the aggregation and application-specific relationships described earlier.
- **Generalization**: One class is the super (parent) class of another class. This relationship is one half of the inheritance relationship described previously.
- **Realization**: One class provides a service for another class.

The Software Life Cycle

The **software life cycle** refers to the steps that one goes through to design, develop, implement, use, and maintain a software system. Within the software life cycle, the developer of the system has some choices to make. In particular, the developer must decide which software development paradigm to use. Once the development paradigm has been chosen, the developer must choose which software development process to use. We have discussed software development paradigms earlier. We will now discuss the software development process.

2.4.1 The Software Development Process

The **software development process** refers to the series of steps one goes through to develop a software system. Although the software development process can be selected independently of the software development paradigm, each paradigm lends itself most readily to a particular software development process. For example, the object-oriented approach is most readily associated with an **evolutionary/incremental** software development process. This association exists because class definitions lend themselves to iterative change [88]. Additional attributes and methods may be added to a class definition without disrupting its original functionality. Adding data elements to a process-oriented system tends to be more disruptive, because certain functions must include these new data elements, frequently requiring algorithm changes to accommodate these new data elements. Consequently, other software development processes are most easily associated with the process-oriented paradigm.

Waterfall Software Development Process

No discussion of software development processes is complete without discussing the classic **waterfall** model [8]. Figure 2.5 shows the waterfall model. This model is useful for discussion because it catalogs the traditional essential phases of software development, namely, **requirements analysis**, **design**, **programming**, **testing**, and **maintenance**. These basic phases of software development are part of every software development process, independent of the software development paradigm. Since each software development process shares the same basic phases, the difference between the various process approaches is in the duration, completeness, and sequence of the development phases. Additional phases such as **risk assessment** and **quality assurance** may be specified as separate phases or may be integrated into each of the basic phases.

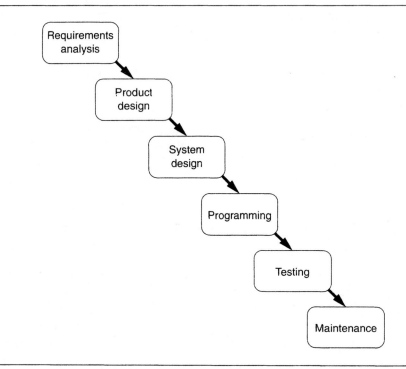

FIGURE 2.5 The Waterfall Software Development Life Cycle

EXERCISE 2.4   Contemplate the process of creating a garden from a previously undeveloped piece of land. What decisions and activities go into this process? Relate these activities to your perhaps sketchy understanding of the phases of software development as defined by the waterfall model.

Two primary types of variations of the waterfall model exist. In the first type, a single development phase is broken into more detailed phases [10]. For example, one may replace the design phase of the basic waterfall model with two distinct phases called **product design** and **detailed design**. Or, one may replace the test phase with **component test**, **integration test**, and **user test** [10]. In the second type of variation, additional phases are added to the traditional waterfall model. For example, one may explicitly specify the addition of a **verification** or **quality assurance** phase of development. In the traditional waterfall model, each development phase is verified before progressing to the next phase of development so that verification is implicitly part of each phase and thus is not shown separately.

The waterfall model has been criticized as overly rigid and therefore risky. In this model, one phase must have been completed before the next can be started. For example, the requirements analysis phase must be complete before any design work begins; the design phase must be complete before any programming can take place; and so on. Such a situation is possible only in the implementation of a system in a very well-defined field, where no experimentation is necessary. Even in such a well-defined field, however, this requirement of completion before moving on engenders huge risk because users will not have an actual, working piece of software to look at until much time and energy have been invested in the system. Although users can give feedback on a requirements analysis or a design, many issues will not become clear to them until they have actually had the chance to use pieces of the system. Therefore, the users may not completely understand the plan for the delivered system and will not see the flaws until the system has undergone testing. This initial investment without substantial user feedback must be avoided. One method for gathering user feedback in a realistic environment is the development of a **prototype**.

Prototyping

Prototyping is the process of building a system mock-up with minimal time investment. The resulting mock-up functions as an evaluation system with which the end users can interact. Prototyping is actually more of a software development technique that can be used in conjunction with any software development process than a software development process in its own right. Prototyping, however, can serve as the focal point of a software development process.

Two types of prototypes exist: **throwaway** prototypes, and **nonthrowaway** prototypes. A throwaway prototype is usually programmed in a programming language other than that intended to develop the production system. One may decide to create a throwaway prototype for a number of reasons, including the following:

- Platforms supporting the prototyping languages are not available for use as the platform of the resulting system.
- The prototyping language is too inefficient for the production system.
- The prototype is too poorly structured to retain.

Prototyping typically involves a dialogue between the end user and the system developers. During its development, the prototype is progressively altered in response to the end users' critique, until a desirable system mock-up results. The advantages to this process are significant. First, the end user has a clear understanding of the functionality of the system to be built. Second, the end user has a critical role in creating the system specifications. It is often the case that the end user does not truly understand the requirements of the system until the system has been completed. Therefore, the idea behind prototyping is to place a system in the hands of the end user as quickly as possible with as little time investment as possible. Third, with the development of a prototype, the system developers have an unambiguous system specification that has already met with the approval of the end users.

Prototypes are created quickly by implementing major features of interface and output only. Issues critical to a production system such as **data integrity** and **security** are ignored during prototype development. An effective prototyping language, therefore, is one that allows quick creation of graphical user interfaces and generation of reports. Programming languages such as Java, Perl, and Tcl/Tk are potential candidates for creating prototypes.

The disadvantage of prototyping is that the end user can easily mistake the prototype for the production system and therefore may not be sympathetic when the production system is not ready for months or years. Depending on the political clout of the end users, such a misunderstanding can pose a serious problem for the technical staff, who are assumed to be unresponsive because they do not deliver the production system immediately. The **20–80 rule** regarding systems development states that 20 percent of the development time is required to create the basic structure of the system, including interfaces and files. The other 80 percent of development time is required to ensure data integrity, security, privacy, and foolproofing of the system.

Although some refer to prototyping as a type of development process [88], prototyping does not address issues pertaining to software structure. Prototyping includes no techniques to describe overall software structure or the design of software components, and, therefore, a modular, robust, extensible system is not guaranteed as a result of prototyping alone. We strongly suggest, however, that prototyping be utilized in conjunction with other development process approaches.

Incremental/Iterative Development Process

The object-oriented paradigm naturally lends itself to an incremental development process because of the ease with which class definitions may be **evolved** to contain increasingly more attributes and methods. In addition, new classes may be integrated into the solution easily and gradually. The phrase "evolving the system" means that an initial system consisting of a subset of functionality of the final target system is first created and is then incrementally modified to include more functionality until the final target system results. Note that this development process is completely different from the traditional waterfall development process in which each phase must be completed before moving onto the next phase. One may, however, select the traditional waterfall development process or any other approach to implement an object-oriented conceptualization of a system.

An incremental software development process still requires careful requirements analysis to produce a well-structured, quality software system. The difference between requirements analysis following a waterfall development process and analysis following an incremental development process is the timing, thoroughness, and frequency of the requirements analysis. In the waterfall model, the requirements analysis occurs once and is to be completed as the first phase of development. Thus the analysis is extensive and requires the systems analyst to understand the system in great detail before design work can proceed. In an incremental/iterative development process, an initial requirements analysis phase exists, but it is shorter and does not require a similar level of detailed understanding before design work can begin. The initial analysis is followed by design, programming, and testing resulting in a partial system, as shown in Figure 2.6. After verification by the end users, the partial system is enhanced with additional functionality, requiring additional analysis to take place. The analysis, design, programming, testing, and verification cycle then repeats itself until the target system is achieved.

The incremental/iterative development process has many advantages. It has the advantages of prototyping because the end users have portions of the system to critique early in the development cycle. The end users provide invaluable proof of concept by assessing finished portions of the system. When it follows the object-oriented or process-oriented paradigm, the incremental development process ensures modularity that produces a well-structured, robust, maintainable

FIGURE 2.6 A Depiction of the Cyclical Nature of the Incremental/Iterative Software Development Life Cycle

system. Finally, in conjunction with object orientation, the incremental development process is likely to flow smoothly between each iteration of the system implementation. Assuming the system begins with a well-conceived initial class structure, there is no need to restructure existing portions of the system between the development iterations because well-designed classes are easily extended.

Simply combining an incremental development process with an object-oriented paradigm is no panacea, however. Careful preliminary analysis is critical to allow the development team to gain sufficient understanding of the target system to produce a class structure that will accommodate system evolution without restricting the emerging iterations of the system. The initial analysis must therefore have significant breadth, considering the entire system rather than simply the first iteration to be implemented.

EXERCISE 2.5   Contemplate how a garden may be developed incrementally. How would you define each developmental increment? Would this process help ensure the success of your garden more so than the waterfall model of gardening?

Hybrid Software Development Processes

A number of software development processes that combine the previously mentioned software development approaches have been proposed (see Summary Points box 2.2) [11, 28, 77]. The **spiral model** [11] combines an iterative approach with the control and structure of a more linear, sequential process like the waterfall model. The spiral model explicitly addresses issues of **quality assurance** and consists of six **task regions**. These regions convey the importance of the customer in the entire development process:

- Customer communication
- Planning
- Risk analysis
- Engineering
- Construction and release
- Customer evaluation

This task domain represents tasks that are repeated as the software project progresses in the spiral model. The customer is therefore the focal point throughout the entire software development process. The spiral model progresses by achieving a series of objectives or **deliverables**. These objectives embody the structure or sequential nature of the process. The first objective of the process is to produce a **requirements statement**, which specifies the functionality that the final system must contain. Each task of the task domain is applied to achieving this end. The

Types of Software Development Processes

1. Top-down, e.g., waterfall
2. Prototyping
3. Incremental/iterative
4. Hybrid, e.g., spiral

next objective is to produce a **software design document**, which again involves exercising each of the six tasks. The development process progresses through the series of deliverables, which include a **development schedule**, a **test plan**, and a **maintenance schedule**.

Object-Oriented Modeling

In this section, we will discuss **modeling** as a set of techniques for expressing the target system before the target system has been complete. Using these techniques, we will build a **model** of the target system. The model will express various aspects of the system to be developed. The representation chosen for communicating the model is a **notation**. The role of such a notation is to allow the expression of a series of representations that model various aspects of the system to be developed. The modeling of a software system requires the use of a particular notation that will unambiguously communicate a variety of aspects of the system to be developed.

2.5.1 Role of Model Building

The necessity of building models may be rationalized in a number of ways. One reason for modeling is to support the building of software systems whose complexities exceed our mental capacities. For example, most of us are unable to multiply multi-digit numbers together in our heads, but with the aid of a pencil and paper the task is trivial. Our unaided mental capacity has limitations, which can be augmented by techniques that allow us to record previous thinking. Such augmentation permits the shifting of our mental focus to unsolved portions of the problem. We will use a software engineering notation to record previous analysis and design decisions so that we may focus on new areas of the software system.

Model building addresses the complexity of the system to be developed by facilitating the creation of a series of models. The first model begins with an abstract representation of the system. Later models contain progressively more detail. Subsequent models are made to contain more detail than their predecessor models by focusing on a smaller portion of the system and extending the analysis to produce additional depth in that portion. The process of model building, therefore, parallels the system developers' understanding of the system. As the system analysts begin their study of the target system, their understanding is very general. During the model-building process, the models become increasingly detailed, and the system developers' understanding also increases. Modeling software systems also creates concise and unambiguous representations, which facilitate communication between collaborating system developers. These precise representations can also be evaluated, verified, and corrected before significant time is invested in programming a poorly conceptualized system.

2.5.2 Creating Quality Modules

A modeling notation consists of representations of the elements from which the software system will be built. An important aspect of the notation expresses the units of modularity, which, in an object-oriented notation, are classes. When we focus our models on classes, which are software modules, the resulting software is likely to be modular. However, this focus on software modules is no guarantee of a successful software system. The modules must be well designed. Good module design requires that the modules be

- Cohesive
- Loosely coupled
- Encapsulated
- Reusable

For a module to be **cohesive**, its functionality must be well defined and well focused. A class must have a clear, easily expressed objective. Cohesion refers to the degree to which the internal elements of a module are bound to or related to each other. For example, a *Book* class is likely to be a cohesive module because the concept of a book is clearly delineated in the minds of most people. An additional requirement for cohesiveness in an object-oriented system is that each class contains methods that relate only to that class. For example, the *Book* class should contain attributes and methods associated with a single book. Therefore, the *Book* class should not contain a method to list all books alphabetically or an attribute that represents the total number of books in the library.

For a module to be **loosely coupled**, the module must be minimally connected to other modules. Coupling, therefore, refers to the degree to which modules are interconnected [101]. For example, the *Book* class is tightly coupled if it must invoke excessive numbers of methods of other classes in order to accomplish its tasks. Assume the *Book* class does not have an attribute to indicate whether the book is currently available, checked out, or waiting to be reshelved. To determine the status of a particular *Book* object, the book must check for itself on a list of checked-out books and on a list of books waiting for reshelving. If the book does not find itself on either of these lists, the book can assume that it is available. In this example, the *Book* class is tightly coupled with the *Checked-out List* and with the *Reshelve List*. The *Book* class requires the use of other classes in order to accomplish a standard *Book* operation.

Encapsulated modules are those that engage in **data hiding** [83]. The attributes of an object should not be directly available to other objects. The attributes of the object are available only through a predefined interface that consists of the object's public methods. A user of a class, therefore, must only understand how to use the methods of the class in order to successfully interact with objects of that class. Encapsulation implies that knowledge of the implementation of a particular class is not necessary for users of the class so that users of a class are insulated from the details of the inner workings of the class. Modules that are not encapsulated allow users direct access to their attributes or require understanding of how the class is implemented in order to use it successfully.

Software module **reuse** is a strategic objective of software engineering and is viewed as an essential approach for improving software development productivity [87]. Reuse, therefore, should be a driving motivation in module design. The implication of designing for reuse is that class functionality should be as broad and general as possible. To achieve maximum reuse, a class may require a few extra attributes or methods beyond the immediate scope of the target system. For example, designing a *Book* class for a library management system does not require the inclusion of the *suggested retail price* of the book as an attribute. The design of a *Book* class for a book store would require that this attribute be added. Conversely, the book store *Book* class does not require a *due date* attribute, while the library application clearly requires that this information be part of the *Book* class. Figure 2.7 shows the two different application areas for the *Book* class that require different attributes. A reusable book class should include all commonly required attributes and methods, encompassing all anticipated applications. The design of a class for all possible applications adds a great deal of overhead to a system development process and therefore may not be practical in all situations.

If the application areas for a particular class are sufficiently distinct, the creation of a class hierarchy may be necessary. For example, in Figure 2.7, a generic *Book* class is defined to contain the attributes and methods shared by all books, such as *title*, *author*, *ISBN*, and the respective methods using these attributes. Using inheritance, two additional book classes are derived from the more general *Book* class to accommodate the specific needs of each application of the class. In particular, a *Retail Book* class is created for the bookstore application, and a *Library Book* class is created for the library application. The *Retail Book* class contains the retail price and any other attributes relevant in a retail context but not relevant in a library

FIGURE 2.7 Software Module Reuse

context. Similarly, the *Library Book* class contains library-specific attributes, such as due date.

Another strategy for creating reusable classes is to create classes that operate on very general data types. In Java, for example, all classes are derived from the same super class, which is called the *Object* class. Similarly, C++ has an explicit **template** mechanism, which allows the creation of a parameterized class. The template parameter determines the data type of the variables inside the class. For example, instead of creating a container class that serves as a sorted list of books, we can enhance the reusability of our sorted list by defining it as a template class that will allow the type of item to be sorted to be passed in as a parameter. The sorted list class can then be used any time we have a list of objects that we would like to sort.

2.5.3 Modeling Notation

Each software engineering paradigm has at least one associated notation for representing systems designed using the paradigm. The object-oriented paradigm has several notational options. These options differ primarily in the symbols used to represent various object-oriented concepts. For example, Figure 2.8 shows two different notations for object-oriented systems. The left side of the figure shows Booch notation [14], while the right side of the figure shows the Unified Modeling Language (UML) notation [15]. Both show the same relationship between the *Patron* class and the *Book* class.

Throughout the rest of this textbook, we will use UML [15, 16, 36] to represent our software system conceptualizations. UML is widely accepted in industry. According to its creators, prior to the existence of UML, there were several modeling languages with minor differences in their overall expressive power. These languages shared a common core of object-oriented constructs but differed slightly in their notation. This disagreement in notation discouraged software engineering practitioners from engaging in object-oriented modeling. The creators of UML set out to define an industry-standard notation to encourage object-oriented software development [15].

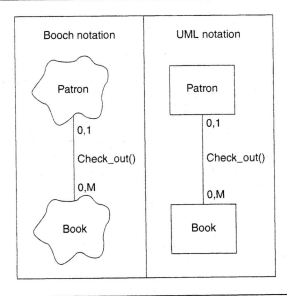

FIGURE 2.8 An Illustration of Two Different Notations for Class Diagrams

The stated goals [15] of UML are as follows:

- To provide users of UML with a ready-to-use, expressive visual modeling language so they can develop and exchange meaningful models.
- To provide extensibility and specialization mechanisms to extend core object-oriented concepts.
- To be independent of particular programming languages and development processes.
- To encourage the growth of the object-oriented tools market.
- To support higher-level development concepts such as collaborations, frameworks, patterns, and components.
- To integrate the best software engineering practices.

The creators of UML wish to facilitate the evolution of the object-oriented paradigm by proposing a clear, easy-to-use notation for software modeling that practitioners can agree to use. If practitioners are using the same notation for their conceptualizations, they can easily exchange software models. The UML creators also wish to support a wide range of application types and have thus made provisions for extensions to UML in order to accommodate specialized areas such as real-time system development [15].

2.5.4 Use of Models in Software Engineering

The goals of model building during the software life cycle are these:

- To create a nonnarrative, unambiguous expression of objects, classes, and their interrelationships.
- To model a variety of perspectives of the target system for use during analysis and design.
- To express a series of system models that are initially abstract, then refined to be increasingly detailed.
- To facilitate communication and collaboration among technical personnel.
- To create complete, verified, and unambiguous programming specifications.
- To serve as system documentation to be modified to reflect changes made during system maintenance.
- To assist in project planning and management.
- To support quality assurance and verification activities.

As this list of objectives suggests, the set of models used in software engineering is central to the whole software life cycle. Figure 2.9 summarizes the associations between UML models (as expressed in UML diagrams) and the critical phases and tasks of software engineering. We will present a precise characterization of how

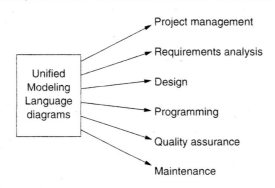

FIGURE 2.9 UML Diagrams and the Software Life Cycle

models are used to support software engineering activities as we discuss each software development phase in greater detail.

EXERCISE 2.6

Consider the process of building a toolshed again. How would you express the desired end product to a builder to ensure that the resulting toolshed meets the precise specifications you need? How does this act of modeling compare to the goals of model building during software engineering?

Qualities of a Good Object-Oriented System

The primary objective of applying good software engineering practices to a software project is to produce quality software in a timely, predictable manner. Two questions arise out of this statement. The first question is "What is quality software?" The second question is "Are the objectives of object-oriented software engineering any different from those of the process-oriented software approach?"

A feature that distinguishes object-oriented software development projects from process-oriented projects is that object-oriented development emphasizes the ability of the software to evolve smoothly over each software release. This emphasis implies that the software is easily extensible. The process-oriented approach emphasizes modularity in design so that maintenance is accomplished easily. Object-oriented development also emphasizes modularity, but the modules must also evolve easily. Extensibility of modules is, therefore, an objective of object-oriented development and is a quality of a good software system.

The desire for reusable software modules transcends the particular choice of software development approach. Certain mechanisms, however, are particularly conducive to the creation of reusable code. Many of these mechanisms are available in object-oriented programming languages. In particular, the inheritance mechanism, unique to object-oriented systems, suggests a strategy for software module reuse. One way of thinking about inheritance is that shared characteristics in a group of classes are extracted to form the parent classes and then the characteristics that differentiate classes are implemented in the child classes. The common code in the parent classes is used over and over (as inherited methods and attributes) in the child classes. Thinking of inheritance in this manner suggests that optimal use of inheritance hierarchies is another quality of a good object-oriented software system.

In the early 1990s, the International Standards Organization (ISO) produced a standard model for assessing the quality of all software independent of paradigm. This standard model, called ISO 9126, is shown in Figure 2.10. The model consists of six major characteristics, each of which has additional properties. The model indicates the qualities good software should possess but does not show how to assess these qualities. A good software development process must incorporate procedures for assessing the elements of quality software.

The ISO 9126 model serves to define the elements of quality software against which all software development methodologies should be compared. If a software development process has mechanisms for ensuring that software resulting from the development process possesses the qualities in the ISO 9126 model, we can feel more comfortable that the result of our development process will be quality soft-

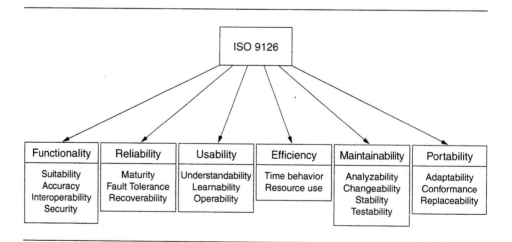

FIGURE 2.10 The ISO 9126 Qualities of Good Software

ware. **Functionality** addresses how well the resulting software product conforms to the client's stated and implied needs. Functionality also addresses additional organizational requirements, such as security and interoperability. The domain experts are unlikely to request these qualities explicitly. **Reliability** relates to the robustness of the software and its relative functionality in the context of equipment and media failure. **Usability** describes how easily users learn to use the software, its intuitiveness and ergonomics, and its ability to interact with other systems used by the client organization. **Efficiency** relates to efficient computer resource utilization. **Maintainability** requires software to be easily modified and tested without compromising its stability. Finally, **portability** addresses the ability of the software to run on multiple platforms and its conformance to organizational standards.

 ## Working in Teams

We will address additional information concerning holding effective team meetings, but first we will address a bit of computer science history and look at other ideas concerning how to structure a software engineering team.

2.7.1 The Chief Programmer Team

In the context of a course in software engineering it is advisable that all students have exposure to all aspects of the SE process. Industry has other priorities and consequently has a variety of strategies for creating teams. One classic team structure is based on Harlan Mills' work [68, 19] and is known as the **chief programmer team**. This team structure capitalizes on the idea that programming productivity varies between professional programmers by as much as an order of magnitude [91]. Another goal of the chief programming team structure is to minimize the interpersonal lines of communication necessary to develop the software system.

The chief programmer team, as the title suggests, centers on one highly productive programmer, the **chief programmer**. The remaining positions on the team exist to serve the chief programmer in some capacity. The following list describes Frederick Brooks' variation on this classic team structure [19]:

- The **surgeon** is the chief programmer who "cuts" the problem into smaller pieces. This person does it all from creating functional specifications to testing the code, and carries responsibility for the entire project.
- The **copilot** is the surgeon's able assistant who can engage in all the activities of the surgeon but has no ultimate responsibility for the project.
- The **administrator** takes care of any organizational tasks necessary for the team to operate.

- The **editor** edits any documentation produced by the surgeon.
- The **program clerk** maintains all files associated with developing the system.
- The **toolsmith** is responsible for installing, maintaining, and possibly creating any support tools necessary for the team to operate optimally.
- The **tester** creates test cases for testing the system.
- The **language lawyer** is expert in the languages and tools used to develop the system.

The communication pattern proposed by this team structure requires everyone to communicate directly with the surgeon and thus reduces the number of lines of communication.

It is important to keep in mind that the proposal for this software engineering team structure was created prior to the existence of any real software engineering methodology. While the surgeon does engage in the creation of software specifications, this phase of development is not yet recognized as essential to the success of the overall project.

EXERCISE 2.7   Gather in your software engineering teams and discuss the following questions:

- Would a chief programmer team utilize people effectively? Why or why not?
- Would people in the various positions each have high levels of job satisfaction? Why or why not?
- Would you structure your team according to the chief programmer team model? Who on your team would fill each role? Would everyone be happy with this choice?
- Is it appropriate to place so much emphasis on programming by giving the team structure the name "chief programmer team"?
- Would you enjoy the role of editor? Why or why not?

2.7.2 Holding Effective Team Meetings

As mentioned in the previous chapter, a number of precautions can be taken to ensure that team meeting time is well spent. One of these precautions is to create and adhere to an agenda for every meeting. This of course presumes that the agenda addresses the tasks the team must accomplish for the coming week. The question to be answered here is, How does one create an effective agenda?

The process of software engineering is punctuated by a number of deliverables that result from the tasks that make up a particular software engineering methodology. In fact, when we teach a software engineering course, we time the topics to coincide with project deliverable due dates. Thus, the deliverables determine the content of our classes. In the same way, these deliverables should be in the forefront of your mind when you are creating an agenda. You should ask yourself, "What deliverables must be completed in the coming week, and what group decisions are necessary in order to ensure they are completed?" Which tasks need to be assigned to team members to ensure the due dates are met? In fact, each meeting should end with each teammate having a clear understanding of what he or she needs to accomplish prior to the next class or team meeting. It is also important to make an effort to ensure that tasks are equitably assigned to each team member.

In order to give you a sense of the deliverables that will be required throughout the semester, Figure 2.11 lists each deliverable and the week that it is due. Your instructor may have additional deliverables or may allow you to revise specified deliverables after you receive feedback. For example, scenarios are due in week 2 and week 3. Thus students can receive feedback on their first attempts at scenarios and resubmit them in the third week for a grade. See also Summary Points box 2.3.

Development Phase	Deliverable	Due Date
Analysis	1. Refined requirements specification	Week 2
	2. Scenarios	Week 2 and week 3
	3. Primary class list	Week 2
	4. Class diagrams	Week 4
	5. Use case diagrams	Week 4
	6. Structured walk-through (in class)	End of week 4
Product Design	1. Object diagrams	Week 5
	2. Refined class diagrams	Week 5
	3. User interface mock-ups	Week 5–6
	3. State machines	Week 5
Class Design	1. Collaboration diagrams	Week 6
	2. Sequence diagrams	Week 7
	3. Object diagrams	Week 7
	4. Refined class diagrams	Week 8
	5. Class skeletons	Week 8
	6. Informal walk-through (in class)	End of week 8
Implementation	1. Implementation plan	Week 8
	2. Source code	Beginning of week 12
Testing	1. Test plan	Week 9
	2. Test analysis report	End of Week 12
	3. System integration	Week 14
	4. System delivery and demo	Week 15

FIGURE 2.11   Class Project Deliverables and Approximate Due Dates

SUMMARY POINTS 2.3

Effective Teams

1. Use the completion of deliverables as objectives when creating agendas for your team meetings.
2. Do not end a team meeting unless each team member has a clear idea of what he or she should accomplish.
3. Keep team meetings well focused on specific objectives.
4. Assign tasks to team members as equitably as possible.

2.8 Questions for Review

1. Create an object-oriented conceptualization for an object-oriented personal finance system. Sketch out the primary classes that you find necessary and explain how each relates to the others. Are there any intangible classes included? Is a class hierarchy possible? What class aggregation exists?
2. Outline a software development process that is structured like the waterfall model but uses prototyping as a technique. Does prototyping necessarily alter the sequence of software development techniques?
3. Create a software development process that has prototyping as its main technique. Which phases do you include?
4. Role-play with a classmate. One of you is an end user who wants an automated music system. The other is the systems analyst. How do you use prototyping to elicit the system requirements?
5. Why is an iterative/incremental development approach associated with the object-oriented paradigm?
6. Can the use of single inheritance introduce any redundancy in a class hierarchy? If so, describe the redundancy. Sketch out an inheritance hierarchy that illustrates this.
7. What characteristics do well-structured modular systems share?
8. What considerations are necessary to create reusable modules? Why is it advantageous to maximize reusability?
9. Compare and contrast the programming constructs of Java and C++ that relate to objects.
10. How are software models used in the process of software development?
11. Why is a unified software modeling notation important?

12. How are the objectives of object-oriented software engineering different from process-oriented software engineering?

13. For the class project, design a window to be used by each player to keep track of the evidence shown and the questions asked.

Object-Oriented Analysis

 Key Concepts

- Requirements analysis
- Requirements specification
- Participatory analysis
- Requirements elicitation
- Evaluating the requirements statement
- Verifying the requirements statement
- Modeling the requirements statement

- Primary class
- Support class
- Class diagram
- Collaboration
- Use case
- Use case diagram
- Scenario

 Introduction to Requirements Analysis

We have discussed a variety of software development processes, each of which consists of a number of different development phases. Although software development processes vary according to which phases are included, they all include a requirements analysis phase. During requirements analysis, the software analyst begins to understand the nature of the software system that is to be developed [88]. A **requirement** is a feature of the system to be developed. Therefore, when we speak of **requirements analysis**, we mean that the software analyst begins to analyze the software features that are necessary if the software system is to solve the problem at hand. Requirements analysis is a set of activities that include learning about the problem that needs a solution and specifying the required behaviors that must be present in a system that can solve the problem [29]. The completeness and duration of requirements analysis varies with the specific development process selected. For example, an iterative development process entails multiple analysis phases of shorter duration, whereas a waterfall approach includes a single, longer analysis phase. The iterative approach is usually associated with the object-oriented paradigm; therefore, in the object-oriented approach, the analyst usually completes several short analysis phases.

Although the precise nature of requirements analysis varies depending on the software development process, its basic objective always remains the same. The basic goal of the requirements analysis phase is to assess and specify the behavior of the final software system. During the initial phase of requirements analysis in an iterative development process, the analyst does not achieve the same depth of understanding as he or she would achieve in an exhaustive requirements analysis. During iterative software development, the objective of the first analysis phase is to abstractly characterize the **breadth** of functionality of the final system.

The purpose of assessing the system in terms of its breadth of functionality rather than its depth of functionality is to develop the system's **architectural vision** [14]. An architectural vision establishes the primary classes and interrelationships that comprise the software system. The goal is to create a set of classes that are likely to remain stable and unchanged throughout the development of the system. By viewing the system broadly early in the development process, we seek to avoid the need to restructure the classes in the system late in the development process. In other words, as the system evolves and areas of functionality are added, the core classes developed during initial analysis should evolve through the addition of attributes and methods rather than through the restructuring and rewriting of existing code. We will give a detailed example of an architectural vision of the library system later in this chapter.

The Importance of Requirements Analysis

As was discussed in Chapter 1, large-scale software development projects are fraught with risks and all too frequently fail to produce a useful end product. Boehm has studied software development projects and has concluded that correct and thorough requirements analysis is critical to producing a successful, cost-effective final software system [10, 12]. In fact, Boehm claims that by investing more up-front effort in verifying and validating the software requirements and specifications, software project developers will see reduced integration and test costs as well as higher software reliability and maintainability [10]. This conclusion should not be startling. It should be intuitive that in order for a software project to be successful, the developers of that project must understand what the users expect the final system to do.

Frederick Brooks has also studied a wide range of software projects and written about successes and failures. In discussing requirements analysis he has said,

> The hardest single part of building a software system is deciding precisely what to build. No other part of the conceptual work is as difficult as establishing the detailed technical requirements, including all the interfaces to people, to machines, and to other software systems. No other part of the work so cripples the resulting system if done wrong. No other part is more difficult to rectify later. [19]

The primary question addressed in this chapter is: What comprises good requirements analysis? We can facilitate our study of good requirements analysis by investigating recent success stories. Many software development success stories attribute the success of the project to involving the domain experts, the users of the software being developed. A technique called **participatory analysis** [70] has been successfully applied to the development of software for the radiology department in a hospital [58]. Participatory analysis involves staff members of all levels of the application area interacting with the software development team to establish a set of **functional requirements**, which is a description of how the system should behave in certain situations [87]. All employee needs are heard without regard to where the employee fits in the organizational structure. In other words, the needs of a radiology technician are just as important to the success of the software project as the needs of a hospital administrator.

The University of Southern California Center for Software Engineering has developed a negotiation-based technique for software system requirements analysis [13]. This approach also involves end users in the requirements analysis process in a central and collaborative manner. USC has had great success applying this model during the development of a multimedia application for the school's integrated library [13].

The importance of successful communication between the end users of a system and the software development team has resulted in a new professional specialization. Professionals specializing in this area serve as liaisons between the domain experts and the software development team and work to facilitate communication between the two groups. For example, a company called PeopleSoft provides consultants who behave as "translators." These consultants first engage in conversation with domain experts, gathering information concerning user needs and software requirements. The consultants then explain these requirements to technical staff [34].

These success stories relate to one critical aspect of requirements analysis, the **elicitation** of requirements from end users. Requirements elicitation entails a dialogue between end users and technical staff. The importance of this dialogue

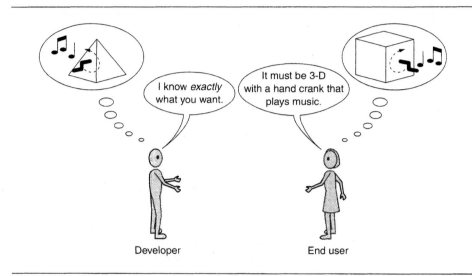

FIGURE 3.1 Miscommunication between End Users and Developers

suggests that successful software developers must possess effective communication skills.

Requirements analysis begins with elicitation of requirements from the domain experts. The information gathered during this process must then be recorded in a clear, succinct, unambiguous manner. This recording of requirements is called **requirements modeling**. The requirements model becomes part of a document called the **requirements specification**. If the specification does not correctly reflect the needs of the users, there is no chance for the software system to be successful in the long run.

Figure 3.1 illustrates a typical scenario in which a developer communicates with an end user to determine his or her needs. In the depicted situation the developer thinks he or she has successfully determined the needs of the end user, when in reality both parties are picturing a very different end product. This confusion can occur even when the end user is speaking in less ambiguous terms.

EXERCISE 3.1   Pair up with a classmate and role-play requirements elicitation for a piece of software. One student should think of a piece of software that he or she is familiar with while the second student asks questions concerning the functionality of the software. When the second student is satisfied that he or she is sufficiently familiar with the software, he or she should describe the software in terms of informal scenarios. The first student should then rate the accuracy of the second student's understanding.

Pair up with a classmate. One student should sketch the design of a house on a piece of paper. This student should then describe the house to the second student in strictly functional terms. For example, the first student might say that the house allows someone to prepare a meal while interacting with guests and provides private sleeping accommodations for one couple and two individuals, rather than describing the house as having a kitchen that is open to the living room and three bedrooms on the second floor. The second student should then sketch this house based on the functional description. Compare the two sketches. How close are the sketches to each other? Why should software be described in strictly functional terms, but not houses?

Requirements Specification

The objective of requirements analysis is to characterize the behavior of the system to be developed in a complete, consistent, correct, and unambiguous manner. The behavior of the system must meet the needs of the system's end users. For example, recall the book-tracking system introduced in Chapter 1. A user of this system would probably require the system to determine which library patrons should receive notices that they have books overdue. The final system should facilitate this task by generating lists of patrons along with their addresses and appropriate correspondence concerning overdue library materials. A software system that does not facilitate this task is less useful than a system that does.

The needs of the end users are formally expressed in a document called the **requirements specification** or **requirements statement** (see Summary Points box 3.1). This document may be drafted by the end users and given to the software development team. Even when the users themselves have drafted the requirements specification, an important step in requirements analysis involves verifying that the requirements-specification document accurately characterizes the needs of the users. However, the users may give nothing in writing to the software development team. In these situations, the technical staff must establish the contents of the requirements specification by interviewing the user community to elicit requirements.

A requirements specification may include the following items:

- The **supported activity list** is a characterization of the user activities that should be supported by the final system. Nearly every requirements specification includes such a list, but a common problem is the omission of certain details or even major areas of functionality.
- The **human-computer interface description** most commonly includes pictures of the critical windows comprising the final system. Such information is

extremely useful because these illustrations can often be translated directly into the final system design. This illustrative description also conveys a tremendous amount of information concerning the functional structure of the final system.

- The **solved problems list** specifies the problems present in whatever current system is being used that will be solved by the new system. This information provides the motivation for undertaking the development of the new system.

- The **information sources list** specifies the location of information necessary to support the new system. If there are any issues of interconnectivity or data translation between systems, they are listed here. Any data-entry or data-acquisition bottlenecks will also be listed here.

- The **Information-requesting organizations list** details any organizations or departments that depend on the current and/or the future system. The list also specifies whether these needs are currently being met and whether any anticipated needs are known. In addition, this list describes the kinds of information needed by these groups.

- The **checks and balances list** details known data integrity checks for both the current system and the new system. If additional information is needed to carry out these checks, the details are given here. Finally, the need for and feasibility of checking data integrity online versus in a batch manner are specified.

- **Security and fault-tolerance requirements:** The need for special security is examined in this section of the requirements specification. Any proprietary, classified, or private information is listed. In addition, if parts of the system support life-critical functions, details concerning what occurs if these parts fail are given here.

- If any other systems transfer control to or use portions of the current system or the new system, they are listed in the **interoperating systems list**. Details concerning known future expansion are also given.

- **Estimates of present information capacity and projected growth:** Any system capacity issues related to the volume of data handled by the system are described. If large files are to be transmitted over a network, issues concerning growth are examined. Any special limitations in the amount of data that can be handled by databases or disk drives are also described.

- **Project time frame:** This section of the specification gives a time frame for completion of the project milestones. Constraints on the time frame, such as changes in law or life endangerment because of the existing system, are also listed.

- **Prioritization of requirements:** This section of the specification details which requirements are needed first in order for a smooth transition from the old system to the new. In addition, this section will list any requirements that are desired but not critical for a sufficiently functional final system.

- Any concerns about ethics are set forth in the **ethical concerns list**. For example, if there are privacy issues relating to the information handled by the system, details concerning steps to guard individual privacy are listed.

Although the preceding list contains items that *may* be included in a requirements specification, they are not likely to be part of a requirements specification authored by end users. The list should therefore serve as a generic checklist of topics that must be resolved in discussions of the final system. Many of these topics may not be adequately covered in an end-user-authored requirements specification even if they have been addressed. More discussion is likely to be necessary for such topics.

SUMMARY POINTS 3.1

Possible Elements of a Requirements Specification

1. Supported activity list
2. Human-computer interface description
3. Solved problems list
4. Information sources list
5. Information-requesting organizations list
6. Checks and balances list
7. Security and fault-tolerance requirements
8. Interoperating systems list
9. Estimates of present information capacity and projected growth
10. Project time frame
11. Prioritization of requirements
12. Ethical concerns list

To see what an actual requirements specification looks like, we will now return to the library system that was introduced in Chapter 1. We will expand upon the functional requirements to create a system that is more generally useful to library staff. We will assume that the initial specification, as presented in the next section, was written by the library staff rather than by a group of technical staff. An evaluation, refinement, and verification of the sample specification follows to show how these specifications are used in the design of a software system.

3.5 *Case Study:* **Library Management System Specification**

The college library needs a new Library Management System (LMS) to track and manage its resources. The most obvious resource the library must manage is its books. Books are checked out, checked in, and requested by library patrons. Books

CASE STUDY

can also have special status if they are placed on reserve or if they are reference books. In either case, such books may not leave the premises. Reminders are mailed to patrons when resources are more than two weeks overdue. Patrons are fined $0.25 per day that books are overdue, to a maximum of $5.00 per overdue item. The library also has other resources that may be checked out, including music CDs, software, and videos, each of which may only be checked out for one week at a time.

Patrons also have a variety of statuses that influence how long a book may be checked out. A patron's status also determines what services are available to her. Students may check out books for four weeks, and faculty may check them out for three months. Library staff may keep a book for an entire year. Any checkable library resource may be renewed as long as no other patron has requested it. Faculty and library staff may place a book on reserve for the period of one semester, or they may bring in foreign resources (books, papers, disks, music CDs, magazines, or tapes that do not belong to the library) and put them on reserve.

The library must also manage a large selection of weekly, monthly, and quarterly magazines, which may not be checked out but are available as reference materials. These magazines are annually bound into volumes or recorded as microfiche. Additional activities of the library staff include reshelving books, renewing magazine subscriptions, and ordering new library resources.

Library staff members also provide a number of other services supporting activities in the research community and for the general public. Two dozen computers are scattered throughout the library. These computers provide access to a variety of databases and indexes as well as to the Internet via up-to-date web-browsing software. Designated library staff are available to assist patrons with their research needs using these computer-based tools as well as standard hard-copy indexes. The library must also connect to the holdings of other libraries so that interlibrary loan requests can be fulfilled. A subset of these libraries allow patrons to directly browse their selections.

A final responsibility of the library staff is the acquisition and retirement of books in the collection. In acquiring new books, a balance between meeting the requests of patrons and achieving a representative breadth in the collection is sought. Books are retired when their content is deemed to be out of date and of no historical value. Ideally, when a book is out of date, it will not be retired until a more up-to-date resource has replaced it in the library's collection.

Create a requirements specification for a computer-based game of ticktacktoe. Address all the possible items that may make up a requirements specification.

Evaluating the Requirements Specification

A classic, and dangerously wrong, response to a requirements specification is to take it at face value and not engage the end users in a continuing dialogue to flesh out detail and find errors. "We gave them what they asked for, so we are not to blame if the system is not being used." We have heard these very words from too many software developers in our careers. We hold that the software development team is to blame whenever unusable software is developed. The software developers are responsible for the verification of the adequacy and accuracy of the requirements specification. The domain experts were hired to perform their respective job functions, not to write technical specifications. Therefore, the buck stops with the software development team.

When a requirements specification is being evaluated, a number of perspectives should be considered. The specification must be clarified for ambiguities, errors, or implicit assumptions. Professionals with different backgrounds have different vocabularies and often have difficulty in communicating with each other. For this reason, implicit assumptions from one professional background may not translate into the same assumptions for professionals in a different field. In order for these ambiguities, errors, and implicit assumptions to come to light, much discussion must occur among the various groups involved in the system development.

To prepare for these discussions, the software development team must make a list of questions that arise while reading the requirements specification. These questions will address ambiguous or potentially erroneous aspects of the specification. These questions are the "easy" ones to come up with. The more difficult task is to determine whether there are major functional areas that are simply not addressed in the specification. Domain experts are frequently so entrenched in their area of expertise that they feel certain things are too obvious to mention, or such obvious items simply do not occur to them. Therefore, the true requirements of the final system may not be limited to those items formally documented by the end user.

Exchange your ticktacktoe specification with one of your classmates. How did your specifications differ from your classmate's? Elaborate on the comparative strengths and weaknesses of each specification.

The following are potential questions formulated in response to the sample library management system requirements statement:

1. What sort of interface is envisioned? Naturally, some sort of graphical user interface will be recommended by the software development team. How should library resources be presented to and browsed by library patrons?
2. Does the system need to allow patrons to search the holdings of the library online?
3. Will library patrons be required to have a library number? In other words, will there be a unique number associated with each person allowed to borrow resources from the library? If yes, do these numbers ever expire?
4. Should the system allow interlibrary loan requests to be filed electronically?
5. Are there any limits on patrons' use of research databases or indexes because of cost incurred by the library? Should the costs of using these resources be tracked? If so, how will the results be used, and therefore, how should they be presented? Does the status of the library patron determine which research resources he or she is allowed to use?
6. Does the system need to advise library staff regarding books with potential for retirement? If yes, what criteria should be used? What kind of notification would the library staff require?
7. How long is a requested resource held for a patron before it is returned to general circulation?
8. Are the overdue fees the same for all types of items?
9. What computerized indexes and databases are provided to library patrons?

These questions represent a wide spectrum of question types that must be asked to clarify a requirements specification. The specification did not address the human-computer interface, so the purpose of question 1 is to flesh out an omitted topic. Questions 2 through 5 attempt to determine whether there are any unstated assumptions concerning the use of the online catalog, borrowing of library resources, interlibrary loan requests, and research resources. Question 6 attempts to determine if there is a large area of functionality that has been omitted from the requirements specification. The remaining three questions clarify relatively minute aspects of the system. There are, of course, many other questions that might be asked (see Summary Points box 3.2).

EXERCISE 3.5   Create a series of questions that will clarify the ticktacktoe specification written by your classmate. Exchange lists of questions with your classmate. Are you surprised by the number of ambiguities in your statement?

Creating Quality Requirements Specifications

1. Requirements specifications must be correct, complete, unambiguous, and verified.

2. Requirements specifications must be verified by the development team.

3. Developers should strive to produce a system that is better than the system requested by the end users.

4. Developers must be in close communication with the end users throughout the development process.

3.7 Refining the Requirements Specification

The requirements specification is an evolving document. The answers to the questions found during the evaluation should be added to the specification. The process of asking questions, getting answers, and updating the requirements specification may take several iterations until the specification is relatively complete. With practice, fewer iterations are required because the software development team will be able to target their questions more precisely in the first or second iteration. In any case, the refinement of the requirements specification requires much communication between the software development team and the domain experts.

We have included here the first refinement of the requirements specification for the library management system. This refinement combines the previous version of the specification with answers to the questions listed in the previous section. The format of this specification is somewhat different from the previous version because it has been written by the technical staff rather than the library staff. In this version, requirements are itemized into the lists that were discussed previously.

Based on the questions written by your classmate in response to your ticktacktoe requirements statement, revise your specification.   **EXERCISE 3.6**

3.7.1 Prototyping as a Refinement Tool

The most foolproof means to refine a requirements specification is to create a **prototype** based on the existing specification [56]. Recall that a prototype is a small version of the system, usually with limited functionality [87]. Ambiguities will make themselves known during the creation of the prototype as the prototype developers are unclear how to proceed. It is appropriate to enlist the assistance of a range of end users to clarify the requirements statement and jointly evolve the prototype. Because the users can interact with a mock-up of the proposed system, prototypes provide an unambiguous vehicle for communicating with the end users. The users can thus critique the adequacy and accuracy of the mock-up system, providing invaluable feedback from a relatively small amount of work.

DELIVERABLE
3.1

Supported Activity List for Refined LMS Specification

1. Allowing library staff to perform activities that are not available to the general public. Such activities include all activities other than searching the catalogs. For example, the general public cannot change the status of a resource in the computer or validate that a patron has a valid library number.
2. Validating that a patron has an up-to-date library number, no resources more than two weeks overdue, and not too many checked-out resources.
3. Giving library numbers to patrons.
4. Deleting expired library numbers and associated patrons. A library number is valid until the patron graduates when the patron is a student. A library number for faculty and library staff is valid as long as employment at the college continues.
5. Checking out books for varying loan periods. Students can check out books for four weeks, faculty for three months, and library staff for one year.
6. Checking out other resources, such as music CDs, videos, and software. All of these resources may be checked out for one week, regardless of the status of the patron. Note that reference resources cannot be checked out.
7. Checking in resources.
8. Changing the status of a resource from "reshelve" to "available."
9. Putting a resource owned by the library on reserve. Only faculty and library staff can put resources on reserve. Reserved resources cannot be checked out.
10. Putting a resource owned by someone other than the library on reserve. These items cannot be checked out.
11. Requesting a resource for a particular patron. A requested resource will be held for two weeks for a patron. If it has not been checked out within two weeks, the resource will be returned to general circulation.
12. Searching the online catalog by author, subject, keyword, resource title, or Dewey call number.
13. Interacting with online research resources such as InfoTrac, Wilson's Guide to Periodicals, and FirstSearch.
14. Adding a resource to the online catalog.

15. Deleting a resource from the online catalog. The determination of when to delete a particular resource is made manually without input from this system.
16. Generating lists of overdue resources.
17. Generating form letters for patrons with resources more than two weeks overdue.
18. Determining the fee amount for a particular overdue resource. The fee structure is $0.25 per day for each overdue resource to a maximum of $5.00 per resource.
19. Linking to the online catalogs of other libraries for searching.
20. Generating interlibrary loan requests.

Human-Computer Interface Description

The interface between the users and the system has two modes. The public mode is available to all patrons. The private mode is available only to users who have a password. All library staff must have passwords. The public mode allows the user to search the current online catalog, including the computerized databases and indexes. The private mode allows the user to view the library record of any patron, to add resources to and delete resources from the catalog, to enter work productivity information, to request lists of overdue items, and to initiate transactions to check out and check in library resources.

The initial public mode interface screen is shown in Figure 3.2. When the patron enters the requested information, a new screen, shown in Figure 3.3, is

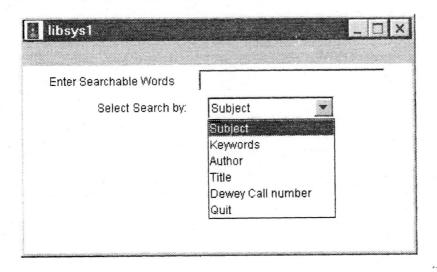

FIGURE 3.2 Initial Screen in Public Mode Interface

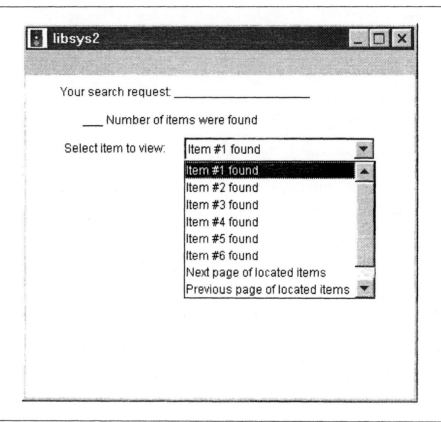

FIGURE 3.3 Second Screen in Public Mode Interface

displayed. When a patron chooses a particular item to view, a new screen showing the author, title, status, Dewey call number, and a short summary of the resource is displayed.

The initial private mode interface screen requires a library staff identification number and a password to be entered. If a valid number is entered, the second private mode interface screen, shown in Figure 3.4, is displayed. When a particular task is chosen from this screen, an appropriate information-gathering screen is then displayed for that task.

Solved Problems List

In this section of a requirements specification, the problems with the existing system that gave rise to the desire for a new system should be enumerated. For our example, however, we have not indicated that the new system is going to take the place of some existing system. The range of existing systems that could be

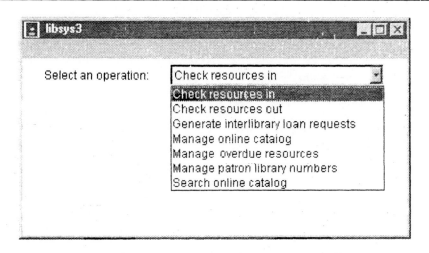

FIGURE 3.4 Second Screen in Private Mode Interface

in place is very large, and for that reason we will not include a comprehensive solved problems list in this requirements specification. During the analysis phase, the development team must gain an understanding of the things the users do not like or find inadequate in the existing system. Without this knowledge, the developers may simply create a new version of the existing system, problems and all.

Information Source List

The new system must receive information from the following sources for the following purposes:

1. **Other libraries**: The online catalogs of other libraries will be available for browsing by patrons of this library.
2. **Online research resources**, such as InfoTrac, Wilson's Guide to Periodicals, and FirstSearch: These databases of resources will also be available for browsing by patrons of this library.
3. **Existing online catalog**: The current system presumably has an online catalog that exists as some sort of database of all of the resources owned by the library. When creating the new system, the existing catalog must be converted to a format that can be read by the new system. This conversion happens only once, and, therefore, the existing catalog is not a source of ongoing information.
4. **Existing patron database**: When creating the new system, the existing patron database must be converted to a format that can be read by the new system. This

conversion happens only once, and, therefore, the existing patron database is not a source of ongoing information.

5. **Student record database**: Since students are allowed to be patrons of the library only as long as they are students of the college, the new system must have access to student records for the college. This information is used to determine when a patron should be added to or deleted from the patron database.

6. **Employee record database**: Since faculty and library staff are allowed to be patrons of the library only as long as they are employees of the college, the new system must have access to employee records for the college. This information is used to determine when a patron should be added to or deleted from the patron database.

Information-Requesting Organizations

Just as our system must give patrons the ability to browse the online catalogs of other libraries, it must also give patrons of other libraries the ability to browse the online catalog of this library.

Automated Checks and Balances

All dates in the system must be checked for their validity. For example, the month, day, and year should be check so that a date of February 31, 1999, is not allowed to be entered. Publishing dates for resources must be the current year or earlier. In addition, only a person who exists on either the student database or the employee database can be added as a patron of the library.

Security and Fault-Tolerance Requirements

In this section of the requirements specification, the following questions should be answered. What happens if the system is down? Can patrons still borrow resources? Is there a way to browse resources when the system is down? Is there some sort of manual backup to take the place of the system? Are multiple copies of the software and online catalog kept on a variety of machines to provide a backup system in case of a crash? The answers to these questions vary considerably from application to application. For example, a system that determines how much oxygen should be pumped into the space shuttle must be completely fault-tolerant, with many redundancies built in. The answer to the question for our library management system will vary from institution to institution. Of course, we would like our system to be totally fault-tolerant, but at some point the cost of making the system more robust outweighs the risk of failure. The line between cost and fault tolerance varies considerably. For the purposes of this requirements specification, we will simply assume that there is no redundant information but that in the case of a crash the library staff will move to paper and pencil for allowing patrons to check out resources. No browsing of the catalog will be possible in such an event.

Interoperating Systems List

For our library management system, there are no interoperating systems.

Present Information Capacity and Projected Growth

This section of the requirements specification is very important for the development of a successful system. Through conversations with users, the developers must get a sense of how much information is currently maintained and what the capacity of the present system is. During these conversations, the developers should also get a sense of how fast the amount of information is growing as well as how long the new system must be in place before it might be replaced. For example, perhaps our library is undergoing renovations to the building in order to be able to house twice the current number of resources. And perhaps the library is also in a financial position to acquire that many resources. In such a case, the system that is developed must be able to withstand huge growth in a short amount of time. If it cannot withstand such growth, yet another new system will likely need to be created in the very near future, probably very soon after our new system is completed. Users will likely see our new system as a failure because it needs to be replaced so quickly. For the purposes of this requirements specification, we will assume that our library is unlikely to undergo very much growth in the near future, discarding nearly the same number of resources as are acquired.

Projected Time Frame

The software developers must discuss with the users any requirements they have in terms of completion of the project. For our library management system, we will assume that the library staff and college administration require that the conversion from the old system to the new system take place over the summer so that the new system will be in place by the next fall semester.

Prioritization of Requirements

Very often, users want some piece of the new system to be finished immediately because that piece involves some critical functionality. Through discussions with the users, the developers should gain a sense of the stages that might be involved in the system development based on user need. For our requirements specification, we will assume that the users have no priorities for the requirements. We will develop the system in phases, nonetheless, because we have chosen the iterative approach to software development. But the users do not care which features of the system are done when.

Ethical Concerns

In this section of the requirements specification, any ethical concerns that have come up during conversations with the users are enumerated. For the library management system, some of these concerns might include the following:

1. Will the system keep track of past checked-out resources for patrons? If so, what happens in the case of a subpoena to view this history? Who has access to look at the borrowing history for a particular patron? Does the answer to the last question change when the patron is a minor? Does the answer change when the patron is not a minor but is still a dependent of another person?
2. Does our system use any Internet-based search engines to find materials on the World Wide Web? If so, how do we protect children from web sites they ought not see while allowing free access to materials for adults?

Verifying the Requirements Specification

The objective of evaluating the requirements specification is to clarify and elaborate on the initial document. The next step in the analysis process, verification of the requirements specification, should begin with a relatively complete specification, which has gone through the evaluation stage and been updated with the results. The goal of verification is to attempt to confirm the correctness and completeness of the requirements specification. The tool for verifying a requirements specification is the **structured walk-through** [35], which may be preceded by an **informal walk-through**.

An informal walk-through is used to correct obvious problems with a requirements specification before the large meeting for the structured walk-through is scheduled. The informal walk-through typically involves a structured presentation of the behavior of the proposed system by one member of the software development team to one or more other members of the development team. Through the informal walk-through, glaring errors in the requirements specification can be corrected without wasting the time of a large number of users.

A structured walk-through typically involves the entire software development team with a wide spectrum of individuals representing every area of expertise and responsibility expected to interact with the final system. Individuals from throughout the organizational hierarchy of the user community should attend the structured walk-through. Before a structured walk-through is scheduled, the requirements specification must be refined and well understood by the software developers. Any interaction with end users to clarify domain-specific questions should already have taken place.

The key objective of a structured walk-through is to present the refined contents of the requirements specification as understood by the software developers. This presentation to the user community should proceed in an ordered and thorough manner, so that errors and omissions are apparent and resolvable. Although walk-throughs are very beneficial to software developers, care must be taken so as to avoid wasting the time of the end users. There are a number of questions, then, that we must answer:

- When should a structured walk-through take place?
- In what form is the system presented to the end users?
- How do we ensure that the walk-through is well structured?

The question of when structured walk-throughs should take place is answered by attempting to strike a balance of needs (see Summary Points box 3.3). The success of the final system requires communication to clarify functional requirements. End users, however, are busy with their primary responsibilities, which frequently do not allow extra time for explaining organizational procedures to software developers. For the sake of the end users, walk-throughs should be scheduled sparingly. Because of the number of end users required to make the structured walk-through useful to the developers, the software developers should have gained a fair amount of expertise in the application domain before the walk-through is scheduled. In addition, the original requirements statement should already have gone through a series of refinements so that glaring errors and omissions have been eliminated.

The questions concerning the form of the structured walk-through and how to ensure that the presentation is well structured can be addressed simultaneously if one chooses to portray the requirements in the form of **use cases**. The notion of a use case will be more formally discussed in section 3.6. Briefly, a use case characterizes a succinct and complete real-world task of the final system. The software

---

SUMMARY POINTS 3.3

Holding Effective Structured Walk-Throughs

1. The entire development team should be present.
2. Representatives from all possible user types should be present.
3. Developers should verify their understanding of the requested system by presenting their understanding of the system to the end users.
4. The walk-through should be structured around use cases.
5. The requirements specification should be refined before a structured walk-through is held.

developers structure the functional needs expressed in the requirements specification as use cases through an associated modeling notation called **collaboration diagrams**. In the next section, we discuss use cases and how they answer our final two questions about the form and structure of the structured walk-through. Collaboration diagrams will be discussed in the next chapter.

Propagating Requirements throughout Development

As discussed before, the ultimate criterion for the success of a software system is whether or not it meets the functional needs of the end users. Indeed the ISO 9126 quality model depicted in Figure 2.10 specifies two categories that address meeting user needs, **functionality** and **usability**. If great care is taken to assess these needs during the requirements analysis phase and then no procedure in the software development process ties these requirements to future products of the development process, the analysis is potentially futile. Therefore, it is essential that the needs assessed during analysis are propagated through the delivery of the software system.

In order to do so, the elements of design and implementation must relate back to the requirements statement. This purpose can easily be achieved if the models produced during analysis are tied to specific user needs, and if these references to the user requirements are propagated as the models are evolved and enhanced as the development process progresses. Because design not only evolves models produced during analysis but also introduces new kinds of diagrams, special attention must be placed on ensuring that the association to the requirements statement is propagated to all relevant models.

A simple means to cross-reference the models produced during development is to enumerate the individual requirements as is done in Deliverable 3.1. These numbers are then placed in all models that address that particular need. As these models are refined and new models are derived from them, the numbers are propagated to the new models as well. Mnemonics or other symbols may be used in place of the numbers if preferred.

3.10 The Process of Requirements Analysis

Before proceeding further, let us review why we are going through the process of analysis. A software system begins its existence as a request to automate a set of related tasks to support the needs of a number of individuals associated with an organization. The ultimate objective is to produce a well-structured, robust, extensible, efficient, object-oriented system. Object-oriented analysis specifies a series of steps and techniques through which a requirements specification is created, refined, and verified to be adequate and accurate.

We have thus far limited our discussion of object-oriented software engineering to the essential issues motivating and generally describing the field. The reader should now have an understanding of the benefits of software engineering as well as a vague sense of how one begins the software engineering process. The discussion will now become more concrete as we incorporate specific techniques and notation. In particular, we will use the **Unified Modeling Language** [15] (**UML**) as our modeling notation for the rest of this textbook. In addition, the particular software engineering methodology we will use is **Use Case Centered Development** (UCCD). In this methodology, use cases play a central role in the entire software development process. We feel that UCCD distinguishes itself from other software engineering methodologies in its clarity and simplicity.

Figure 3.5 shows the steps of the UCCD analysis methodology. Through these steps, the class definitions for the final system are developed and refined. These class definitions represent the architectural vision of the final system. The figure shows the system developers and domain experts working together to create and refine the requirements specification. From the requirements specification, the software developers create a list of primary classes and a set of informal scenarios. The informal scenarios will be used to create use cases, which in turn will be the basis of what is presented to the users during the structured walk-through. Both the use cases and the primary classes are modeled in a variety of diagrammatic notations taken from UML [15]. The entire process is described in the following subsections.

3.10.1 Identifying Classes of UCCD

The first step of the UCCD analysis methodology is the initial analysis of the requirements specification, the result of which is a list of **primary classes**. Primary classes are classes that are necessary to conceptualize the final system. If the initial analysis is successful, no more than one or two of the classes that are central to the functionality of the system will be omitted. Other classes are expected to be needed throughout the development process. These nonprimary classes, called **support classes**, are not crucial to conceptualizing the system.

Support classes serve as building blocks for other classes to reduce complexity, as container classes to organize or aggregate instances of other classes, or as transient classes that exist to perform a service and then are deleted. Support classes may also serve some technical need such as establishing a network connection, or they may be other incidental classes whose need is not apparent from initial system conceptualization. These support classes are developed during later stages of analysis and during the design phase.

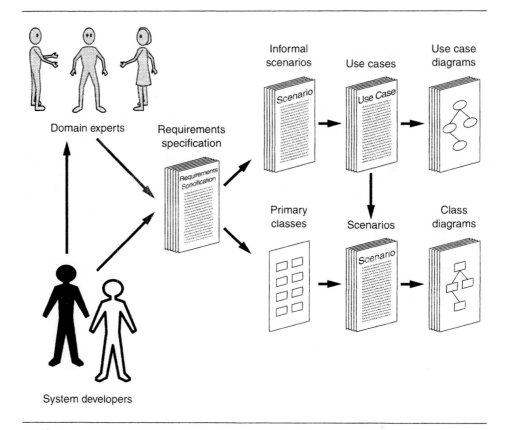

FIGURE 3.5 The UCCD Analysis Process

The identification of primary classes and the interrelationships among them requires skill in analyzing system requirements. Such skill often comes as a result of extensive experience. Novice software engineers can begin to gain experience and skill in requirements analysis by keeping certain guidelines in mind. One useful starting point, proposed by Coad and Yourdon [25], is to create a list of all nouns from the requirements specification. This list can be used as a starting point for class identification because classes and nouns are simply representations of things in the real world. To determine whether a particular noun should be used as a class in the software system, each noun can be examined for the following characteristics:

- **Retained information:** Potential classes require information to be stored about them. For example, assume that the noun is *system user*. To determine whether a class should be created to represent system users, one may ask if a system user is strictly external to the system or if there are certain attributes of the user that must be stored in the system. If the system is a single-user system and no history of use is recorded, it is unlikely that a *system user* class is necessary. However, if multiple concurrent users exist or a history of use is recorded about individual users, then a *system user* class is probably necessary.

- **Needed services:** Does the potential class have a set of operations that may provide services to other classes? Is there a set of information to be manipulated or retrieved by methods in order to protect the integrity of this data? For example, in a game you allow each user to inquire the current score of each opposing player. The information characterizing the state of the game such as each players' score, amount of time elapsed, and so on, may be stored in an instance of the *Game* class.

- **Multiple attributes:** Does the potential class have more than a single attribute? If not, this noun should probably serve as an attribute of some other class. For example, in the description of a banking application, the noun *balance* plays an important role. Despite its importance, a balance is simply represented as a double or integer, if one represents the balance as cents as opposed to dollars. So, balance is likely to be an attribute in an *Account* class as opposed to being a class itself.

- **Common attributes:** Do all instances of this noun share the same attributes? If not, this noun should probably not be a class in the system. For example, a bank keeps track of customers by recording their name, address, phone number, and list of active accounts. Because each customer has the same categories of information, *Customer* should be a class. However, the external entities that the banking system interfaces with, such as a TCP/IP connection, an external database, and an indexed file, share no common attributes, so an *External entity* class should probably not be created.

- **Common operations:** Do the operations defined for this noun apply to all other instances of the noun? If not, the noun should probably not be a class in the system. Just as in the preceding criterion for deciding whether a noun should be a primary class of the system, if a class like the *Customer* class has a set of common attributes, one would expect to have a common set of methods to operate on those common attributes, like *getName()*, *getAddress*, and so forth.

- **Essential requirements:** Are there external entities known to the system that produce or consume information? If so, a class is typically needed in the final system in order to complete the required information exchange. Rather than having a single *External entity* class as was deemed inappropriate previously, each external entity should have its own class definition. For example, if one created a *Database* class, a set of easy-to-learn methods could be provided to the developers so that each developer using the database would not need to be familiar with the technical details of utilizing the database. In fact, the type of underlying database could be switched, and the methods of the *Database* class need not change.

Identify the primary and secondary classes from your ticktacktoe specification, and explain briefly your rationale for selecting each class.

3.10.2 *Case Study:* Identifying Classes for LMS

The following is a list of all the nouns found in the requirements specification for the Library Management System: *Patron, Library Number, Student, Faculty, Library Staff, College, Book, Loan Period, Resource, Music CD, Video, Software, Status, Reference Resource, Reserved Resource, Requested Resource, Online Catalog, Author, Subject, Keyword, Title, Dewey Call Number, Online Research Resource, InfoTrac, Wilson's Guide to Periodicals, FirstSearch, Overdue Resource, List of Overdue Resources, Overdue Form Letter, Overdue Fee, Fee Structure, Other Libraries,* and *Interlibrary Loan Request*. We now must examine this list of nouns using the list of characteristics from the preceding subsection to determine which of the nouns should become primary classes in our system.

Consider the noun *Patron*. Each patron of the library has much information that must be retained by the system. For example, the system needs information concerning the name and address of each patron along with information about the resources that the patron currently has checked out. In addition, the system may need to keep track of any resources the patron has requested and any overdue resources the patron may have, along with the overdue fees that have been charged and not yet paid. A patron also provides services to other potential classes. For example, a patron object should keep track of any fees that are owed by that patron as well as any resources that are currently checked out or requested by the patron. The question of multiple attributes for a particular class is related to the issue of whether information about the class must be retained. For example, for the patron class, we saw that much information must be retained by the system. This information is stored in multiple attributes in the patron class. For example, the patron class requires a name attribute and an address attribute along with an attribute to keep track of checked-out resources for the patron. All instances of the patron class share these attributes. In other words, for each patron object in the system, we need to know the patron name, address, and list of checked-out resources. All instances of the patron class must be able to check out, check in, and request resources as well as be charged and pay overdue fees. In other words, all patron objects have a set of common operations. From this brief discussion, it should be clear that our first primary class is *Patron*.

Next, consider the noun *Library Number*. The library number is a single attribute. In fact, each patron must have one, so library number is probably an attribute of the *Patron* class rather than a class in its own right. *Library Number* does not make it onto our list of primary classes.

Students, Faculty, and *Library Staff* are all types of patrons. There is information that must be retained about each of them (see the discussion of *Patron*). Some of the information retained about them varies, however. For example, the length of time that resources can be checked out is different for students than it is for faculty. These three nouns are added to our list of primary classes as children of the *Patron* class. In other words, a patron is a **generalization** of each of these three classes. Although these nouns have made it onto our list of primary classes, we may find, during the design phase, that creating classes for these nouns is not the best design for our software. We may decide that a better way to handle these nouns exists.

We are creating the library management system for the library of the *College*. From the standpoint of the library management system, we find there is no information about the college that we must retain. The college, as an entity, does not provide services to other potential classes in our system. As a result of this analysis, we determine that *College* is not one of our primary classes.

Primary Classes for LMS

1. *Patron*
2. *Student, Faculty, Library Staff* (all children of the *Patron* class)
3. *Resource*
4. *Book, Music CD, Video, Software* (all children of the *Resource* class)
5. *Reference Resource, Reserved Resource, Requested Resource, Online Research Resource* (all children of the *Resource* class)
6. *Interlibrary Loan Request*

DELIVERABLE 3.2

In addition, during our analysis, we find some unique features of our system. The *Online Catalog* is not a class by itself because there is no need for multiple online catalogs. Instead, the *Online Catalog* turns out to be simply a list of all the *Resource* objects in the library. In addition, during the analysis of the notion of an *Overdue Fee*, we discover that the fee itself is fairly static with a set amount charged for each overdue resource for each day. The total amount charged to a particular *Patron* for a particular *Resource* is something that the system must track. The total amount charged disappears from the system only when the fee is paid, not when the resource is returned, because a patron may put the resource in the return box without speaking to a library staff member. Therefore, the *Patron* class must have an attribute that associates an overdue charge to a particular *Resource*. We create a primary class called *Overdue Charge* that has a *Dewey Call Number* (an attribute of the *Resource* class) as an attribute. The *Overdue Charge* is an attribute of the *Patron* class. Finally, the library staff member must have the ability to generate *Overdue Form Letters*. These letters are created in a transient class called *Overdue Form Letter*. Objects of this class exist from the request to generate the letter until the letter is printed.

When we examine the notion of an *Interlibrary Loan Request*, we see that we have two nouns to consider: *Other Libraries* and *Interlibrary Loan Request*. Other libraries are entities that are external to the system we are developing. We may need to keep track of what has been loaned to the patrons of our library from other libraries because we may be charged fees (other than overdue fees) for these loans. From the requirements specification that we have seen, this possible requirement is not clear. The question of fees for interlibrary loans must be brought back to the users for clarification. For the purposes of our system, we assume that no fees are charged for any interlibrary loans. Therefore, *Other Libraries* is not on our list of primary classes.

DELIVERABLE 3.2 (cont.)

More Primary Classes for LMS

7. *Overdue Charge* (a list of these is an attribute of the *Patron* class)
8. *Overdue Form Letters*

3.10.3 Identifying Use Cases

While the list of primary classes is being developed, the requirements specification is also used to develop a set of **use cases**. A use case is description of a scenario (or perhaps a set of closely related scenarios) in which the system to be developed interacts with the users of the system [20]. Through the development of use cases, the behavior of the system can be expressed without specifying how the behavior is implemented [16]. In other words, a use case specifies, from an outside perspective, what the system does but not how the system should accomplish its tasks. The manner in which the system will be used is the focal point of use case analysis. Typically, use cases are first described narratively. As the understanding of the system's requirements increases, use cases are represented graphically by **class diagrams**, which are discussed in section 3.10.8, and **interaction diagrams**, which are discussed in section 5.3.2.

A use case interacts with **actors**. The actors represent a set of roles that users of use cases play when interacting with the use case. An actor can be a human, a hardware device, or another software system that interacts with the system to be developed. The initial use case description specifies how and when the use case begins and ends, when the use case interacts with the actors and what objects are exchanged, and both the basic and alternative flows of events [16]. Each use case describes a set of sequences of events. One of these sequences is the basic flow of events, while the other sequences represent similar flows of events that differ from the basic in the particular circumstances.

Use cases decompose the system into coherent categories of functionality. The term **coherent** implies that each use case can be analyzed as a quasi-autonomous unit. Use cases are not truly autonomous because, as building blocks of the system, they are interdependent. For example, a *player move* use case requires a *game initiation* use case to execute first.

Use case development follows informal scenario development. Informal scenarios are a good starting point for use case development, because they have few restrictions and thus allow individuals who are new to systems analysis to be productive immediately. Use case development can be viewed as a process of organizing and restructuring the informal scenarios. Use cases are also initially narrative in form just as the informal scenarios are, but differ from them in the following respects:

- Use cases are more abstract than informal scenarios. They characterize the behavior of the system in less specific terms than the scenarios, avoiding reference to hypothetical values.
- A single use case may encompass multiple scenarios.
- Use cases avoid redundancy, whereas a set of scenarios may address redundant system behavior while exploring different user options.
- Use cases are more formally structured than informal scenarios.
- In a use case, exceptional flows of events are explicitly specified separately from the normal flow of events. In a scenario, such separation may not exist.
- Because informal scenario development is less rigorous than use case development, informal scenarios may omit certain important system behavior. Use cases, however, express the complete breadth of functionality of the system.

3.10.4 *Case Study:* **Identifying Use Cases in LMS**

Examination of the requirements specification for the library system reveals that one of the interactions that must occur between the final system and the library staff is *ValidatePatron*. This interaction occurs when a patron is attempting to check a resource out and the patron's library record must be found in the system. The

CASE STUDY

ValidatePatron use case, therefore, is a piece of a larger use case that might be called *CheckOutResource*.

Use Case: *ValidatePatron*

Main flow of events: The use case starts when the system prompts the *Library Staff* for the *Patron*'s library number. The *Library Staff* can either scan in a card or type in a number and then commit the entry by pressing the Enter key. The system then checks to see whether the library number entered is valid. If it is valid, the system displays the library record for the *Patron*, thus ending this use case.

Exceptional flow of events: If the *Library Staff* enters an invalid library number, the system cancels the entire transaction, and this use case ends.

Exceptional flow of events: If the *Library Staff* enters a library number that has expired, the system cancels the entire transaction, and this use case ends.

Exceptional flow of events: If the *Patron* has too many library resources checked out he or she may not check out any additional resources. A message that tallies and lists the resources currently held by the *Patron* is displayed on the screen, and this use case ends.

Exceptional flow of events: If the *Patron* has any library resources that are more than two weeks overdue, then these resources are listed on the screen, and this use case ends.

The preceding use case description is written in informal but structured text. Use cases may also be described using formal, structured text with **preconditions** and **postconditions**. A precondition is a statement of the conditions that must exist before the use case can successfully take place. A postcondition is a statement describing the modified state of the system as a result of executing a use case. In addition, notice that certain words are in italics in the preceding use case. These words represent **actors**, or roles played by users of the system who are interacting with the system. One of the actors is *Patron*. A patron is a role played by students, faculty, and library staff when they interact with the system for a particular purpose. The final thing to notice about this use case is that all four exceptional flows of events are very similar. What probably differs between them is what use case will be invoked when the current use case ends. In other words, this use case interacts with other use cases for the library system. The interactions among use cases are captured through **use case diagrams** [16], which will be discussed in detail in section 3.10.10. A use case diagram will also show the relationship between the

ValidatePatron use case and the *CheckOutResource* use case, which might be described in the following manner (note the precondition and postcondition).

Use Case: *CheckOutResource*

Precondition: The *Library Staff* member has successfully identified himself or herself to the library system by entering a valid library staff identification number and password. A library database, containing information concerning the library holdings and the patrons of the library, has been created and initialized.

Main flow of events: The use case starts when the *Library Staff* requests the *CheckOutResource* function from the system main menu. The system then initiates the *ValidatePatron* use case. If that use case ends successfully (with a valid patron number having been entered into the system), the system initiates the *EnterResource* use case. If the *EnterResource* use case ends successfully, the *DetermineDueDate* use case is initiated. The *EnterResource/DetermineDueDate* use case pair is executed over and over until the *Library Staff* commits the entry by pressing the Enter key. The system then displays a list of valid resources that have been entered along with due dates for each resource, thus ending this use case.

Exceptional flow of events: If the *ValidatePatron* use case does not end with a valid patron library number having been entered, the system cancels the entire transaction, and this use case ends.

Exceptional flow of events: If the *EnterResource* use case does not end with a valid resource Dewey call number having been entered, the system displays an appropriate warning message and continues the *CheckOutResource* use case by skipping the *DetermineDueDate* use case and initiating the next instance of the *EnterResource* use case.

Postcondition: If the *ValidatePatron* use case does not end with a valid patron library number having been entered, nothing in the entire system has changed when this use case ends. If a valid library patron number was entered, then the *Patron* object is updated with the Dewey call numbers of the *Resource* objects that have been checked out along with their due dates. In addition, the *Resource* objects are updated to have a status of checked-out along with the library number of the *Patron* who checked it out.

The following is the *GenFormLetter* use case, which is the use case that generates form letters to library patrons, informing them of their overdue library resources.

Use Case: *GenFormLetter*

Precondition: The file or database containing patron and resource information is initialized and populated with valid information and is ready for read/write access.

Main flow of events: Each patron's list of checked-out resources is checked to determine if any resources are more than two weeks overdue. If so, a form letter is generated containing the patron's address, his or her list of overdue resources, and the fine currently owed the library. The form letters are then folded and sent.

Postcondition: A series of form letters is generated.

EXERCISE 3.8   Write the following use cases for the ticktacktoe game: *initiate game*, *player move*, and *terminate game*. For each, identify the main flow of events and any exceptional flows of events. In addition, specify any preconditions and postconditions.

A somewhat complex system, such as the library management system, might require a few dozen use cases to capture its behavior. We leave the determination of the rest of the use cases for this system as an exercise for the reader. For each use case, there may be several **scenarios**, each of which specifies the behavior of the system in a slightly different context. For example, within the *DetermineDueDate* use case, there are several different scenarios. If the patron is a student trying to check out a book, the system will behave in a particular manner, setting the due date for the book to be four weeks in the future. If the student is checking out a music CD, the due date is set to one week in the future. If a book is checked out by a faculty member, the due date for the book is set to three months in the future. Each of these situations is a scenario, related to the same use case, that illustrates the behavior of the system in a particular context.

3.10.5 Scenario Development

Now that the overall general behavior of the system has been laid out in terms of use cases, these use cases need to be verified by deriving a set of scenarios from each one. This process is more formal than the informal scenario development. In fact, the informal scenarios may be modified to serve this purpose. Scenario development is carried out by using narrative text to describe a scenario as a specific possible sequence of events that the final system must handle. This sequence of events should center on a particular use case. Scenarios involve concrete instances of objects that might exist in the system. These objects may be fictitious, but must be plausible. Scenarios may also have **preconditions** and **postconditions**. Recall that a precondition is a statement of the conditions that must exist before the scenario can successfully take place and a postcondition is a statement describing the modified state of the system as a result of executing a scenario.

As stated earlier, if a use case is very general, more than one scenario may be necessary to characterize the use case effectively. For example, the *CheckOutResource* use case is somewhat abstract because the resource checked out must be handled differently if it is a book rather than a music CD. One scenario with a book and another scenario with a music CD may be necessary to analyze this use case properly. A scenario involving a specific library patron checking out a specific library book and being assisted by a specific library staff member may serve as a scenario for the *CheckOutResource* use case. The following is a narrative description of such a scenario.

3.10.6 *Case Study:* Sample Scenarios in LMS

CASE STUDY

DELIVERABLE
3.6

Scenario: *CheckOutResource*

Precondition: The librarian on duty, Maria Blanco, has identified herself to the library system by entering her library staff identification number. A library database, containing information concerning the library holdings and the patrons of the library, has been created and initialized.

Library patron: Greta Smith, who is a student of the college, wishes to check out *Gone with the Wind*. She hands her selection and her library card to the librarian, Maria Blanco, who determines Greta's status as a patron by scanning Greta's library card. Scanning the library card reads in the patron's library identification number, which is used to access the library database. The patron object associated with the library identification number is returned from the library database. Greta's patron object indicates that her student library membership is currently valid, but since she is scheduled to graduate in a month, her membership expires in one month. A message concerning the expiration flashes on the librarian's screen, which prompts her to alert Greta to this fact. Next, the bar code on the book is scanned, reading the book's identification number. This number is used to access the book object for *Gone with the Wind* from the library database. Based on the fact that a student is borrowing a book, the due date for the book is determined. The book object is then sent a *check-out* message, which changes the book's status to *checked out* from its previous status of *available*. The patron's library identification number is also sent with the *check-out* message, and the patron ID is recorded in the book's check-out-history list.

The due date of the book is also sent to the book object and is stored in the due date attribute of the book. The patron object is sent a *check-out* message along with the book ID so that the book ID can be added to the checked-out-resources list for the patron object.

Postcondition: The status of the book is *checked out*, and the current borrower for book object is the patron ID. The due date for the book has the appropriate date. The patron-object checked-out-resources list is updated with the book ID.

DELIVERABLE 3.7

Scenario: *GenFormLetter*

Precondition: The LMS database is ready for sequential access by patron ID, is populated with valid patron data, and is ready to read the first patron ID.

The first library patron ID number is LMS0001, which is owned by Harry Potter, who is a faculty member. Harry has three books and one music CD checked out. Each resource is queried for its due date, which is compared to the current system date. If the due date is more than 14 days before the system date, a form letter is generated. Harry has one book that is three days overdue, so Harry will not receive a form letter. The next patron ID number is LMS0004, which is owned by Berta Goldman, who is a library staff member. She has five books checked out, none of which is overdue, so no form letter is generated. The next patron ID is LMS0011, owned by Wanda Wirtschaft, who is a student and has three books, all of which are three weeks overdue. So, Wanda will receive a form letter. An *OverdueFormLetter* object is created that contains the current system date, the patron name and address, and a list of resources that are over two weeks overdue. This information is used to generate a form letter that is mailed to the patron. The remainder of the patron objects are queried.

Postcondition: A series of form letters results, and all *OverdueFormLetter* objects are deleted. No change to the database results.

EXERCISE 3.9   The preceding scenario embodies the library's policy on overdue resources. How would you change this policy so that patrons are less likely to ignore the form letter? How must the use case be changed in order to reflect the new policy? Write a new scenario with your new overdue resource policy.

During the formulation of scenarios for each use case, it is appropriate to highlight any potential **technical vulnerabilities**. A technical vulnerability is an aspect of implementation of the final system in which the development team perceives a lack of expertise. For example, a system may require some sophisticated graphics, and the system development team may not have a team member with the necessary experience to implement the graphics.

Create a scenario for the following use cases in the ticktacktoe game: *initiate game*, *player move*, and *terminate game*. Do any of the use cases require multiple scenarios? If so, create the additional scenarios as well. **EXERCISE 3.10**

3.10.7 Modeling the System with UML

Figure 3.5 shows that the first step in the UCCD analysis process involves creating a list of primary classes and a list of use cases. The figure also shows that in the next step of the analysis process, a number of diagrams are created. These diagrams express a variety of aspects of the proposed system and are shown to the users during the structured walk-through. In order to create the diagrams, we must use a notation. The notation used in this textbook is the Unified Modeling Language [15], which is fast becoming an industry standard and is a valuable tool for the aspiring software engineer.

The role of UML, or any notation for that matter, is to provide an unambiguous, concise, and effective means to represent the system from a number of perspectives, supporting various levels of specificity. In other words, UML provides a number of modeling techniques that are realized through a variety of diagrams. UML allows the system modeler to represent the system to be developed in an abstract or progressively more detailed manner. As the system developers understand the final system in increasing detail, UML allows this detail to be effectively represented. The modeling process, therefore, parallels the progress of understanding the system and thus helps to control complexity. The desired result of analyzing and designing a system with UML is a kind of blueprint for implementing the system.

Since modeling a system requires the representation of a number of different perspectives, one must learn several diagramming methods, each of which expresses a different aspect of the final system. In the rest of this chapter, we will focus on two types of UML diagrams, **use case diagrams** and **class diagrams**.

In a successful use of the object-oriented methodology, the transition from use cases to class diagrams should flow seamlessly. Class diagrams are a common element shared between the analysis and design phases in which class diagrams started during analysis are refined and enhanced during design. Implementation proceeds by fleshing out class definitions that are derived directly from the class diagrams. Thus class diagrams function as a mechanism that integrates all phases of software development. When the class definitions have been coded, tested, and verified, the system is complete.

3.10.8 Class Diagrams

Class diagrams model one aspect of the system, the composition of classes. Given that class definitions are static when the system is in use, class diagrams model a static perspective of the system. A given system may have many class diagrams, and a given class may appear in different class diagrams for different purposes. For example, a particularly complex class may be modeled as an aggregation hierarchy in a special class diagram that portrays the various attributes and classes that comprise the class. Each component class may in turn be further broken down into its constituent attributes and classes. The same class may appear in another class diagram that models a group of classes that collaborate to accomplish a particular task. Class diagrams, therefore, model a variety of structural aspects of a system.

The objective of the class diagram is to portray the elements that are part of a class and the essential relationships that exist between classes. The notational building blocks of the class diagram—**classes**, **interfaces**, **relationships**, and **collaborations**—are shown in Figure 3.6. The notation used throughout this section is standard UML [16].

A class may be portrayed in various class diagrams with varying levels of detail. In one class diagram, it may be sufficient to specify only the class name, whereas in another, it may be necessary to specify the class name along with all attributes and

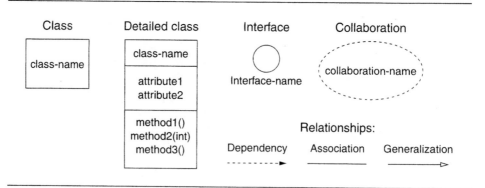

FIGURE 3.6 Notational Elements of Class Diagrams

methods that make up the class. During the analysis phase, most classes are likely to be modeled with just their class names. The attributes and methods comprising the class may not be known until the design phase and will be added to the appropriate class diagrams at that time.

The relationships that exist between classes must also be shown in class diagrams. The three possible relationships between classes in class diagrams are **association**, **generalization**, and **dependency**, and each is represented by a different type of line and arrow, as shown in Figure 3.6. An association is a labeled relationship between two classes. For example, a patron checks out a resource. Therefore, the *Patron* class and the *Resource* class are associated with each other through the *Checks-Out* relationship. A generalization is a hierarchical relationship between two classes in which one class is the parent of the other class, as in an inheritance hierarchy. For example, the *Patron* class is a generalization of the *Student* class. In other words, a student is a particular type of patron. Finally, a dependency is a relationship between two classes in which one class depends on another in some way so that changing one class might require that the second class also change. For example, recall that we decided that *Online Catalog* is not one of the primary classes for the library management system. Assume that for some reason, we do indeed need to have a class called *Online Catalog*. An *Online Catalog* object is then a collection of *Resource* objects. If the *Resource* class were to change, it is very likely that the *Online Catalog* class would have to change. At the very least, we must examine the *Online Catalog* class to determine whether the *Resource* class change affects the *Online Catalog* class. In this manner, the *Online Catalog* class depends upon the *Resource* class.

Many behaviors in a system require several classes to interact with each other. The manner of interaction between these classes can be specified using a class diagram element called an **interface**. By specifying interfaces, software developers can ensure that one of the fundamental object-oriented principles, **encapsulation**, is followed. Encapsulation is the principle that in order for one class to interact with another, no knowledge of the implementation of the two classes need be known. Instead, the two classes interact with each other by means of a specified interface. Interfaces are represented in class diagrams by small circles with the interface name underneath, as shown in Figure 3.6. Interfaces are typically not added to the class diagrams until the design phase. During the analysis phase, the class diagram is typically much simpler, specifying just enough detail to explain system behavior to the users. Accordingly, interfaces will not be discussed in detail here.

Although many of the detailed elements of class diagrams do not come into play until the design phase, elements called **collaborations** are very important for explaining system behavior. A collaboration specifies that two elements of the class diagram must interact with each other to produce a particular behavior. A collaboration names a set of classes, interfaces, and other elements that work together to produce a particular behavior. In the class diagram, a collaboration is represented by a dashed-line ellipse with the collaboration name inside. A collaboration has two parts, the **structural** part and the **behavioral** part. In a class diagram, we represent only the structural part of the collaboration. The behavioral part of the collaboration will be discussed in section 5.3.2.

The structural part of the collaboration specifies which classes, interfaces, and other elements are required to carry out the collaboration. A collaboration is an abstract entity, used solely for the purposes of expressing behavior. An examination of the code of the final system will reveal that the collaboration does not exist there. Rather, the components comprising the collaboration are present, and the software causes these components to work together to carry out the intended behavior. For example, each use case is modeled as a collaboration by means of a class diagram. When a use case specifies behavior that is part of a larger use case (as was the situation with *ValidatePatron*), the smaller use case is represented in the class diagram of the larger use case using the dashed-line ellipse. In other words, a collaboration is modeled by means of a class diagram, and it can also be an element in a class diagram.

3.10.9 *Case Study:* Class Diagrams for LMS

For any given system, a series of class diagrams must be created to capture the system structure as fully as possible. Deliverable 3.8 shows the overall class diagram for the library management system. This class diagram was created from our list of primary classes. It specifies all of the primary classes in the system along with their relationships to one another. This diagram, however, does not give any information about which classes must interact to produce particular behaviors.

To show which classes interact to produce particular behaviors, additional class diagrams must be created. These additional class diagrams typically contain some subset of the classes from the overall class diagram. For example, in the library management system, a behavior to be modeled is *CheckOutResource*. The collaboration consists of the classes necessary to check a resource out of the library as well as the relationships among those classes. Deliverable 3.9 shows the class diagram for this collaboration. The collaboration consists of seven classes, which are a subset of the classes in the overall class diagram. Not all of the child classes of *Resource* are shown because not all of them can be checked out. Notice also that the class diagram in Deliverable 3.9 shows only a subset of the relationships among those classes. In particular, although the *Patron* class is a generalization of the *Library Staff* class, that relationship is not shown here because it is not necessary for illustrating the *CheckOutResource* behavior. There should be a class diagram for each use case that has been specified.

Library Management System Overall Class Diagram

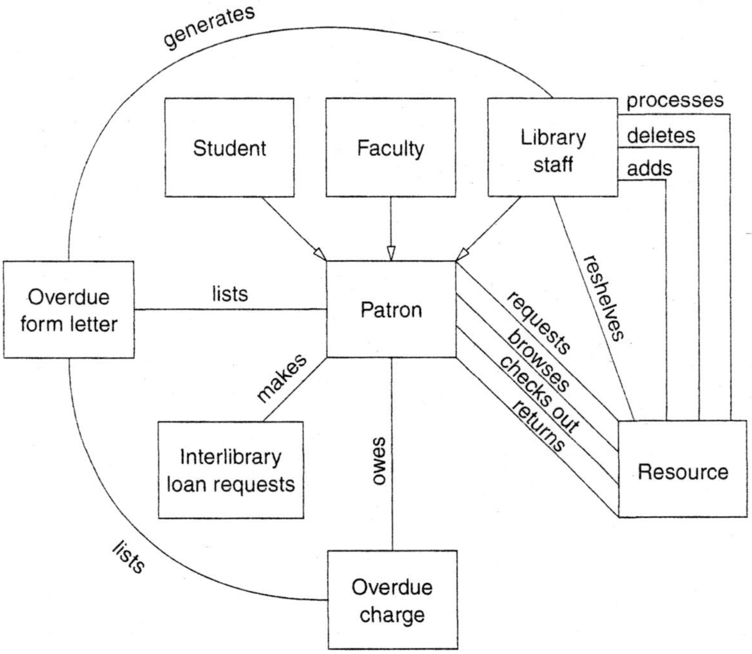

generates

Student   Faculty   Library staff

processes
deletes
adds

Overdue form letter — lists — Patron

requests
browses
checks out
returns

reshelves

makes

Interlibrary loan requests

owes

Resource

lists

Overdue charge

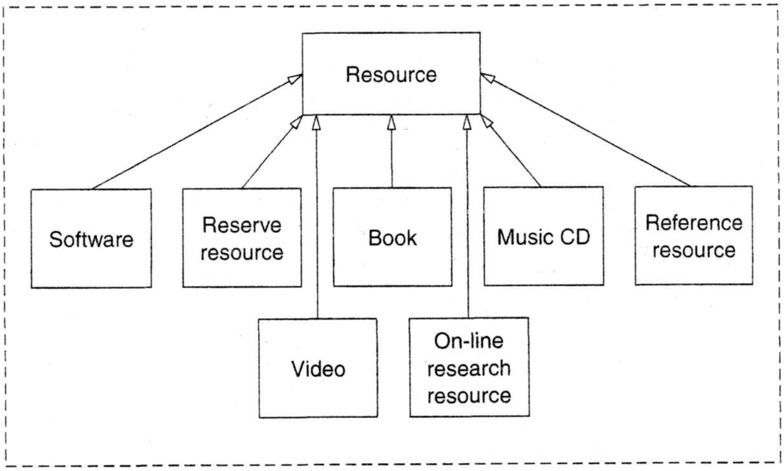

Resource

Software   Reserve resource   Book   Music CD   Reference resource

Video   On-line research resource

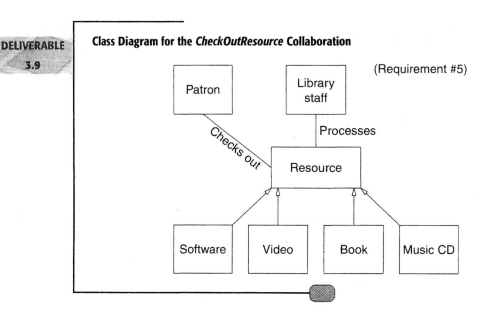

DELIVERABLE 3.9

Class Diagram for the *CheckOutResource* Collaboration

(Requirement #5)

Deliverable 3.10 depicts the class relationships required to fulfill the *GenForm-Letter* use case, which creates a series of form letters for patrons who have library resources that are over two weeks overdue. Although the overall class diagram depicted in Deliverable 3.8 includes the *OverdueFormLetter* class with its relationships to other primary classes, the class diagram in Deliverable 3.10 conveys additional detail pertaining to the *GenFormLetter* use case. The relationships between the *Patron, Resource,* and *OverdueFormLetter* indicate that the form letter does not list all library resources, but only those that are checked out by the patron. An additional constraint on the resources that are listed in the form letter is expressed in the braces next to the *List* relationship between the *OverdueFormLetter* and *Resource* classes; it indicates that only resources over two weeks overdue are listed on the letter. The reference to requirement #17 in Deliverable 3.10 ties this diagram to a specific goal stated in the supported activity list of Deliverable 3.1.

Because classes are the central consideration in an object-oriented software system, class diagrams are a critical aspect of object-oriented systems analysis and design. Recall that the first formal software engineering activity that we described was the creation of a list of primary classes. The class definitions for these primary classes evolve throughout the development of the system. All subsequent modeling activity is undertaken to better understand the overall system and to more fully define each class. The class diagrams are complete only when the final system is complete.

Class Diagram for the *GenFormLetter* Collaboration

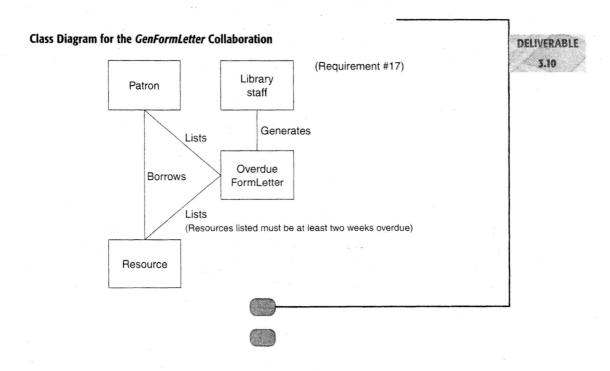

Create a class diagram for the ticktacktoe game that embodies the primary class   **EXERCISE 3.11**
interrelationships. Are there opportunities for inheritance?

Divide into groups to discuss this exercise. Refer to Figure 3.7, and determine the   **EXERCISE 3.12**
functionality of the system that is being modeled. If the class diagram is meant
to be comprehensive, what does this intention indicate about the scope of the
system? (Hint: Is the electronic funds transfer system part of the banking system
being modeled?) How did you make this determination?

3.10.10 Use Case Diagrams

A use case, as described in section 3.10.3, is a description of the manner in which
the system should behave in a particular type of situation. Each use case is described
narratively and then modeled more formally using class diagrams. What has not
yet been modeled, however, is how the behaviors of the system fit together. In
other words, we need a mechanism for describing the overall behavior of the
system and how the various behaviors interact with external actors and with

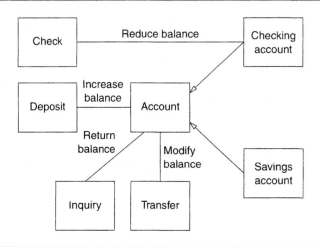

FIGURE 3.7 Determine the Meaning of this Class Diagram

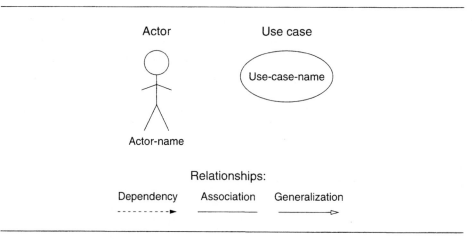

FIGURE 3.8 Notational Elements of Use Case Diagrams

each other. To describe these interactions, we use a modeling technique called **use case diagrams** [16]. Figure 3.8 shows the notational elements found in use case diagrams. Notice that, just as in class diagrams, use case diagrams can model three types of relationships, **dependency**, **association**, and **generalization**. In addition, use case diagrams contain representations of **use cases** and of **actors**, which are external elements interacting with the system.

3.10.11 *Case Study:* Use Case Diagrams for LMS

Deliverable 3.11 shows a use case diagram for part of the library management system. In this diagram, the external entities, called **actors**, that interact with the system are connected to each use case by a solid line with no arrows. This connection represents an **association** relationship between the actor and the use case. Some of the actors represent real-world entities, such as a *Patron*, that are represented by a class within the software. Other actors, such as a *Shelf*, are real-world entities that have no analogous entity in the system but that are important to understanding the behavior of the software in some situation. Two actors that are connected to the same use case by association relationships interact with each other through the use case. For example, a *Patron* is associated with the *CheckOutResource* use case, as are the *Resource* and the *Library Staff* actors. This piece of the use case diagram models the fact that patrons can check out resources and that library staff assist them in this process. No label is placed on the association relationship because the meaning of the relationship is contained in the use case name.

Use cases are central to our software development methodology. Therefore, a mechanism for modeling use cases is important. To verify the requirements specification, the functionality of the system must be communicated in a form upon which the domain experts and the systems developers can agree. Use case diagrams are, therefore, intended to serve as an unambiguous means to express the behavior of the final system in terms that a nontechnical audience can understand.

Use cases express both the functional requirements of the system and the **functional partitioning** of the system. The role of functional partitioning in system development is to specify well-defined subsets of functionality. These functional subsets of the system identify logical **iterations** of the development of the final system. The use case can help to determine a series of development goals. In other words, given an iterative development process, use cases express the manner in which the final system is to evolve during development. Each stage of system evolution consists of the development of software to implement one or more use cases. This functional partitioning is, thus, another means to control complexity during development. A particularly complex class may be partitioned into the attributes and methods that apply to particular use cases in order to facilitate the analysis and design of that class. This partitioning establishes different **roles** for the class.

For example, library patrons may be considered as playing at least two roles in the library system. The first role is as a borrower of library resources. The second is as a user of reference, research, and database facilities as a researcher. So, certain attributes and methods are necessary for one role and not the another. The same is true for certain attributes. Thus, as the system evolves, one role of a class may be analyzed, designed, and implemented before any others. Future iterations of the software system include additional roles of the class.

A Library Management System Use Case Diagram

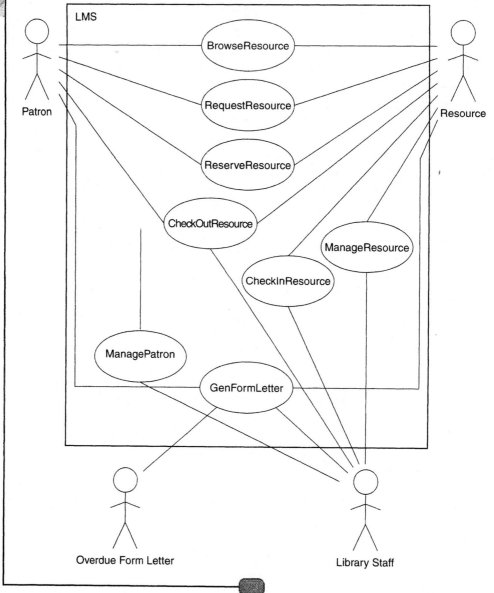

3.10.12 Requirements Analysis Summary

The object-oriented software engineering methodology proposed here, called Use Case Centered Development (UCCD), has an explicit analysis phase (see Summary Points box 3.4). As its modeling notation, UCCD uses UML, which provides a wide array of diagrams for a variety of modeling purposes. This text focuses on a core of critical modeling techniques, although UML contains many more. Now that a core set of UML diagrams has been introduced, let us summarize the process of UCCD requirements analysis:

1. A requirements specification must be created. The initial specification may be created by a committee of users of the final system, or it may be created by the system developers who engage the users in a dialogue about their needs. In either case, the system developers must begin by familiarizing themselves with the domain in which the system is to be used. A useful technique to assist in the process of familiarization with the domain of expertise is the creation of informal scenarios.

2. The requirements specification must be evaluated for ambiguities, errors, and implicit assumptions. This evaluation process involves clarification of the specification so that the software developers understand the requirements as well as the users understand them. One of the main techniques used for this clarification is the development of a list of questions about the requirements specification. These questions are answered by the users in ongoing conversations with the software developers.

3. When the answers to the preceding questions are well understood by the software developers, they refine the requirements specification, creating a new document. Of course, during the refinement process, more questions may arise. These questions must be written and answered by the users. Prototyping is a useful tool for refining the requirements specification because users can interact with a prototype and get an idea of what the developers understand in terms of required final system behavior.

4. Once the requirements specification is reasonably complete, it must be verified for consistency, plausibility, and completeness. This verification may be accomplished through an informal walk-through. Before a walk-through is scheduled, some initial modeling of the system must be done. Through ongoing discussion with the users and review of the requirements specification, the developers create a tentative list of primary classes. In addition, the system requirements are restructured in the form of use cases. One or more scenarios are created for each use case to characterize the specific behaviors represented by each use case.

5. Once the basic functionality of the requested system is generally understood, the system developers begin the process of developing class diagrams for the

purpose of representing basic interclass relationships and class composition. Thought should be given to possible inheritance hierarchies and class reuse. Class diagrams will continue to evolve until the final system is completed.

6. The use cases from step 4 must now be transformed into use case diagrams, which begin to describe the interactions of the use cases with each other and with external actors interacting with the system.

7. Using the class diagrams developed in step 5 and the use cases from step 4, a second set of class diagrams is created. These class diagrams illustrate the subset of classes that interact with each other to produce the behavior described in each use case. One use case may be represented by several class diagrams, illustrating the basic flow of events along with any exceptional flows of events.

8. Once the software developers have created enough diagrams to illustrate a complete understanding of the system to be developed, a structured walk-through should be scheduled with a wide spectrum of domain experts. The system should be presented to the future users of the system by means of the diagrams created in the previous steps. The scenarios developed during analysis of the use cases are used to facilitate discussion of the system. Any corrections by the domain experts should be factored in to the scenarios, class diagrams, and use case diagrams.

An expected result of requirements analysis is that the system developers understand the application domain in enough detail to be able to assess and implement the specified requirements in a software system and to discuss the proposed system with the domain experts in an effective manner. Another consequence of requirements analysis is the emergence of a verified and accurate requirements specification, which both the domain experts and the systems developers can understand. The final result of requirements analysis is the creation of definitions for many fundamental classes required for implementation of the final system. These

SUMMARY POINTS 3.4

Steps in the UCCD Analysis Process

1. Create and/or refine the requirements specification.

2. Create informal scenarios.

3. Create list of primary classes.

4. Create use cases.

5. Create scenarios for the use cases using the primary classes.

5. Create class diagrams showing basic interclass relationships.

6. Model key class collaborations.

7. Create use case diagrams showing use case interactions.

definitions, however, are expected to continue to evolve during the course of system development.

3.10.13 Evolving the System

The process of system analysis as presented to this point entails understanding and assessing the needs of the end users. Certain practical issues are appropriately addressed during this phase of software development. For example, in the analysis phase, the time frame for completion of various stages of the system development should be determined. The determination of the time frame is best done in conjunction with the end users, who may need certain capabilities of the system earlier than others and could, therefore, benefit from a system delivered in phases. The negotiation of the time constraints on the delivery of a partial system should be entered into as soon as the requirements analysis is complete.

In the event that end users have no need for a partial system and that no other time constraints dictate the delivery of a partially completed system, the evolution of the system is determined by the system developers. The use cases developed during analysis are useful for identifying subsets of functionality that define the stages of the evolving system. The use cases can be clustered according to the classes required to implement them, and these clusters can serve as the basis for system evolution.

3.11   Analyzing the *Class Project*

The requirements statement provided in section 1.10 is the formal requirements specification for the class project. Since class members do not have direct access to users who requested the development of the class project, the course instructor serves as the primary domain expert. This scenario is idiosyncratic because software developers typically have a number of different domain experts to consult. To get a potentially more realistic scenario, students may also interact with the textbook authors over the Internet, if preferred, through a chat room created by the authors at the following URL:

CLASS PROJECT

http://oz.plymouth.edu/~estiller/SEproject.html

The students should have created a list of questions from their first reading of the requirements specification. After these questions have been refined during team discussion, they should be directed either to the instructor or to the authors through the chat room. The resolution of these questions should be documented. After gaining familiarity with the project and resolving any questions, the team should continue the analysis process through the following sequence of steps.

- A list of primary classes should be created and refined as illustrated by the case study in section 3.10.2 and Deliverable 3.2.
- A set of basic class diagrams should be developed using these classes. The class diagrams should show aggregation and inheritance.
- Use cases should be developed concerning the major functionality of the system.
- Class diagrams modeling the use cases should be created.
- Use case diagrams, in which the use cases are shown in relationship to each other, should be created.
- Scenarios relating to each use case should be created.
- Each team should engage in a structured walk-through, with their instructor serving as the end user. The structured walk-through should verify the completeness and correctness of the proposed system.

The formal deliverables resulting from the analysis phase are the refined requirements specification, use cases, scenarios, class diagrams, and use case diagrams. Each project team should discuss any technical vulnerabilities and bring these issues to the attention of the instructor.

3.12 Working in Teams

As we know, software development teams must meet at least once a week to share and coordinate work efforts. Each team member should make substantial effort to become familiar with the breadth of the project. Responsibilities should be divided among team members very early in the semester. Each team member should develop a list of use cases for the system. These use cases should be presented in an abstract use case diagram to be brought to the first analysis meeting. Each team member should also bring a list of potential primary classes to this meeting as well. A set of use cases for the system and a list of the primary classes to be used in the system should be agreed upon in an early team meeting. Responsibility should then be given to particular team members for creating class diagrams for scenarios in specific use cases.

The objective of the second set of analysis team meetings should be to review, refine, and approve the class diagrams that were produced. At this point, responsibility for the development of specific classes should be assigned to each team member. The rationale for this strategy of dividing the labor of the project is that classes are the basic unit of modularity for object-oriented software development. In addition, coordination among several individuals modifying the same module would be overly complex.

Some additional pointers on trying to make the most out of your team meetings are as follows:

1. The role of the chair of the meeting is to facilitate discussion.
2. Each team member should have an equal opportunity to be heard.
3. The meeting chair should make an extra effort to recognize less aggressive team members to ensure that they are heard.
4. Unless someone is being long-winded, team members should never be interrupted while speaking.
5. Everyone should strive to make his or her points as concisely as possible during team meetings.

3.13 Questions for Review

1. Why is requirements analysis considered to be the most important phase of software development? What are the possible consequences for software development initiatives that do inadequate requirements analysis?
2. What are the objectives of requirements analysis? What are the deliverables of requirements analysis?
3. Given a requirements statement, what procedure would you use to develop a list of important classes for the final system?
4. To ensure the completeness of a requirements specification, what items should you look for?
5. What sort of ethical concerns may appear in a requirements specification for a credit reporting system, a medical information system, a banking system, a library information system, or a missile guidance system?
6. What clarifications are necessary for the library information system based on the requirements specification in this chapter?
7. Attempt the following role-playing exercise to gain experience eliciting information from end users. Pick a classmate and ask him or her to envision a personal butler robot. Engage in a dialogue with this classmate to determine functional specifications for this robot. How do you get started? What sorts of leading questions are the most effective? How do you flesh out the details? How are you organizing the information elicited from your classmate? After the requirements have been elicited and enumerated in a requirements specification, how will you verify the quality of your specification?
8. What are the objectives of a structured walk-through?

9. Conduct an informal walk-through of the results of your requirements analysis of the class project with your software development team members. How does the nature of the information presented and gathered differ from a structured walk-through?

10. How are objects and classes identified in a requirements statement? If a potential object is rejected, what other role may it serve in the final system?

11. What are support classes, and how are they derived during analysis and design?

12. How do use cases influence the structure of a proposed system? What transformations of information are necessary to modify a class definition based on a use case?

13. What types of class diagrams are there? What are the objectives of each? How are they used?

14. What relationships exist between classes? Give an example of each.

15. How are use case diagrams used to model a software system? Can they be functionally decomposed?

16. What practical issues of software development should be factored in during requirements analysis?

17. If you were the project manager for the class project, what steps would you take to ensure that the analysis phase of the class project stays on schedule? How much time would you allocate for analysis?

18. Research the Frederick Brooks reference [19] to determine the evidence behind his conclusion that the initial stages of software development have the most significant influence on the overall success of the project.

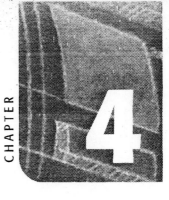

Product Design

Key Concepts

- External versus internal software structure
- Object persistence
- Object serialization
- Deployment diagram
- Interprocess communication
- State transition diagram
- State machine

- Resource distribution
- Network utilization
- User interface
- Graphical user interface
- User-friendliness
- User profiles
- User interface design principles
- Interaction styles

Objectives of Design

The software development process may be either evolutionary or top-down in nature. The choice of development process determines what information has been gathered and created in the analysis phase and, therefore, what information is available at the start of the design phase. For example, an evolutionary development process implies that the analytical output entering the design phase will be a subset of the whole problem, whereas in a strict top-down development process, both the analysis and design phases will encompass the entire software project. The techniques discussed in this chapter can be used in either an evolutionary or a strict top-down development approach.

The objectives of analysis are to understand the functional requirements of the system to be developed and then to unambiguously portray those requirements. In carrying out these objectives, information relevant to system design emerges. The design phase of the software development process then takes the information resulting from the analysis phase and evolves it further. The result of the design process then feeds directly into the implementation phase of development. The goal of the Unified Modeling Language (UML) and the Use Case Centered Development methodology proposed in this textbook is to provide a seamless progression from one development phase to the next.

The ultimate objective of the design process is to represent the proposed system so that the resulting models serve as effective implementation blueprints. In order to achieve this objective, we will discuss the use of some additional UML diagrams as well as some UML notational enhancements for existing diagrams.

 ## Class Design versus Product Design

This text divides the topic of design into two components: product design and class design. The goal of **class design**, which is the topic of the next chapter, is to define the classes comprising the system along with the interrelationships among those classes. Class design is concerned with the attributes, method signatures, and semantics of each class in the system to be developed. The goal of **product design**, the topic of this chapter, is to create effective interactions. These interactions may be among various processes within the system, between this system and other systems, or between this system and human users of the system. In particular, product design addresses process architecture design, design of interprocess communication, and user interface design.

 ## Product Design Overview and Objectives

Product design addresses the external structure of a piece of software, whereas class design addresses the internal structure of the software. The **external structure** of software includes all software components that interact with external resources. For example, the user interfaces of a software system are considered external because they interact with users of the software to input data into the system and output information from the system. Other external components of the software interact with outside elements, such as databases and files. A system may also comprise remote processes communicating over a network, such as with client/server applications. Because of the communication among remote processes, how to effectively distribute the processes of the software over multiple machines is considered a product design issue. Figure 4.1 shows an abstract representation of the division between the internal and external structure of software.

The **internal structure** of the system consists of the classes that do not directly interact with elements outside the software system. Class design, therefore, deals

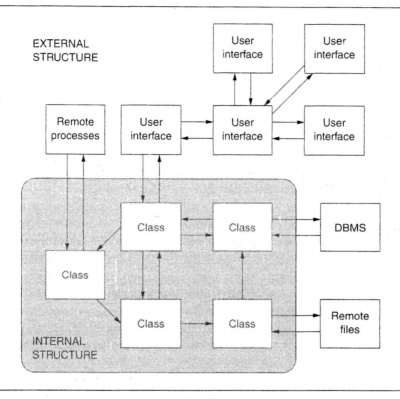

FIGURE 4.1   Internal Structure versus External Structure of Software

with determining the attributes and method signatures of the internal classes rather than classes that form the foundation for the user interfaces of the system. Product design, however, entails designing classes used in the user interfaces as well as classes used to interact with other external entities.

EXERCISE 4.1

Consider a car in terms of its internal versus its external structure. Certain parts of the car are designed to interact with external resources while other parts are designed to interact internally to ensure the car runs. Describe the automobile's external structure, and compare notes with your classmates. Now describe your understanding of the automobile's internal structure, and again compare notes with your classmates. Which description varied the most between class members? Why?

The objectives of the product design phase of object-oriented software development include

- Effective object persistence to facilitate efficient storage of data
- Effective design of process architecture to facilitate distributed, coordinated computation and resource use
- User-friendly, effective, and efficient user interfaces to facilitate human-computer interaction

Object Persistence

Object persistence is the notion that the information represented in an object (the **state** of the object) must be stored on a storage device if the information is to be permanently maintained. Object persistence (or more generally, **data persistence**) is an important design issue for object-oriented systems. Most mechanisms for permanent storage are not object-oriented and therefore do not explicitly accommodate objects. If an object-oriented software project is to succeed, we must find an adequate solution to the problem of how to go back and forth between the object-oriented software system and the non-object-oriented storage of the object information.

Several solution options exist. The most convenient solution is to use a database management system (DBMS) for storing information. By using a commercial DBMS, we have no need to worry about issues such as concurrent access, locking of records during update, and security. The difficulty with employing such a solution in an object-oriented system is that most commercially available DBMSs are relational and not object-oriented. The commercial DBMSs, therefore, cannot explicitly store objects. Typically, therefore, when a commercial DBMS is to be used, the software design must include mechanisms for putting objects into a relational form and restoring objects from that relational form.

Some alternative solutions, whose adoption depends upon the volume of information that needs to be stored and used by the system, exist. Certain object-oriented languages, such as Java, provide **object streaming** (also called **object serialization**), which facilitates storing objects in files and recreating those objects from files. This solution is attractive when all objects can be held in memory during the system execution. When memory is not large enough to hold all the system data at the same time, other solutions must be used.

The class project provides an excellent opportunity to effectively apply object serialization. If project developers wish to allow the state of the game to be saved and resumed at a later time (not a necessary requirement of the project), the state of the game, which is represented in the state of the individual objects in place during game execution, could be serialized and streamed to a file for later use. The real complexity in orchestrating the resumption of a game is coordinating the next meeting of the original game players. This complexity presents a logistical rather than technical problem.

A third alternative to solving the object persistence problem is used when memory is not large enough to hold all the system data at the same time. This solution employs a commercial object-oriented database management system. The functionality provided by such a DBMS is highly desirable. Unfortunately, although object-oriented DBMSs exist [6, 82], the commercially viable DBMSs continue to be relational, and, therefore, finding a commercial object-oriented DBMS may be difficult or impossible. Because of this difficulty, most solutions to the data storage problem employ a relational DBMS that interacts with the object-oriented software system.

4.5.1 Object Serialization

Database management systems are solutions for object persistence when the information in the object-oriented system is highly structured, is too large to reside simultaneously in memory, or requires concurrent access by multiple users. For example, an application that contains thousands of instances of a relatively small number of different classes is a good candidate for a DBMS. However, if the application consists of a small number of objects that do not need to be accessed by multiple users concurrently, then **object serialization** is a potential candidate solution for attaining object persistence.

To see the power of object serialization, let us consider an example from the Library Management System. Deliverable 4.1 shows the inheritance hierarchy for the various resources owned by the library. Each resource type contains the attributes from the *Resource* class plus some attributes that are specific to the resource type. For example, *Software* probably contains a *Version* attribute but no *Author* attribute. A *Book*, on the other hand, contains an *Author* attribute but no *Version* attribute. A *Patron* can check out many *Books*. In fact, the relationship between the *Patron* class and the *Book* class can more generally exist between the *Patron* class and the *Resource* class. That is, a *Patron* can check out many *Resources*, of various types. The *List* class, therefore, can contain a reference to any type of *Resource* object, not just *Book* objects. The *List* attribute associated with a *Patron*, therefore, is really a *List* of *Resources*, but each individual element of the *List* can actually be an instance of a child class of *Resource*.

A Class Diagram Showing an Inheritance Hierarchy in the LMS

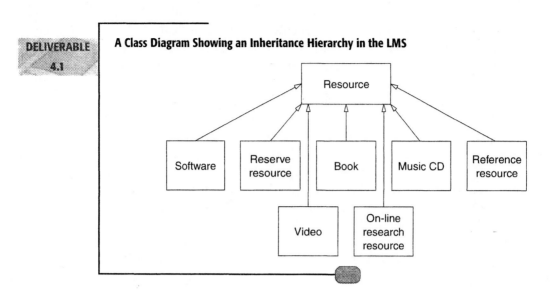

If we want to save information concerning checked-out resources to a file (or a relational table), we must first save the type of *Resource* and then the data that define the current state of that object. When we then read the information back from the file, we must first read the type of the object, create a blank object of that type, and finally, fill that object with the data that we stored in the file. We may write the code to implement this process for every class in our object-oriented system, but that job would be extremely tedious. With Java's object serialization mechanism, this process becomes trivial. Of course, in the case of the Library Management System, the amount of data in the system is too large to be held in memory all at once; therefore, object serialization is not a good solution to the problem of object persistence for that system. Our class project, Galaxy Sleuth, in contrast, represents an excellent candidate for the object serialization solution to the object persistence problem.

Using Java's object serialization mechanism, extremely complex interobject relationships are efficiently stored. For example, Deliverable 4.2 shows a partial representation of the **game state** of Galaxy Sleuth. The user may wish to save the game state in order to resume the game at a later time. The game state shown in Deliverable 4.2 associates several lists with the game state. One list contains references to *Player* objects, each of which contains a list of *Card* objects representing the player's hand of cards. An additional *Player* object reference, called *Current-Player*, refers to the player whose turn it currently is. Another list consists of *Card* object references, representing the state of a murder scenario *Hypothesis* put forth by the *CurrentPlayer*.

Partial Object Diagram of the Game State of Galaxy Sleuth

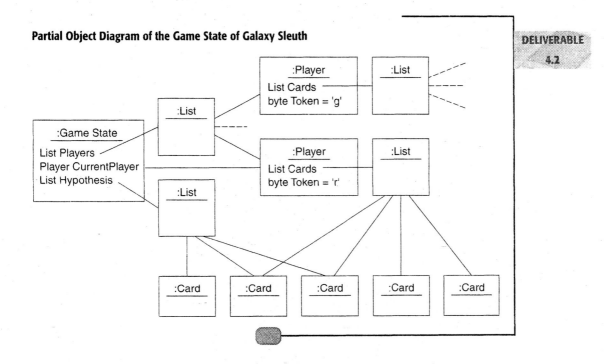

In Deliverable 4.2, notice that in several cases a single object is referred to by two other objects. For example, a *Player* object is referenced as the *CurrentPlayer* and as an element in the *Player* list. In addition, two of the *Card* objects associated with a particular *Player* object are also part of the current murder *Hypothesis Card* list.

Java's object serialization mechanism successfully and easily handles such multiple object references. Regardless of how many references to a particular object exist, a single serialized representation of each object is stored. Java also creates the necessary object identification numbers required for object persistence and subsequent object restoration. When an object is stored to disk, the object identification number replaces all references to that object, since an object reference is relevant only when an object resides in memory (since a reference is simply a memory address). For example, when the Galaxy Sleuth game is in memory, the list of *Player* objects contains the memory address of each of the players. When the game state is stored to disk, each *Player* object is assigned a unique object identification number (automatically by Java), and any reference to a particular *Player* object's location in memory is replaced by that object's unique identifier. When the game is restored to memory, the object identification numbers in the list of *Players* are replaced by the memory addresses to which the *Player* objects have been restored. If an object-oriented language does not provide automatic object serialization, such translations must be coded by the software developers.

4.5.2 Evaluating Object Persistence

The quality of the persistence solution should be judged against the following issues and extrapolations. The solution must adequately accommodate the following:

- Security: Hackers and malicious technical staff or end users cannot directly alter or access the stored data.
- Information growth: The solution will be efficient despite larger than anticipated growth in the volume of information processed by the system.
- Additional users: The solution is still viable if the pool of concurrent users grows.

EXERCISE 4.2   You have been engaged in a ferocious game of chess with your favorite aunt for the last two hours, but she has to catch a train home, and you won't see her again for a month. How do you preserve the state of the chess game so that you can pick up the game when she returns one month later without monopolizing the chess board for the entire month? If this game were played on a computer, how would you suggest saving the state of the game electronically?

 Case Study: **Object Persistence in LMS**

The Library Management System may contain tens if not hundreds of thousands of book entries, as well as thousands of other library resources tracked by the system. The data required by this system cannot be held in memory all at the same time. In addition, library staff and patrons may be concurrently accessing this data, and the system requires some security features because the various users have a variety of access levels and update privileges for the data. Some sort of DBMS provides the most convenient solution to the object persistence problem in the Library Management System.

Figure 4.2 shows a comparison of the representation of a *Patron* and its associated data as a set of interrelated objects and in a relational database context. The translation of objects into relational tables is one of the difficulties encountered when attempting to use commercial relational DBMSs for storing data from an object-oriented software system. One possible solution to this problem is to introduce into the object-oriented system an intermediate class, which is used to translate the state of objects into relational tables when the objects must be stored. This class acts as an intermediary between the object-oriented software system and the commercial relational database management system.

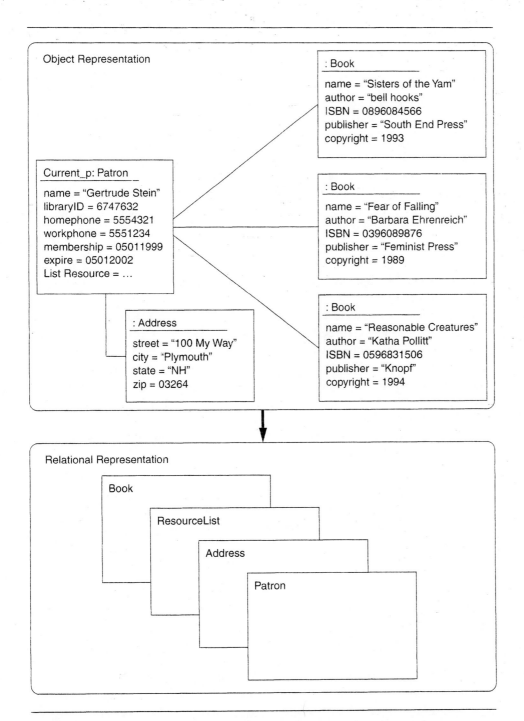

FIGURE 4.2 Object versus Relational Representation of a Patron in the Library Management System

From Figure 4.2, one might conclude that the translation from objects to tables is simple. In the figure it appears that each class in the object-oriented system might simply comprise a table in the relational representation. The translation, however, is a bit more complex. For example, in Figure 4.2, there is a line from the rectangle containing the *Patron* object to the rectangle containing the *Address* object. This line (like the other lines connecting rectangles) is implemented in the final software system as a pointer or reference from one object to another. When translating from objects to tables, these references must be translated into **key** values that allow **join** operations to bring all of the information together. Key values are designed to uniquely identify one record in a relational table. In other words, no duplicate values are allowed for key values in relational tables. In particular, the *PatronID* might be designated as the key value for the *Patron* class so that each *Patron* object is uniquely identified by his or her *PatronID* when translated to the relational table. This key value must also be an attribute in the *Address* table so that we can find the address associated with a particular *Patron* (by joining the *Patron* table with the *Address* table).

Another interesting feature jumps out from Figure 4.2. Notice that between the *Patron* object and the three *Book* objects, there is a *List* object, which has no attributes. The relationship between patrons and books is one-to-many. In other words, one patron can check out many books, but a book can be checked out by at most one patron. To translate this relationship from objects to tables, we must create a new table, called BookList. This new table contains two attributes, the key value for the Patron table (presumably *PatronID*) and the key value for the Book table (probably *CallNumber*). The *BookList* table is therefore introduced for the sole purpose of associating a variable number of *Books* with each *Patron*.

This one-to-many relationship results in the introduction of a new class, *List*, to our object-oriented system. The *List* class has the purpose of creating an object-oriented interface to a relational DBMS. We should note that the *List* class provides an application-specific solution to translating between object-oriented and relational representations of data.

Process Architecture

Software systems may comprise cooperating software processes executing on one or more machines. The design of the process architecture determines how the processes are structured within a system. In other words, process architecture lays out the machines, known as **nodes**, that will host the various processes making up the software system and what the functions of the separate processes will be. Unified Modeling Language (UML) provides a notation, called a **deployment diagram**, to allow modeling the processes comprising a system [16]. Through the use of modeling, we can specify both the processes that comprise the software system and the manner in which the processes will communicate with each other.

Concurrent portions of code in a single process may execute in distinct **threads of control** or simply **threads**. Separate threads may communicate with each other through a shared address space by way of shared memory locations or parameter passing during method invocation. Separate processes, however, do not share any address space and therefore cannot communicate by way of the same mechanisms as threads. In UML, a special kind of class, called an **active class**, is used to represent multithreaded processes, while deployment diagrams represent communication among separate processes.

4.7.1 Modeling Multiple Nodes

When a system consists of processes distributed over multiple nodes, the design of the process architecture must specify the functionality of each separate process, on which node the process runs, and how the processes communicate with each other. The breakdown of the functionality of the overall system into separate processes can be difficult to accomplish in an effective manner. The design goals of such a breakdown include an elegant partitioning of functionality from a software engineering standpoint and an optimal utilization of each node in the system. These design objectives remain more of an art than a science, however.

Deliverable 4.3 shows a sample deployment diagram for the Galaxy Sleuth class project. The cubes in the diagram represent the nodes that comprise the system. Each cube is labeled with the names of the processes that will be hosted on the corresponding node during execution of the system. The deployment diagram also shows how the nodes are connected to each other. In the example the nodes are shown as being connected through the Internet, which is shown as a cloud.

Deployment diagrams accommodate a great deal of notational flexibility. If the system consists of heterogeneous nodes, the software engineer may select special icons to represent various types of machines comprising the system. For example, the software developer may know that the system to be developed will be implemented on a network of midrange Unix-based machines and low-cost IBM-compatible personal computers running the latest flavor of the Microsoft Windows operating system. The developer can choose to represent the Unix machines with a particular icon (a cube, for example) and the Windows machines with another icon (a plain rectangle, for example). Appropriate labels can be used to assist in distinguishing these nodes. Deliverable 4.4 shows a deployment diagram modeling another processor topology using different icons to represent different types of processors.

Deployment Diagram for the Class Project

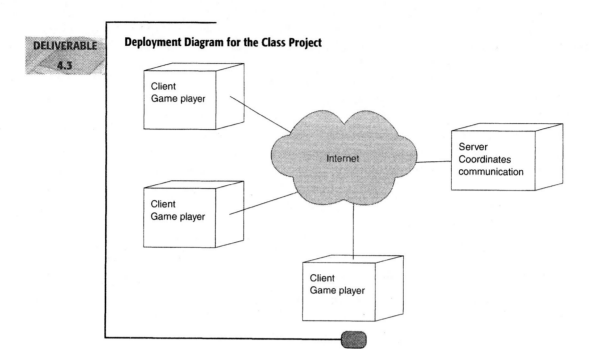

A Deployment Diagram Using Icons

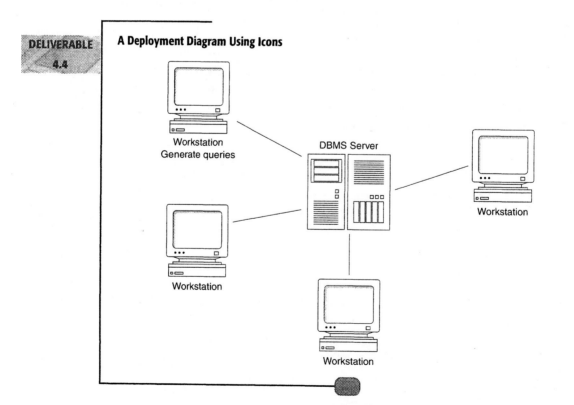

One vital aspect of system architecture not addressed by deployment diagrams, however, is **interprocess communication**. Interprocess communication is concerned with how the various processes will communicate with each other. It is addressed in the next subsection.

4.7.2 Modeling Interprocess Communication

Deployment diagrams do not suffice for expressing interprocess communication. Additional notation, therefore, is needed in order to model the manner in which different processes in a system communicate with each other. Processes can communicate with each other in a variety of ways, but we will focus on communications that are based on message passing over sockets.

To model interprocess communication over sockets, we will use **state machines** [16]. In UML, these state machines allow us to model dynamic aspects of the system to be developed. When interprocess communication is complex, as it is with the Galaxy Sleuth class project, modeling the communication by means of state machines is particularly important. State machines have been used in many computer science subdisciplines for modeling a variety of complex algorithms. They are discussed in more detail in the next subsection.

4.7.3 State Machines

Figure 4.3 shows the basic notational elements that make up state machines in UML [16]. State machines model behavior. In a state machine, processing in the system begins at the **initial state**. Processing typically moves to an **intermediate state** when given some trigger event. These intermediate states are given meaningful names. The system moves from state to state by means of *transitions*. A transition simply provides a way to leave one state and enter another. If a transition carries a label, it represents a **trigger**, which specifies the condition or event causing a transition to take place. For example, Figure 4.4 shows that an authenticated password serves as a trigger to advance the state from *user login* to *check out resource* in the Library Management System. A transition without such a label is said to be **unconditional** in that the movement from one state to the next will occur regardless of input. The transition from the initial state to the first intermediate state typically occurs unconditionally. Processing proceeds between intermediate states until a transition to the final state of the state machine occurs. Once the state machine enters the final state, the functionality of this subset of the system concludes.

Interprocess communication, which consists of several types of messages passed between two or more classes, can be effectively modeled with state machines. The algorithm for the interprocess communication is divided into several distinct states or phases. These states are represented in the state machine, and

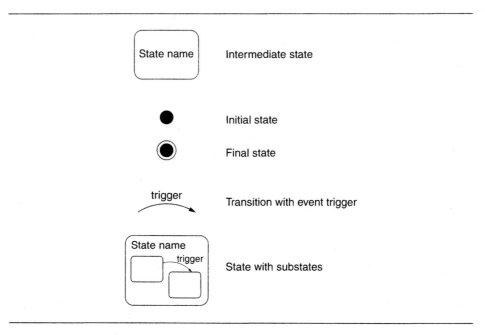

FIGURE 4.3 Notational Elements of State Machines

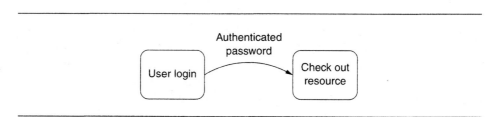

FIGURE 4.4   State Machine with a Trigger

when the algorithm moves from one state to another in response to input either from another process or from another part of this process, a labeled transition is represented in the state machine. State machines that represent interprocess communication can appear to be quite complex.

In certain instances in which states are complex or numerous, designers may wish to have a hierarchical representation of states. Figure 4.3 shows that one of the notational elements of state machines is an aggregate state that contains **substates**. Such a hierarchical representation, in fact, aids in the breakdown of a problem into subproblems. For example, in Galaxy Sleuth, potential players join the game by identifying themselves and then selecting one of the remaining player tokens. Deliverable 4.5 shows these steps characterized as a state called *player joining game*. The client process moves unconditionally from the initial state to a state called *get name* in which the process waits for the user to enter his or her name. Once the name has been entered, it is communicated to the server process state called *communicate remaining tokens*. The server process sends the list of unchosen tokens back to the client process, which transitions into a state called *select token* and waits for the user to choose a token. The selected token is then communicated to the next state outside of *player joining game*. This aggregate state can then be used as a single state in later state transition diagrams, such as the one shown Figure 4.5.

State Machine for Player Joining a Game

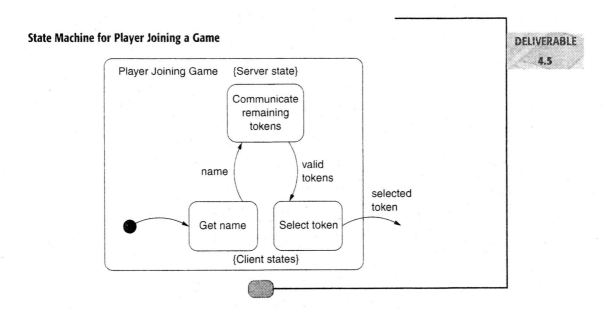

Imagine trying to program a robot to systematically traverse a labyrinth. Your robot has a simple sensing device that can perceive if a wall is present or not. Also, the sensing device may be positioned to sense *ahead*, *right*, or *left*. Conceptualize the feedback from the sensing device as an external process to the program that determines the robot's moves. The robot recognizes the following commands: *move forward*, *turn right*, *turn left*, *if <condition>*, and *return to last turn*. Assuming a recursive programming language, create a state machine that illustrates the communication between the sensing device and the navigation program.

EXERCISE 4.3

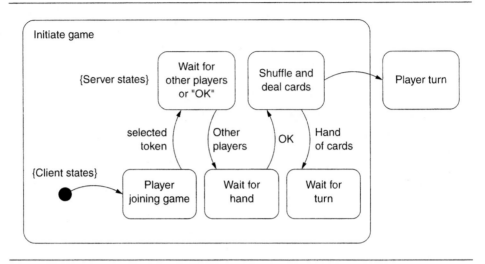

FIGURE 4.5   State Machine for Initiating a Game

4.7.4 Modeling Multiple Threads of Control

A single process that contains multiple threads of control is implemented with at least one multithreaded class. Such a class is called an **active class** and is distinguished from nonactive classes in a class diagram by rendering the rectangle representing the class with thick lines. Figure 4.6 shows an active class called *PlayerListener*. The *PlayerListener* class interacts with a nonactive class called *GalaxySleuthServer* by means of method invocations. The *GalaxySleuthServer* class also interacts with another nonactive class called *GameBoard*. All three of these classes will run on the server machine.

The *PlayerListener* class must be multithreaded because it is the class that will listen to the socket connections on the server for communication from the individual players or client processes. Since each player's communication may occur at unpredictable times, this class must have its own thread of control to be able to respond to the player immediately. An instance of this class will be created for each player so that the system will be responsive to each player.

4.7.5 Effective Use of Network Resources

Networks are frequently an application bottleneck and may be unreliable. Applications that depend on communicating information over networks should use efficient data representations and compress as much information as possible to reduce the volume of data transmitted over the network. Contingency plans must also be

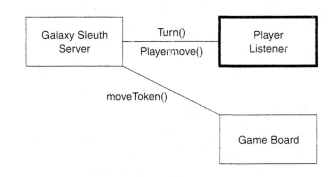

FIGURE 4.6 An Example of an Active Class

implemented to maximize application availability in the face of network or node failure. The issues involved in effective use of network resources are beyond the scope of this textbook but are mentioned here so that the reader will understand that such concerns must be considered.

 ## *Case Study:* Interprocess Communication in LMS

The Library Management System must also handle concurrent access to centrally stored information. No interprocess communication design is required for this system, however, because concurrent client requests are handled by the database management system itself rather than by software that we are building. In other words, by using a commercial DBMS for the storage of data, we get the benefit of all the features of the DBMS. The software that we build, therefore, may be structured as a set of distributed client processes making requests from the centralized DBMS.

 ## *Class Project:* Interprocess Communication in Galaxy Sleuth

One of the objectives of the class project, Galaxy Sleuth, is to coordinate the playing of the game between remote players over the Internet. Accordingly, this system takes on a **client/server** architecture. Each client represents a remote player, and the server coordinates the game playing among the players. Deliverable 4.3 is a simple deployment diagram suitable for the class project. The classic client/server system partitioning involves the server process disseminating centralized information to the client processes, and each client process creating the user interface for its client user. Beyond that intuitive division of responsibility in client/server systems, determining the comprehensive functionality of the client versus the server is more challenging.

For example, the software developed for the class project must embody the rules for Galaxy Sleuth. Does each client process individually enforce these rules, or should that logic reside on the server? Either scenario seems reasonable, and there are many such decisions that the software designer must make. For example, each client process can determine which player should take the next turn, or the server can execute the sequence of player turns.

A very basic rule for dividing tasks among clients and a server involves determining the number of clients that would need to execute a given set of logic at a given time. That is, in the case of determining which player should take the next turn, if the logic resides on the client, then every client process must execute that logic at the end of every turn. This logic, therefore, is an excellent candidate for residing on the server. However, the logic embodying the rules of the game is a good candidate for residing on the client since only the client whose player is currently taking a turn would need to execute this logic at a particular time.

After the responsibility of game playing has been distributed among the client and server classes, the communication between these components must be designed. Deliverable 4.5 shows a state machine that represents the *initiate game* aggregate state. The initial state, represented by the black dot, unconditionally transitions into the *player joining game* substate (which is shown in more detail in Figure 4.5). Once the *player joining game* state has executed, the token selected by this new player is communicated to the server substate called *wait for other players or "OK."* The transitions between substates represent information passed between client and server processes over a socket connection. Figure 4.5 therefore represents the communication between the client and server processes to accomplish the initiation of the game.

Looking at Figure 4.5 and Deliverable 4.5, the *initiate game* state begins at the *player joining game* substate, which in turn begins at the *get name* substate, part of the client. This substate then communicates the player name to the server, and a transition is made to the *communicate valid tokens* substate, which sends a list of valid tokens to the client. The transition is then made to the *select token* state, which communicates the user-selected token to the server. The transition is then made from the *player joining game* state to the *wait for other players or "OK"* state, which waits for additional players to identify themselves. Once at least three players are ready to play the game, the first player who logged on may start the game at any time by selecting an OK button. As players log on to the system, their presence is communicated to each client. Once sufficient players are logged on and the first player initiates play, the *Shuffle and deal cards* substate is entered. This substate communicates the hand of each player to that player, and then unconditionally enters the *player turn* state. The *player turn* state may be broken down similarly to the way the *initiate game* state has been broken down in this example.

Deliverable 4.6 shows the entire *Galaxy Sleuth* interprocess communication. Notice that the *initiate game* state shown in detail in Figure 4.5 is placed in context in Deliverable 4.6. The *initiate game* state is entered unconditionally from the initial state. The transition to the next state, *player turn*, is unconditional. Which state is entered next depends upon the action taken by the player on his or her turn. If the player makes no hypothesis or conclusion, the state machine enters the *player turn* state again (for the next player, of course). If, however, the player formulates a hypothesis, the state machine enters the *attempt to refute hypothesis* state and then unconditionally returns back to the *player turn* state. Finally, if the player formulates a conclusion, the state machine enters the *verify murder scenario* state. If the user has guessed incorrectly, the state machine enters the *remove player* state and then returns unconditionally to the *player turn* state. If the user has guessed correctly, the game is over, and the state machine enters the final state.

High-Level State Machine Representing Galaxy Sleuth

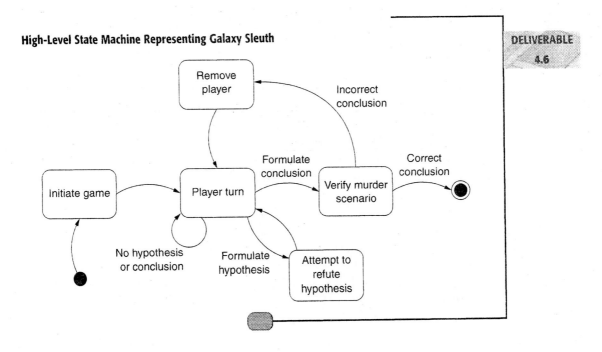

DELIVERABLE
4.6

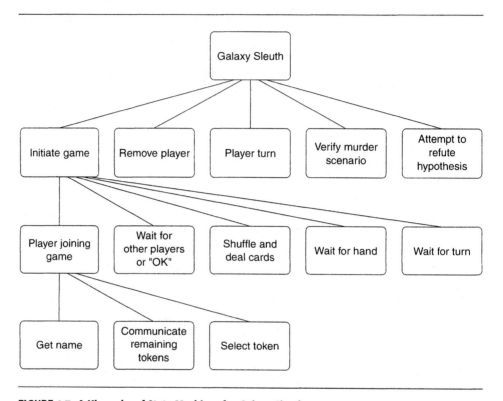

FIGURE 4.7 A Hierarchy of State Machines for Galaxy Sleuth

Deliverable 4.6 consists of very abstract states, each of which may be broken down into its respective substates as has been done with the *initiate game* state. Some of the substates shown in Figure 4.5 may themselves be deemed too abstract, and may be broken down into their substates as has been done with the *player joining game* state. In fact, an entire hierarchy of state machines may be created until only very self-explanatory states are specified as building blocks of more complex states.

Figure 4.7 shows a partial hierarchy of state machines, where the parent node in the hierarchy is the state machine that is made up of substates that are represented as child nodes in the hierarchy. The **root** node represents the system as a whole and consists of the set of sets expressed at its most abstract level. In this case, each state merits decomposition into substates, but in the illustration only one of the second-level states is decomposed.

Decompose each of the states shown in Figure 4.7 until the label on the state is **EXERCISE 4.4**
self-explanatory.

4.10   User Interfaces

The user of a software system has a set of tasks that he or she must accomplish. In the mind of the user, the software system is a tool that will help to accomplish these tasks. We can think of the software system as a set of functions that the system is capable of executing. These functions are the **semantics**, or meaning, of the software system. In order to execute these functions, the user must input information into the system through a set of syntactic rules [92]. The **user interface** of a system can be thought of as the mapping of these user inputs to internal representations of these inputs as well as the mapping of internal representations of information to external representations of the information that the user can understand [59]. Figure 4.8 shows how the user interface of a system relates to both the user of the system and the functionality of the system.

The user interface is more than these mappings, however. The user interface also consists of **interaction techniques** [59]. The interaction techniques are the input devices that the user uses to input data and information into the system. For example, we may design the user interface of a system such that a user manipulates a mouse to interact with menu options. Or we may decide to have the user input

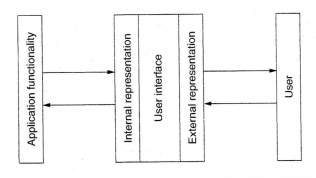

FIGURE 4.8 The Role of the User Interface

choices with a keyboard. In the Library Management System example, the librarian may be required to type the patron ID into a text field, or we may decide that the librarian should use a bar code reader to input the patron ID from the patron's library card.

It is very important to note that the user interface for a system is separate from the functionality of the system. The choices for user interfaces for a system are many. The development of the functionality of the system and the user interface for the system should be kept relatively independent. This independence will allow pieces of the functionality to be reused in slightly different user situations [64]. For example, in the Library Management System, we could develop an interface for users who are searching the catalog in the library using machines in the library. In the future, we may want to rewrite our interface so that users can access the catalog through the World Wide Web. By keeping the search application code separate from the interface of the search application, we can reuse that functionality when we move the search to the World Wide Web.

One way of keeping the user interface design separate from the application functionality design is to focus on the difference between **information content** and **information form** [59]. The content of the information is determined by the application's functionality, while the form of the information is determined by the application's user interface. In other words, the functionality determines what information is to be communicated via the user interface, and the user interface determines how that information is to be communicated.

User Interface Design

The user interface of a software product is its most visible external component. Through this interface, the human user interacts with the software. No matter how well designed the internal structure of a piece of software is, the software will fail if the user interface is perceived to be difficult to understand. In fact, a major subarea of computer science, called **human-computer interaction**, addresses the issues of good user interface design.

The source code required to implement the user interface may comprise 70 percent or more of the source code for the entire system [92]. Like all software, the user interface must be designed to be effective. There is no "right" or "wrong" user interface. Because good user interface design has much to do with user perceptions of the interface [59], much of this design topic falls into the realm of psychology.

There are, however, five general factors that relate to user interface quality [73]:

- Ease of learning
- Speed of use
- Frequency of user errors

- User satisfaction
- Knowledge retention

The ease of learning of a user interface refers to how long it takes a user to learn enough about the interface to begin to use the system effectively. The speed of use of a user interface refers to how long it takes a typical user to carry out specific tasks. The frequency of user errors refers to how often a user makes mistakes in attempting to carry out particular tasks. User satisfaction refers to the user's attitude toward the system. In other words, a user who likes the system a lot has high satisfaction, while a user who does not like the system has low satisfaction. Knowledge retention refers to how easy it is for the user to remember how to complete some task after not having used the system for some amount of time.

Ultimately, we would like to design a user interface that is of high quality in each of these five areas. In most cases, however, we must sacrifice performance in one of the areas to get the desired performance in another area [73]. For example, to increase the speed of use, we may need to sacrifice in the area of learning ease, since to increase the speed of use, we will typically create shortcuts that may be difficult for a user to learn. Once they are learned, however, the speed at which the user can interact with the system will increase. No matter what interface we design, however, we should try to maximize user satisfaction. Of course, one user may be satisfied with the interface that we design, while another user may not be satisfied. Such personal preference issues can be hard to predict. A user's satisfaction with a software system has to do with the two main parts of the system: its functionality and its user interface [73]. In other words, the system must actually do what it is supposed to do, and it must be **user-friendly**.

4.11.1 User-Friendliness

The main property of a good user interface is **user-friendliness**. See Summary Points box 4.1 for guidelines for making a user-friendly interface, and the following description [96]:

- Use instructions that are easy to learn and remember. If the instructions for an application are difficult to learn, many users will choose not to learn the instructions and will look for other ways to accomplish tasks. For example, the arcane command language that is the interface of the Unix operating system has significantly inhibited its adoption by many users. The various Windows-based operating systems, however, with their graphical user interfaces, are easier to learn and have been more popular with average, nonexpert users.
- Make help functions context sensitive. Different help texts should be displayed based on the current state of the application. For example, if a user is attempting to use a copy command in a particular application and asks for help, help information about the copy command should be displayed. The user should not

have to search through a lot of irrelevant "helpful" information to find information relevant to the task at hand. By definition, helpful information is relevant to the task at hand.

- Present logically connected functions together and consistently. By presenting logically connected functions together, we enable the user to use the user interface in a more effective manner because the user does not have to search for the appropriate function. For example, in Windows-based applications, there is a menu bar at the top of the application. On the menu bar are a set of relatively standard menu items, one of which is *Edit*. In the *Edit* menu, we can find additional menu items that will allow us to edit the current document. In particular, the *Edit* menu contains the *Cut*, *Copy*, and *Paste* menu items. These menu items are placed near each other because they are logically related to each other.
- Create graphical user interfaces whenever possible. In general, the graphical symbols of graphical user interfaces trigger faster recognition than do textual input and output devices.
- Allow actions to be activated quickly. If every action requires the traversal of several menus, frequent users of the application will soon become dissatisfied with the interface. These users require mechanisms that will allow them to increase their speed of use and thus their productivity. Intermittent users, however, appreciate reminders (such as lists of instructions in menu form) about how to accomplish a variety of tasks.

EXERCISE 4.5   Choose your favorite application. Evaluate the user interface of the platform using the preceding guidelines for user-friendliness. Compare your evaluation with the evaluation of a student who has chosen a different application. How similar are your evaluations? Can you think of ways to incorporate the strengths of the user interface of one application to improve the weaknesses of the other application?

SUMMARY POINTS 4.1

Guidelines for User-Friendly Interfaces

1. Use instructions that are easy to learn and remember.
2. Make help functions context sensitive.
3. Present logically connected functions together and consistently.
4. Create graphical user interfaces whenever possible.
5. Allow actions to be activated quickly.

User Interface Design Principles

There are two broad principles that should be taken into account when designing user interfaces. First, before you can design an effective user interface, you must understand who will be using the interface and how those users will be using it. Second, you should follow some tried and true rules of interface design that have been gained from years of experience. We will now examine each of these principles in more detail.

4.12.1 Know the User

Users of software systems have varying amounts and types of background knowledge. Some users may have lots of experience with computer systems, while others may have no experience. Some users may use a system all day every day, while others may only use a system once or twice a year. Designing an interface to accommodate all the potential experiences of users of the system is a very difficult task. When creating a user interface for a software system, we need to know who the users of the system will be. To find out this information, we must create **user profiles** [92].

User Profiles

There are three broad categories of users [73]:

- The novice user, who has rarely used a computer system
- The knowledgeable intermittent user, who has used a variety of systems on a sporadic basis
- The frequent user, who is completely comfortable with using computer systems in general and our computer system in particular

The user interfaces designed for each category of user will vary. For example, novice users require lots of feedback and very clear, constructive error messages. In addition, one should minimize the chances for the user to make an error and the number of user commands or actions that are required to perform a particular task. In contrast, a knowledgeable, intermittent user typically can remember the underlying structure of the software system but has problems recalling the details of any one system. For such users, the ability to explore the system without fear of doing something dangerous may be very important. Menus, consistent commands and terminology, and help screens are particularly useful to the knowledgeable, intermittent user. Finally, the frequent user typically wants very little feedback and many shortcuts [73].

These descriptions serve only as broad categories, and additional information about the particular users of the system must be gathered. User interface designers should gather user population profiles that reflect age, gender, physical abilities, education, cultural or ethnic background, training, motivation, goals, and personality. In addition, users can be tested for a variety of skills such as understanding of Boolean expressions, knowledge of set theory, insurance claims concepts, and map reading. In other words, the designer of a user interface must understand the future users of the system in great depth before beginning to design the interface [92].

EXERCISE 4.6   Choose your favorite application. Does the application have features that are designed to help novice users? What are they? Does the application have features for intermittent and expert users? What are they?

Most user interfaces must accommodate a variety of user types. Designing such interfaces is much more difficult than designing interfaces for only one category of user [92]. When designing a user interface for more than one user type, two basic strategies exist.

The first possible strategy for dealing with a variety of users is the **layered** approach. Novices can be taught a small set of skills that will allow them to interact with the system in a very basic manner. Once novice users have become comfortable with the initial set of tasks, a second layer of more complex tasks and its associated interfaces is added to their training. Eventually, the users can progress to the most complex tasks and their associated interfaces [73]. An individual user's progress through such training is determined solely by his or her learning progress. Users with strong a priori knowledge and understanding of the task and interface concepts will progress rapidly through the training.

The second strategy for dealing with a variety of users with a single interface is to allow the users to control how much and what type of information is given to them at a particular time [92]. For example, the novice user can (relatively slowly) walk through a series of well-structured choices to accomplish a task. At each step in the process, the novice user receives a lot of informative feedback to confirm his or her actions. The expert user attempting to complete the same task can do so much more quickly with far fewer steps and with much less feedback. To achieve this speed, however, the expert user is required to remember more about the interface and the functionality of the task. An example of such a strategy can be seen in most applications that run on the Windows 95/98/Me/NT platform. These applications typically include some sort of tool bar that will allow advanced users to click on a small image in order to complete a particular task. The same task may be accomplished in at least one other manner by following a set of choices on menus. In addition, most modern user interfaces have sophisticated help facilities to help novice users figure out how to use the system without overburdening more advanced users with information they already know.

Multiuser domains (MUDs) are very cryptic applications. Class members who are familiar with one or more MUDs should explain the basics of their favorite MUDs, so that others less familiar with these applications can have a sense of them. One common characteristic of MUDs is that they are very intimidating for new users. Create a list of user types that a new MUD should accommodate in order to be a satisfying experience for a wider range of users.

4.12.2 Rules for Interface Design

Much work has been done to determine what constitutes an effective user interface. Summary Points box 4.2 lists the rules that come out of that research, and each of the rules is described in the following subsections [92].

Be Consistent

Many types of consistency exist; therefore, following this user interface design principle can be difficult. In fact, this principle is perhaps the one that is most often violated [92]. The interface should be consistent in syntax, terminology, action sequences, and layout. Inconsistent interfaces are difficult for users to learn to use. For example, if a user can *delete* a character, he or she should not *remove* a word, *destroy* a line, and *kill* a paragraph. Each of these options should result in similar fates for the intended item, namely, that the item is removed from the interface. The user should instead be able to delete a character, delete a word, delete a line, and delete a paragraph. All menus should follow the same format, and all error messages should use similar terminology and appear in the same location [73].

SUMMARY POINTS 4.2

General Design Guidelines for User Interfaces

1. Be consistent.
2. Provide shortcuts.
3. Offer useful, meaningful feedback.
4. Design a beginning, middle, and end for each sequence of actions.
5. Prevent catastrophic mistakes.
6. Verify deletion tasks.
7. Allow easy reversal of most actions.
8. Make user focus on task, not interface.
9. Do not rely on user memory.
10. Display only currently relevant information.

Provide Shortcuts

Frequent users want to work as quickly as possible through a given task. One of the simplest mechanisms to allow increased speed for such users is to provide shortcuts for the completion of various tasks. A shortcut reduces the number of steps required to complete a task. Because these shortcuts increase the speed at which frequent users interact with the system, they also increase productivity. Some possible shortcuts include abbreviations, special keys, hidden commands (like pressing Shift while clicking on the *Reload* button in Netscape to force the web page to be reread from the host), and macro facilities (to allow frequent users to create their own shortcuts) [92]. For example, in Microsoft Word, a popular word-processing program, a novice user can highlight some text, use the mouse to choose the *Edit* menu, and then choose *Cut* to remove the text from his or her Word document. An intermittent user might remember that the icon on the tool bar that contains a picture of scissors is a shortcut for cutting text, and an expert user might remember that pressing *Ctrl-X* is another shortcut for cutting text.

Offer Useful, Meaningful Feedback

Every action, successful or unsuccessful, should result in some sort of feedback to the user. Major actions should produce more substantial feedback than minor actions. The feedback can be some sort of audio tone, the display of some text, a change in the object being modified (removal of text from a word-processing document, for example), or a change in an icon that represents a portion of the task.

Design a Beginning, Middle, and End for Each Sequence of Actions

Every sequence of actions should have a clearly marked beginning and ending, leaving the remaining actions to be classified as the middle. The ending of the sequence gives the user a sense of completion, indicating that the next task can be begun. For example, on web pages that require the user to enter information, there is often a *Submit* button at the bottom of the form. The user knows that when the button has been pressed, the task is complete, and any chance to recover from possible errors is gone.

Prevent Catastrophic Mistakes

The system should, as much as possible, protect itself against mistakes. For example, if a field requires the user to enter a number, do not allow the user to enter letters into the field. If the user does make an error, a simple, useful error message should be displayed. The error message should pinpoint exactly where the error occurred and what the user must do to fix the error. If possible, erroneous actions should not change the state of the system. If the system state does change in response to erroneous actions, give the user clear instructions about how to restore the original state.

Verify Deletion Tasks

Do not delete any major item without asking the user whether he or she is sure about the deletion.

Allow Easy Reversal of Most Actions

As much as possible, user actions should be reversible. An "undo" command increases user productivity by allowing the user to reverse the most recent actions without having to start the entire operation over again in the case of mistakes. In addition, easy reversal relieves user anxiety because the user knows that errors can be undone. With less anxiety, the user is more likely to explore additional features of the software.

Make User Focus on Task, Not Interface

Users should see themselves as the initiators of tasks rather than responders in the human-computer interaction. The computer is the tool that helps the user complete a variety of tasks, and the interface should reflect that fact. A well-designed interface that puts the user at the center of the human-computer interaction is said to be **transparent** to the user. In a transparent system, the user is able to focus on the task at hand, and the computer becomes invisible.

Do Not Rely on User Memory

Humans have a limited-capacity short-term memory. Therefore, the user should not be required to remember huge amounts of information as he or she accomplishes a task. Any information the user is required to remember should be task related rather than computer related. For example, the user should not have to remember names and numbers from page to page in multipage displays. To aid in reducing short-term memory load, online help should be provided.

Display Only Currently Relevant Information

When a user asks for information of a particular type, display only the information that is useful at the moment if possible. The user should not have to wade through extra information to find the nugget that is needed. For example, help facilities should be context sensitive so that the user who is asking for help will get a response that is relevant to the task at hand.

EXERCISE 4.8   Investigate a multiuser domain (MUD) like LambdaMOO or another familiar to you. Create a list of user interface design principles violated by this MUD, and briefly describe how the MUD violates each principle.

4.12.3 Interaction Styles

Although there are general guidelines that should be followed when designing user interfaces, specific types of user interfaces have specific sets of design guidelines. There are five primary interaction styles for user interfaces. These interaction styles are listed in Summary Points box 4.3 and described in the following subsections [92]. In some situations, a combination of the interaction styles is appropriate.

Menu Selection

In **menu selection** user interfaces, the user is presented with a series of lists of items corresponding to possible actions. The user selects the appropriate item to complete a task and then observes the result. In order to complete a particular task using a menu selection interface, the user does not have to learn or memorize very much, as long as the list of items clearly represents the possible actions to be undertaken and the actions can clearly and intuitively be linked to particular tasks. The difficulty of developing such interfaces is that the menu structure for the possible tasks is not necessarily clear.

In Windows 95/98/Me/NT, most applications have similar menu structures. For example, nearly every application has a *File* menu on which the user will find familiar tasks such as *New*, *Open*, *Save*, *Print*, *Close*, and *Exit*. If a user has never used a Windows-based application, the difference between *Close* and *Exit* (closing the current file as opposed to completely exiting the current application) may not be clear. But once the user understands that difference, *Close* and *Exit* in every application encountered on a Windows-based system will make sense.

In addition to the common menu items (*File*, *Edit*, *View*, *Tools*, *Windows*, and *Help*), an individual application on a Windows-based system must have some unique menu items in order to accommodate any application-specific tasks. The meaning of the these new menu items may not be clear to new users. To develop effective, well-structured menu selection interfaces, designers must completely understand the tasks that must be supported by the application and how a user might typically attempt to accomplish these tasks. Choosing the names of menu items is an art rather than a science. Summary Points box 4.4 shows a set of simple but widely violated guidelines for such choices, each of which is described in the following list:

- Be consistent. Choose terminology that is familiar to the potential users, and use this terminology in a consistent manner.
- Use distinctive items. Be clear about the distinction between one menu item and the next. For example, the set of menu items *Musical Interludes*, *Harmonious Recitals*, and *Instrumental Performances* is much less distinct than *Classical Recordings*, *Folk Recordings*, and *Jazz Recordings*.
- Be concise. The menu items should have short names such as *Help* rather than longer names such as *Information you might find to be helpful*.
- Put keywords first in the item name. The first word of the item name can help the user distinguish among menu items. For example, the set of menu items *Set Font Size*, *Set Font Type*, and *Set Font Color* is difficult to scan and find the appropriate choice for the task at hand. A better set of menu items is *Size of Font*, *Type of Font*, and *Color of Font*. The user can now scan this list of items more quickly to find the appropriate choice.
- Create groups of logically similar items. Each item on a menu should be related to the other items on the same menu. For example, assume we are creating menus for the Library Management System user interface. The menu items that allow us to manage patron information, such as adding a new patron, updating a patron's address, and checking the resources currently held by a patron, should appear on the same menu. However, we do not want to mix menu items for managing patrons with menu items for managing resources.

SUMMARY POINTS 4.4

Guidelines for Designing Effective Menus

1. Be consistent.
2. Use distinctive items.
3. Be concise.
4. Put keywords first in the item name.
5. Create groups of logically similar items.

EXERCISE 4.9   Design a set of menus to help facilitate issuing DOS or Unix commands. Because of the quantity of such commands, it is necessary to develop an effective hierarchy for these commands.

Form Fillin

When data entry is required, menu selection typically becomes too cumbersome for effective interaction. Form fillin is a much more appropriate user interface for such situations. In a form fillin user interface, the user sees a series of related fields through which he or she moves the cursor, entering data whenever necessary. Users must understand the labels associated with each field in which data can be typed, know what values are allowed in each field, and be able to respond to any error messages that may arise. Typically, novice users do not have enough knowledge or training to be able to interact effectively with form fillin user interfaces. Nevertheless, empirical studies suggest that the form fillin approach is faster than command language user interfaces. In addition, most users seem to prefer the form fillin interface over the command language interface [79].

The form fillin user interface strategy is used widely on the World Wide Web. Many sites that deal with electronic commerce have some type of form into which the user must enter information. Although these interfaces have not been studied very much, there are some basic guidelines for designing effective forms. Summary Points box 4.5 highlights these guidelines, which are explained in detail in the following list.

SUMMARY POINTS 4.5

Guidelines for Designing Effective Forms

1. Use a meaningful title.
2. Give instructions that are understandable but brief.
3. Use logical sequencing and grouping of fields on the form.
4. Lay out the form in a visually appealing manner.
5. Use familiar field labels.
6. Use consistent terminology and abbreviations.
7. Create boundaries around the data-entry fields.
8. Allow the cursor to be moved in a convenient way.
9. Allow easy error correction.
10. Prevent errors whenever possible.
11. Provide error messages when invalid values are entered.
12. Clearly mark any optional fields.
13. Give explanations of the individual fields.
14. Clearly signal the completion of data entry.

- Use a meaningful title. The title of the form should clearly identify the topic of the form and not use computer jargon. For example, if we create a form to allow the entry of data pertaining to a new patron in the Library Management System, we call the form "Enter New Patron Information." Such a title is far preferable to "Patron Database, PInformation Table." This second title reflects the fact that our patron information is stored in a relational database in a particular table but does not provide much useful information to the user entering data for a new patron.
- Give instructions that are understandable but brief. If more detailed instructions are required by novice users, provide help facilities. Avoid the use of the word "Enter," as in "Enter the address," since a user can get confused and think the word refers to the Enter key on the keyboard. Instead use "Type," as in "Type the address," or simply "Address" followed by a box delineating where the data are to be typed.
- Use logical sequencing and grouping of fields on the form. Related fields should be next to each other, on the same line, if possible. In addition, related fields should be placed on the form in an order that makes common sense. For example, since we typically think of an address as a city, state, and zip code, these fields should be placed on a form next to each other in the specified order.
- Lay out the form in a visually appealing manner. The fields on the form should be spaced in a somewhat uniform manner rather than crowded together in one part of the form. If the user is entering data from a hard copy, the fields on the form should match the hard copy as closely as possible.
- Use familiar field labels. The labels for each field should be commonly used names rather than terms that are unfamiliar to most users. For example, the field label *Patron Name* is much more common and familiar than *Patron Appellation*.
- Use consistent terminology and abbreviations. To ensure such consistency, the designer of a form should create a list of acceptable terms and abbreviations. For example, the term "Patron ID" might appear on this list. When creating forms for the Library Management System, the designer should use this term and not "Patron Number," "Identification Number," "Library ID," or any other term when referring to the patron identification number. New terms or abbreviations should be added to the list only after very serious consideration of whether such an addition is absolutely necessary.
- Create boundaries around the data-entry fields. A visible delineation of the boundaries of a field on a form allows the user to determine whether abbreviations or other trimming techniques are necessary to enter the appropriate data in the field. In a graphical user interface, such a boundary can be created using some sort of box. In a text-based interface, the boundary can be indicated by using the underscore character to specify the length of the field.
- Allow the cursor be to moved in a convenient way. To allow the user to move the cursor from field to field, use some very simple mechanism. In Microsoft

Windows-based applications, the Tab key typically allows the user to move from field to field.

- Allow easy error correction. Allow the user to use the Backspace key to correct individual characters as well as some mechanism for overtyping to correct an entire field. In graphical user interfaces that use the mouse for some input, the mouse can be used to highlight all text in a particular field so that overtyping can occur.

- Prevent errors whenever possible. For example, if the only valid input for a particular field is numeric, do not allow the user to enter any nonnumeric data. In addition, if there are a limited number of valid entries for a particular field, consider using a list box. For example, in the Library Management System, we may have a form that allows the user to enter data about new resources. One of the fields that the user must enter specifies which type of resource this new one is. There are only a limited number of valid resource types, such as *book, music CD, video, journal*, and *software*. Since these are the only possible values to be entered into the type field, if our interface type can handle list boxes, we should create a list box with the values in it. The user then simply chooses from the list when entering the resource type. The list box minimizes the chance of error in the data entry. Of course, the user could still make an incorrect choice for a particular resource, but at least the choice is a valid one.

- Provide error messages when invalid values are entered. Sometimes, it is not possible to prevent invalid values from being entered into a particular field. In such situations, if the user does enter an invalid value, a meaningful error message, suggesting what is wrong with the value, should be displayed to the user. For example, perhaps all patron identification numbers contain eight digits. If the user enters five digits in a Patron ID field, an error message stating that the Patron ID requires eight digits should be displayed.

- Clearly mark any optional fields. Optional fields should be labeled with either the word "optional" or by some other mechanism. The mechanism must be consistently applied throughout the system. If possible, optional fields should follow any required fields on a form. For example, in the Library Management System, the field containing a new patron's work phone number may be entered. This field should be clearly marked as optional. Since the work phone number is logically related to the home phone number of the patron, these two fields should appear near each other on the form. Since the home phone number is probably a required field, the work phone number should appear after the home phone number on the form.

- Give explanations of the individual fields. If possible, some brief explanatory information about a particular field should appear in a standard location whenever the cursor is in that field. For example, when the cursor moves into a particular field, a short explanation of what the field contains can appear at the bottom of the window (in the status bar on a Windows-based system) in which the form appears.

• Clearly signal the completion of data entry. Users should be able to see that the form has been completed. Avoid automatic completion of forms when the last field is entered because a user may wish to review the entered data before committing it. On many web page forms, for example, the bottom of the form contains a *Submit* button that the user must press in order to send the entered information to the Web site. Until the *Submit* button has been pressed, the user has the opportunity to change the entered information.

Design a GUI for an automobile driving simulation program in which the user does not have a joystick or steering wheel device, but only a standard mouse and keyboard. How will the user interact with the system? What sort of operations does the user need to perform, and how effective is your proposal in facilitating those operations. How error prone or foolproof is your proposal? Are the interfaces proposed by your classmates significantly different from yours?

EXERCISE 4.10

Command Language

A command language is a set of syntactic statements that a user may enter in order to accomplish a specific set of tasks. Each command has a specific, well-defined syntax that corresponds to the specific functionality of the system. Command languages require that the user learn and remember the syntax of the language. In addition, the user must be able to type each command effectively. Command languages are typically fairly arcane and appear complex to the uninitiated user. As such, a command language is not an appropriate interaction style for a system designed for novice users. In fact, because error rates are typically quite high for command languages, only interfaces designed for expert users should require the use of a command language.

Many command languages exist today. The Unix operating system, for example, has a command language that allow users of the operating system to accomplish many tasks. The command language in Unix is quite arcane and difficult to understand. For example, although not obvious, the following Unix command counts the number of nonblank lines in a file called *outline.txt*:

```
grep -v ^ $ outline.txt | wc -l
```

SUMMARY POINTS 4.6

SUMMARY POINTS 4.6

Design Guidelines for Command Languages

1. Limit the number of commands.
2. Choose meaningful, distinctive command names.
3. If abbreviations are used, be consistent.
4. Structure of the command syntax should be consistent.
5. Use prompts to help intermittent users.
6. Consider command menus to help intermittent users.

Summary Points box 4.6 shows a set of guidelines for the design of effective command languages. Each of these guidelines is described in the following list:

- Limit the number of commands. A major design flaw of many command languages is that they have too many commands with too many options. An effective command language must be designed to represent all the user's tasks and nothing more. Excess functionality slows learning and introduces more possibilities for user error. Tasks that must be performed over and over should be accomplished easily with a minimum of errors. For example, if a command for copying files is likely to be used often, a single-letter command, or a command that does not require the use of the Shift key or the Ctrl key, will be appreciated by the user.
- Choose meaningful, distinctive command names. The command names should be as meaningful to the human user as possible (therefore, grep is not a very good command name). For example, the command copy is used in DOS to allow a user to copy one file to another. Frequent, expert users, however, appreciate shorter commands. Abbreviations for many commands can be used to satisfy expert users.
- If abbreviations are used, be consistent. There are many strategies for abbreviating commands. The strategy for abbreviation should be consistent across commands. The prevalence of graphical user interfaces has reduced the necessity of using abbreviation strategies, but if they are needed, testing the abbreviations on users, if possible, is the safest route to take.
- Structure of the command syntax should be consistent. In other words, the various components of the command should consistently appear in the same position across commands. For example, in the Unix operating system, the command name appears first. If there are options for the command, these appear next following a − sign. Any arguments for the command appear after the options. The following Unix command is used to add read permission to all files in a subdirectory called *Home*:

```
chmod −R a+r Home
```

The name of the command is *chmod*, not an obvious choice for the name of a command that will change the permissions of subdirectories and files. The option chosen is *R*, which means to recurse into the subdirectory to be named later in the command. In other words, read permission will be added to the subdirectory and all the files in the subdirectory. The first argument, *a+r*, means to add read permission. The last argument is the name of the subdirectory for which read permission is to be added. Although the structure of this Unix command is consistent with the structure of other Unix commands, it is still very difficult for nonexpert users to learn and remember.

- Use prompts to help intermittent users. To help intermittent users learn to use a command language, consider adding prompts. For example, if a user wants to move a file from one directory to another but cannot remember the syntax and structure of the command, he or she might type the name of the move command and then be prompted to enter the rest of the command. Thus, the user types *move* and the user interface responds with `File Name:` and the user types the name of the file, *outline.txt*. The user interface responds with `Move To:` and the user responds with the new location, *Home*. If, however, the user is an expert, he or she can simply type in the entire command at once: *move outline.txt Home*.

- Consider command menus to help intermittent users. Command menus make a command language easier to learn and can also make the system more attractive to intermittent users. For example, *pico*, a Unix-based text editor, has a command menu at the bottom of the text window (Figure 4.9). Because of this menu, users do not have to remember the commands for various tasks.

Natural Language

Natural language user interfaces have long been the dream of software designers and developers. Because natural language interaction typically provides little context for issuing the next command, the success of such interfaces has thus far been limited to situations in which intermittent users are knowledgeable about specific tasks. If

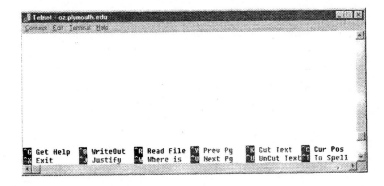

FIGURE 4.9 Pico Command Language Menu

the users are expert users, a command language interface is typically much faster. If the users are novice users, they probably need more structure and feedback than is provided with either a command language or natural language interface.

There are significant difficulties in trying to develop natural language user interfaces. The first difficulty lies in the lack of structure presented to the user and how the user might respond to that lack of structure. Typically, natural language interfaces present the user with some sort of prompt to which the user is supposed to enter a natural language statement. The user must know a significant amount about the types of tasks and permissible actions that can be accomplished with this system. Users who are knowledgeable about the tasks and actions frequently prefer a concise command language because of the imposed structure. The second difficulty also lies in the previously mentioned lack of structure. Developing a system that will respond appropriately to the wide variety of potentially ambiguous natural language statements that might be entered by the user can be very difficult. If the range of tasks and permissible actions is too large, developing such an interface might in fact be nearly impossible.

Natural language user interfaces have been most successful in situations where the user is very knowledgeable about the task domain, where the task domain is very limited, and where the user uses the system only intermittently. In particular, many relational database management system developers have created natural language front ends for their systems to allow users to perform queries on the data in the database. Studies have shown, however, that structured query language interactions are most effective, efficient, and satisfactory [55, 94].

Direct Manipulation

In a direct manipulation user interface, the user sees a visual representation of the real world, and the user manipulates the representations of familiar objects of the real world to accomplish a particular task. Such user interfaces are typically fairly easy for a user to learn how to use, but relatively difficult and complex for the user interface developer to create. By interacting with visual representations of the world, users can accomplish many tasks very quickly and see the results of their actions immediately. Summary Points box 4.7 shows some guidelines for creating

---

SUMMARY POINTS 4.7

Design Guidelines for Direct Manipulation Interfaces

1. Use easy to understand icons.
2. Avoid misleading analogies.
3. Do not violate population stereotypes.
4. Use icons for appropriate purposes.
5. Carefully design the iconic interaction.

direct manipulation interfaces. Each of these guidelines is discussed in detail in the following list:

- Use easy to understand icons. The meaning of the icons should be as obvious as possible. A poorly chosen icon does not convey its message very well. For example, in Windows-based systems, the trash bin represents the location of deleted (or thrown away) items. The meaning of this icon is easy to understand.
- Avoid misleading analogies. The icons should behave in expected ways. For example, in the case of the trash bin on the desktop of Windows-based systems, if the items placed in the trash bin could not be retrieved, the icon would not behave as expected. Users know that items placed in real-life trash bins can be retrieved until the trash bin is emptied by the trash collector. Therefore, items placed in the Windows trash bin can also be retrieved until the trash bin is emptied.
- Do not violate population stereotypes. Different user populations may have different expectations about how an icon will behave. For example, in the United States, a green left arrow indicates that a left turn is allowed because oncoming traffic has a red light. In Canada, however, an allowed left turn is indicated by a blinking green light.
- Use icons for appropriate purposes. Icons may not be faster or easier to use than input from the keyboard. The speed at which the user can point the mouse at an icon and choose it may not be as fast as typing. For example, experienced typists can probably type arithmetic expressions more quickly than they can choose numbers and operations on an iconic calculator numeric pad. To satisfy both novice typists and skilled typists, the creators of the calculator program that comes with Windows 95/98/Me have opted to allow data entry either from the keyboard or by clicking the mouse on the calculator keypad.
- Carefully design the iconic interaction. The manner in which an individual icon is used in the interface is less important than the overall design of the interaction with the icons. The semantics, consistency, layout, and ease of learning of the interface are much more important than the style of the chosen icons.

There are several potential difficulties with direct manipulation interfaces, however. First, users must learn what the visual representation means. Each icon represents something, and although the representation may be clear to the creator of the interface, it may not be clear at all to the user. Second, the visual representation of the real world may be misleading. Because much of the interface may look like familiar, similar items in the real world, the user may think he or she understands the meaning of a particular representation, but may in fact be drawing incorrect conclusions concerning such meanings. The user may overestimate or underestimate how deeply the computer-based analogy to the real world actually goes. Third, the keyboard may be the most effective direct manipulation device for certain tasks, so that pointing at icons with a mouse or a finger may actually be slower than using the keyboard. This problem is likely to occur especially when the user in question is a very experienced typist who is used to entering complex, compact instructions on the keyboard. Finally, choosing the correct representations for real-world objects and actions is not a trivial or easy task. A simple metaphor or analogy to the real world must be chosen. Mixing metaphors can cause confusion. Metaphors can have negative connotations. Users may not understand the real-world entity on which the metaphor is based. Because of such difficulties, direct manipulation user interfaces require significant amounts of testing with many users.

Many examples of direct manipulation user interfaces exist, and as the speed of personal computers continues to increase, such interfaces are becoming increasingly popular. Windows 95/98/Me/NT, with the desktop metaphor, use direct manipulation user interfaces. The main operating screen represents a desktop on which items are placed. The user then manipulates those items in various ways to accomplish various tasks. For example, to move a file from one folder on the desktop to another, the user simply picks the file up using the mouse, drags the file from one folder to the other, and then drops the file into the second folder. Many games, such as Myst and Riven (from Broderbund), also have direct manipulation user interfaces. Direct manipulation user interfaces can also be found on paint and drawing programs, flight simulators, authoring tools, and presentation graphics programs.

4.13   *Case Study:* User Interface for LMS

Recall that no user interface can be determined to be either "right" or "wrong." Therefore, which type of user interface we should choose for a particular application is not obvious. We must determine whether to build a user interface with menus, forms, command language instructions, natural language instructions, or graphical objects that are manipulated directly, or some combination of those choices. The main factor in determining which type to build is the user.

In order to build an effective user interface, we must understand as much about our users as possible. In the Library Management System, our users will vary widely. The library staff must use the system. These users may begin as novice users (although most of them are probably not novices). They will, in any case, become expert users over the course of time because they will likely use the system every day to perform a wide variety of tasks. The part of the interface that we build for the library staff must allow these users to move from their current level of knowledge about the system to expert knowledge over a period of time. Library patrons, however, must also be able to use the system effectively. Some patrons will be novice users who use the system so infrequently that they never gain more knowledge about the system. Others will be knowledgeable users who understand how library systems work but use this system very intermittently, so that they never become expert users. Finally, some library patrons will use the system very frequently and will become expert users who are likely to want shortcuts to do the things they do often. In order to satisfy as many of these users as possible, the user interface that we build must have a variety of features.

Deliverable 4.7 shows a menu for a command language to be used by our library staff. Recall that command languages are typically used when the majority of users are expert users. To allow knowledgeable, intermittent users to use a command language effectively, menus are often added. In our first design of the interface for the Library Management System, it may seem to be a good idea to create a command language with menus, since the majority of our library staff will eventually become at least knowledgeable, intermittent users. There are several difficulties with using a command language interface for the Library Management System. First, although the majority of our library staff will not be novice users, many of our library patrons are likely to be novice users. If we use a command language, we probably will have to design a user interface for the patrons that is entirely different from the one that the library staff will use. Second, we assume that the Library Management System is going to run on Windows-based and Macintosh computers, because the library has these machines available for Internet searches. As a result, the user interface that we develop should look like other Windows-based and MacOS-based applications. This requirement means that the application should be menu based. The menu-based interface will probably be mixed with other interface types, however, to allow easy input of information.

Before we can design the menus for the user interface for the Library Management System, we must look at the tasks that must be accomplished by the users of the system. An examination of the requirements specification helps us determine which tasks the users must be able to accomplish. Deliverable 4.8 shows the initial logon screen that will be seen by users of the system. If the user enters "guest" as a user name and "guest" as a password, he or she will be allowed to choose only from a limited number of items, as shown in Deliverable 4.9. If the user enters something other than "guest" for the user name and password, he or she will see the screens shown in Deliverables 4.10–4.13. These figures show the menus along with the items on those menus that will allow the library staff to accomplish their tasks.

Library Management System: Command Language Menu

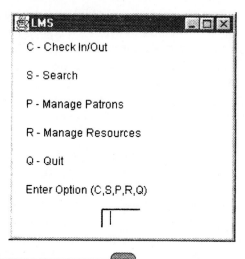

Library Management System: Password Entry Form

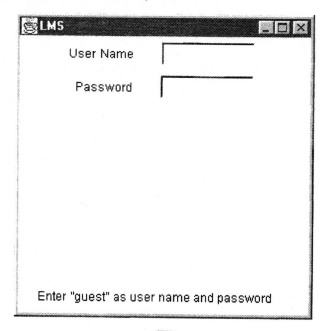

Library Management System: Public Search Interface

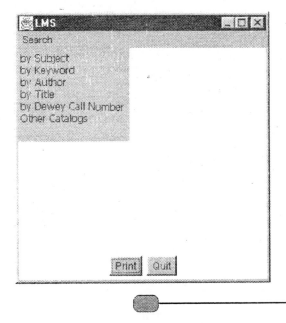

Library Management System: Check Menu Items

DELIVERABLE 4.11

Library Management System: Search Menu Items

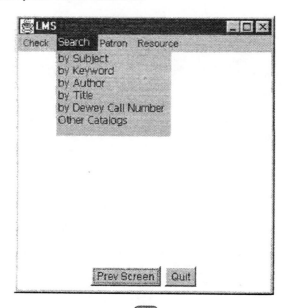

DELIVERABLE 4.12

Library Management System: Patron Menu Items

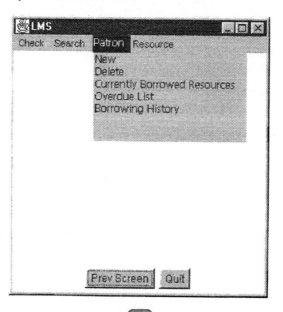

Library Management System: Resource Menu Items

DELIVERABLE
4.13

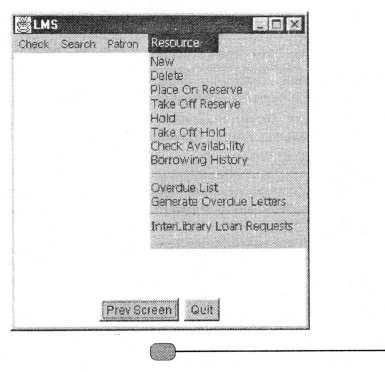

To test whether these menus (and the screens that are displayed when a particular menu item is chosen by the user) are adequate, we build a **user interface prototype**. This prototype is very simple, with no functionality beyond bringing up the appropriate screens in response to user input. We then ask a set of users, some novice, some knowledgeable, intermittent, and some expert, to attempt several tasks using the prototype. Based on the user feedback, we revise the user interface and then retest with the users. This iterative development process mirrors the iterative development process of the rest of the application. When the users are satisfied with the interface prototype, we connect the interface to the application functionality.

For example, in our prototype, when the library staff user chooses the *Check* menu, he or she sees the screen shown in Deliverable 4.10. If the user then chooses the *Out* option from the *Check* menu, he or she will see the form shown in Deliverable 4.14. The user can either type the patron ID number into the textbox or scan the patron's library card with a bar code reader. In either case, the patron's ID number appears in the patron ID textbox. The user can then either type the resource ID number into the next textbox or scan the bar code of the resource through a bar code reader. In either case, the ID number of the resource appears in the resource ID textbox. In addition, the title, author, call number, and due date for the resource appear in the corresponding textboxes. The items cannot be edited by the user. If the resource is the correct one, the user presses the *Accept* button, and the item appears in the scrollable text area in the middle of the screen. If the resource is not the correct one, the user presses the *Cancel* button and enters the resource ID number again. If there are no more resources to be entered for this patron, the user presses the *Finish* button.

DELIVERABLE 4.14

Library Management System: Resource Check Out Form

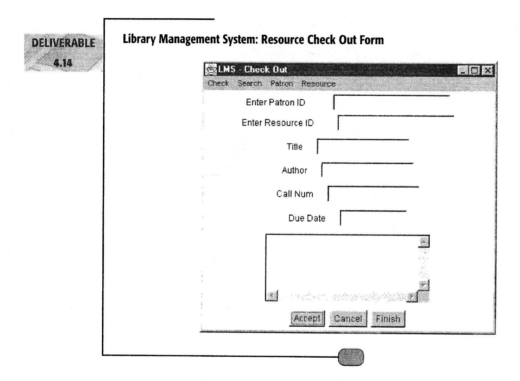

EXERCISE 4.11   Evaluate the Library Management System screens shown in Deliverables 4.8–4.14 according to the principles laid out in this section. Do any of them violate any of the design principles? If so, what would you do to fix the user interfaces?

During the testing of this prototype, the library staff may discover that something is missing in the user interface. In the example of checking out resources, perhaps the library staff determines that mistakes are sometimes made when the patron ID number is entered by typing. Since no information about the patron is displayed after the patron ID number is entered, these mistakes cannot be caught. In other words, if the library staff types the patron ID into the system incorrectly, the resources checked out are attributed to an incorrect patron. One solution to this problem is to disallow the typing of the patron ID by requiring the patron ID to be entered with the bar code reader. Such a requirement will certainly minimize mistakes. The problem with this solution, however, is that sometimes bar code readers fail to read a bar code. In such instances, the library staff would still like to allow the patron to check out resources by simply typing the patron ID into the system. A better way to minimize mistakes is to display some information, such as the patron name, about the patron whose patron ID has been entered. Through testing of the prototype user interface, such problems can be discovered and corrected relatively easily.

Redesign the *Check-Out Resource* form, shown in Deliverable 4.14, to allow the library staff user to determine whether the patron identification number that has been entered belongs to the patron who is actually attempting to check out this resource. How will the library staff user notify the system that the patron identification number belongs to the correct patron? If this is the correct patron, how will the library staff user then move on to enter the resource identification number?

EXERCISE 4.12

When a library patron wants to use the Library Management System to search for resources in the library catalog, he or she enters "guest" as the user name and password on the screen shown in Deliverable 4.8. He or she then sees the screen shown in Deliverable 4.9. The patron then enters the necessary search information. Deliverable 4.15 shows the results of an example search. In this example, the user has chosen "by Subject" from the search menu and entered "amber" as the search subject. The Library Management System has found two resources that match the entered subject and lists those resources in the text area. If the user wants to see more detail (such as the call number) for either of the resources, he or she clicks on the resource in the text area and then presses the *Get Item* button. This example illustrates that sometimes combinations of the various interface types are required. This particular interface is a combination of the form interface and the menu interface.

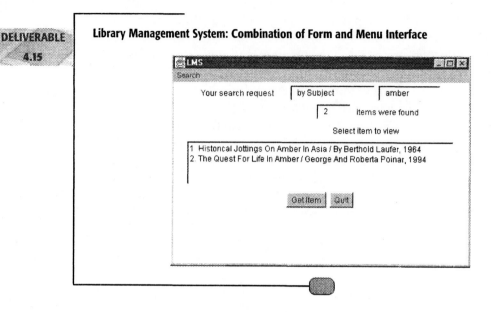

DELIVERABLE 4.15

Library Management System: Combination of Form and Menu Interface

Figure 4.10 summarizes the UCCD process to the extent that it has been covered here. The two development phases discussed thus far are represented as ovals, with the results of each phase listed under its respective activity. In an iterative development process each development activity is visited several times.

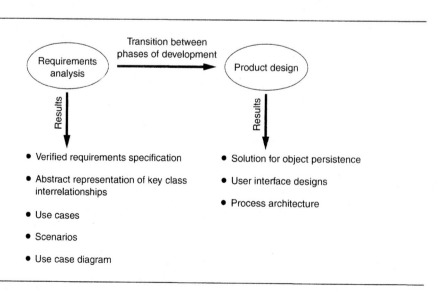

FIGURE 4.10   A Summary of Steps in the UCCD Process

Working in Teams

In order to improve on team meetings, it can be useful to engage an impartial observer to provide feedback. Some possible ways to get impartial feedback are as follows:

- One or more teams may agree to hold all or part of one team meeting during regularly scheduled class time and have the remaining class serve as the observer.
- All teams may meet during class time, and the instructor may observe and provide feedback.
- The instructor may designate team pairs, in which each team agrees to observe the other. This activity may or may not take place during class time.

The observers of the development teams should try to identify obstacles to successful meetings. Some possible causes of ineffective meetings are as follows:

- The team may have a poorly written agenda. The agenda does not adequately address completing project deliverables.
- Communication between team members may be dysfunctional. One or more team members may either dominate discussion or not contribute to discussion.
- The discussion may not adhere to the agenda.
- The substance of the discussion may be peripheral to the agenda items, rather than focused on how to accomplish a specific task.
- Team members may each be speaking, but no one appears to be listening to what is being said. In other words, after one teammate speaks, the substance of the communication is not addressed or reacted to by the next speaker.

It is important that the critique be expressed in a constructive and professional manner, and that the team being critiqued understand that this review process is in place to help them succeed with their class project and learn to work in groups effectively.

Class Project Product Design

The elements of product design are as follows:

- Object persistence
- Process architecture
- User interface design
- Resource distribution
- Network utilization

The requirements specification for Galaxy Sleuth provides an illustration of one user interface, specifically the game board to be seen by the players, so all other interfaces must be designed by the system developers. Because the class project is an example of a client/server system, the network-based communication between the clients and the server constitutes an essential aspect of the software structure. In addition, the client/server interaction also determines several interfaces for the client. The server does not directly interact with human users, and thus it requires no human-computer interfaces to be designed.

The steps for designing the user interface for Galaxy Sleuth are these:

- Storyboard the primary functionality of the system.
- Determine which objects of the system require a graphic representation, and design these. For example, *Card* objects require such a representation.
- Add the secondary functionality of the system to the storyboard.
- Create mock-up (prototype) interfaces.
- Get user feedback.
- Refine interfaces.

4.16 Questions for Review

1. Consider the internal and external structure of a banking system whose functionality and user interfaces are similar to those you encounter at your bank's automatic teller machine. What elements make up the external structure?
2. Outline an object persistence strategy for the banking application of question 1. What characteristics of the banking system predicate your choices and why?
3. Develop a deployment diagram that characterizes a very abstract view of an ATM banking system.
4. Create a state machine that portrays the information communicated between an ATM banking client and a centralized server process that handles transactions from the ATM.
5. Characterize a set of user interfaces that you are most familiar with. Critique them according to the criteria outlined in the chapter.
6. Propose an ATM interface that is language neutral (but perhaps not culturally neutral). In other words, develop a set of icons that guide a person who is reasonably knowledgeable about banking through the options of a typical ATM machine.
7. Characterize the different types of users an ATM banking system should accommodate. Create a user profile description for each type of user.
8. In this age of newly created e-commerce systems, we are still experiencing growing pains. Find a web-based system that is particularly frustrating from a navigation standpoint. (Hint: I have wanted to pull my hair out frequently when trying to book airline flights on the web.) Specify the navigational problems,

and outline how you propose to improve the system. Also, give the URL of the system, so your instructor knows what web-based services to avoid.

9. Consider web-based applications that are frustrating because of their user interface design, rather than navigational difficulties. Find interfaces that are frustrating because they permit users to enter erroneous information, that may otherwise be avoided, or that are cumbersome or confusing to use. Specify how the interface may be improved, and give the URL of the site.

10. Characterize a system in which a command language interface is appropriate. Specify the type of application and its users.

11. Propose an e-commerce application that is predominantly direct manipulation. Specify its user interfaces, and characterize the application's objectives.

Class Design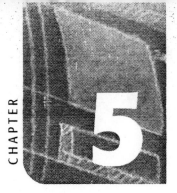

 Key Concepts

- Class design
- Class role
- Class skeleton
- System decomposition
- Pattern scavenging
- Data integrity
- Cardinality
- Constraint

- Tagged value
- Collaboration diagram
- Sequence diagram
- Object diagram
- Design verification
- Abstract base class
- Informal walk-through

 The Class Design Process

Figures 5.1 and 5.2 show the relationships between the analysis, design, and implementation phases of software development through their deliverables. In the analysis phase, we produce use cases and scenarios as well as class diagrams. At the beginning of the design process, we have these products of the analysis process available to us for refinement and input into the deliverables of design.

During the design process, the products of analysis must be expanded in order to ensure that the entire range of functionality in the final system is considered. For example, we may need to develop additional scenarios in order to address all the issues in each use case. Various aspects of the scenarios are modeled through class diagrams, **object diagrams**, and **interaction diagrams**. Object diagrams and interaction diagrams are additional UML notational tools that help the developers

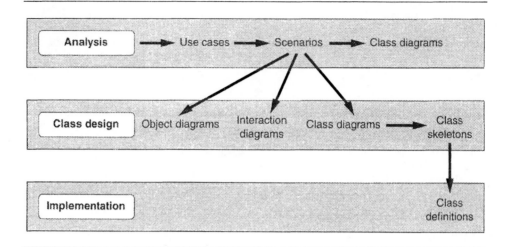

FIGURE 5.1 The Interrelationship of Certain Products of the Development Process

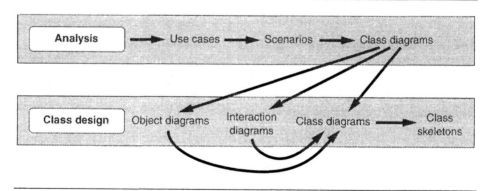

FIGURE 5.2 More Interrelationships of Deliverables from the Development Process

record and represent various aspects of the system to be developed. During design, detail must also be added to the class diagrams. This detail will include the signatures for the methods in the class as well as the attributes in the class. These method signatures and attributes make up a **skeleton** for the class. A class skeleton serves as the basis for creating class definitions in the implementation phase of the development. The class skeleton serves as the blueprint for beginning to implement the system. The ultimate goal of class design is to decompose the detailed class diagrams into class skeletons, which serve as a starting point for writing actual code for the system.

Although not shown in Figures 5.1 and 5.2, there may be multiple analysis and design phases in an iterative development process. In such a development process, the distinction between what happens during analysis and what happens during design is more fluid than is shown in the figures. In addition, Figures 5.1 and 5.2 show that in the class design phase, information from the object and interaction diagrams is used to enhance the class diagrams. Object diagrams, interaction diagrams, and the aspects of the system that they model will be discussed later in this chapter.

An interclass association is frequently carried out through a method that is defined within one class and invoked from another. In some instances, a more complex implementation is required, involving additional objects, which provide intermediate services between them. For example, the relationship between the *Patron* class and the *Book* class may be modeled as *checks out*. In reality, the library patron presents the book and his or her library ID to the library system through a library staff member. Thus, no message is directly sent between a patron object and a book object, although at an abstract level, it is correct to model this relationship.

5.2.1 Class Skeletons

The ultimate goal of the class design process is the creation of a class skeleton for each class comprising the system. A class skeleton includes the following items:

- A list of the **roles** the class plays within the system
- Information concerning when objects of the class are created and deleted
- For each role, the **semantics** of the class
- All attributes, including access modifiers, types, names, and semantics (if the attribute name is not self-documenting), that constitute the class
- All constructors with preconditions and postconditions
- For each method, its signature, semantics, preconditions, and postconditions

5.2.2 *Case Study:* Class Skeletons in LMS

Deliverable 5.1 shows a class skeleton for the *Patron* class. The order in which the elements of the class skeleton are listed should be decided upon and made consistent throughout the set of class skeletons. In our sample skeleton, the semantics of the *Patron* class in various situations is described first. Part of the semantic description should be the roles the class plays in these situations.

CASE STUDY

Skeleton for the *Patron* Class

```
public class Patron
{
  // Class semantics and roles:
  // Library patrons function in two primary roles,
  // as researchers who use index,
  // reference, and database materials, and as borrowers
  // of loanable resources
  // Information maintenance
  // Creation: New patrons are introduced into the system
  // by library staff when
  // presented with a library membership application,
  // or from information retrieved
  // from a web-based application form.
  // Deletion: Patrons are removed from the library database
  // 3 years after their membership has expired.

  // Instance variables:
  private String name;  // name of Patron in Last name,
                             First name, MI format
  private long PatronID;  // Patron's library identification
                               number sequentially generated
  private long homephone;  // format area code (3) local
                                exchange (9)
  private Date memberDate;  // date of first membership in
                                 mmddyyyy format
  private Date expireDate;  // date membership expires in
                                 mmddyyyy format
  private List resourceList;  // Object reference to Patron's
                                  list of  checked out resources
  private Address homeAddress;  // patron's home Address

// Class variables
  private static long nextPatronID;
// Keeps track of the next Patron ID to be assigned

  // Constructors
  public Patron(String n, long home, Date m, Date e, String
  street, String city, String state, long zip)
```

```
{// Parameters: n = name, home = homephone, m = memberDate,
e = expireDate,
 // PatronID = getnextPatronID()
 // street, city, state, and zip are used to create an Address
 // object for homeAddress, resourceList is null
 // Precondition: Library database can accept an additional
 // entry and memory allocation succeeds
 // Postcondition: Library database will contain an addition
 // Patron and Address entry
 }


//Static methods
  public static long getnextPatronID()
  { return nextPatronID; nextPatronID++;}


//Nonstatic Methods
public boolean validatePatron(Date e)
{ // precondition: expireDate is not null
  e = expireDate;  //pass expiration date through parameter
  list for validation
  // if expireDate <= Today return false else return true
 }
public boolean checkout(Resource ResourceID)
{ // precondition: ResourceID points to a legitimate Resource
  // object, available for check out.
  // postcondition: if resource list is null one is created,
  // otherwise a new Resource reference is added
  // The patron's List of checked Resources checked out is
  // updated to reflect the parameter object
 }
} // end class Patron
```

A **role** of a class is the behavior of the class in a particular context [16]. A role played by a class represents a functional partitioning of the behavior of the class in the system. We can then design and implement all of the attributes and methods for a class to allow it to play a particular role and ignore the attributes and methods necessary for the class to play a different role in the system. For example, while designing the attributes and methods for allowing the *Patron* class to check out resources, we do not have to pay attention to attributes and methods that track how many interlibrary loan requests a patron has made. The tracking of those requests is important when keeping track of the research costs incurred by a particular patron playing the role of a researcher and will be dealt with when we design and implement that portion of the system.

The **information maintenance** portion of the skeleton describes when objects of the class are created and deleted. The **instance variables** for the class are a list of data required for each object of the class. These variables help the object play its various roles in the system. By dealing only with a subset of the instance variables (the subset required for the object to play a particular role) at a particular time, development of the system can proceed along functional lines, with attention being paid to one role at a time. **Class variables** are pieces of data that are shared among all objects of a certain class. For example, in the *Patron* class, there is a class variable called *nextPatronID*. All objects of the class share this variable. When a new *Patron* object is created, the *PatronID* instance variable for the new object is given the value currently stored in the *nextPatronID* class variable and the *nextPatronID* class variable is incremented. This sequence of events occurs when the **constructor** of the *Patron* class is called. In the constructor, the *PatronID* instance variable is assigned the value that is returned from a call to the *getnextPatronID* static method. The *getnextPatronID* static method retrieves the value in the *nextPatronID* class variable, returns it to the calling method, and then increments the *nextPatronID* variable. A **static method** is shared among all objects of a class, just as a class variable is. Finally, the class skeleton contains a list of all **nonstatic methods** for the class. Nonstatic methods are those that are not shared among all objects of the class, just like instance variables.

EXERCISE 5.1   Think about your life, and make a list of all the different roles you play. Which of your attributes must be considered to allow you to play each of the roles? Are any of the attributes necessary to more than one of your roles?

5.2.3 System Decomposition

The analysis phase of software development results in system models that facilitate the system developers' understanding of the system. In addition, these models allow the system developers to communicate, in an unambiguous manner, their understanding of the system to the domain experts. During the analysis process, these models tend to remain relatively abstract. Throughout the design process, the system is modeled in increasing detail, which demonstrates the system developers' increasingly detailed understanding of the system. To get at the more detailed models of the system, the less detailed models must be **decomposed**, or broken down into smaller pieces that are more precise in their specification of some aspect of the system. The less detailed models are more abstract than the more detailed models in that they specify the functional requirements of the system in a more abstract manner.

There is a cost-benefit line that must be examined when deciding what level of detail should be used to represent models of the system. Very abstract models are created early in the software development process and allow the domain expert to respond to the potential system very early. However, the functional requirements may be specified so abstractly that the domain expert does not see that relevant information has been omitted. The fact that information is missing is likely to be caught later in the development cycle, but fixing such errors late in the development cycle is costly and difficult. Very detailed models specify the functional requirements of the system in significant detail so that if anything is missing, the domain expert should be able to catch it. The downside of such detailed models, however, is that they take significant time to produce, and if they model some aspect of the system incorrectly, a large amount of energy may be expended heading down an incorrect path. The timing of when to get user input concerning the models of the system is critical. Such input must be sought late enough in the development process so that the model has enough detail to allow domain experts to catch errors but early enough so that any errors in the models will not have wasted a huge amount of development time.

Regardless of when domain expert feedback is sought concerning the system representation, a major objective of design is to decompose the representation to a level of detail that will allow the resulting representation to be used as a blueprint for implementation. As the design phase progresses, additional details concerning the system surface. The models of the system, such as class diagrams and use cases, must change to reflect these new details. Summary Points box 5.1 discusses system decomposition. The process of decomposition requires that class diagrams evolve,

---

SUMMARY POINTS 5.1

System Decomposition

1. System decomposition adds detail to the previous system representation.

2. System decomposition can be done iteratively or in a traditional, waterfall manner.

3. Each phase in the system development process decomposes the system further.

4. System decomposition leads to a blueprint for implementation.

but certain aspects of the system that are discovered during the evolution cannot be adequately modeled with class diagrams. To model these new aspects of the system, UML has two additional types of diagrams, **interaction** and **object** diagrams, which are discussed in the next section.

 ## More UML

The UML notational features discussed in the previous chapter represent a subset of the overall UML notation. During the design process, the details of the system to be developed begin to be understood at increasing levels of detail, and therefore, more notational expressiveness is required to be able to represent the details. This notational expressiveness is accomplished through the use of several additional types of diagrams. In addition, some of the diagrams used in the analysis phase will be enhanced with notational elements called **adornments** [16]. These adornments allow the existing diagrams to represent more detailed perspectives of the system.

5.3.1 Notational Adornments for Class Diagrams

Adornments are notational detail added to a UML element's basic graphical notation [16]. For example, an adornment to the basic element, class, is a symbol that represents the **access modifier** for the methods in the class. Specifically, the + character placed before a method name indicates that access to the method is public, the − character indicates that a method is private, and the # character indicates that the method is protected.

Another adornment on class diagrams represents the **multiplicity**, or cardinality, of an association relationship. For example, the cardinality on the *checks out* relationship between the *Patron* class and the *Resource* class is zero or one to zero to infinity. A patron can check out as many resources as he or she would like, while a resource can be checked out by only 0 or 1 patrons (at one time). To represent this detailed information on a class diagram, one simply puts the numbers for the cardinalities on the line representing the relationship between the two classes. Figure 5.3 shows the cardinality adornment on the *checks out* association relationship.

Another adornment on association relationships represents a role that a class plays in the association. For example, the *Patron* class plays the role of a borrower in its *checks out* association relationship with the *Resource* class. Figure 5.3 shows that the *Borrower* label is put on the line that represents the *checks out* relationship between the two classes.

UML also provides two additional notational adornments that may be applied to any UML diagram. They are **constraints** and **tagged values**. Both of these

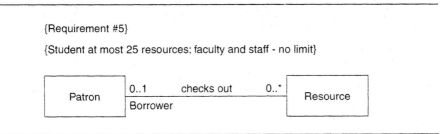

FIGURE 5.3 **Examples of Notational Adornments for Class Diagrams**

adornments are specified by surrounding the element in curly braces. A constraint represents a restriction on a class, an interclass relationship, or an attribute value. For example, Figure 5.3 shows a constraint on the cardinality of the *checks out* relationship between the *Patron* class and the *Resource* class. This constraint specifies that only faculty and staff can check out an unlimited number of resources. Students, however, actually have a limit of 25 resources that they can check out. Tagged values are a means to enhance diagrams with nonstandard information. For example, as the diagrams that we use in our analysis and design change, we may want to begin to put version numbers on the diagrams. A version number is an example of a tagged value. If we have two different diagrams that are supposed to represent the same aspect of the system, we can determine which of the diagrams illustrates the more recent one. Tagged values are also a means to associate a particular functional requirement with a diagram. Such a tagged value is shown in Figure 5.3.

During class design, one may find that an attribute for a class is a reference to another class. For example, the *OverDueFormLetter* class contains a reference to a *Patron* object and another reference to a *Resource* object. This type of containment relationship, called **aggregation**, is a special type of the association relationship. Therefore, the representation of aggregation on a class diagram is by means of an adornment to the association relationship. To represent an aggregation relationship between two classes, a diamond is placed on the end of the association relationship near the aggregate class. For example, in Figure 5.4, a diamond is on the line representing the two list relationships at the end closest to the *OverDueFormLetter* class because the *OverDueFormLetter* class contains both the *Patron* class and the *Resource* class. The *OverDueFormLetter* class is the aggregate of the *Patron* class and the *Resource* class (and perhaps other attributes and methods). Note that the diamonds adorning the lines connecting the classes are empty in this case.

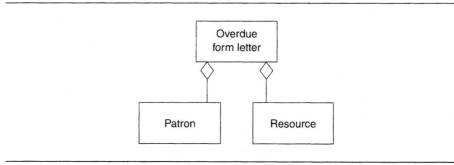

FIGURE 5.4 The *OverDueFormLetter* Class as an Aggregation

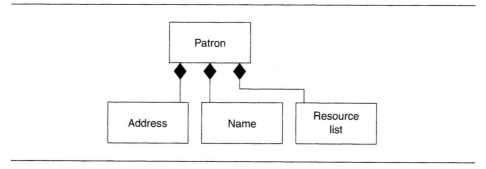

FIGURE 5.5 The *Patron* Class as an Aggregation

Figure 5.5 demonstrates another kind of aggregation relationship between classes. In the aggregation relationship shown in Figure 5.5 the diamonds adorning the connecting lines are solid, or filled in. The purpose of using an empty versus a filled-in diamond is to signify whether the aggregated classes exist in the absence of the aggregating class or not. The solid diamond indicates that the aggregated class, the patron address for example, does not exist without the presence of a specific instance of the *Patron* class. Consider the library patron Emma Goldsmith. If she moves and is no longer in the library database, it would make no sense to retain her address. Therefore, the address is deleted with the patron, and thus a solid diamond is used to depict this aggregation relationship. Similarly, the *Name* and *ResourceList* classes are also dependent on the existence of a particular *Patron* object for their existence. Although the *Resource* objects persist beyond the presence of a specific patron, the particular aggregation of these resources, representing what a particular patron currently has checked out, will not persist.

EXERCISE 5.2

Examine some of your old programs in which you have used multiple classes. Create a class diagram showing the relationships between the various classes. Put cardinalities on the class diagram. Can you find any examples of aggregation relationships? If so, put those on the diagram as well.

5.3.2 Interaction Diagrams

Class diagrams model a static perspective of a system, while interaction diagrams model dynamic aspects of a system [36]. In particular, class diagrams can be used to express the structural aspect of a collaboration, in which multiple classes interact to produce a particular behavior. A class diagram specifies the classes that collaborate to produce a particular behavior. For example, a class diagram shows that the *Patron* class and the *Resource* class work together to produce the *checks out* behavior. The manner in which that behavior is produced is not specified by a class diagram.

An interaction diagram, however, specifies the interaction among the classes that are required to produce a particular behavior. Two types of interaction diagrams are defined in UML, **sequence diagrams** and **collaboration diagrams**. A collaboration diagram emphasizes the structural organization of objects that send and receive messages via the method invocations. A sequence diagram emphasizes the time ordering of those messages. For example, a collaboration diagram would show a particular *Patron* object checking out a particular *Resource* object along with the methods that must be invoked to allow the checking out to occur. A sequence diagram would show the order in which the methods must be invoked so that the *Patron* object can check out the *Resource* object. The information about particular methods is not shown on a class diagram. For example, to be allowed to check out another *Resource* object, the *Patron* object will probably need to be checked for overdue resources and will not be allowed to check out this new *Resource* object if money is owed. This step in the check-out process has probably not been noted elsewhere.

EXERCISE 5.3

Think about starting a car. List the items that are needed to start the car. List the relationships among these items. From these two lists, could you figure out how to start the car? What's missing?

The graphic elements comprising interaction diagrams are shown in Figure 5.6. An object is an instance of a class and is represented by a rectangle with the object name as a label. A link is an instance of the association relationship between two classes and is represented by an arrowless line in an interaction diagram. When

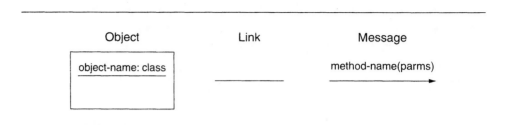

FIGURE 5.6 Notational Elements of Interaction Diagrams

a class diagram shows two classes related to each other by an association, an interaction diagram will show two objects (whose types are those classes) related to each by a link. The link will ultimately be implemented in the system by a method invocation.

Recall that a set of use cases is created during the analysis process. These use cases represent general situations that should be able to be handled by the final system. Recall also that for each use case, a scenario (or set of closely related scenarios) is developed to aid in the analysis of the use case. In a sense, a scenario is an instance of a use case. During the design phase of software development, use cases are modeled as class diagrams while scenarios are modeled as interaction diagrams, which capture some of the dynamic aspects of message passing that must occur to realize a particular behavior.

5.3.3 *Case Study:* Interaction Diagrams for LMS

To create an interaction diagram, the elements of a scenario must be translated into objects and the messages passed between those objects. Recall from the last chapter that the Library Management System has a *CheckOutResource* use case and that this use case represents one of the functional requirements of the system. The class diagram that structurally represents this use case is shown in Deliverable 3.9. Deliverable 3.6, repeated for reference as Deliverable 5.2, is a narrative description of a scenario for the *CheckOutResource* use case.

DELIVERABLE 5.2

Scenario: *CheckOutResource*

Precondition: The librarian on duty, Maria Blanco, has identified herself to the library system by entering her library staff identification number. A library database, containing information concerning the library holdings and the patrons of the library, has been created and initialized.

Library patron: Greta Smith, who is a student of the college, wishes to check out *Gone with the Wind*. She hands her selection and her library card to the librarian, Maria Blanco, who determines Greta's status as a patron by scanning Greta's library card. Scanning the library card reads in the patron's library identification number, which is used to access the library database. The patron object associated with the library identification number is returned from the library database. Greta's patron object indicates that her student library membership is currently valid, but since she is scheduled to graduate in a month, her membership expires in one month. A message concerning the expiration flashes on the librarian's screen, which prompts her to alert Greta to this fact. Next, the bar code on the book is scanned, reading the book's identification number. This number is used to access the book object for *Gone with the Wind* from the library database. Based on the fact that a student is borrowing a book, the due date for the book is determined. The book object is then sent a *check-out* message, which changes the book's status to *checked out* from its previous status of *available*. The patron's library identification number is also sent with the *check-out* message, and the patron ID is recorded in the book's check-out-history list. The due date of the book is also sent to the book object and is stored in the due date attribute of the book. The patron object is sent a *check-out* message along with the book ID so that the book ID can be added to the checked-out-resources list for the patron object.

Postcondition: The status of the book is *checked out*, and the current borrower for book object is the patron ID. The due date for the book has the appropriate date. The patron-object checked-out-resources list is updated with the book ID.

Deliverable 5.3 shows a collaboration diagram that models the *CheckOutResource* use case scenario (Deliverable 5.2). The diagram shows particular objects interacting with each other via message passing (method invocations). One object invokes the method and is the sender of the message, while the object to which the message is directed is the recipient of the message. Note the differences between this collaboration diagram and the class diagram illustrating the *CheckOutResource* use case. The first major difference between these diagrams is that the class diagram shows the *Patron* class interacting with the *Resource* class through a *checks out* association, while the collaboration diagram shows a particular *Patron* object interacting with a variety of objects, but *not* interacting with a *Book* object (since *Book* is a child class of *Resource*). The second major difference between these two diagrams is that the class diagram shows the *Library Staff* class participating in the use case while the collaboration diagram shows the Library Staff as an external actor in the scenario. In this particular scenario, the real-world library staff plays an important role, but no messages are sent to or from the *Library Staff* class in the software. Therefore, from the perspective of the final software system, in this scenario, the *Library Staff* is an external entity interacting with the software.

Finally, the collaboration diagram in Deliverable 5.3 shows instances of two new classes, *Library System* and *Library Database*, interacting with the *Student* and *Book* objects.

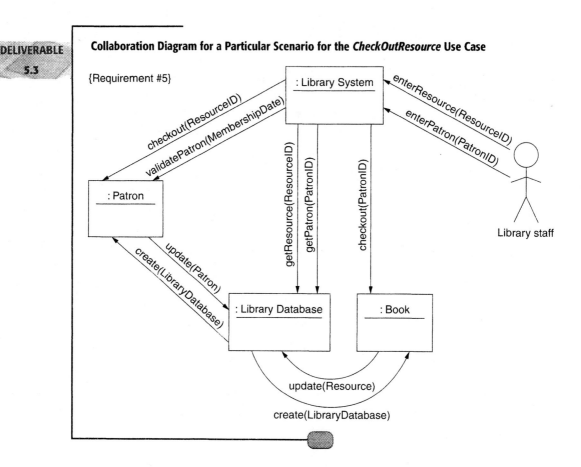

DELIVERABLE 5.3

Collaboration Diagram for a Particular Scenario for the *CheckOutResource* Use Case

{Requirement #5}

The transition between the class diagram in Deliverable 3.9 and the collaboration diagram in Deliverable 5.3 represents the process of model evolution in which relatively abstract representations are made increasingly more concrete and detailed. The class diagram shows a *checks out* relationship between the *Patron* and *Resource* classes. This diagram is sufficient to characterize the desired behavior of the system to allow patrons to check out resources. However, as we design a scenario for the use case, we realize that instances of new classes will be necessary to implement the scenario. In particular, the *Patron* object has no mechanism for sending a *check-out* message to a *Book* object because there is no reference to the desired *Book* object in the *Patron* object. In order to accomplish this task, we must change the design of the system. The *Library System* object is used to serve as an intermediary between the *Patron* object and the *Book* object by containing references to both objects. The *Library System* object is simply the graphical user interface that controls the activity within the Library Management System software. Therefore, the collaboration diagram does not show the *Patron* object sending any messages directly to the *Book* object. The *Library System* object is required to coordinate this communication.

Recall that in Chapter 3 you created scenarios and class diagrams for a ticktacktoe game. Create a collaboration diagram for the *player move* scenario. Compare your collaboration diagram with that of another student. Are there differences? Are these differences important?

EXERCISE 5.4

When developing collaboration diagrams from class diagrams, it is not unusual to introduce additional entities to control the message passing that occurs among objects. For example, in Deliverable 5.2 the due date for the *Book* object being borrowed by the *Student* is determined. The due date depends upon the fact that a *Student* is borrowing a *Book*. If a *Faculty Member* borrowed the same *Book*, the due date would be different. If the same *Student* borrows a *Music CD*, the due date is different. The due date, therefore, cannot be determined by either the *Student* object or the *Book* object alone. The due date is determined by the interaction between the two objects. The *Library System* class provides a mechanism for controlling and managing such interactions. Therefore, the class diagram for the overall system must be modified as a result of this bit of design work. Such continued modification is desirable in the iterative software development process.

Also note the *create( )* message that is sent from the *Library Database* object to the *Patron* and *Book* objects. Recall from Chapter 4 that the Library Management System is an example of a system that has a lot of data, too much to exist in memory all at the same time. We therefore have had to create some mechanism to ensure the persistence of the data. The mechanism we have chosen is to create a relational database that will interact with the object-oriented LMS. All the data from the relational database exists on disk somewhere, and when the LMS requires a particular piece of data, an object is instantiated in memory using the data that reside in the relational database. The *Library Database* object exists as an intermediary between the relational database and the object-oriented system. The mechanism for creating this object depends upon the relational database management system used to store the data and the programming language used to implement the object-oriented system. We will not go into the details of how to create this *Library Database* object. We simply need to understand that this object is used to pass messages between the relational database and the object-oriented system.

EXERCISE 5.5   Think about the ticktacktoe game. Is a persistence mechanism needed for this application? If so, why? If not, why not? What characteristics of a software system indicate that some sort of persistence mechanism is needed?

The *create( )* message sent from the *Library Database* object is an abstraction of an invocation of a constructor method. When the system is implemented, the *create( )* method will ensure that the parameters for the constructor have the appropriate values and will then invoke the constructor of the appropriate class. In addition, notice that Deliverable 5.3 shows the *create( )* message sending a *Library Database* object reference to both the *Patron* and *Book* objects. Once the information for the *Book* or *Patron* object is properly updated in memory, the reference to the *Library Database* object allows the information to be properly updated on disk.

Deliverable 5.4 shows a collaboration diagram for the *GenFormLetter* use case, which was described in section 3.10.4. The scenario associated with this use case is left as an exercise for the reader, but it entails a library staff member initiating the generation of overdue form letters by specifying a date. The specified date determines which overdue resources will prompt the creation of the form letter. If the database contains any resources that are due on or before the date specified, a letter will be sent to the patron who holds a resource, reminding him or her to return it. Of course, measures are taken to ensure that multiple overdue resources held by a single patron will generate only one letter listing all resources.

Inspecting Deliverable 5.4 makes it clear that the class skeleton for *Patron* must be enhanced to accommodate this collaboration diagram. The *notifyODR(ResourceID,Date)* method must be added to the class, and an associated attribute of class *Date* that records when the patron was last notified of overdue resources must also be added. The method updates this new attribute when an overdue resource form letter is generated. An additional required method of the *Patron* class is *getResourceList*, so that the patron's other holdings may be checked to determine whether they are also overdue.

5.3.4 Collaboration Diagram Creation

Summary Points box 5.2 lists the steps required to create a collaboration diagram for modeling the behavior of a particular apsect of the system to be developed. These steps are described in the list on page 180.

Collaboration Diagram for the *GenFormLetter* Use Case

DELIVERABLE
5.4

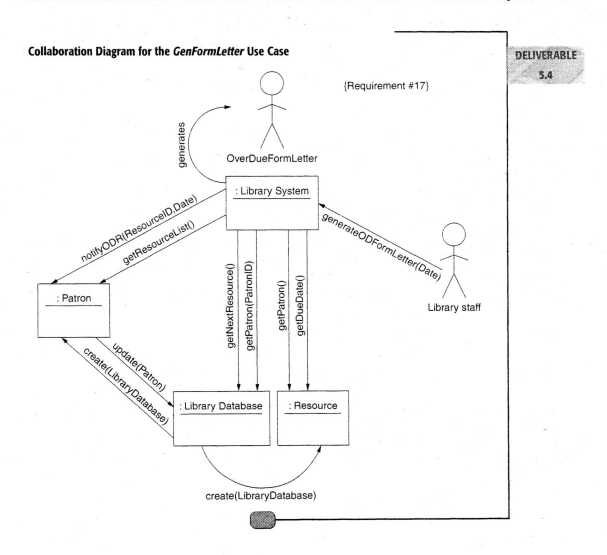

{Requirement #17}

Steps for Creating Collaboration Diagrams

1. Identify a behavior to model.
2. Identify participating classes and their relevant interrelationships.
3. Identify a specific scenario to model.
4. Determine the necessary message passing to carry out the behavior.
5. Introduce solution for object persistence, if needed.

- Identify a particular behavior to be modeled. The behavior should have previously been represented by a use case. In the LMS example of the previous subsection, we modeled the *CheckOutResource* behavior.
- Identify the classes and other elements comprising the behavior to be modeled and identify relationships among these elements. The classes should already have been modeled in a class diagram for a use case. For example, the class diagram for *CheckOutResource* shown in Deliverable 3.9 identifies classes and relationships that constitute the *CheckOutResource* behavior.
- Identify a scenario related to the use case, and select specific instantiations (objects) of the classes represented in the class diagram.
- Determine how message passing between various objects will occur. For example, if one object is to send a message to (invoke a method of) another object, does the first object contain a reference to the second object? If not and if it is not practical for such an object reference to be added to the first object, introduce an intermediary object to carry out the communication. For example, the collaboration diagram in Deliverable 5.3 shows the introduction of a *LibrarySystem* object to act as an intermediary between the *Patron* and *Book* objects.
- If it is impractical for all data to reside in memory at once, introduce a solution for object persistence. For example, a *LibraryDatabase* object is introduced to facilitate object persistence in the LMS system. Instances of class *Patron* and *Resource* are constructed by the *LibraryDatabase* object in response to requests from the *LibrarySystem* object.

5.3.5 *Case Study:* More Interaction Diagrams in LMS

Sequence diagrams, like collaboration diagrams, show the messages that are passed between objects during the execution of a scenario. Unlike collaboration diagrams, sequence diagrams also specify the time ordering of messages and show the life span of each object taking part in a particular scenario. Deliverable 5.5 shows a sequence diagram for the *CheckOutResource* scenario. The time order of the messages can be seen by looking at the diagram from top to bottom. The earlier messages, or method invocations, are at the top of the diagram, and the later messages are at the bottom of the diagram. In Deliverable 5.5, the first message generated is *getResource(ResourceID)*, sent from the *LibrarySystem* object to the *LibraryDatabase* object, and the last message generated is *update(Patron)*, sent from the *Patron* object to the *LibraryDatabase* object.

Several notational elements of sequence diagrams are identical to those of collaboration diagrams. For instance, in both sequence diagrams and collaboration diagrams, objects are shown as rectangles with an optional, underlined object name separated by a colon from its underlined class name. Message passing is also shown in the same manner, as labeled arrows, in both types of diagrams. The label specifies the method to be invoked, and the arrow points from the originator of the message to the recipient of the message.

Sequence Diagram for the *CheckOutResource* Use Case Scenario

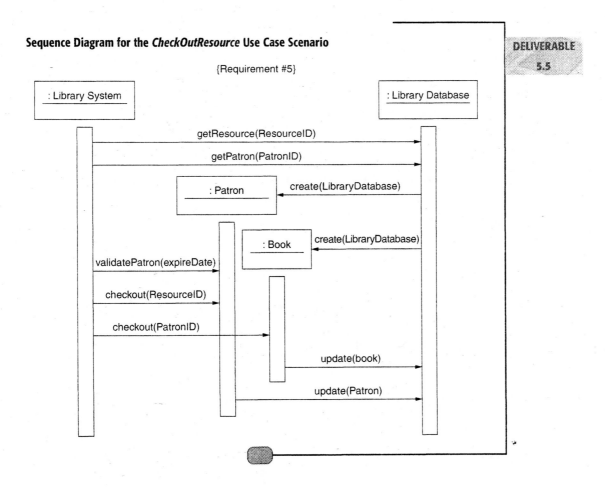

{Requirement #5}

In order to represent the time ordering of messages, however, sequence diagrams differ from collaboration diagrams. In collaboration diagrams, objects are arranged in any manner that shows message passing with a minimum of crossed lines. In sequence diagrams, we place objects in an arbitrary horizontal sequence, but vertical progression from the top of a sequence diagram to the bottom represents the progression of time. Thus, objects appear in their horizontal position at various points in time during the execution of a scenario. For example, in Deliverable 5.5, the *Patron* object comes into existence before the *Book* object, and so the rectangle that represents the *Patron* object is vertically above the rectangle that represents the *Book* object. Of course, in this example, we could just as easily have decided that the *Book* object should be created before the *Patron* object. The order of these *create()* messages does not matter. It does matter, for example, that the *create()* message for the *Patron* object occurs before the *validatePatron()* message is sent to the *Patron* object.

Deliverable 5.6 shows a sequence diagram for the *GenFormLetter* use case, in which form letters reminding patrons of their overdue resources are sent out. The *LibrarySystem* class orchestrates the generation of form letters by iterating through the library holdings in the database.

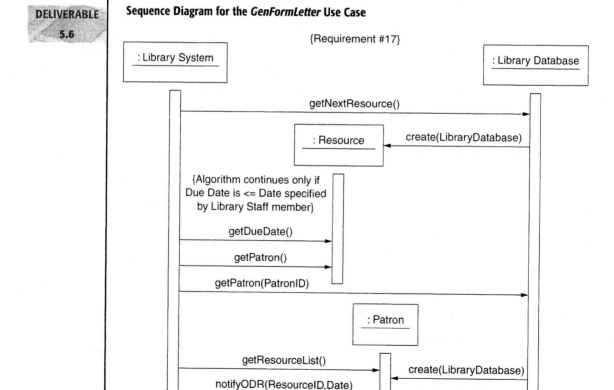

DELIVERABLE 5.6

Sequence Diagram for the *GenFormLetter* Use Case

EXERCISE 5.6

How would the sequence diagram in Deliverable 5.6 change if instead of iterating through the library resources, the system iterated through the list of patrons, checking their respective holdings? Would this algorithm be more efficient?

EXERCISE 5.7

Create a sequence diagram for the *player move* scenario in the ticktacktoe game.

5.3.6 Evaluating Design

There are several reasons for modeling software before embarking on writing code. One reason is that to produce well-structured, modular, and correct code requires some planning. A second reason is that the models allow us to evaluate the quality of the proposed solution without too large an investment of effort. A system may be well structured but also contain vulnerabilities that may introduce data integrity problems. A sequence diagram that models a scenario may highlight some of these sources of potential data inconsistency.

5.3.7 *Case Study:* Evaluating Design of LMS

CASE STUDY

If we examine the model shown in Deliverable 5.5, a clear design flaw emerges. This flaw relates to the two distinct method calls that are required in order to update information concerning the borrowing of a resource. When we look at the semantics of the *update(Resource)* and *update(Patron)* methods, it is clear that both methods record the fact that a book is checked out by a particular individual. In order to maintain data integrity, these separate method calls must be coordinated. What happens if the system crashes after the *update(Book)* method has completed but before the *update(Patron)* method has completed? The fact that these updates occur as separate transactions should motivate an examination of the data integrity issues involved.

The *update(Patron)* method stores an object reference to the *Book* object in a list of checked-out resources, while the *update(Book)* method records a reference to *Patron* object in the *Book* object. These updates may occur in separate method invocations if the invocation of one is dependent on the successful completion of the other. For example, if some error occurs after the successful completion of the first update, then the initial update can be backed out and logged for future update after the database access problem has been resolved.

5.3.8 Object Diagrams

An **object diagram** models a set of objects and their interrelationships during a system **snapshot** [16]. A system snapshot is the state of the software system at a selected moment in time. The notational elements that make up object diagrams are objects and links. An object diagram models the states and interconnections of objects and serves as another static design view of the system. Unlike other diagram types encountered thus far, an object diagram may contain multiple instances of a particular class. The representation of multiple objects shows that more than one instance of a class may be allocated at a particular point during execution.

5.3.9 *Case Study:* Object Diagrams for LMS

Deliverable 5.7 shows the relationship between *Patron* and *Book* objects. The semantics behind this representation is that *Gertrude Stein*, a *Patron*, has three books checked out at this time, and that each book has a link back to the patron who has it checked out. By consulting the class diagram in Figure 5.3, the software developers realize that the system must accommodate a one-to-many (cardinality) relationship from *Patron* to *Resource*. To facilitate this relationship, a *List* class is used to aggregate all *Resources* checked out by a *Patron*. The class diagram in Deliverable 5.7 further specifies that a *Resource* can be checked out by at most one *Patron* at a given time. Therefore, each *Resource* must have an attribute that holds the *PatronID* of the *Patron* who currently has the *Resource* checked out. If the *Resource* is not currently checked out, the *PatronID* attribute on the *Resource* object is **null**.

EXERCISE 5.8   Create an object diagram for the *player move* scenario in the ticktacktoe game.

An Object Diagram for the Library Management System

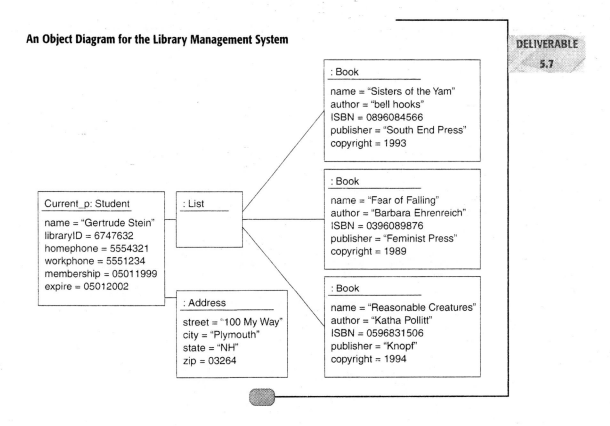

DELIVERABLE
5.7

5.3.10 Object Diagram Creation

Summary Points box 5.3 shows the steps required to create an object diagram modeling the object structure of a particular aspect of the system to be developed. These steps are described in the following list:

- Identify a context for the object structure to be modeled, such as a particular scenario. In the preceding case study, for instance, the relationship between *Patron* and *Resource* objects is modeled in the context of a *Patron* checking out one or more *Resources*. In this situation, the *CheckOutResource* scenario is the context of interest.
- Identify the classes and other elements comprising the modeling context, and identify the relationships among these elements.
- Identify the objects related to this particular scenario. The state of these objects represents the snapshot of the system that will be modeled by the object diagram.
- Show the state of each object in the diagram at the time of the snapshot in each object representation.
- Finally, portray the interobject links, remembering that links are instances of association relationships.

Steps for Creating Object Diagrams

1. Identify a system snapshot within a scenario to model.
2. Identify participating classes and their relevant interrelationships.
3. Identify all allocated objects at the time of the snapshot.
4. Show the state of each object in the snapshot.
5. Determine all interobject links.

5.4   Objectives of the Class Design Phase

Objectives of the class design phase of software development include

- Code reuse
- Well-designed classes and methods
- Assurance of data integrity

We will now examine each of these objectives in detail.

5.4.1 Code Reuse

Code reuse is a constant consideration during object-oriented system development. Reuse is initially considered during project conceptualization to determine whether any primary classes intuitively form an inheritance hierarchy. During class design, system developers have the results of analysis to use as a basis for identifying potential opportunities for code reuse. Collaboration diagrams are of particular use in **pattern scavenging** [14].

Pattern scavenging involves studying class diagrams, interaction diagrams, and object diagrams to identify patterns in class interaction. These patterns should be evaluated to determine whether these mechanisms for interaction may be effectively reused rather than reinvented in similar collaborations. Additionally, classes may be evaluated in terms of commonality of behavior to determine whether they should share methods through a common abstract base class. Finally, as the design phase progresses, the method signatures may be assessed for similarity as another source for code reuse.

5.4.2 *Case Study:* Code Reuse in LMS

In the Library Management System, the *CheckOutResource* functionality is similar to a patron-requesting-reserve resource. In both cases, the patron must present his or her library card and be verified against the library database. In both cases, a tangible library resource is presented to the patron who is then responsible for returning that resource in the time frame specified. The only differences in the two scenarios are that the reserve time frame is measured in hours rather than days and that the reserve resource may not leave the premises even during the checked-out time frame. Clearly, reserve resources and checkable resources share a great deal in common in terms of their interactions with library patrons.

A typical strategy to consolidate the similar methods between the *CheckableResource* class and *ReserveResource* class is to place the *ReserveResource* in the inheritance hierarchy with *CheckableResource*. Deliverable 5.8 shows a possible means to reuse common methods that must be defined in a more general *Resource* class.

Inheritance Hierarchies in the Library Management System

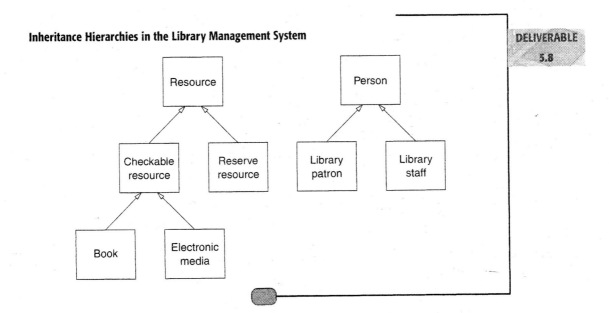

Another example of class redesign motivated by reuse of methods involves the *Patron* and *LibraryStaff* classes. Because library staff can function both as employees and patrons of the library, reconsideration of these class definitions is in order. These classes share a number of attributes. In particular, for both classes the essential properties of people must be represented, such as *name*, *address*, *home telephone number*, *work telephone number*, and *identification number*. Each class then has additional attributes that are not appropriate for the other. To allow reuse of code between these classes, we introduce a parent class called *Person* that contains the attributes common to the *Patron* and *LibraryStaff* classes. Deliverable 5.8 shows this inheritance hierarchy.

5.4.3 Well-Designed Classes and Methods

The consequences of designing classes and methods well include software extensibility, reliability, maintainability, and flexibility. In addition, here are a few guidelines [47] for class design:

- Always keep data private.
- Always initialize data in a constructor.
- Do not use too many related primitive types. If many related attributes are primitive types, they should probably be aggregated in their own class. For example, perhaps there should be a class called *Address* so that the related address attributes can be aggregated. The *Patron* class then contains an attribute whose type is *Address* rather than several individual attributes, such as *street* and *city*, whose types are primitive.
- Not all attributes need individual **accessor/mutator** methods. Accessor methods are methods that return the value in a particular attribute in the object. Mutator methods allow the modification of a single attribute value in the object. These methods are sometimes called **get** and **set** methods.
- Order the elements comprising each class consistently. For example, first define constants, then constructors, then static methods, then other methods, followed by instance variables, and finally static variables.
- Break up overly complex classes into multiple classes.
- Name classes, methods, and attributes well, so that they are self-documenting.

EXERCISE 5.9   With a group of other students, examine one of your old object-oriented programs with the preceding list of guidelines in mind. Have you followed these guidelines for well-designed classes? Using suggestions from your classmates, rewrite the code.

5.4.4 Data Integrity

A well-structured, modular, and otherwise robust system may have data integrity vulnerabilities even if all algorithms and calculations are tested and correct. The potential vulnerability stems from updating interrelated information in separate transactions or method invocations. Interrelated information refers to multiple data values that must be updated together in order to maintain data integrity. For example, in LMS, when a *Patron* borrows a *Resource*, both the *Patron* and the *Resource* object must be updated with similar information.

Data integrity can also be at risk from malicious or inappropriate user access. In most applications, not all users should have the same access to all the information embedded in the system. The manner by which this security is implemented is a matter of design. Under certain circumstances, security can be handled by the database management system or operating system rather than being carried out at the application level. Otherwise, end users must be represented within the system associated with some information access profile.

Verification of the Class Design

Verifying the design entails three separate verification objectives. One objective is to ensure that all requirements developed during analysis are accounted for through design. The second objective is to ensure that all required attributes and methods are used properly. For example, if an attribute is to be passed as a parameter in a method invocation, we must ensure that the attribute has a valid value before the method is invoked. The third type of verification ensures that the separate components comprising the system work together properly.

The first verification objective is also called **traceability to requirements**. A systematic process of module decomposition will ensure that the requirements developed during analysis are traceable through design, which will in turn allow us to determine whether our design has accounted for all requirements. For example, consulting the requirements specification from Chapter 3, item 16 specifies that the system must accommodate lists of overdue resources. Further analysis is likely to establish that several types of overdue resource lists are necessary. Therefore, what is initially encoded as a single use case is decomposed into a series of scenarios, each of which vary the specific nature of the overdue resource listing.

Figure 5.7 shows an example of how a specific requirement can be traced from analysis through design. The requirement is first identified within the requirements specification and associated with a unique number. The requirement *List overdue resources* is associated with the number 16. This requirement is first developed into a use case. After clarification with end users, three different scenarios are created from the original use case. Each of these three scenarios is labeled with the requirement number and an alphabetic extension. The three scenarios then contribute to the development of class diagrams for the *Resource* and *Patron* classes. The attributes and methods added to a class definition in response to a specific scenario carry a comment connecting them with the scenario that motivated it.

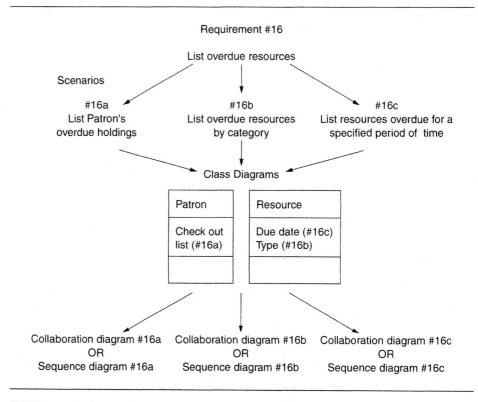

FIGURE 5.7   Tracing Requirements throughout the Development Process

A collaboration or sequence diagram is then developed for each scenario and the label of the scenario is propagated through each diagram.

The second design verification criterion requires the application of checks and balances to the attributes and methods defined for each class in such a manner that the creation of every piece of information can be accounted for. The origin of a piece of information can therefore be traced to its source. For example, in the method *CheckOutResource*, the reference to a *Patron* object can be traced to its transmission in the parameter list of that method. Such verification is best accomplished by using **Computer Aided Software Engineering** (CASE) tools. Object-oriented CASE tools are emerging [95] and, like their predecessor tools, automate the checks and balances required for this type of verification.

The third type of class verification is critical to ensure that the classes being created by separate developers fit together and function effectively as a system. This aspect of the verification is most effectively accomplished through an informal walk-through. The objective of an informal walk-through is to follow the system execution from beginning to end, scenario by scenario, ensuring that the message passing between objects is being adequately accommodated. This process ensures that the developers of one class are using the methods of another class correctly by being in agreement with the method signature. Because the objective of the design walk-through is to ensure agreement in method signatures between invokers of the methods and the developers of the methods, it is not necessary to involve domain experts in this process. The walk-through should, however, consist of the entire development team.

5.6   Designing the *Class Project*

At this point in the software development process, all members of the development team should have clearly delineated responsibility for developing the class project. The delineation is most effective if it is along class boundaries so that development responsibility is assigned in terms of classes. Each team member should have responsibility for classes that constitute a functional partition of the project. Of course, each functional partition will require services from classes being developed by other team members. This interaction among functional partitions means that it is essential that development team members be in close communication during this period, so that each may express his or her needs to the appropriate teammate.

CLASS PROJECT

The primary design process for the project is to further develop models of the system behavior so that definitions for the classes comprising the system can evolve. Further refining the class diagrams and creating collaboration, sequence, and object diagrams will establish a more complete portrayal of the attributes and methods necessary for each class. Each development team member must independently develop the diagrams necessary for his or her functional partition of the project.

There is a tremendous amount of work to do during the design phase. In a semester-long project, only about three weeks may be devoted to design. Given that the classes designed must interoperate effectively, one must accommodate class design revision during this brief period. To allow for class refinement, team members should try to complete a preliminary design in time for an informal walk-through after the second week of design. Such a target will allow one week for revisions made apparent during the walk-through.

The design period addressed here encompasses both class design and product design. Thus, the graphical user interfaces, the game board, and the client/server architecture need to be designed in these three weeks as well. These responsibilities can be distributed to development team members who have smaller functional partitions and thus fewer or less complex classes to develop.

The steps for completing class design are as follows:

• Review the set of scenarios to determine whether any additional scenarios need to be created to model significantly different aspects of any use cases.

- For new scenarios, create a class diagram showing the necessary interclass relationships for each scenario.
- For each scenario, consult its associated class diagram and develop either a collaboration or sequence diagram.
- Update the class diagrams of the classes that require additional attributes or methods to accommodate the interobject links portrayed in the collaboration or sequence diagrams.
- Translate the resulting class diagrams into class skeletons to begin the implementation phase.

5.7 Questions for Review

1. What are the objectives of class design? How do they differ from the objectives of analysis?
2. What steps comprise the design process? Do these steps differ between an incremental development process and a top-down process?
3. What deliverables result from the design process? Which deliverable embodies all information developed during design?
4. What information comprises a class skeleton, and where does this information come from?
5. How are the elements of design linked back to the functional requirements?
6. Identify all UML adornments shown in Figure 5.3.
7. How is the information that is embodied in the cardinality of a relationship between two classes relevant to class design?
8. Compare and contrast sequence diagrams with collaboration diagrams. Do they convey the same information? If not, what information is embodied by one that is not embodied by the other?
9. How are collaboration diagrams used during design? What do they model? Who should view them and how are they verified?
10. How are sequence diagrams used during design? How are they verified?
11. What role do object diagrams play during the design process? What information is embodied in object diagrams that is not present in sequence or collaboration diagrams?
12. What are the qualities of well-designed classes? Methods?
13. What is pattern scavenging?

Case Study: Game2D with Method Design

This chapter has two objectives. The first is to review the use case centered development (UCCD) steps introduced in previous chapters in the context of a new case study, a game called Game2D. The second objective is to discuss the process of **method design**. Only the new concepts introduced in this chapter are listed in the Key Concepts section.

CASE STUDY

6.1 Key Concepts

- Timer objects
- Method design
- Qualities of well-designed methods

- Pseudocode
- Decision tables

6.2 Overview

This chapter introduces a new case study that will be utilized to examine the process of software development. The new case study is smaller in scale than either the Library Management System or the class project. However, it represents a reasonably sophisticated problem that requires objects of several different classes to work together over a network. The Library Management System, in contrast, represents a realistic industry problem, which, if it were to be completely solved, would double the number of pages in this book.

The case study in this chapter will be solved from beginning to end, covering each software engineering step introduced thus far and introducing the topic of method design. That is, this chapter discusses the following topics in the context of the new case study:

- Requirements specification
- Requirements analysis
- Product design
- Class design
- Method design
- Implementation and testing (to be covered in a later chapter)

 Requirements Specification

You work for a software development company. In the mail, you receive the following letter:

> Dear Alysha,
>
> You said if I ever had anything I wanted you to work on for me, I should contact you, and that's the purpose of this letter. My father, who has never used a computer before, has just bought one. He's having serious difficulty learning to use and control the mouse. I have come up with a simple game that would allow him to work on his reflexes and practice using the mouse.
>
> The game, as I said, is very simple. When he begins the game, he will see a grid. As the game progresses, dots appear in the rectangles of the grid. The goal of the game is to use the mouse to click on the dots and make them disappear. If two dots appear next to each other (in the same row or column), then the game ends. For each dot he makes disappear, he gets a point. When the game ends, his score is displayed. To make the game more interesting, I think he should be competing against someone else on a different computer, probably over the Internet. Then the first player to have two of his or her dots next to each other loses the game.
>
> I hope this is a project you will consider taking on.
>
> Thanks,
> Kyle

You decide that you would like to work on this project and use it as a model for your coworkers showing how software engineering ought to be done.

 Refined Requirements Specification

The first goal of requirements analysis is to understand the functionality of the software to be developed and produce a refined requirements specification. Because this project is relatively small and clearly described, understanding what the customer is asking for is not as difficult as it is in most software engineering projects. Despite the apparent clarity, it is still advisable to schedule a meeting with the eventual users of the system to present your understanding of the system's functionality and help to ensure that you are clear on what the users intend.

Because we cannot emulate the process of interacting with end users to confirm our understanding of the requirements specification, we propose that the class engage in a role-playing exercise to clarify any possible ambiguities and misunderstandings. The class should break into project teams, or groups of two or three depending on class size. Each group should meet and create a consensus description of the project's functionality and a list of omitted, ambiguous, or conflicting information. Because no actual user is present, each team should propose a resolution to any necessary clarification to the requirements statement. After each team has developed its statement, teams should present their findings to the class as a whole, and any discrepancies should be resolved by the class, creating a consensus project description.

One issue that requires clarification is whether more than two players can play the game. Although the game itself is structured as a two-player game, are multiple sets of two-player games facilitated by this software? The solution addressed in this chapter will allow any number of games to be initiated with two players each. Of course, other resolutions of this problem are possible. The following is a refined requirements specification for Game2D.

DELIVERABLE 6.1

Supported Activity List for Game2D Specification

1. Allow registration of two players for each game. The players will play against each other over the Internet.
2. Display a simple table of initially empty cells.
3. When two players have been registered and one of them clicks the Start button, the game begins.
4. Randomly display dots in the cells at regular intervals. The dots appear alternatingly in one of two colors, red and blue.
5. Allow the player to adjust the interval at which dots are displayed.
6. Assign one of two colors to each player so that each player is concerned with dots of only one color. That is, one player seeks to click the mouse on the blue dots to make them disappear, while the other seeks to click on the red dots.

7. Respond to mouse clicks. If either player clicks on a dot, the dot disappears in response to that click. That is, even if a player clicks on a dot that belongs to his or her opponent, the dot disappears.
8. Keep track of points (the score). Each time a player clicks on a dot of his or her color, he or she earns a point.
9. If two dots of the same color appear next to each other, the game ends. The player whose color corresponds to the color of these dots is the loser of this game. Notify each player who the loser is. Dots are considered to be next to each other if they are adjacent horizontally or vertically. Dots in a sequence diagonally are not considered to be next to each other.

Human-Computer Interface Description

Deliverable 6.2 shows the basic interface for Game2D. The player clicks the *Start Game* button to register with the server. The player is then assigned a dot color, either red or blue. Once two players have been registered, red and blue dots begin to be displayed on the grid. The players use the mouse to click on the dots, which disappear in response to these mouse clicks.

DELIVERABLE 6.2

The User Interface for Game2D

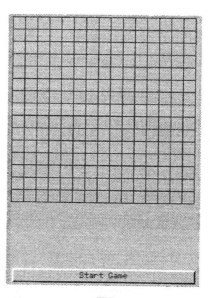

Start Game

Game2D Requirements Specification

Solved Problems List

The major problem that we hope to solve with this software has to do with skill in use of the mouse. Through this software, new computer users should be able to practice using the mouse in an entertaining manner.

Information Source List

This software receives no information from any outside system. The software that runs on the client machine receives information from the software that runs on the server machine and vice versa.

Information-Requesting Organizations

No outside organizations will request information from this software.

Automated Checks and Balances

The server software ensures that two players have been registered before beginning the game.

Security and Fault-Tolerance Requirements

There is no need for any security or fault tolerance built into this system. There may be problems with the server or client machines crashing in the middle of a game, but since the information involved in this software is not critical, the software will not be designed to deal with such situations in any special manner.

Interoperating Systems List

This software does not interoperate with any other systems.

Present Information Capacity and Projected Growth

The server will be designed to be able to handle any number of two-player games. There are no plans to upgrade the software to be able to handle a single game of more than two players at one time, and we anticipate no demand for such games.

Projected Time Frame

The development of this software will take no more than one month.

Prioritization of Requirements

The one requirement that can be pushed off into the future is the one that stipulates that player scores will be calculated (requirement 8). All other requirements have equal priority.

Ethical Concerns

There are no ethical concerns regarding this software.

Requirements Analysis

Once each student has a consistent understanding of the functionality of Game2D, the next step is the creation of the primary class list.

6.5.1 List of Nouns

The next goal of project development stipulated by UCCD is to establish the primary classes for the software. First, a list of potential primary classes is derived from the list of the nouns occurring in the list of supported activities in the requirements specification. Each noun is then scrutinized for qualification as a class according to the Coad and Yourdon rules [25]. The following is a list of the nouns in the requirements specification for Game2D. Note that your list of nouns may differ from the following list because you should have rewritten the requirements specification as a result of discussions during the in-class exercise.

- Player
- Game
- Internet
- Table
- Cell
- *Start Game* button
- Dot
- Interval
- Color
- Mouse
- Mouse click
- Point (score)
- Loser

6.5.2 Analysis of List of Nouns

To determine which nouns from the preceding list should make it onto our list of primary classes, recall the list of characteristics described in section 3.10.1. The characteristics are

- Retained information
- Needed services
- Multiple attributes
- Common attributes
- Common operations
- Essential requirements

Using these characteristics, we now analyze the nouns from the requirements specification to determine which of them are likely to be classes in the final software product.

The first noun on our list is *player*, which turns out to be a likely candidate for class definition. For each player of the game, a significant amount of information, such as the dot color assigned to the player and the machine on which the player is playing the game, must be stored. In addition to this retained information, the *Player* class might provide services to other classes. In particular, the *Player* class might embody the user interface for each human player. Each *Player* object will contain several attributes, and these attributes are common to all players. From this analysis, we can see that a *Player* class is necessary in the Game2D software.

The next noun is *game*. Each game has a current state. For example, when the game is just beginning, there are no dots in the cells, and as the game progresses, dots are placed in the various cells. The location of the dots is part of the current state of the game. This information must be retained throughout the progress of the game. *Game*, therefore, represents a potential class and belongs on our list of primary classes.

The user has specified that he would like the game to be played over the *Internet*. The Internet is the means for connecting the machines on which the players are playing against each other. It exists independently of this game and represents an external actor with which the game must communicate. We probably do not need to record any information about the Internet, and therefore it does not require a class definition in our software system.

Table is the next noun in the requirements specification. The table is the organization of the cells comprising the game. There is no information about the table that must be stored. In fact, the organization of the cells can be handled with a two-dimensional array, as an attribute of some other class. *Table*, therefore, does not require a class definition.

A *cell*, the next noun in the requirements specification, consists of attributes determining the position of the cell on the table (or grid), whether the cell contains a dot or not, and what color the dot is. This information must be retained and manipulated, and therefore *Cell* is a clear candidate for becoming a class.

The Game2D game requires that the player press the *Start Game button* in order to begin the game. This button is part of the graphical user interface of the software. The Java Development Kit (JDK) has *Button* as one of its graphical classes. Therefore, the *Start Game button* will be an attribute of the class that embodies our graphical user interface and will not be a new class for which we must create attributes and methods.

The next noun in the requirements specification is *dot*. Each dot has at least one attribute, *Color*, whose value must be retained. In addition, information about the *Cell* in which the *Dot* appears must be kept. There are several operations that every *Dot* must be able to accomplish. For example, when the *Cell* in which a *Dot* appears is clicked upon, the *Dot* must disappear. *Dot* will be one of our primary classes.

The players of Game2D are allowed to increase or decrease the level of difficulty of playing the game by altering the *interval* at which dots are displayed on the table of cells. An *Interval* is a single piece of information that represents part of the current game state. In other words, *Interval* is an attribute of the class that contains the game state and is not a class itself.

The next noun in the requirements specification is *Color*. The JDK has a class called *Color*. In Game2D, *Color* is used as an attribute of a *Dot*. There is no other information about *Color* that must be retained. Therefore, we will use the *Color* class from the JDK as an attribute of *Dot*.

The game must handle *mouse* events, such as *mouse clicks*. Mouse movements must, therefore, be recorded, but there are no mouse attributes that must be retained, and so *mouse* will not be a class in the Game2D software. The JDK has several classes, such as *MouseListener*, that we can use to handle the capture of and response to mouse events.

The next noun in the requirements specification is *point* or *score*. The game must keep track of the score for each player. The *Score* is a simple numeric value that is incremented as the player clicks on *Dots* of his or her *Color*. *Score* will, therefore, be an attribute of the *Player* class.

The final noun in the requirements specification is *loser*. One of the two players of the game will be the loser at the end of the game. Since the game ends when one player is designated the loser, no information about the loser must be retained. Therefore, *loser* is not a good candidate for becoming a class.

6.5.3 List of Primary Classes

DELIVERABLE 6.4

Primary Classes for Game2D

- Player
- Game
- Cell
- Dot

6.5.4 Use Case Development

The next step of requirements analysis in the UCCD development process is to develop a set of use cases. These use cases will characterize the software system's interaction with external actors, such as the users of the system. Because client/server systems consist of at least two processes communicating over network connections, these process-to-process interactions are also considered candidates for use case formulation. By examining the refined requirements specification for Game2D, we develop the following list of use cases:

1. Client communicates player sign-on.
2. Client communicates player action (mouse click on a particular cell with/ without a dot).
3. Server communicates that dot is to be removed from a cell.
4. Server communicates that dot is set in a cell.
5. Server communicates that game is won/lost.

Notice that this list could be broken down into a number of additional use cases. For example, the first use case listed could be split into two smaller ones. The first could be called *user signs on* and would involve interaction between the user and the system. The second could be called *client process communicates player sign-on to server* and would involve interaction between the client and server processes. We have chosen to create one use case that subsumes both of these smaller use cases because the user-client process interaction is not very complicated in this particular interaction.

Using the preceding list of use cases, determine a complete set of smaller use cases **EXERCISE 6.2** that capture all the interactions of the system with external actors.

After each use case is briefly described, it is then fleshed out through the development of individual scenarios. Through the development of these scenarios, we expect to discover that additional classes must be introduced to our list of classes. We also expect to identify additional detail in previously defined classes. In other words, through the process of developing scenarios, we expect to evolve our list of primary classes. Scenarios for the use cases are developed in the following paragraphs.

Use Case: Client Communicates Player Sign-On

In thinking about the first use case, *client communicates player sign-on*, issues of product design are pushed to the forefront, exposing ambiguities of the requirements statement. In order to think about the process of how a player signs on to the game, we must establish the basic process architecture for the game. In other words, we must determine how multiple remote players may communicate with each other and where the various processes are running. Nontechnical users do not typically prescribe the hardware configuration and distribution of the software processes beyond specifying what hardware resources are currently available and what kind of budget for additional hardware exists. In this particular application, however, the user has requested that the game be able to be played over the Internet. This requirement suggests either a peer-to-peer or client/server process architecture.

Because Java is the selected programming language for this text, a client/server process architecture is a good choice. Java applets running through web browsers can only connect to the host that served the applet [48]. This security restriction means that general peer-to-peer connections cannot be accomplished using applets. Instead, a game server must run on the host that transmits the applets, and each player interacts with an applet (which in this case is the client software), which in turn communicates with the game server software. The game server then transmits the necessary information to the other applets.

Use Case: Client Communicates Player Sign-On

Preconditions: Given a client/server process architecture, the server must be running and ready to accept socket connections from game players.

Main flow of events: A potential player initiates a game by selecting a web page containing the player applet using a World Wide Web browser. The user presses the *Start Game* button, and a socket connection between the player's machine and the game server is created. The game does not begin until a second player has also connected to the server. The server informs this first player of the game's status, which is either waiting for a second player or initiating the game. If a game is initiating, the server assigns the first player the color blue and the second player the color red. The players are notified by means of dialogue boxes. With the display of these dialogue boxes on the players' machines, this use case ends.

Exceptional flow of events: If the server is not running when the player presses the *Start Game* button, the message "Sorry the server is currently down; please try later" appears in the browser's status area, and this use case ends.

Exceptional flow of events: If a second player does not connect to the server for a period of five minutes, the game server allows the player to play the game without an opponent. The player is notified of this situation by a dialogue box. With the display of the dialogue box, this use case ends.

Exceptional flow of events: If the first player loses his or her socket connection while waiting for a second player, this use case ends. If a second player connects but the first player disconnects before the game can be initiated, then the second player is considered to be the first player, and the use case continues in the main flow of events until a second player connects.

Use Case: Client Communicates Player Action

DELIVERABLE
6.6

Main flow of events: This use case begins when the player clicks the left mouse button in the applet window. The goal of each player is to erase as many dots of his or her associated color as possible. In other words, the blue player wishes to erase blue dots, while the red player wishes to erase red dots. A player erases a dot by pressing the left mouse button over a cell containing that dot. When the mouse button is clicked, the event is trapped, and the coordinates of the mouse event are translated into a specific reference to a *Cell* object. The *Cell* object is queried to determine whether a *Dot* is present in that *Cell* and what its color is. If no *Dot* exists in this *Cell*, the use case ends. If a *Dot* matching the player's color is present, the player receives a point. If a *Dot* of any color is present, the *Dot* is removed from the *Cell*, and the information to remove the *Dot* from the *Cell* is transmitted to the server. The use case then ends.

Exceptional flow of events: If a player clicks the mouse on an area of the applet where no *Cell* object is rendered, the use case ends with no information being transmitted to the server.

Use Case: Server Communicates That a Dot Is to Be Removed from a Cell

DELIVERABLE
6.7

Main flow of events: This use case begins when the server has received information from one of the clients that a *Dot* is to be removed from a *Cell* as a result of a player's mouse click. This use case ends when the server communicates the received information to the other client process.

Exceptional flow of events: If the player to whom the information is being communicated has disconnected, either intentionally or unintentionally, the use case ends without the server communicating the received information. The remaining player (if there is one) will continue to play until a game-ending condition occurs for either player.

Use Case: Server Communicates That Dot Is Set in a Cell

Main flow of events: This use case begins when the interval of time for generating random dots has transpired. To keep track of the interval, a timer class must be created. A *Timer* object is created and sleeps for a minimum number of milliseconds (the interval). When the *Timer* object wakes up, it sends a message to the server process, which then generates a random number. This random number corresponds to a *Cell* on the graphical game interface, and a *Dot* of the appropriate color will appear in the random *Cell*. The server alternates *Dot* colors, starting with blue. As the *Dot* is generated, the server process checks to see if a neighboring *Dot* of the same color exists. If two *Dots* share an edge, they are considered to be neighboring. That is, diagonal *Dots* are not considered to be neighboring. If a neighboring *Dot* of the same color exists, this use case ends, and the *Server Communicates Game Is Won/Lost* use case begins. If neighboring *Dots* of the same color do not exist, the *Timer* object goes back to sleep, and information concerning the location of this *Dot* and its color is transmitted to the client process. The client process updates the graphical user interface to reflect the new *Dot*, and the use case ends.

Exceptional flow of events: If the randomly selected *Cell* object already contains a *Dot*, then the use case ends without transmitting any information to the client processes.

Exceptional flow of events: If a player has disconnected, either intentionally or unintentionally, the server communicates with the remaining player (if there is one) who will continue to play until a game-ending condition occurs for either player. In this situation, the use case ends when the generated information has been transmitted and reflected on the graphical interface of the remaining player.

Use Case: Server Communicates Game Is Won/Lost

Main flow of events: This use case begins when a *Dot* is generated in a *Cell* that is next to a *Cell* that already has a *Dot* of the same color. The information concerning who has won and who has lost the game is transmitted to each client process and is displayed on the graphical user interfaces. The use case ends when the game ends.

Exceptional flow of events: If a player has disconnected, either intentionally or unintentionally, the server communicates with the remaining player (if there is one). The use case ends when the game ends.

6.5.5 Scenarios

Scenario: Client Communicates Player Sign-On

DELIVERABLE
6.10

Emma connects to a web page containing the *Game2DClient* software and presses the *Start Game* button. This action creates a socket connection to the game server, *Game2DServer*, which is running on the host machine. The server sends back a message indicating that it is waiting for a second user to sign on to the game before the game is initiated. A *Timer* object is initiated to time how long Emma is waiting. The *Timer* object queries the second player *Socket* object every 10 seconds to determine whether it is still null (no one has connected to the socket). After the first two minutes, no one has started another game. Before the third minute elapses, a second player, Fred, starts the *Game2DClient* software from a web page served from the computer running the game server. Now that two players have connected to the server, a *Game* object is created. Both Emma and Fred are sent a message informing them that the game will begin in ten seconds. Emma is informed that she is the blue player, while Fred receives a message that he is the red player. The game begins when the *Game* object creates a *Timer* object that will keep track of the interval at which *Dots* will be generated at random locations on the graphical user interface. At regular intervals, the *Timer* object alerts the *Game* object to randomly pick a *Cell* for the placement of a *Dot* of alternating blue and red color.

Additional scenarios are useful to portray exceptional flows of events, such as a second player not signing on to the game in the five-minute limit. Because the exceptions do not appreciably influence the nonexceptional scenario, we can simply add partial scenario descriptions that address a particular exceptional situation rather than reiterating the entire scenario.

One of the exceptional flows of events described in the use case is the situation in which no second player starts the game. In this case, the *Timer* object would determine that after five minutes the socket connection to the second player is still null, and would create a connection over the loop back address (127.0.0.1) to the game server, thus allowing the game to begin without a second human opponent. Although this solution creates a game that is less challenging for Emma (the first player), it solves the need for a second player rather easily.

DELIVERABLE
6.11

Scenario: Client Communicates Player Action

Emma and Fred both see the same game state on their respective client applets. Emma, the blue player, is attempting to click on *Cells* containing blue *Dots*, while Fred is attempting to click on *Cells* containing red *Dots*. Emma clicks her left mouse button on a position in her applet window. The coordinates of this click (123,235) are extracted from the *MouseEvent* object (*MouseEvent* is a class from the Java Development Kit) and are translated into the index values of the two-dimensional array of *Cell* objects. The value 123 represents the coordinate along the x-axis, while 235 is the coordinate along the y-axis. In the applet window coordinate system, (0,0) is the upper left-hand corner of the window. The *Cell* object containing the (123,235) point is queried to determine if it contains a *Dot*. In this particular case, there is a blue *Dot* in that *Cell*, and therefore the *Dot* is removed. Emma receives one point for removing this *Dot*. The information that the *Dot* has been removed is communicated to the server software, which in turn communicates this information to Fred's client applet.

A second scenario for this use case involves Emma, who is the blue player, clicking on a *Cell* that contains a red, rather than blue, *Dot*. In this situation, the *Dot* disappears, Emma's point total does not change, and the removal of the *Dot* is communicated to the server software, which in turn communicates this information to Fred's client applet.

A third scenario for this use case involves Emma clicking on location (123,235) in the applet window. In this scenario, the *Cell* that contains this location does not contain a *Dot* of either color. The client applet does not transmit any information to the server software in this situation but instead simply waits for the next *MouseEvent* to occur.

DELIVERABLE
6.12

Scenario: Server Communicates That a Dot Is to Be Removed from a Cell

Emma has clicked on a *Cell* that contains a blue *Dot*. Her client applet has transferred this information to the server software. Once the server software receives this information, it must pass it onto Fred's client applet. Once Fred's client applet receives the information to remove the *Dot* from the *Cell*, the local applet window is updated so that the *Dot* no longer appears in the *Cell*.

An alternate scenario is that Fred has disconnected, either intentionally or unintentionally, from the game server before this information can be transmitted to his client applet. In this situation, the server attempts to send the information, finds that the *Socket* connection has been closed by the client and, therefore, simply does not attempt to retransmit the information.

Scenario: Server Communicates That a Dot Is Set in a Cell

DELIVERABLE
6.13

Every 350 milliseconds, the game server picks two random numbers that represent the location of a *Cell* in the server's two-dimensional array representation of the game board. The server picks *Cell* (4,9) to put a *Dot*. There currently is a *Dot* in that *Cell*, and therefore the server must pick another pair of random numbers. This time, the server picks *Cell* (7,3) and finds that currently there is no *Dot* in that *Cell*. The server then checks the *Cells* at locations (6,3), (7,2), (7,4), and (8,3) to see if they contain blue *Dots*. None of these *Cells* contain a blue *Dot*, and therefore the server transmits a message to the *Socket* objects for each client applet specifying that a blue *Dot* is to be drawn in *Cell* (7,3).

An alternate scenario is that Fred has disconnected from the game server. In this case, Emma's client applet is given the message specifying that a blue *Dot* is to be drawn in *Cell* (7,3).

Scenario: Server Communicates Game Is Won/Lost

DELIVERABLE
6.14

The server picks *Cell* (5,5) and finds that currently there is no *Dot* in that *Cell*. The server then checks the *Cells* at locations (4,5), (5,4), (5,6), and (6,5) to see if they contain blue *Dots*. *Cell* (5,6) contains a blue *Dot*, which means that Emma has lost the game. The server informs Emma that she is the loser and informs Fred that he is the winner.

6.5.6 Refined Class List

Through the process of developing use cases and scenarios, we expect that new classes will be added to the list of primary classes. In developing the use cases, we realize that two new classes are necessary, a *Timer* class and a game server class, called *Game2DServer*. The *Timer* class is necessary to prompt the creation of random dots at regular intervals, and the *Game2DServer* class is necessary to allow multiple games to take place concurrently.

DELIVERABLE
6.15

Refined List of Classes for Game2D

- Player
- Game2DServer
- Game
- Timer
- Cell
- Dot

During the design phase of this piece of software, we will probably find that additional classes are necessary.

6.5.7 Modeling

The first step in modeling the software to be developed is to create an initial class diagram, which will be enhanced throughout the software development process. Deliverable 6.16 shows an initial class diagram containing the classes of the refined class list for *Game2D*. Two classes, *Thread* and *Applet*, which are not on the refined class list appear in the class diagram. Both classes are defined in the Java programming language and serve as super classes for the *Timer* and *Player* classes, respectively. That is, a *Timer* is a *Thread*, and a *Player* is an *Applet*. The Timer class will be discussed in more detail in section 6.7.3.

The class diagram in Deliverable 6.16 shows a number of relationships between classes. Several of the relationships illustrate containment and can be implemented by creating references to the contained class as attributes in the containing class. For example, both the *Player* and *Game* classes contain a *Two-Dimensional Array* instance, which in turn contains references to *Cell* objects. Instances of the *Cell* class contain a reference to a *Dot* object. The class diagram does not formally represent the multiplicity of the interclass relationships. Adding multiplicity notation is left for the design phase.

An Initial Class Diagram

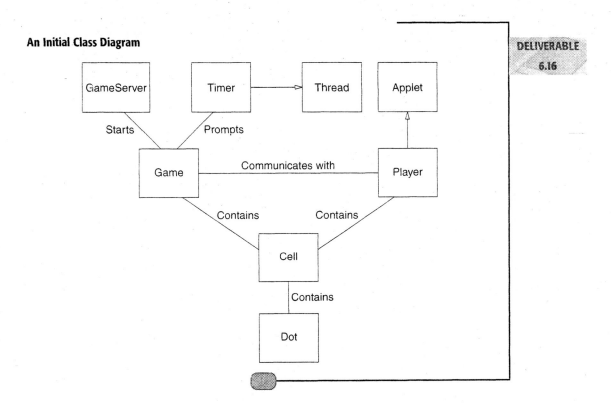

The two noncontainment, noninheritance relationships portrayed in Deliverable 6.16 are *prompts* and *communicates with*. These relationships are worth noting because of their varying abstractness. The *prompts* relationship can be implemented with a reference to the *Game* object in the *Timer* object. After invoking the Thread.sleep( ) method (found in the *Thread* class from the Java Development Kit) for a fixed interval, the *Timer* object can invoke a method in the *Game* object to generate the random numbers representing a particular *Cell*. In contrast, the relationship *communicates with* cannot be implemented as a simple method invocation. Because this application has a client/server process architecture, the *Player* and *Game* classes will be part of separate processes executing on separate machines. Therefore, additional classes must be introduced to facilitate communication between the *Player* and *Game* classes. The details of bringing this interprocess communication about can be resolved during the design of the process architecture and the individual classes. Therefore, the abstract characterization of this relationship is completely appropriate at this time during the analysis phase of software development.

While the initial class diagrams are being created, we must also create use case diagrams to represent the use cases developed earlier. Use case diagrams model a different aspect of the system than the class diagrams. Deliverable 6.17 shows how the use cases fit together and interact with external actors to create the Game2D system.

DELIVERABLE
6.17

A Use Case Diagram for Game2D

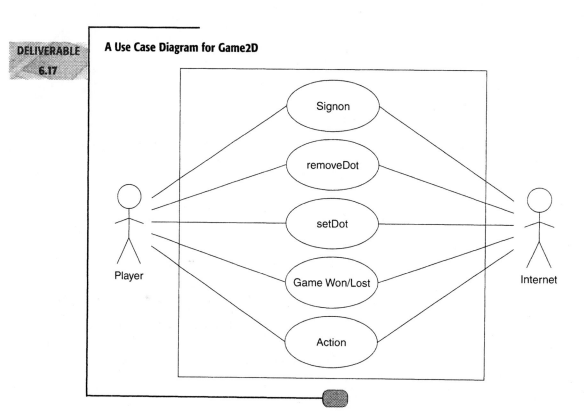

6.6   Product Design

Recall that the objective during product design is to establish the software system's external structure, which includes the following elements:

- Object persistence
- Process architecture
- User interface design

Because of the simplicity of this project, a number of the elements of the external structure need not be considered. For example, we need not consider object persistence because we do not allow a game to be suspended and then restarted at a later time. In addition, our requirements do not include the need to keep a record of games previously played. Nevertheless, because the game is structured as a server interacting with clients, the design of the process architecture is extremely important. Although a user interface was suggested in the requirements specification, this user interface should be reviewed for its usability. Therefore, the primary considerations for product design in Game2D are the design of the process architecture and associated network utilization issues, with a brief review of the relatively simple graphical user interface.

Assume that the requirements specification for Game2D includes a request to maintain a record of the 100 best games played. Such a record includes who played the game (requiring player identification at sign-on) and the total points won by each player. In addition, assume that the requirements specification details a need to freeze a game and resume play at a later time. Outline an object persistence strategy to accommodate these needs.   **EXERCISE 6.3**

6.6.1 Process Architecture

During the analysis phase we determined that Game2D requires a client/server architecture. The design of the process architecture determines a more precise division of responsibility between distinct processes and specifies the need for separate threads of control within particular processes. In addition, during the design of the process architecture, we develop the strategy for interprocess communication. For this case study, message passing is the selected communication mechanism because the processes execute on machines remote from each other.

We use a state machine to model the interprocess communication. This model allows us to divide computational responsibility between the processes and characterizes the content of the information being passed between processes. Deliverable 6.18 shows the state machine for Game2D. The server states in the figure represent all the possible states for the Game2D server process, while the client states represent all the possible states for the Game2D client. In other words, the overall functionality of each server and client process is the composite of its respective substates.

DELIVERABLE
6.18

A State Machine for Game2D

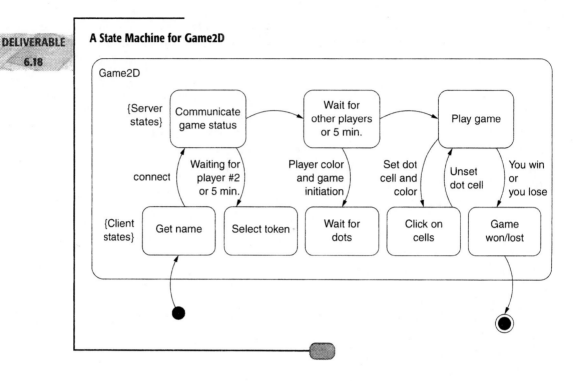

We believe the labels on most of the states in Deliverable 6.18 are self-explanatory. The exception is the *Play Game* server state. This state encompasses the generation of random dots, the communication of unset dot actions between players, and the determination of who has won or lost the game.

EXERCISE 6.4   Recall that complex states in a state machine can be broken down into more detail. A large portion of the functionality of the server is embodied in the *Play Game* state, shown in Deliverable 6.18. Create a state machine that models the *Play Game* state.

Interprocess communication that must occur asynchronously lends complexity to a software system. In the case of Game2D, the server process must be able to communicate with each client asynchronously, with the ability to listen for and send messages at the same time. These message will be generated and received in an unpredictable order. To handle these conditions, separate threads of control for listening and sending are required. In other words, the server process must contain an additional class whose sole purpose is to listen for messages from the clients by way of a socket connection. In fact, the server process needs two instances of this *Listener* class, one for each client. In addition, the client processes must contain a separate *Listener* class to listen for messages from the server process. Deliverable 6.19 shows an updated class diagram for the Game2D system.

A Revised Class Diagram for Game2D

DELIVERABLE
6.19

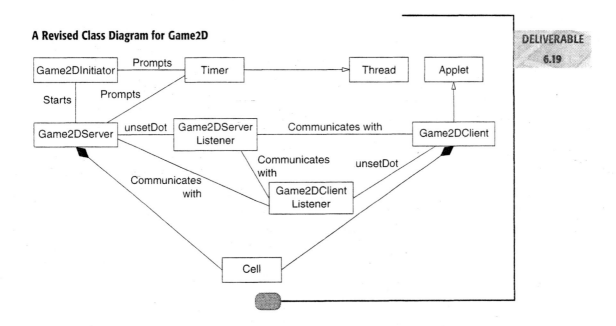

Note that class names in Deliverable 6.19 are slightly different from those shown in the initial class diagram in Deliverable 6.16. In particular, the *Player* class has been renamed *Game2DClient*, the *GameServer* class has been renamed *Game2DInitiator*, and the *Game* class has been renamed *Game2DServer*. This renaming ensures reusability and coexistence with other software by reflecting that these classes are not generic but are instead the client and server classes specific to the Game2D application. The *Game2DInitiator* simply instantiates the *Game2DServer* class when contacted by a *Game2DClient* object. The *Game2DServer* object coordinates the playing of the game once two *Game2DClient* objects have been associated with the *Game2DServer* object by the *Game2DInitiator*.

Enhance the class diagram in Deliverable 6.19 to show multiplicity on the relationships between classes and to identify active classes.   **EXERCISE 6.5**

Network Utilization

Network utilization is the last major issue to be considered as part of the design of the process architecture. All information exchanged between client and server processes can be easily communicated as text, which can then be parsed by the recipient. For example, the server may issue the following messages to the client (note that all italicized words are replaced by integer values in an actual message):

- setDot *row column color*
- unsetDot *row column*
- Game2D Welcome! You are player Blue
- Game2D Welcome! You are player Red
- Congratulations! You win!
- Sorry, you lose.

The client only sends a single message type to the server, the *unsetDot* message. Its format is the same as that specified for the server's *unsetDot* message.

6.6.2 Graphical User Interface Review

The graphical user interface described by the requirements specification and shown in Deliverable 6.2 appears to be quite functional. Recall that the overall goal of Game2D is to give the player some practice manipulating the mouse. In order to win the game, the player must be fairly adept at moving the mouse and clicking on a particular point. Messages to the player are communicated in a standard location, between the grid of cells and the *Start Game* button, which represents a very clear way to begin the game. Given the simple context of Game2D, the selected user interface appears suitable. Of course, to be entirely sure that it is suitable, a prototype of the interface should be built and tested using potential users.

Class Design

The objective of the class design phase of software development is to take the class representations developed during analysis and add any necessary new classes as well as to add detail to existing classes. Two types of diagrams, interaction diagrams and object diagrams, are used to model the system during class design.

6.7.1 Interaction Diagrams

Recall that there are two types of interaction diagrams, collaboration diagrams and sequence diagrams. Deliverable 6.20 shows a collaboration diagram for Game2D. This diagram encompasses the functionality of all use cases. Typically, each scenario for each use case is modeled with a collaboration diagram. Because of the simplicity of this case study, Deliverable 6.20 shows a single aggregate collaboration diagram for the entire system.

A Collaboration Diagram for Game2D

DELIVERABLE
6.20

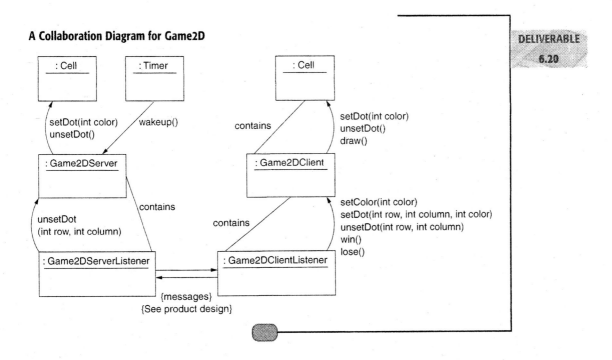

EXERCISE 6.6

Trace through each scenario on the diagram shown in Deliverable 6.20 to verify that the collaboration diagram supports all the use cases for Game2D.

Also note that the collaboration diagram in Deliverable 6.20 shows three *contains* links between objects. These links ensure that objects passing messages contain a reference to the object that is to receive the message. These links, therefore, give detail about the attribute lists of the relevant classes. For example, the *contains* link between the *Game2DServer* and the *Game2DServerListener* specifies that the *Game2DServer* class must have an instance variable whose type is *Game2DServerListener*.

Because sequence diagrams convey all the information contained in collaboration diagrams and also portray the order sequence of all interobject message passing, it is not advisable to consolidate more than one or two scenarios in a single diagram.

Thus, Deliverable 6.21 shows the sequence diagram of two use cases: *Client Communicates Player Action* and *Server Communicates That Dot Is to Be Removed from a Cell*. The sequence of actions begins when the user clicks the mouse on a cell. The *Game2DClient* object invokes the *unsetDot* method of the corresponding *Cell* object, which is identified as *grid[i][j]* in the diagram. Next, the *Game2DClient* object communicates text over a socket connection to the *Game2DServerListener* object. Note that the *i* and *j* of the socket message are the index values of the grid element whose dot is being unset. The *Game2DServerListener* object then propagates the same message to the *Game2DClientListener* object of the opponent, which invokes the *unsetDot* method of its corresponding *Game2DClient* object. Finally, the corresponding *Cell* object is sent an *unsetDot* message with an invalid color value so that the opponent does not receive points.

DELIVERABLE 6.21

A Sequence Diagram for Two Use Cases: *Client Communicates Player Action* **and** *Server Communicates That Dot Is to Be Removed from a Cell*

{mouse click on a cell initiates this sequence diagram}

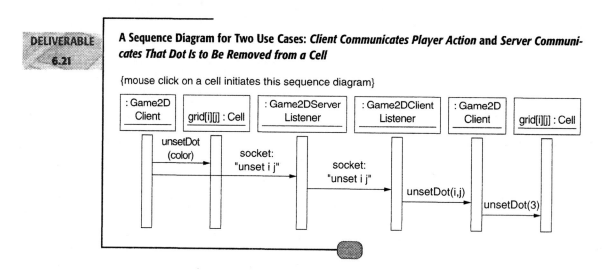

EXERCISE 6.7   Develop sequence diagrams for the remaining use cases: *Client Communicates Player Sign-On, Server Communicates a Dot Is Set in a Cell*, and *Server Communicates Game Is Won/Lost*.

6.7.2 Object Diagrams

An object diagram shows a snapshot of the executing system, including possible attribute values for particular objects. If more than one object of any class is in existence during the snapshot, the object diagram shows multiple instances of the class. These diagrams help the software designer refine the attribute list of each class and determine whether additional classes are necessary. Although attributes may be recorded at any time during the development process, the creation of the object diagram stresses refinement of the attribute list more than the preceding steps do.

Deliverable 6.22 shows an object diagram consisting of allocated objects associated with a particular *Game2DClient* object at a particular moment in time. During the course of a game, two *Game2DClient* objects will be allocated, one for each player. Since each player is using a separate machine, however, only one *Game2DClient* object will typically be allocated on an individual processor. Deliverable 6.22 shows the two-dimensional array, called *grid*, that contains the *Cell* objects. In order to save space, however, only one *Cell* object (*grid[0][0]*) is shown with its specific attribute values. Each *Cell* object contains an attribute for its *x* coordinate and one for its *y* coordinate on the applet window. The *Cell grid[0][0]* has *x,y* coordinates of 0,0, meaning that it appears in the upper left-hand corner of the applet window. The *Cell grid[1][0]*, on the other hand, has *x,y* coordinates 15,0 and the *Cell grid[0][1]* has *x,y* coordinates of 0,15 (because the *width* and *height* attributes for each *Cell* contain the value 15). Each *Cell* object also has an applet attribute whose value is the *Game2DClient* object itself, which is an applet. This applet reference allows each *Cell* to draw a circle (a *Dot*) of a particular color on the applet window when necessary. Recall that there is only one attribute (*color*) of *Dots* that must be kept. To keep our design simple, we have decided that it is not necessary to create a separate class for *Dot*. Instead, the *Cell* object now has a boolean attribute that specifies whether the *Cell* currently has a *dot*. In addition, the *Cell* objects contain an attribute called *color*. When the *Cell* does not have a *dot*, the value in *color* is 0. If the *Cell* does have a *dot*, the value in *color* will be 1 if the *dot* is blue and 2 if the *dot* is red.

Also associated with the *Game2DClient* object are instances of *Game2DClientListener* and *Socket*. The *Socket* class is standard in the Java Development Kit and allows communication over the Internet between processes. The *Game2DClientListener* object is instantiated by the *Game2DClient*, but the *Game2DClient* does not contain a reference to the listener object in its attribute list. Instead, the listener object contains an applet object in its attribute list, and this attribute refers to the *Game2DClient* object, which is an applet. When the *Game2DClient* object instantiates the *Game2DClientListener* object, it passes a reference to itself (using the key word *this*) and a reference to its *Socket* object to the constructor of the *Game2DClientListener* object. The *Game2DClientListener* object executes in a separate thread of control, and when it receives a message via the *Socket* object, it passes this message to the *Game2DClient*, which responds appropriately.

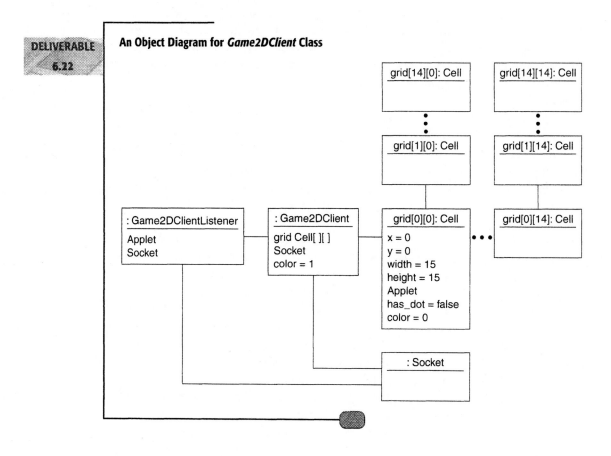

DELIVERABLE 6.22

An Object Diagram for *Game2DClient* Class

EXERCISE 6.8   Create an object diagram for the *Game2DServer* class. Model this class immediately after game initiation when both players and associated *Game2DServerListener* instances are created.

6.7.3 Reuse

At the conclusion of every development phase, it is useful to scrutinize the current model of the system for possible code reuse opportunities. One strategy commonly employed during design is to look for possible inheritance hierarchies. In reviewing the class diagram in Deliverable 6.19, one notices that both the *Game2DClient* and *Game2DServer* classes contain *Cell* objects. Recall that the *Game2DClient* class embodies the graphical user interface, with its grid of *Cells*, seen by the user. The

Game2DServer class, however, executes on the server machine, with no graphical representation of the *Cell* objects.

The primary question to be answered is whether the *Cell* objects used by the GUI-based *Game2DClient* class are the same as the strictly logical representation of the *Cell* objects contained in the nongraphical *Game2DServer* class. Is it possible to create a single *Cell* definition, including the graphical rendering necessary for the *Game2DClient* class, and allow it to be used by the nongraphical *Game2DServer* class? The answer to this question is no. The primary use of *Cell* objects is to *set* and *unset dots*. The methods to accomplish these tasks must make calls to graphical drawing methods in the *Game2DClient* class. Such calls made from the *Game2DServer* class on the server machine make no sense. In other words, when the *Game2DClient* class sets or unsets a dot in a cell, a boolean flag must be set, and a dot must be graphically rendered or erased, while the *Game2DServer* class only resets the boolean flag.

This dual role of the *Cell* class suggests that at least two distinct classes are called for, preferably organized in an inheritance hierarchy. Selecting the nongraphical version as the base class is appropriate because the graphical rendering can be considered additional detail added to the class. Figure 6.1 shows a detailed portrayal of a possible inheritance hierarchy accommodating both types of cells. The *Game2DServer* class, therefore, must contain a two-dimensional array of objects whose type is *Cell*, while the *Game2DClient* class contains a two-dimensional array of objects whose type is *GraphicalCell*. The *GraphicalCell* class contains all the attributes of the *Cell* class plus some additional ones to allow graphical rendering of a *dot*. The *GraphicalCell* also contains all of the methods of the *Cell* class, although it overrides the *setDot( )* and *unsetDot* method, again, to allow graphical rendering or erasing of the *dot*. The *GraphicalCell* class contains one additional method, *draw( )*, which renders the *Cell* as a rectangle on the applet window.

Another challenge for code reuse is the *Timer* class. Note that in Deliverable 6.19, both the *Game2DInitiator* and the *Game2DServer* are *prompted* by the *Timer* class. In other words, both classes are timed classes. The *Game2DInitiator* requires a *Timer* to determine whether a player has been waiting long enough to begin the game without an opponent. The *Game2DServer* requires a *Timer* to determine whether a sufficient interval has passed for the generation of a new *dot*. Rather than creating a timer inheritance hierarchy, we will create a single *Timer* class that addresses several needs. To maximize its utility, the objectives of this class are conceptualized in a general manner. For example, the timing interval must be specifiable by the class that uses the *Timer*, and therefore the *Timer* constructor should accept a time interval. The class that uses the *Timer* is called the timed class. The event that is to occur after the time interval has passed varies as well and should be coded in the timed class rather than in the *Timer* class. The *Timer*

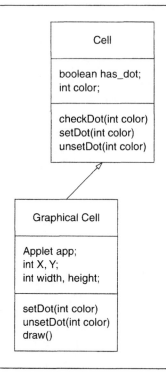

FIGURE 6.1 An Inheritance Hierarchy for the *Cell* Class

object, when the interval has passed, will invoke a method from the timed class. In other words, every timed class must have a method with a particular name, for example, *wakeup( )*, that can be called by the *Timer* class when the time interval is over. One means to facilitate the invocation of a method from an unknown set of classes is to create an *Interface* called *Timed*. The timed class then *implements* the *Timed* interface. Note that an *Interface* is a special mechanism included in Java that allows multiple inheritance without the major issues usually involved in multiple inheritance. Such a situation stipulates that a particular method, for example, *wakeup( )*, must be overridden. In other words, the class that implements the *Interface* is obligated to override all the methods inherited from the *Interface*.

EXERCISE 6.9 Design the *Timer* class, the *Timed* interface, and the two timed classes, *Game2D-Initiator* and *Game2DServer*, in accordance with the given specifications.

6.7.4 Class Skeletons

The final step of design is to integrate all the information derived from the entire set of models created thus far and produce a set of class skeletons for each new class required by the software system. The possible categories of information that comprise a class skeleton are

- Class semantics and roles
- Information maintenance
- Instance variables
- Class variables
- Class constants
- Constructors
- Static methods
- Nonstatic methods

Information about the semantics of a class and the roles it plays in the system specifies the purpose of the class in the system. Information maintenance is concerned with the persistent information that is found in the system and how that information is kept current. The instance variables for the class detail the data that are allocated for each individual instance of the class. The class variables contain information that is allocated for the class as a whole and are, therefore, shared among instances of the class. The class constants are similar to class variables except that their content cannot be varied (hence, the word *constants*). The constructors for a class specify the actions that must occur when an instance of the class is allocated. The static methods for a class are methods that belong to the class and therefore do not operate on any particular instance of the class. The nonstatic methods for a class are methods that perform actions on individual instances of the class.

Deliverables 6.23–6.25 show the class skeletons for the classes *Game2D-Client*, *Game2DServer*, *Game2DServerListener*, and *Game2DInitiator*. Categories of information not relevant to these class definitions are simply omitted from the skeletons. For example, the category *constructor* is omitted from the class *Game2DClient* because the class extends the class *Applet* and applets do not require a constructor. The category *information maintenance* has also been omitted from all classes because no record of games played, players, or game state is kept between system invocations. The constants *MAX*, *WIDTH*, and *HEIGHT* have been defined in the *Game2DServer* class because the *Game2DServer* instance sends these values to the *Cell* constructor.

A Class Skeleton for the *Game2DClient* Class

```
public class Game2DClient extends Applet implements
MouseListener, ActionListener
{
// Class semantics and roles:
// This class embodies the GUI through which a player
// interacts with the game, and thus
// displays a graphical representation of the game board

// Instance variables:
private Graphical_Cell grid[][]; // Two-dimensional array of
// Graphical_Cells representing the game state
private int color; // The player's color (either 1 for blue
// or 2 for red)
private Socket sock; // Socket object connecting to the game
// server
private PrintWriter out; // An output stream built over the
// above socket connection

// Nonstatic Methods
public void paint(Graphics g)
// Override Applet method. Render the array of Graphical_Cells
// with their dots.

public void setColor(int c)
// Update the instance variable, color, to the value of the
// parameter, c, and communicate that the player is
// Blue (c=1) or Red (c=2) on the Applet window

public void setDot(int i, int j, int c)
// send a message to the Graphical_Cell object which is
// element at row i and column j in the grid array
// set the dot to color c. precondition: the 2-D array of
// Graphical_Cells has been instantiated. c has value 1
// or 2 only. postcondition: Graphical_Cell object
// reflects a dot is set with color c.

public void unsetDot(int i, int j)
// send a message to the Graphical_Cell object which is at row
```

```
// i and column j in the grid array removing the dot.
// precondition: the 2-D array of Graphical_Cells has been
// instantiated. postcondition: Graphical_Cell object reflects
// a dot is not set.

public void win( )
// communicate to the player that he/she won the game and
// remove the MouseListener

public void lose( )
// communicate to the player that he/she lost the game and
// remove the MouseListener

public void actionPerformed(ActionEvent e)
// implements abstract method of ActionListener
// If the Start Game button has been pressed and no Socket
// object has been created, establish the Socket connection
// to the server process at port 8120. Also create a
// ReaderBuffer and PrintWriter over the Socket, and create
// and start a Game2DClientListener. precondition: a
// Game2DServer is executing on the specified remote
// machine on port 8120. postcondition: a Game2DClient
// Listener object is ready to accept
// communication from the server.

public void mousePressed(MouseEvent e)
// implements abstract method of MouseListener. Get coordinate
// of mouse press and send unset message to Graphical_Cell
// object rendered around that point in the Applet window.
// Send message to server communicating the index values of
// the Graphical_Cell object being unset.
// precondition: a Game2DServerListener is reading information
// over the socket connection.
// postcondition: Specified Graphical_Cell object is unset at
// server, player's and opponent's game representation.

}// end class Game2DClient
```

A Class Skeleton for the *Game2DServer* Class

```
public class Game2DServer
{
// Class semantics and roles:
// This class orchestrates a single game between two remote
// players. It is created by Game2DInitiator. Game2DServer
// embodies a logical representation of the game board and
// communicates the removal of dots from one player to the
// other. Game2DServer has an associated timer class that
// prompts it to pick random cells to place blue and red
// dots. The placement and color of the dots is then
// communicated to both players. At game initiation, this
// class assigns the color blue or red to each player.

// Instance variables:
private Socket player1, player2; // A socket connection to
// each remote player
private PrintWriter p1out, p2out; // Output stream to player1
// (p1) and player2 (p2)
private Timer t; // The timer object that prompts the setting
// of a new dot
private int Player_Turn
private Cell grid[][]; // logical representation of the game
// board

// Class Constants
public static final MAX = 15;
public static final WIDTH = 15;
public static final HEIGHT = 15;

// Constructors
public Game2DServer(Socket p1, Socket p2)
// This constructor accepts two socket objects created by the
// class Game2DInitiator and creates PrintWriter objects
// built on top of these to communicate change in game status
// to the remote players. It also allocates a two-dimensional
// array of Cell objects (grid), assigning an x,y coordinate
// and dimension to each Cell object. MAX determines the
// dimension of the array, grid. It also creates and starts
```

```
// a Timer object, passing a self-reference and interval
// in milliseconds.


// Nonstatic Methods
public void unsetDot(int i, int j, int c)
// send a message to the Cell object which is at row i and
// column j in the grid array removing the dot, and add
// points to the appropriate player if color matches player
// color(c). precondition: the 2-D array of Cells has been
// instantiated. postcondition: Cell object reflects a dot
// is not set, and play points may change.


public void wakeup( )
// pick two random values between 0 and MAX-1 inclusive to
// serve as index values in the 2D array of Cells (grid),
// selecting a Cell and setting an alternating blue or red
// dot. then scan neighboring cells to determine if the
// game has been lost or won, if so communicate the winning
// or losing of the game. Communicate the setting of the
// dot to both players.


} // end class Game2DServer
```

A Class Skeleton for the *Game2DServerListener* and *Game2DInitiator* Classes

DELIVERABLE
6.25

```
public class Game2DServerListener extends Thread
{
// Class semantics and roles:
// This class is created by Game2DServer to read messages
// sent from one of the two client processes. It reads
// and writes over the socket connection to its connected
// player and passes along the messages from its player to
// the opponent. It also sends a message to the Game2DServer
// object to allow the updating of the state of the logical
// game representation in response to unsetDot messages.


// Instance variables:
private Socket me, you; // socket connections to player (me)
```

```
    // and opponent (you)
    private int color; // color of player
    private Game2DServer game; // reference to communicate
    // unsetting dots

    // Constructors
    public Game2DServerListener(Socket s1, Socket s2, int c)
    // Assigns the parameters to associated instance variables.
    // s1 is the player socket, s2 is the opponent socket, and c
    // is the player's color

    // Nonstatic Methods
    public void run( )
    // Create input and output stream over player socket.
    // Communicate the player's color and that game is starting.
    // Until the socket connection is closed loop reading lines
    // over the socket input stream (unsetdot messages).
    // Communicate these lines to your opponent over the
    // previously created output stream (youout).

    } // end class Game2DServerListener

    public class Game2DInitiator
    {
    // Class semantics and roles:
    // This class creates a server socket and connects to one or
    // two client processes before a Game2DServer object is
    // created passing the socket objects to the constructor; the
    // server continues to create Game2DServer objects as
    // additional clients connect. After the first player
    // connects a Timer object is created which checks after 5
    // minutes to determine if a second player has connected to
    // the game and if not creates the connection so that
    // the game can proceed

    // Static Methods
    public void static main(String[] args)
    // implements the above class semantics

    } // end class Game2DInitiator
```

Create class skeletons for the *Timer*, *Cell*, and *Game2DClientListener* classes.   **EXERCISE 6.10**

 ## Method Design

The class skeletons produced during the class design phase reflect the necessary methods and attributes that are apparent from previous modeling steps. The methods specified in the skeleton may vary widely in abstractness. In other words, certain method definitions may be self-evident, whereas others may require careful design and efficiency assessment. For example, the *unsetDot( )* method in the *Game2DClient* class is precisely described in the method narrative of the class skeleton, while the *wakeup( )* method of the *Game2DServer* class is more complex and may benefit from a more precise specification. The process of specifying more detail in the method definitions frequently makes the need for additional attributes or methods apparent. One may not assume, therefore, that class skeletons are not modified after their creation. These class skeletons continue to be refined as the software development progresses.

6.8.1 Specifying Methods

A number of techniques exist for specifying algorithms. Some common techniques include **Nassi-Shneiderman** charts [74], **flowcharts** [93], **pseudocode** and **decision tables** [49]. For the sake of expediency, only pseudocode and decision tables will be considered here.

Pseudocode is a means to concisely characterize the steps of an algorithm with an informal syntax rather than the formal syntax of programming languages. For example, one may write "while socket is open" to specify that a block of code is executed iteratively until a socket connection closes. When this line of pseudocode is translated into programming language instructions, more than one instruction may be necessary. For example, we may need to introduce a boolean variable for the loop condition, check the various circumstances under which a socket connection may be closed, and reset the boolean variable accordingly.

We will specify blocks of pseudocode through indentation. For example,

```
while socket is open
    read String over socket connection.
    communicate String to opponent
terminate thread
```

means that the two lines of pseudocode following the `while` statement are part of the block to be iterated and that `terminate thread` is outside the `while` statement.

Decision tables are used to supplement pseudocode, making it easier to represent a series of related conditions. For example, the condition under which the game can be lost can be concisely characterized with pseudocode followed by a decision table as follows:

```
pick random numbers i,j between 0 and MAX-1
Set dot in Cell grid[i][j] to color c
```

grid[i+1][j] has dot color c	Player c loses game
grid[i-1][j] has dot color c	Player c loses game
grid[i][j+1] has dot color c	Player c loses game
grid[i][j-1] has dot color c	Player c loses game

This table is an example of an extremely simple decision table. The first two lines of pseudocode preceding the table represent the context of the decision, specifically that a *dot* of color *c* is being set in *Cell grid[i][j]*. The first column of the decision table represents the *condition*, and the second column represents the *consequence* to be carried out if the condition is true. The table, therefore, expresses the conditions under which *Player c* loses the game. Decision tables typically involve multiple conditions and multiple consequences, making them more complex than the one shown.

6.8.2 Method Design for Game2D

Only methods that are not self-evident need to be pseudocoded, so we will only address methods that embody some amount of complexity. Recall from Deliverable 6.25 that the *Game2DInitiator* class contains a single method called *main( )*. This method must accept socket connections from two remote clients, create listener objects for each of these clients, create a *Game2DServer* object that contains the socket references for the clients, and create a *Timer* object that will begin the game if a second player has not connected in a certain amount of time.

The pseudocode for the *main( )* method of *Game2DInitiator* is

```
create server socket: S
loop forever    // this creates infinitely many games
    accept client connection, called P1, on Socket S
    create listener object using
         Game2DServerListener(P1,null,Game2DServer.BLUE)
    create Timer object using
         Timer(300000,this)
```

```
accept client connection, called P2, on Socket S
create listener object using
        Game2DServerListener(P2,P1,Game2DServer.RED)
create Game2DServer object using
        Game2DServer(P1,P2)
```

Examining this pseudocode, three outstanding issues arise. These issues, as follows, must be accommodated with design changes:

- The constructor for the *Game2DServerListener* requires references to two socket connections. When the first *Game2DServerListener* object is created, we have a reference to only one socket connection, *P1*, while the other socket connection gets the value *null*. When the second *Game2DServerListener* object is created, the second socket connection, *P2*, must be passed to the first *Game2DServerListener* object. Therefore, an *updateSock(Socket)* method must be defined in the *Game2DServerListener* class.
- Since the *Game2DServer* object created in the last step in the pseudocode coordinates the playing of the game between the two clients, both listener objects must contain a reference to the *Game2DServer* object. The *Game2DServer* object is created after the two listener objects; so the *Game2DServerListener* class requires another update method, called *connectGame(Game2DServer)*.
- The *Timer* constructor requires a reference to the timed object in order to be able to notify the timed object that the time interval has ended. In the case of the preceding pseudocode, the timed object is the *Game2DInitiator* object. Recall that the *Game2DInitiator* contains the *main()* method, the place where execution of this software will begin. In Java, the class that contains the *main()* begins execution, but no object of that class is allocated in memory. In other words, the *Game2DInitiator* class is not instantiated, and therefore no object of that type exists. The call to the *Timer* constructor with a reference to *this*, as specified previously, is invalid. Resolving this problem requires restructuring the class definition for *Game2DInitiator* so that the timed class is instantiated.

Restructuring the *Game2DInitiator* class so that it is instantiated is most easily done by simply creating another class to contain the *main()* method where execution begins. This new class must create an instance of *Game2DInitiator*. Of course, an alternative solution is that *Game2DInitiator* can create an instance of itself. This solution is somewhat confusing, and we have decided it is simpler to create another class for this purpose. Therefore, the class *G2DLaunch* is added to the design. Deliverable 6.26 shows the newly restructured class skeleton for *Game2DInitiator* and the new class *G2DLaunch*.

Revised Class Skeleton for *Game2DInitiator* and Skeleton for New Class *G2DLaunch*

```
public class G2DLaunch
{
// Class semantics and roles:
// This class creates an instance of the Game2DInitiator
// and starts the Thread

// Static Methods
public void static main(String[] args)
// creates an instance of Game2DInitiator and starts the
// Thread

} // end class G2DLaunch

public class Game2DInitiator implements Timed
{
// Class semantics and roles:
// This class creates a server socket and connects to one
// or two client processes before a Game2DServer object is
// created passing the socket objects to the constructor.
// The server continues to create Game2DServer objects as
// additional clients connect. After the first player
// connects a Timer object is created which checks after
// 5 minutes to determine if a second player has connected
// to the game and if not creates the connection so that
// the game can proceed.

// Instance variables:
private Socket p2_sock; // Opponent's socket reference is
// checked in wakeup( )

// Constructors: default used

// Nonstatic Methods
public void run( )
// This method creates a server socket and connects to one
// or two client processes before a Game2DServer object is
// created passing the socket objects to the constructor.
// After the first player connects a Timer object to
// potentially interrupt the blocking
```

```
// for a second client connection.

public void wakeup( Timer t)
// check the opponent's Socket reference (p2_sock) for null.
// If null, create a local loop-back connection so that the
// game may proceed. unconditionally stop the timer (t)

} // end class Game2DInitiator
```

Notice that the *Game2DInitiator* class no longer contains a method called *main()* but instead contains a method called *run()*. The *run()* method now contains the algorithm for creating socket connections as described previously (and containing the modifications required to solve the first two issues in the preceding list). After the *Game2DInitiator* object is created, its *run()* method is called. In addition, two other changes have occurred in the class skeleton to allow *Game2DInitiator* objects to be timed. The first is that the class *Game2DInitiator* now implements the *Timed* interface. The second is that the class now overrides the *wakeup()* method, specifying the actions to be performed when the time interval has ended.

6.8.3 Creating Quality Methods

Recall that good module design requires that the modules are

- Cohesive
- Loosely coupled
- Encapsulated
- Reusable

Although the modules of primary interest in previous chapters were classes, methods constitute another type of module, and these principles also apply to good method design.

To illustrate the listed principles of good module design in context of the Game2D case study, consider the *run()* method of the *Game2DServerListener*. The objective of this method is to read a *String* from a socket connection to one of the clients, to pass the *String* to the other client by way of a socket connection, and to unset dots in cells in response to the content of the *String*. To determine the content of the *String* in order to respond to it, the *run()* method of the *Game2DServerListener* must parse the *String*. Pseudocode for the *run()* method might therefore be `parse and handle client message`. This statement actually encompasses two related but very different subgoals. To allow maximum cohesion and reusability, it is probably advisable to extract the logic required for the parsing of the *String*, creating a new method called *parseUnset(String)*. The cumulative changes made to the *Game2DServerListener* class are shown in the class skeleton in Deliverable 6.27.

DELIVERABLE
6.27

Revised Class Skeleton for the *Game2DServerListener* Class

```
public class Game2DServerListener extends Thread
{
// Class semantics and roles:
// This class is created by Game2DServer to read messages
// sent from one of the two client processes. It reads and
// writes over the socket connection to its connected
// player and passes along the messages from its player to
// the opponent. It also sends a message to the Game2DServer
// object to allow the updating of the state of the logical
// game representation in response to unsetDot messages.

// Instance variables:
private Socket me, you;
// socket connections to player (me) and opponent (you)
private PrintWriter youout; // Output stream over opponent's
// Socket
private int color; // color of player
private Game2D game;
// reference to Game2D to communicate unsetting dots

// Constructors:
public Game2DServerListener(Socket s1, Socket s2, int c)
// Assigns the parameters to associated instance variables.
// s1 is the player socket, s2 is the opponent socket, and c
// is the player's color

// Nonstatic Methods
public void run( )
// Create input and output stream over player socket.
// Communicate the player's color and that game is starting.
// Until the socket connection is closed loop reading lines
// over the socket input stream (unsetdot messages).
// Communicate these lines to your opponent over the
// previously created output stream (youout).
```

```
public void updateSock(Socket y)
// Used by listener for first player to update socket
// reference to second player. Updates instance variable
//  (you) and creates the PrintWriter (youout)

public void connectGame(Game2D g)
// Assign parameter to instance variable (game)

public void ParseUnset(String s)
// Parse String read over the player socket and extract
// Cell index values and player color. invoke the unsetDot
//  method of Game2D to update its logical representation.


} // end class Game2DServerListener
```

6.9   Questions for Review

1. Create the requirements specification for a program that manages the personal finances of an individual, so that it conveniently handles the income and expenditures of a typical student on a monthly basis.

2. Review your requirements specification for the personal finance management system created in question 1, and remove any nonessential features. For example, the ability to classify certain expenditures in terms of a list of predefined categories is essential to the system, while predicting expenditures per category for future months is not essential. Compare notes with a classmate to determine how different your essential versions of the system are.

3. Create a list of primary classes for your personal finance management system.

4. Create two key use cases for your personal finance management system. One use case should involve calculating the current monthly balance.

5. Create a class diagram showing the relationships between your primary classes as portrayed in the use cases developed in question 4.

6. Design the user interface for your personal finance management system, and update your primary class list created in question 3, if necessary. Compare your interface with that of a classmate.

7. Create either a collaboration diagram or sequence diagram portraying the interclass relationships discussed in the use cases of question 4.

8. Design the method that calculates the current monthly balance. Specify the remaining methods and attributes of the class where this method is defined.

9. Create the requirements specification for a client/server, two-player version of the game Battleship. Battleship is a game in which two players have a two-dimensional grid of points and a fleet of ships of varying lengths, so that each ship takes up two to five points on the grid and no ships may overlap. Each player places his or her ships on the grid along a row or column of points on the grid. Each player takes turns specifying a point on his or her opponent's grid. If that point contains a part of a battleship, the opponent must say "hit"; otherwise the player indicates that the specified point misses. If that point hits a battleship and causes each point of the battleship to have been hit, then the player indicates that the battleship has been sunk. A player wins when he or she has sunk every battleship of his or her opponent.

10. Make a list of questions that you would ask the users in order to clarify your understanding of the Battleship game. Designate a classmate or the instructor to serve as the user, and pose your questions to him or her.

11. Exchange your requirements specification for Battleship with a classmate, and critique each other's solution. Identify significant areas in which your solution differs from your classmate's solution. In which cases did the difference minimally impact the game, and in which cases were the differences significant?

12. Create a list of primary classes from your requirements specification of Battleship.

13. Create a class diagram showing the essential relationships between the primary classes of Battleship.

14. Design the user interface for Battleship. Compare your interface with that produced by a classmate. Based on a critique of both interfaces, suggest improvements.

15. Specify the responsibilities of the client and server classes of the Battleship game. Design the client/server socket communication scheme, and identify any new classes necessary to support the transmission of information over the socket. Create a state machine that models the client/server communication.

16. Specify the complete design in the class skeleton (everything except the method algorithms) of the client class that embodies the graphical user interface for Battleship.

17. Contemplate a text-only version of Battleship. Which classes are affected, and which are not? Is the primary class list changed as a result of moving to a text-only user interface?

18. Contemplate a single-user version of Battleship, in which the computer serves as the opponent. Which classes are affected, and which are not? Is the primary class list changed as a result of moving to a single-user version of the game?

Implementation

CHAPTER **7**

Key Concepts

- Implementation
- Big Bang implementation
- Top-down implementation
- Bottom-up implementation
- Thread implementation
- Implementation plan

- Programming style
- Internal documentation
- Header comment block
- Line comments
- Coding standards

Introduction

Until now, all of our activities have been geared toward representing the functionality of our software system in ways that can be easily understood by human beings. In the implementation phase of software development, we must make a shift toward representing our software in a manner that can be understood by the computer. Implementation involves the creation of code in a programming language that can be executed by the computer. To implement the system, the design documents that have been created must be translated into the chosen programming language so that all the functionality specified in the design works properly in the implemented system. To ensure that the functionality is there, a significant amount of organized, well-structured testing must be done. As soon as coding begins, formal testing must also begin.

Implementation Approaches

Recall that in the object-oriented software development paradigm, classes can be organized in inheritance hierarchies in which the child classes reuse code that was written for the parent classes. The classes represent the modularity of the software system. The methods for the classes represent a second level of modularity. In implementing the software, we must decide the order in which the modules are to be built. In particular, do we start with the top-level modules, with the highest level of abstraction, and code those first? Or do we start with the bottom-level modules, with the lowest level of abstraction, and code those first?

A major advantage of using the object-oriented paradigm in developing software is that the software can be **evolved**. The software can be built in stages, one upon the other. In fact, we can move back and forth between the various phases of the object-oriented software development process as needed. For example, we may analyze part of the system to be developed, then design a solution for that part of the system, and then move back to the analysis phase for the next part of the system. This ability to move back and forth between development phases carries over into the implementation and testing phases as well. In fact, there is no way to separate the implementation phase of software development from the testing phase. The point is that we will implement and test the pieces of the software system that have been designed up to this point. If the entire system has been designed, then we will implement and test the entire system, again through an evolutionary process. If only a piece has been designed, then we will implement and test just that piece of the system in an evolutionary manner. In any case, we can begin our implementation and testing in either a top-down or a bottom-up manner.

Figure 7.1 shows four approaches to implementation and the advantages and disadvantages of each approach. Each of these approaches to implementing and testing software is discussed in the following subsections.

7.3.1 Big Bang Implementation

Beginning programming students and masochistic programmers typically attempt to build software using the **Big Bang method** [73], in which every module in the system is coded separately. Once the entire system has been coded, the individual modules are thrown together to see what happens. This method leads to disastrous failures. Finding bugs in software that has been built using the Big Bang method is extremely difficult, if not impossible. The Big Bang method has nothing to recommend it and should be avoided.

Approach	Advantages	Disadvantages
Big Bang	None	1. Difficult to debug 2. Much throwaway code 3. Critical and peripheral modules not distinguished 4. User does not see product until very late
Top-Down	1. Separately debugged modules 2. System test by integrating previously debugged modules 3. Stubs easier than drivers 4. User interfaces are top-level modules	1. Stubs must be written 2. Low-level, critical modules built last 3. Testing upper-level modules difficult
Bottom-Up	1. Separately debugged modules 2. System test by integrating previously debugged modules 3. Testing upper-level modules easier	1. Drivers must be written 2. Upper-level, critical modules built last 3. Drivers more difficult than stubs 4. User interfaces are top-level modules
Threads	1. Separately debugged modules 2. System test by integrating previously debugged modules 3. Critical modules built first 4. Users assess critical modules early	1. Which modules to implement first?

FIGURE 7.1   **Implementation Approaches—Some Advantages and Disadvantages**

7.3.2 Top-Down versus Bottom-Up Implementation

In a top-down implementation, we start at the top of the hierarchy of modules and proceed to the lower levels. When dealing with object-oriented systems, a top-down implementation means that, first, the class where execution will start [the class that contains the *main( )* or *init( )* method] is implemented. In implementing this class, we start with the *main( )* or *init( )* method itself, leaving all classes it allocates and methods that it calls as **stubs**. A stub is a **dummy method** or **dummy class**. A dummy method is a method whose body does not yet function fully because it is not completely coded. A dummy class is one that contains all its necessary constructors with incomplete method bodies along with any other dummy methods necessary to test the initial class.

For example, assume we decide that the first piece of the Libray Management System that we will implement is an applet that will allow the entering of information about new *Resource* objects that have been purchased by the library. To implement this simple applet, we will need three classes, as shown in Figure 7.2. The *NewResourceApp* class is a child class of the applet class that is a standard part of Java. Its primary purpose is to provide a graphical user interface for entering information about new resources. Execution begins in this class, and therefore our implementation will begin here. A *Resource* object is created by the *NewResourceApp* with the information that is entered by the user by means of the GUI. Once the *Resource* object is successfully created, it is added to the *Library Database* object, where it is permanently stored. To begin the implementation of this functionality of the LMS, we code the three classes with their instance variables and all the methods that we know we will need. These methods have no instructions yet in their bodies. For example, the *checkDuplicates( )* method of the *Library Database* class is

```
public boolean checkDuplicates(Resource r)
{
    return true;
}
```

These methods are stubs. The details of the *NewResourceApp* class are implemented next. We start with the building of the GUI in the *init( )* method. We test the GUI to ensure that it looks the way we want it to, and then we proceed to the other methods of the *NewResourceApp* class. In this case, there is only one other method, *actionPerformed( )*, and it is this method which creates the *Resource* object and calls the appropriate methods to add it to the *Library Database*. Once we have completely coded the *NewResourceApp* class and ensured that it works as expected, we can begin the coding and testing of the *Resource* class, and then, finally, we can code and test the *Library Database* class. In this example, our implementation (and testing) proceeded in a top-down manner.

In a bottom-up implementation, we build the software starting at the bottom of the class inheritance hierarchy, although it is not necessarily a strict reversal of the top-down order. The first classes to be coded and tested are those that only allocate or reference primitive or predefined classes. The classes coded first will be nearly complete, except that the classes that utilize them will not be written yet. Therefore, **drivers**, or methods that call the lower-level modules, must be created to test them. The implementation process then proceeds upward through the higher levels, where we define **higher-level classes** as classes that allocate or reference primitive types, predefined classes, and classes that have already been tested. This process continues until we have implemented and tested all classes.

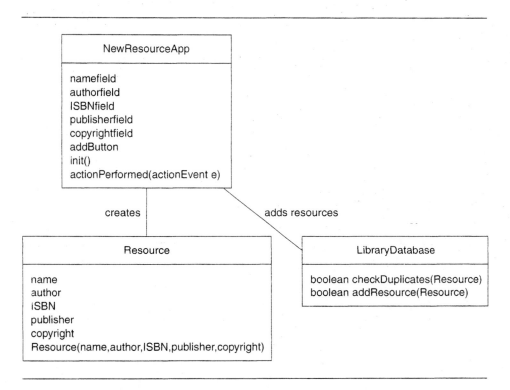

FIGURE 7.2   Implementing the *NewResourceApp* Function in a Top-Down Manner

If we were to implement the capability of a user to add a new resource in a bottom-up manner, we would probably implement and test the *Resource* class first. The testing of that class would require that we write a driver class with a method that creates a *Resource* object. The driver class must display the *Resource* object in a way that allows us to determine whether it was created properly. The code for the driver class is thrown away once we are convinced the *Resource* class has been properly coded. Once we have coded and tested the *Resource* class, we then begin the implementation of the *Library Database* class, again creating a driver class for testing. Finally, we implement and test the *NewResourceApp* class.

Unfortunately, the process of bottom-up implementation and testing is not always as well defined as the top-down process. There will be situations where the next class to be implemented will require not only a driver class but one or more stubs as well. This necessity arises because of mutual references between classes. Figure 7.3 illustrates such a case of class mutual reference, complicating the sequence of coding classes by requiring the creation of stubs. Note in the figure that the classes *M1, M2,* and *M3* each contain a reference to the other two classes.

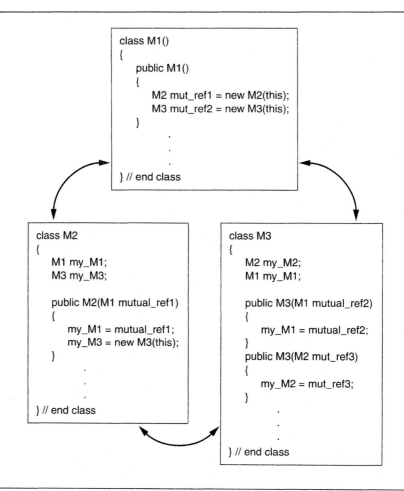

FIGURE 7.3   An Illustration of Class Mutual Reference

So, the first class to be coded requires two stub classes, the second requires one stub, and the last does not require any. The actual order is arbitrary, but may be influenced by the ease with which the classes may be implemented.

When the software is implemented from the top down, testing the higher-level modules requires the creation of stubs for the lower-level modules. The use of stubs means that our testing is also proceeding in a top-down manner. When software is implemented from the bottom up, testing the lower-level modules requires the creation of drivers for the higher-level modules. The use of drivers means that our testing is proceeding in a bottom-up manner. The decision of whether to implement the system in a top-down or bottom-up manner affects the order in which the modules that comprise the system are implemented and tested.

Both top-down and bottom-up approaches are examples of **incremental development**. The system is built a bit at a time rather than in one monumental effort. As soon as a module has been coded, it is tested. The module is then added to the previously coded and tested modules to determine how it works with those modules. If a problem arises, the most likely source for the problem is the most recently added module. In most instances, bugs can be found relatively easily.

7.3.3 Combining the Top-Down and Bottom-Up Approaches

The best order for implementing software modules depends upon a variety of factors. Using a top-down method with stubs, it is often possible to allow users to interact with the system in a fairly realistic manner and get useful feedback very early in the implementation and testing process. Because the use of stubs is similar to the process used when building prototypes, the top-down approach is particularly useful when the design of the system is not complete before the implementation begins. For example, in the *NewResourceApp* example, if the implementation proceeds in a top-down manner, we first create a user interface with which a user can interact. This early interaction can often provide information about how the rest of the system must function.

Although stubs must be written in the top-down approach, these are often easier to write than drivers [73]. In the bottom-up approach, the low-level modules are implemented and tested first. If these low-level modules happen to be critical components of the system, they will receive extensive testing. For example, in the *NewResourceApp* example, the heart of the functionality is the storing of the *Resource* object information in the *Library Database*. This functionality is coded earlier in the bottom-up approach than in the top-down approach and will, therefore, receive more testing in the bottom-up approach. However, because the user interface will not be implemented and tested until relatively late in the bottom-up implementation process, the user cannot assess the operation of the system until much of it has already been built.

In practice, a combination of the two incremental approaches is used during coding of large systems [54]. The top-level modules generally contain both an overall picture of the final system and the user interfaces. By implementing and testing these modules first, the users can give early approval to the look and feel of the final software product. The bottom-level modules often contain the basic operations used by the upper-level modules. By coding these modules early, they can be tested early and often to be sure they are working correctly for each of the upper-level modules. This realization leads us to a third incremental approach to software implementation and testing that gives us the best of both worlds. This approach is called the **threads** approach [73].

7.3.4 Threads Approach to Implementation

Because of the difficulties already described, most software development projects are best implemented using a combination of the bottom-up and top-down approaches. The threads approach to implementation combines the bottom-up and top-down approaches to give us the best of both. A **thread** is a minimal set of modules that performs a critical function [73]. These modules probably come from different levels in our design hierarchy and interact across these levels to accomplish the appropriate function. Once this thread has been built and tested in some initial form, other modules can be added to complete the thread. The major advantage of this approach is that threads can be built and tested in parallel and separately. In addition, the users can experiment with the early, critical pieces of the system and provide early feedback on the system. The difficulty with the threads approach, however, is that the order in which modules should be implemented is not obvious.

How threads are effectively defined for a system is determined by the size and scope of a system in addition to the desired granularity of the threads. The granularity of the threads determines whether testing takes place over a large number of small threads or a small number of large threads. On the one hand, there is a certain overhead incurred by each thread, so an extremely large number of threads is not desirable. On the other hand, the larger the thread, the more difficult it is to test. If one selects a larger granularity of thread, use cases may be the appropriate focal point for thread definition, whereas a collaboration provides the focal point for threads of smaller granularity.

 Implementation Plan

Once the design phase of the software development has been completed, the developers must create an **implementation plan**. The implementation plan specifies which implementation strategy will be used as well as a schedule for **coding, unit testing, integration of units**, and **integration testing**. Figure 7.4 shows an abstract example of an implementation plan. The plan divides a project into phases, each of which must go through coding, unit testing, integration, and integration testing. Each step for each phase is assigned a start and end date within the overall project schedule. The steps through which each phase must pass during implementation are critical to the successful completion of the overall project.

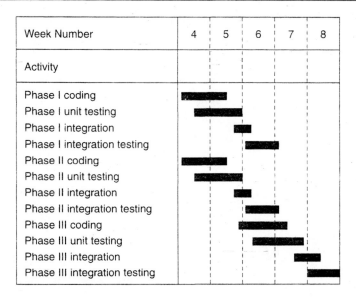

Week Number	4	5	6	7	8
Activity					
Phase I coding					
Phase I unit testing					
Phase I integration					
Phase I integration testing					
Phase II coding					
Phase II unit testing					
Phase II integration					
Phase II integration testing					
Phase III coding					
Phase III unit testing					
Phase III integration					
Phase III integration testing					

FIGURE 7.4   An Abstract Implementation Plan

Unit testing, which is the testing of each individual module, may require the coding of either stub modules or driver modules (or both). Integration involves writing code that combines the coded and tested modules to accomplish larger functions of the system. Integration testing is the testing of the combined modules to be sure that they work together properly.

Developing and disseminating an appropriate implementation plan is critical to the success of the project. The implementation plan organizes the activities that are required to complete the project successfully. All decisions that are made during the development of the implementation plan must be recorded and documented for later reference. To document these decisions in an object-oriented system, we will use the use case diagrams that were created during the design phase of development. Deliverable 7.1 shows a use case diagram for the LMS, as developed in Chapter 3.

To develop an implementation plan for the LMS, we must make some decisions concerning how critical the various functions of the system are. For most systems, no "correct" decision about criticality exists. Many different choices can be made and result in a successful implementation. In the next section, we will make some of these decisions for the LMS.

Use Case Diagram for the Library Management System

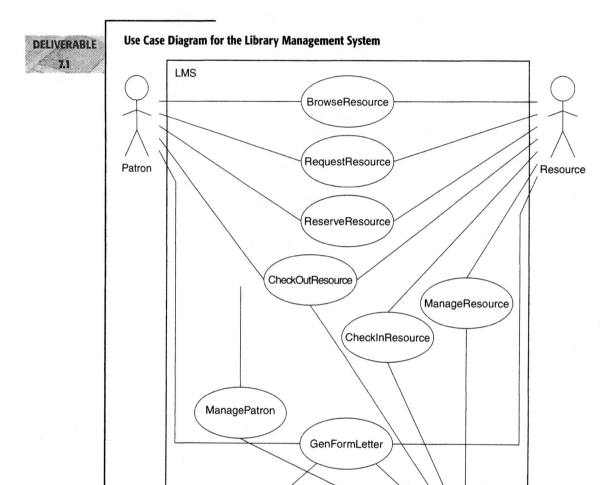

Case Study: **Implementation Plan for the LMS**

In discussions with users of the LMS, we discover that the most important aspect of the system is the ability of patrons to check out and return resources. The ability to add and delete resources is the next most important function of the system. The ability to add and delete patrons ranks next in importance, and finally, the ability to generate overdue form letters and the ability of patrons to request and reserve resources are of least importance. This information is very useful to us in developing our implementation plan for the system. The approach to implementation that we will use is the threads approach, in which we build and test the critical functionality of the system first and gradually add on the other layers of the system.

To document these decisions, we create another diagram, similar to the use case diagram, to be part of our implementation plan. Deliverable 7.2 shows this diagram for the LMS. The diagram illustrates the use cases that are to be implemented in each phase of the development process.

Deliverable 7.3 shows an implementation schedule for the completion of the LMS. To develop this schedule, we must know how many programmers and testers are on our development team. For the schedule shown in the figure, we assume that we have three programmers and three testers. Because Phase I of the project is most critical, at the beginning of the implementation phase two of the three programmers will work on coding these modules, while at the same time the third programmer will begin to code the Phase II modules. These two phases proceed in parallel.

Figure 7.5 shows another view of the implementation schedule. In this view the tasks of each programmer and tester are laid out week by week. Programmers 1 and 2 will begin in week 8 of the project by coding the Phase I modules, as indicated by Ic in the figure. Programmer 3 will begin in week 8 of the project by coding the Phase II modules, as is indicated by IIc in the figure. For the programmers, the letter c stands for coding, the letter i stands for integration, and the letters ci stand for coding and integration—that is, for part of the week the programmer is coding the basic modules, and for the rest of the week the programmer is integrating those modules. For the testers, the letter u stands for unit testing, the letter i stands for integration testing, the letter s stands for supervising user testing, and the letters is mean that for part of the week the user is involved in integration testing, and for the rest of the week, supervising user testing.

DELIVERABLE 7.2

Implementation Plan Diagram for the LMS

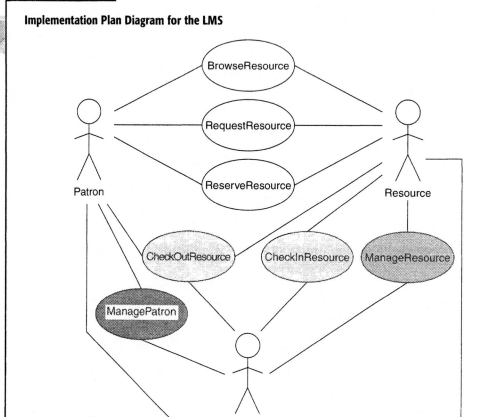

Implementation Schedule for the LMS

Week Number	8	9	10	11	12	13	14	15
Activity								
Phase I coding								
Phase I unit testing								
Phase I integration								
Phase I integration testing								
Phase I user testing								
Phase II coding								
Phase II unit testing								
Phase II integration								
Phase II integration testing								
Phase II user testing								
Phase III coding								
Phase III unit testing								
Phase III integration								
Phase III integration testing								
Phase III user testing								
Phase IV coding								
Phase IV unit testing								
Phase IV integration								
Phase IV integration testing								
Phase IV user testing								

Week Number	8	9	10	11	12	13	14	15
Team Member								
Programmer 1	Ic	Ic	Ici	Ii	IVc	IVc	IVci	
Programmer 2	Ic	Ic	IIIc	IIIc	IIIc	IIIi	IIIi	
Programmer 3	IIc	IIc	IIci	IIi	IVc	IVci	IVi	
Tester 1		Iu	Iu	Ii	Iis	IVu	IVu	IVs
Tester 2		IIu	IIu	IIi	IIis	IVu	IVi	IVi
Tester 3		Iu	Iu	IIIu	IIIu	IIIi	IIIis	IIIs

FIGURE 7.5 **Another View of the Implementation Schedule for the LMS**

When two or more programmers or testers are working on the same phase of the project implementation, much communication between these individuals must occur. For example, programmer 1 and programmer 2 must work very closely together in weeks 8 and 9 of the implementation in order to determine who will work on which parts of the coding of the Phase I modules. Similarly, tester 1 and tester 3 must work very closely together in weeks 9 and 10 while both are involved in unit testing the Phase I modules. In addition, the programmers and testers of these modules must be in constant communication, with the testers giving substantial feedback to the programmers. As is the case in most of the software development process, good communication is key to the successful implementation and testing of the system.

7.6 Programming Style

A programming style is a consistent pattern for carrying out some programming activity. Each programmer has probably learned his or her own unique style of programming. There are literally millions of ways to put together statements to accomplish a particular task, but each programmer tends to consistently choose certain patterns of statements [73].

The matter of defining a good programming style is largely subjective, but two factors related to good programming style are simplicity and readability [73]. **Simplicity** refers to the clarity of the code and the ease with which others are able to understand the code. **Readability** refers to the ease with which someone can scan the code and understand it. These two factors are clearly related, but complex code can be readable, and simple code can be written in a highly unreadable manner. For example, look at the code in Figure 7.6.

The code in Figure 7.6 is a segment of a program that calculates the number of dollar bills, quarters, dimes, nickels, and pennies to be given as change. The idea of this algorithm is very simple, but the way the code is written is extremely unreadable. For example, assume the code is placed into a larger program and compiled. Assume also that the compiler finds a mismatched brace, either { or }. Determining whether the braces in this code segment are all matched is not an easy task. Now, look at the code in Figure 7.7.

The actual statements in Figure 7.7 are exactly the same as those in Figure 7.6. The way the statements are spaced and lined up, however, is very different. If the code from Figure 7.7 were part of a program that the compiler indicates has some

```
while(amount>=1){
amount--;    dollars++;}
while(amount>=.25){
amount-=.25;    quarters++;}
while(amount>=.10 ){
amount-=.10;    dimes++;}
while(amount>=.05){
amount-=.05;    nickels++;}
while(amount>=.01){
amount-=.01;    pennies++;}
```

FIGURE 7.6   Not Very Readable Code

```
while(amount>=1)
{   amount--;
    dollars++;
}
while(amount>=.25)
{   amount-=.25;
    quarters++;
}
while(amount>=.10)
{   amount-=.10;
    dimes++;
}
while(amount>=.05)
{   amount-=.05;
    nickels++;
}
while(amount>=.01)
{   amount-=.01;
    pennies++;
}
```

FIGURE 7.7   More Readable Code

mismatched braces, we can easily scan this code to determine that all of these braces are indeed matched. This code segment is spaced and lined up so that it can easily be scanned to find the statements that belong to a particular block of code. Each programmer should attempt to develop a style of coding that is readable not only for the programmer but also for others who may need to examine the code at a later date.

EXERCISE 7.1   Find a program that you've written. Exchange it with another student in the class. Examine the code of the other student. How readable is the code? Point out techniques used in the code that make it readable. Point out techniques used in the code that make it unreadable. Rewrite the unreadable sections so that they are more readable. Share your ideas with the author of the code.

Simplicity of code is more difficult than readability to define and illustrate. Simplicity of the source code tends to be related to the design of the system. Individual programmers can, however, affect the simplicity of individual modules within the system. We will discuss three guidelines for coding simple individual modules:

- Shorter is simpler.
- Simpler code has fewer decisions.
- Excessively nested logic should be avoided.

7.6.1 Shorter Is Simpler

In general, the more code there is to read, the more complex the piece of software is. Therefore, to create simpler code, the programmer must write less code. Although other factors such as the number of parameters in a module also contribute to the complexity of a piece of code, research into software complexity has shown that the single most powerful factor in code complexity is code length. Like any general guideline, however, there are exceptions. Short code segments may be so terse that they require significant effort to determine their purpose. For example, consider the code segment in Figure 7.8, written in C.

This very short code segment is very complex and, therefore, difficult to understand. The code checks for an a in position i of a character array of length 10. If there is an a, it is changed to a b and the b is printed. If there is no a, the character in position i is simply printed. Compare the code segment from Figure 7.8 with the code segment in Figure 7.9, which accomplishes the same task.

The code in Figure 7.9 is three times as long as the code in Figure 7.8. Figure 7.9, however, is much simpler and easier to understand. Of course, the task can

```
i=-1;
while (i<9)
 printf("%c\n", myString[++i]=='a'?myString[i]='b':myString[i]);
```

FIGURE 7.8   Short but Complex Code Segment

```
i=0;
while (i<10)
{
    if (myString[i]=='a')
        myString[i]='b';
    printf("%c\n", myString[i]);
    i++;
}
```

FIGURE 7.9   Longer but Less Complex Code

be accomplished with many different sequences of statements. The point of this example is simply to show that terseness does not always translate into simplicity. In general, however, fewer lines of code means simpler code.

Look through some of your own programs, and find examples of code that could **EXERCISE 7.2** be made easier to understand if written with fewer statements. Rewrite the code. Find examples of code that could be made easier to understand if written with more statements. Rewrite the code.

7.6.2 Simpler Code Has Fewer Decisions

The number of decisions that must be made in a code segment relates to the complexity of the code segment. Each decision results in two different pathways that can be taken during execution, each of which may contain additional decisions that result in new pairs of pathways. The number of decisions to be made in a module has been proposed as a very simple measure of the complexity of the module [54]. Other researchers have proposed other measures of complexity that are directly related to the number of decisions in the module [67].

```
freqNum = -1;
freq = 0;
for (i=0; i<10; i++)
{   if (myArray[i] == freqNum)
        freq++;
    else
    {  tempFreqNum = myArray[i];
       tempFreq = 1;
       for (j=0; j<i; j++)
       {   if (myArray[j] == tempFreqNum)
               tempFreq++;
       }
       if (tempFreq > freq)
       {   freq = tempFreq;
           freqNum = tempFreqNum;
       }
    }
}
printf("most frequent is %d, occurring %d times\n",freqNum,freq);
```

FIGURE 7.10   Code Segment with Many Decisions to Be Made

When possible, the number of decisions in a module should be kept to a minimum. For example, consider the code segment shown in Figure 7.10. This segment determines which number in an array of ten positive numbers occurs most frequently and how many times it occurs. The code segment requires many decisions and is quite complex. Figure 7.11 shows a code segment that accomplishes the same task as the one in Figure 7.10. The code in Figure 7.11 requires fewer decisions and is easier to understand. Of course, the code segment in Figure 7.11 also has fewer lines of code and therefore follows the first simplicity principle as well.

EXERCISE 7.3   Look through some of your own programs, and find an example of some code that is complex because of the number of decisions. Can the code be rewritten? If it cannot be rewritten, explain why not. If it can be rewritten, do it.

```
        freqNum = -1;
        freq = 0;
        for (i=0; i<10; i++)
        {   tempFreqNum = myArray[i];
            tempFreq = 1;
            for (j=i+1; j<10; j++)
                if (myArray[j] == tempFreqNum)
                    tempFreq++;
            if (tempFreq > freq)
            {   freq = tempFreq;
                freqNum = tempFreqNum;
            }
        }
printf("most frequent is %d, occurring %d times\n",freqNum,freq);
```

FIGURE 7.11 Code Segment with Fewer Decisions

7.6.3 Excessively Nested Logic Should Be Avoided

Nested logic is an indication of poor design. If the nesting is more than three or four levels deep, the logic should be redesigned to reduce the nesting. Nested logic adds to the complexity of the code and, therefore, makes the code more difficult to understand. Figure 7.12 shows a code segment that determines which of three numbers is the largest. This code has three levels of nested *if . . . else* statements.

The code shown in Figure 7.13 also determines which of three numbers is the largest. This code, however, is easier to understand than the code in Figure 7.12 because there are no nested *if . . . else* statements. The code in Figure 7.13 has been redesigned to eliminate the nesting and, as a result, is much shorter and simpler than the original code. Also note that in the redesign we have eliminated the compound conditions on the *if* statements, and doing so has contributed to the greater simplicity of this code.

Look through some of your own programs and find an example of code that has either nested *if . . . else* statements or nested loop statements. Is the code well designed? If not, redesign the code and rewrite it. If it is well designed, can the readability of the code be improved? How would you improve the readability?

EXERCISE 7.4

```
int Max(int i,int j, int k)
{
    int m;
    if (i>j && i>k)
        m = i;
    else if (j>i && j>k)
            m = j;
        else
            m = k;
    return m;
}
```

FIGURE 7.12   Code with Nested *if . . . else* **Statements**

```
int Max(int i,int j, int k)
{
    int m = k;
    if (j>m)
        m = j;
    if (i>m)
        m = i;
    return m;
}
```

FIGURE 7.13   Code Without Nested *if . . . else* **Statements**

 Comments and Internal Documentation

Comments and internal documentation in source code are extremely important. Any successful system has a lifetime of years, and over the course of those years the code will require some modification. For the programmers who must carry out the modification, the major source of information about the code is likely to be the source code documentation. If this documentation is poorly written, the task of modifying the code will be much more difficult because the programmers will then have to rely on the source code itself to understand the system. If the documentation is well written, the modification task will be easier to complete.

When the coding of the system begins, some internal documentation will already have been written. In particular, the designers should have written substantial comments as they put together the class skeletons for the system. The additional comments required for documentation will vary from project to project, but there are several guidelines that should be followed in every project.

7.7.1 Header Comment Block

Each module in the system, whether the module is an entire class or a method in a class, has a header comment block that summarizes the module. This summary information includes such items as descriptions of the roles the module plays in the system; the purpose of the module; descriptions of the module's data structures, variables, algorithms, and flow of control; the author(s) of the module; the date of the final release of the module; and a version number. Deliverable 7.4 shows an example of the header comment block for the *CheckOut( )* method within the *Patron* class in the LMS.

Header Comment Block for *CheckOut( )* Method of the *Patron* Class

DELIVERABLE
7.4

```
// ***********************************************************
// *********** CheckOut() method in Patron class **********
// WRITTEN BY:  Jane Jones
// RELEASE DATE: January 31, 2001
// VERSION: 1.5
//
// PURPOSE: This method adds a resource to the checked-out
// resource list for the patron.  The due date for the
// resource is passed back to the calling method.
//
// DESIGN: The method takes an integer as an input parameter.
// The integer is the resource ID for the resource to be
// checked out.  The method adds this resource ID to the
// checked-out-resource list for the patron by calling the
// List class method addItem().  The method calculates a due
// date for the resource for this patron by first determining
// the type of resource (call to the getType() method of the
// Resource class) and then calling the getDueDate() method
// of the Patron class, passing in the resource type.  The
// method then changes the status of the resource to 'checked
// out' and adds the due date to the resource by calling the
```

```
// checkOut() method of the Resource class.
//
// PRECONDITION: ResourceID points to a legitimate Resource
// object that is available for checkout.
//
// POSTCONDITION: If checked-out-resource list for the Patron
// is null, one is created and this resource is added to it.
// Otherwise, a new Resource reference is added to the
// checked-out-resource list.
//
// MAJOR VARIABLES:
//   ResourceID -- integer passed in as a parameter.
//   Corresponds to the resource object that is to be
//   checked out.
//   ResourceList -- List instance variable for the Patron.
//   ResourceType -- integer for type of the resource to be
//   checked out.  1 = book, 2 = music CD, 3 = software,
//   4 = video, 5 = reserve item
//   DueDate -- Date variable on which the resource is due.
//   Returned from the getDueDate() method of the Patron
//   class and returned to the calling procedure.  The
//   value is also placed into the DueDate instance
//   variable for the Resource object.
//   Status -- String instance variable for the Resource
//   object. Will start as 'available' and end as
//   'checked out.'
//   DueDate -- Date instance variable for the Resource
//   object.
//**************************************************************
```

7.7.2 Line Comments

Line comments are inserted into the actual source code in order to give detailed information about what is happening in the module. These comments can be used to break the module into small, logical chunks of code. The comments explain each individual code chunk. The comments should provide useful information that does not simply repeat what the source code would already tell a programmer. By reading both these comments and the source code, the maintenance programmer should be able to understand very quickly how a code segment works. For example, our understanding of the following Java statement is not augmented by its line comment:

```
i++;          // increment i
```

Well-written line comments should add to our understanding of the source code. The following comment better explains its source code statement:

```
i++;          // set counter to read the next resource in
              // the resource list
```

In fact, the names chosen for variables can aid in the internal documentation process. Rather than using the generic variable name *i* for the counter in the resource list and then commenting it well, we could simply have given the counter a self-documenting name. In particular, we might have used the following line of code:

```
resource_counter++;
```

Line comments can also be used to document blocks of code in a module. These comments should also augment our understanding of the source code. For example, the code segment shown in Figure 7.14 is well documented using line comments. The code in this module calculates the number of dollars, quarters, dimes, nickels, and pennies there are in the amount passed in as a parameter. The figure does not show the header comment block that accompanies the module.

Find a program that you have written in the past. Remove all the comments from the code. Exchange your program with another student in the class. Read through the code of the other student to determine what his or her code does. How difficult is it to do so? Add internal documentation (header block comments and line comments) to the program. Return your programs to each other and compare the comments added by the other student to the original comments in your program. How are they similar, and how do they differ? **EXERCISE 7.5**

 ## Project Coding Standards

The largest cost of owning software comes from maintenance rather than the initial development of the software. Therefore, anything that the software developer can do to make maintaining code easier will save money in the long run. Creation of and adherence to coding standards is a major step in developing software that is easy to maintain. These standards provide uniformity and consistency in the final code that facilitate understanding of the code by programmers who have never seen it before. In addition, these standards can help to ensure that the

```
void CalculateChange(double Amount)
{ int numDollars, numQuarters, numDimes, numNickels, numPennies;
  const int Dollar = 100;
  const int Quarter = 25;
  const int Dime = 10;
  const int Nickel = 5;
  const int Penny = 1;
  // translate Amount from dollars and cents to cents
  Amount *= 100;
  // calculate number of dollars in Amount and subtract the
  // dollar value from Amount to find how much is left over
  numDollars = Amount / Dollar;
  Amount -= numDollars*Dollar;

  // calculate number of quarters left in Amount
  numQuarters = Amount / Quarter;
  Amount -= numQuarters*Quarter;

  // calculate number of dimes left in Amount
  numDimes = Amount / Dime;
  Amount -= numDimes*Dime;

  // calculate number of nickels left in Amount
  numNickels = Amount / Nickel;
  Amount -= numNickels*Nickel;

  // add less than a penny to deal with decimal to binary to
  // decimal conversion errors and then calculate number of
  // pennies left in Amount
  Amount += 0.05;
  numPennies = Amount / Penny;
  Amount -= numPennies*Penny;

  // now communicate results to the user
  System.out.println("%d Dollars %d Quarters",numDollars,
                                  numQuarters);
  System.out.println("%d Dimes %d Nickels",numDimes,numNickels);
       System.out.println("%d Pennies",numPennies);
} // end of CalculateChange method
```

FIGURE 7.14   Line Comments to Document Blocks of Code in a Module

implementation of the software is directly linked to the design of the software. A major focus of the design is modularization, and if this modularization is not carried into the implementation, then it is of little value. Finally, standards facilitate communication among the development and maintenance team members. The code written by one person will be read and used by other programmers and perhaps even testers. Adherence to a set of standards enhances the readability of the code because the readers of the code are already familiar with certain aspects of the code.

The standards developed for each project may vary widely. Most projects, however, have standards concerning the type and scope of the internal documentation to be created for the project as well as standards regarding the style of the source code statements. In addition, most projects have standards concerning the translation of the software design into code to ensure that any changes in the design will be easy to implement in code. Standards of this type specify the manner in which the translation is to occur. In particular, these standards often address issues concerning module flow of control, algorithm development, and data structures. For example, a general rule in structured programming is the avoidance of the *goto* statement. The use of the *goto* statement often results in code that is extremely difficult to follow, since the reader of the code must jump from place to place as execution jumps from place to place. Therefore, one standard regarding flow of control may specify that the *goto* statement should not be used. In fact, the standard may be even stricter, suggesting that whenever possible the flow of control should be linear. Of course, completely linear execution is not possible or even desirable within an object-oriented module, but as much as possible, once a module is entered, execution should flow from top to bottom in the module.

Reproducing a complete set of programming standards here is infeasible. In the next subsection, however, we have included a subset of the kinds of standards one might encounter on a software development project.

7.8.1 *Case Study:* **Programming Standards for the LMS**

General Rules

1. Structured programming techniques should be used in all methods. The primary goal is to produce working modules that are easily read and maintained.
2. Comments should be used to identify the purpose of each method or major part of a method and to clarify obscure processing.
3. Each method must be prefaced with a comment box.
4. Each major block of code within a method should be prefaced with a comment box. In addition, any code that is complex or obscure should also be prefaced with a comment box.
5. Document each major control structure (loop, selection) with a comment line.
6. Keep code simple and straightforward. Do not try to be clever by being terse.

Modularization Rules

1. Each method must perform only one task.
2. Global variables should not be used. Data should be shared only through the parameter list of a method.
3. If, during implementation, a need arises for a class not specified in the design, the design must be reexamined before the new class can be implemented. In other words, implement only classes that have been specified in the design.

Declarations

1. All variables must be declared and explicit types used.
2. Names of variables and methods should describe their content or usage. The only exception is commonly used names such as *i* and *j* for subscripts.
3. Declarations of any files should precede variable declarations.
4. Declarations of instance variables in a class should precede method definitions.

Executable Instructions

1. Align and indent parallel constructs. Normally, each level (except the first) is indented three spaces inside the next outer level. Each line should contain at most one instruction. Use blank lines to set off major control constructs. For example:

```
int power = 1;
// for each digit in the binary number
for(int i = 0; i<MAX; i++)
{
   // determine whether this digit in the binary number
   // representing the value in the variable amount
   // should contain a 1 or a 0
   if((1/(double)Math.pow(2,power)) <= amount)
   {
      digit[i].setText("1");
      amount = amount - 1/(double)Math.pow(2,power);
   }
   else
      digit[i].setText("0");
   power++;
}
```

2. Do not use *goto*.
3. Use the priming-read/looping-read technique for all sequential files.
4. Open and close files explicitly.
5. Avoid negative conditions.

7.9   Implementing the *Class Project*

The class project is almost ready to be implemented. Your instructor may wish to provide you with programming standards that you should review with your development team members. Otherwise, create a simple set of programming standards for your class project, or adopt the standards proposed in the LMS case study. Responsibility for class design has already been assigned to individual members of the project team. Ideally, all students should implement the classes that they designed, but the logistics of orchestrating the implementation process may make this goal impractical, so adjustments may need to be made. Assign responsibility for implementing classes in a manner that maximizes everyone's ability to code and test classes independently and that reasonably distributes the workload.

The most manageable approach to implementation is the threads approach. You should divide the project into partitions of functionality according to the use cases created during analysis. Select one or two use cases for each phase of development. Each member of the development team should create an implementation plan to present at a development team meeting where an implementation plan is adopted. Make sure that time constraints of the course are adhered to and that opportunities for integration testing are scheduled. Time constraints may limit the number of implementation phases that are practical, since the formal completion of a phase requires additional time. Nonetheless, the completion of a stable, reliable phase of the project increases the likelihood of completing the entire project successfully.

In implementing and testing the class project keep in mind the timeline that was proposed in Chapter 2 (Figure 2.11). Notice that approximately half the time for the entire project is devoted to programming and testing, the majority of which is testing. This time frame reflects a realistic time allotment when sufficient analysis and design work precede the programming phase. Outmoded thinking on software development assigns nearly 100 percent project development time to the process of programming and testing. Current thinking assigns time to the processes of understanding and efficiently structuring the problem, thus greatly reducing the amount of time devoted to programming.

7.10   Questions for Review

1. Why should you avoid the Big Bang method of implementation? Have you ever used this method for implementing programs? What was the result?

2. What is the difference between a stub and a driver? Which do you think would be easier to write? Why?

3. What are the major differences between a top-down implementation approach and a bottom-up implementation approach?

4. Are there situations that you can think of in which a top-down implementation approach is better than a bottom-up approach? Are there situations in which a bottom-up approach is better than a top-down approach?

5. Give an example of a situation in which a combination of top-down and bottom-up implementation is the best approach to implementation.

6. In the threads implementation approach, how might use cases and/or collaborations be used to define the threads?

7. Why is it important to establish programming standards?

8. Find a program that you've written for another class. Using the code from this program, write a set of programming standards. Did you follow these standards throughout your program? Look at other programs that you wrote for that class. Did you follow these standards for all the programs in that class?

9. Find a program that you've written for another class. Using the programming standards from section 7.8.1, rewrite the program. What kinds of changes did you have to make? Which style do you like better? Why?

10. Why is creating internal comments for a program a skill that is critical for programmers to learn to do well?

11. Can a comment in a program ever be useless? If so, give an example. If not, explain why not.

Testing

CHAPTER 8

  Key Concepts

- Testing
- Error, fault, and failure
- Test plan
- Test oracle
- Test cases
- White box testing

- Black box testing
- Unit testing
- Integration testing
- System testing
- System configuration
- Regression testing

  What Is Testing?

Ideally, when a programmer writes code, the code does exactly what it is supposed to do in every situation. Unfortunately, we do not live in an ideal world. The number of situations in which the software must work properly is very large. In addition, there are many people involved in the development of the software, and the communication among these people is imprecise. This complexity ensures that faults will appear in the code during implementation. Finding as many of these faults as possible before the software is turned over to the users is the goal of testing.

Testing is defined as "the process of exercising or evaluating a system by manual or automatic means to verify that it satisfies specified requirements or to identify differences between expected and actual results" [50]. In other words, testing is the determination of how close to ideal the system's behavior is. Any deviation from ideal indicates the presence of a bug in the system that must be fixed.

8.3 Principles of Object-Oriented Testing

Is object-oriented testing different from testing under the process-oriented paradigm? In order to explore this question fully, we first must review the elements that make up an object-oriented system and contrast these with the elements of traditional process-oriented systems.

An object-oriented system can be characterized in the following ways:

- A system consists of two or more interrelated objects.
- Objects consist of attributes and operations that may be performed upon those attributes, and classes define these attributes and operations.
- Objects interrelate by message passing, which entails one object invoking a method defined by another object's class definition.
- The result of message passing is either one or more return values, one or more output values, and/or a change in object state. An output value entails a change to the user interface or a value written to a file or database.
- Objects may also relate to each other through inheritance and/or containment.

A process-oriented system can be characterized in the following ways:

- A system consists of one or more interrelated subprograms (functions and/or procedures).
- Subprograms interrelate when one subprogram invokes another subprogram.
- The result of a subprogram call is one or more return values, one or more output values, and/or change in subprogram state. Subprograms may also have side effects and thus cause changes in program state.
- Subprograms may share data values through variables of primitive types and/or structured data aggregations. These variables and data aggregations may be inspected for correctness of their possible states.

Not surprisingly, the object-oriented paradigm shares many testing concerns with the process-oriented paradigm. Although the object-oriented paradigm is centered on objects that are data aggregations with associated operations as defined by their class definitions, the focus of testing is ensuring that the operations on the data are correct and that the aggregate system produces correct results. Thus a great deal of effort is exerted to ensure that methods function correctly. Additionally, each attribute has a range of correct values. Because attribute values should be modified through designated methods, each method must enforce that any attribute it modifies take on only values within the range of correct values. Thus both software development approaches emphasize the testing of subprograms or the object-oriented analogue of subprograms, methods.

Section 8.6 addresses some of the testing distinctions between testing in traditional development approaches and testing in object-oriented systems. Before we can look at the steps involved in testing, we must understand some terminology.

 Definitions

8.4.1 Error, Fault, and Failure

The terms **error**, **fault**, and **failure** are typically used interchangeably. Sometimes, however, these three terms are used to refer to different concepts.

Error is used in two different ways when applied to the process of testing [51]. In the first use, error refers to any discrepancy between an actual, measured value and a theoretical, predicted value. For example, when a *Patron* checks out a *Resource* in the Library Management System, the *status* instance variable of the *Resource* object should change from *available* to *checked out*. If we find that after the *Resource* has been checked out the *status* still indicates that the *Resource* is *available*, then there is a difference between the actual value (*available*) and the predicted value (*checked out*). This difference is an error.

In the second use of the term, error refers to some human action that results in some sort of failure or fault in the software. For example, if the *Library Staff* enters the incorrect *Resource* identification number when a *Patron* is checking out a *Resource*, an error occurs. The *Resource* removed from the library by the *Patron* has a *status* of *available* in the system. The incorrectly entered *Resource*, although still sitting on the shelf, has a *status* of *checked out*. The error in this situation is the entering of incorrect information. Of course, we should design the system so that such errors are difficult to make. To minimize the possibility of entering incorrect identification numbers, we should probably design the LMS so that it uses bar code readers rather than requiring the library staff to type the identification numbers into the system.

A **fault** is a condition that causes the software to fail [51]. The basic reason for software malfunction is a fault. For example, if the *status* of the recently checked out *Resource* does not change from *available* to *checked out*, we may find that the design of the *checkOutResource()* method does not specify that the *status* instance variable must be changed. Such a design flaw is a fault. In practice, when speaking of software, we usually make no distinction between errors and faults.

A **failure** is the inability of a piece of software to perform according to its specifications [51]. Failures are caused by faults, although not all faults cause failures. A piece of software has failed if its actual behavior differs in any way from its expected behavior, as designed in its specifications. It is important to note that a failure may occur and not be detected. Such invisible failures are still failures. The example of the *Resource status* instance variable not changing is an example of a failure. The software does not crash in such a situation, but it does not perform as expected. Although we may not detect the fact that the *Resource* is still shown as being *available*, the software has indeed failed.

These three terms, even when referring to different concepts, are very clearly related. If there is an error in the system, a failure must have occurred, and if a failure occurred, there must be a fault in the system. However, if there is a fault in the system, there is only the potential that the system will fail. The conditions for failure must be precisely correct. This fact is part of what makes testing a difficult task. If a system has not failed during our testing procedure, we still cannot guarantee that no faults exist in the system. Testing can only show the presence of faults, not the absence of faults. In practice, it is difficult, if not impossible, to test all possible conditions to ensure that no faults exist. Many software systems with faults run for years before a failure occurs. A difficult decision during testing is determining when to stop testing. At some point it is no longer cost-effective to continue trying to find faults that may or may not exist. The determination of when testing is no longer cost-effective is one of the very hard issues in testing.

Once a fault has been deduced by observing failures, the system must be debugged. The debugging process can be time-consuming and difficult. A poor design will have many faults that must be deduced by observing many failures. Each of these faults must then be tracked down and removed from the system. This process is much more costly than spending time up front creating a good design. The expense of testing and debugging during implementation of the system is the reason that a good analysis and design process is critical.

8.4.2 Test Plan

A **test plan** specifies how we will demonstrate that the software is free of faults and behaves according to the requirements specification. Through the test plan, we organize all the testing activities that we will undertake. There are several levels of testing, such as unit testing, integration testing, and system testing, and the test plan is a guide to the entire testing process, just as the implementation plan is a guide to the entire implementation process.

In the test plan, the overall testing process is broken down into individual tests that deal with specific items. The test plan includes documentation about each test that is to be performed, as well as the schedule of testing and the personnel allocation for the testing process.

For each test, the documentation includes a test specification. Among the items included in the test specification is a list of requirements that this test addresses. This list is a kind of description of the purpose of the test. The specification also contains a description of the test, which is used as a guide for performing the test. The description must include information concerning the input data and whether these data are automatically generated or not. The input commands are also included in the test description. These commands ensure that the tester knows how to begin the test, how to halt the test, how to resume the test if necessary, and how to terminate the test. The description also explains how to interpret system messages. If possible, the test description must also explain how to distinguish a hardware failure from a software failure. Finally, the description of the test includes a test procedure or test script that explains, step by step, how to perform the test.

For example, Deliverable 8.1 shows the test specification for unit testing the *addPatron( )* method in the context of the *CheckOutResource* functionality.

Test Specification for Adding a Patron While Checking Out Resource

DELIVERABLE
8.1

```
Test #15 Specification: addPatron() while checking out resource
   1. Requirement #3
   2. Purpose: Create a new Patron object when Patron attempting
         to check out a Resource is not a current Patron.
   3. Test Description:
         a) Enter Check Out Resource Screen
         b) Press New Patron button
         c) Enter Jill Smith in Patron Name
         d) Enter New Boston Rd. in Address
         e) Enter Goffstown in City
         f) Enter NH in State
         g) Enter 03045 in Zip
         h) Enter 603-555-8122 in Phone
         i) Choose Student from Status choice box
         j) Press Add button
         k) A Patron ID Number is automatically generated if no
            Patron with the same name exists
   4. Test Messages:
         a) "Patron Added": Patron has been assigned a unique
            Patron ID Number and added to the database
         b) "Patron Duplicate?": a Patron with the same name has
            been found. Ensure Patron is different and press Add
            button again. If Patron is not different, press OK
            button. In either case, the Patron ID Number is
            carried back to the Check Out Resource Screen.
   5. Evaluation: Print the Patron List report to ensure that
            the Patron ID Numbers are unique and that the
            entered data have been stored properly.
```

If the test is to be accomplished by a series of smaller tests, then the test specification describes the relationship between the smaller tests and the larger test. The test specification also makes clear any test conditions, such as the order in which the smaller tests must be performed or other timing limitations, that might constrain the test situation. Finally, the test specification must describe the conditions that indicate that the test is complete and the means for evaluating the results of the testing. For example, perhaps the data generated by the test should be processed manually in some manner before being presented to the tester for inspection. The data might instead be evaluated by an automated tool that produces summary reports to be inspected by the tester.

8.4.3 Test Oracle

A **test oracle** is the set of predicted results for a set of tests [73]. It is used to check the actual results of the tests for their correctness. One way of describing the testing process is that we give the test cases to both the system to be tested and the test oracle and compare the results to determine whether the system is behaving correctly. For example, the test oracle for adding a *Patron* object during the check-out-resource functionality must indicate what is displayed on the screen when a *Patron* is successfully added and what is displayed when the *Patron* already exists and is not added. In addition, the test oracle indicates what will be displayed on the Patron list report after the *Patron* object is added. The test oracle is necessary for proper evaluation of the success of the test.

Test oracles are necessary for testing, but they are extremely difficult to create. Ideally, the oracle is created in an automated manner, but this ideal is rarely achievable. When it is possible to do so, the oracle is created from the requirements specification for the system. Therefore, the oracle is only correct if the requirements specification is correct. In most instances, however, the oracle is created by hand. Humans creating test oracles in this manner often make mistakes. If there is a discrepancy between the oracle and the actual results, therefore, the output predicted by the oracle must be verified before we can say that a failure has occurred. This process is time-consuming, cumbersome, and expensive.

8.4.4 Test Cases

The creation of a good set of **test cases** is critical to successful testing. A test case is a set of inputs to the system or a situation that is used to execute the code being tested [54]. Despite the presence of faults, a system may behave as expected in many situations, given many inputs. Poorly chosen test cases may fail to illuminate the faults in the system. In fact, even when test cases are carefully chosen, existing faults may remain undiscovered during testing. Our goal, then, is to carefully choose test cases so that as much as possible of the code being tested executes in response to the test cases. Ideally, we want to choose our test cases so that successful execution of all of them guarantees a lack of faults.

An ideal test case is one that executes with no errors only if there are no faults in the system. We would like to select a set of test cases so that if there is a fault in the system, it will be exercised by one of the test cases. One possible set of test cases includes a test case for every possible input into the system. Using such a set of test cases is called **exhaustive** testing. Because there are so many possible inputs for all but the smallest systems, exhaustive testing is not practical. Instead, we want to select a set of test cases that is close to ideal. Selection of test cases can proceed in one of two ways, either by examining the internal structure of the code to be tested or by examining the expected outputs or behavior of the code. Examining the internal structure of the code to select test cases is called **white box testing**. Examining the expected behavior of the code to select test cases is called **black box testing**.

8.4.5 White Box Testing

Through careful examination of the code of a piece of software, the tester acquires a good understanding of the internal logic of the software—how it does what it does. In particular, the tester knows what conditions are tested and what kinds of loop structures are executed in certain situations. In **white box testing**, the tester uses this knowledge to determine a set of test cases that is close to ideal. If the tester developed a set of test cases that ensured that every line of code would be executed (an impossible task), then successful execution of all the test cases would ensure that no faults existed in the software. Since it is impossible to select an exhaustive set of test cases, it might appear that white box testing has no value. In practice, however, the tester chooses a limited number of critical logical paths through the software and designs test cases that will execute those paths. Since it is impossible to execute all of the possible paths through the software, white box testing is usually combined with black box testing.

Figure 8.1 shows an example of selecting test cases based on the internal structure of the code. The parameter to the constructor for class *WhiteBox*, *height* should be tested with boundary values so that the *for* loop is executed no times, once, the maximum number of iterations, and too many iterations. In addition, the loop should be tested for some intermediate number of iterations. For example, if MAX is equal to 10, we might test the loop for 4 iterations. If the constructor has specified as a precondition that the values for height and width do not allow it to equal or exceed the constant value *MAX*, the constructor does not need to handle this situation, although it is better to handle too many error conditions than too few. The boundary conditions for loops always require them to be executed

```
class WhiteBox
{
    public WhiteBox (int height, int width, boolean flag)
    {   value = new Table_element[MAX] [MAX];
        for (int i = 0; i < height; i++) ─────────────▶
            for (int j = 0; j < width; j++) ─────────▶
            {   value[ i ][ j ] = new Table_element(i,j,this);
                if (flag == true) ─────────────────▶
                    value[ i ][ j ].setFlag();
            }

    } // end constructor
            .
            .
            .
} // end class WhiteBox
```

Boundary values for
height = 0,1, MAX - 1, MAX;
Same boundary values for width
as for height

Flag values: true, false

FIGURE 8.1   Selecting Test Cases for White Box Testing

zero times, once, and the maximum number of iterations at least. The maximum number of iterations in the example is determined by the constant *MAX*, because of the purpose of the loop, which is to allocate elements of the two-dimensional array *value*, which is allocated to contain *MAX* squared number of elements. The next parameter of the constructor is *width*, and because it serves a similar function to the variable *height*, it has the identical boundary conditions to be tested. The *if* statement in the figure requires the parameter *flag* to take on the values *true* and *false* to be adequately tested.

White box testing is also sometimes called **clear box testing**, **open box testing**, or **structural testing**.

8.4.6 Black Box Testing

In **black box testing**, the tester knows nothing about the internal structure of the code to be tested. Instead the tester understands only the expected external output of the code to be tested. Given this knowledge, the tester designs test cases that will demonstrate that the external behavior observed is the same as the external behavior expected. The tester must generate a set of test cases that represents all possible situations in order to ensure that the observed and expected behaviors are the same in all situations. It may not be possible to generate representative test cases

```
public void setDot(int i, int j, int c)
// send message to the Graphical_Cell object which is the
// element at row i and column j in the grid array.  Set
// the dot to color c.
// precondition: the 2_D array of Graphical_Cell objects has
// been instantiated.  c has value 1 or 2.
// postcondition: Graphical_Cell object shows that a dot at
// row i and column j is set with color c.
```

FIGURE 8.2 Selecting Test Cases for Black Box Testing

for every situation using the black box technique. For this reason, most testing is a combination of white box and black box testing.

Figure 8.2 shows an example of code, taken from the Game2D example, for which we can select test cases without knowing anything about the structure of the code. Instead, we pay attention to what we know about how the code is supposed to work when determining the test cases. For example, we will choose a test case in which i, j, and c are all set to 0. We know that there is no row 0 and no column 0 and that 0 is an invalid color. We know, therefore, that we should see an error message. We should also see an error message if we put in a valid row and a valid column but still put in 0 as the color. Of course, we should also choose a set of test cases in which all three values are greater than their allowable maximums. For example, if we know that there are 14 rows and 14 columns in the grid, we should attempt to set a dot at row 15, column 15 with color 3. Another set of the test cases should address situations in which valid, but boundary, values are chosen. So, we choose a test case in which the dot is to be set at row 1, column 1 and another in which the dot is to be set at row 14, column 14. Although we do not know what the particular implementation for this method looks like, we do know what the behavior of the module is supposed to be, and based on this knowledge, we can design a set of test cases.

Black box testing is also sometimes called **closed box testing** or **functional testing**.

8.4.7 Unit Testing

The first step in testing a system is to test the individual components that comprise the system. Testing these components is called **unit testing**, and the process is similar to the testing that students perform when attempting to find faults in programs assigned in classes. During unit testing, first the code is examined for faults in the algorithm, data, and syntax of the program. Finally, a set of test cases is input into the component to demonstrate the correctness or incorrectness of the component.

The code of a software system represents the programmer's interpretation of the requirements specification of the system. The code review phase of unit testing is best done by an objective group of experts who can look for misunderstandings or inconsistencies in this interpretation. Often, misunderstandings can be uncovered simply by examining the implementation of a particular module.

Using a set of test cases to test a component in a software system is not the same as proving that the component behaves correctly. Unit testing the component of the system simply provides a basis for understanding how the system behaves in certain situations, namely, the situations that are close to the ones that have been tested. The component might still behave incorrectly in a situation that has not been tested. Of course, our goal is to choose test cases that cover all possible situations. But as discussed earlier, choosing a good set of test cases is a difficult task.

EXERCISE 8.1   Find a program that you've written. What kind of testing did you do on this program? Create a set of test cases for this program. For each of these test cases, explain what is being tested. Create a test oracle for the test cases. Exchange your program, your test cases, and your oracle with another student in the class. Evaluate the other student's test cases. Has he or she covered every possible situation? What's missing?

8.4.8 Integration Testing

Once we are satisfied that each individual component of the software behaves as expected, we integrate these components into a working system. The integration must be well planned so that we can determine the cause of any failures that might occur.

Inexperienced programmers might think that if the individual components behave as expected, there is no need to worry that failures might occur when the components are integrated. Recall that the difficulty of building software lies in the complexity of the software. When individual system components are combined, the complexity of the system increases very quickly. Suddenly, as modules communicate with each other, there are many more places where data can be lost or misinterpreted or simply used in different ways. For example, one module may require that a date be passed from another module. In testing the first module, we input the date with the day first, followed by the month, followed by the year. The first module behaves as expected when given a date in this format. The second module, however, outputs a date with the year first, followed by the month, followed by the day. This module also works as expected when tested individually. When we integrate the two modules, however, they do not behave as we expect them to because they do not communicate correctly.

The goal of **integration testing**, therefore, is to ensure that groups of components working together behave as specified in the requirements. As individual components are coded, they are unit tested. Once the component has been thoroughly unit tested, it can be integrated into the currently working subsystem, and integration testing can begin. Unit testing is sometimes called **testing in the small**, and integration testing is often considered the first step in **testing in the large**. The last integration testing done by the developers is a test of the entire system, with all the components of the system having been integrated.

Summary Points box 8.1 shows the four kinds of integration tests described in the following paragraphs [73]. Integration tests should be designed to try to break the system. In other words, the test cases chosen for integration testing should include data that are not typical or average. In addition, the order in which tasks are completed should be varied and include some unusual orders. Successful tests are those that actually cause the software to fail.

Structure Tests

Structure tests use the same basic strategy as white box tests during unit testing. In other words, in structure testing we use knowledge of the code of the components being integrated to determine the test cases for the subsystem. In fact, white box unit testing is also sometimes called structural testing. In designing structure tests, we choose test cases to ensure that every method of every class is called at least once and that all input and output parameters of each method are used. In this way, we can demonstrate that the methods communicate with each other properly and behave as expected.

Functional Tests

Recall that black box unit testing is sometimes called functional testing. As you might have guessed, functional tests are very similar to black box tests in unit testing. No knowledge about the internal structure of the code is used when designing the test cases for functional tests. Instead, we use knowledge of the

---

SUMMARY POINTS 8.1

Four Kinds of Integration Tests

1. Structure tests
2. Functional tests
3. Stress tests
4. Performance tests

requirements specification for the design of test cases. Through understanding how the subsystem in question is supposed to behave in certain situations, we can design test cases to demonstrate whether it does or does not behave as expected in those situations.

Stress Tests

Tests in which the subsystem is pushed to its limits are called stress tests. One way to push the subsystem to its limits is to increase the load on the subsystem far beyond what is considered typical. The subsystem should handle the overload gracefully, without crashing. Stress tests in which files and other data structures are filled to capacity should be performed to ensure that the subsystem does not crash in extreme situations. During these tests, the subsystem should be carefully examined even if it does not fail in order to determine what it does when faced with these extreme situations. The behavior undertaken in such situations should be reasonable.

Performance Tests

Performance tests assess the amount of execution time spent carrying out certain functions of the system. Typical situations should be handled by the system in a timely manner. Situations that are not typical should also be handled in a timely manner.

For example, if the Library Management System is designed to provide the ability to check out 500 resources each day, a performance test should be designed to evaluate how the system handles 5,000 checkouts a day. Design of such a test may require many computers to access the centralized database of resources at the same time. The system should be able to handle concurrent access in a reasonable amount of time, so that no one request goes unanswered forever. If the system cannot handle these situations, then perhaps the efficiency of one or more components should be reexamined.

A wide variety of performance tests may be executed to verify the performance of the system. **Regression tests** are an important class of performance tests. Regression tests are performed any time a system is changed. For example, when a new system replaces an old system, a regression test should be performed in order to guarantee that the new system performs the same functions as the old system without the introduction of faults. Regression tests are designed to verify that the new system performs at least as well as the old system.

8.4.9 System Testing

In unit testing and integration testing, our goal was to be sure that the code actually implemented the design correctly. During **system testing**, our goal is to ensure that the system that we have implemented actually does what the customer would like it to do. We hope that misunderstandings between the customer and the developer would have been found and eliminated during the design phase. It is entirely possible, however, that some misunderstandings made it through the design phase and have been implemented into the code of the system. System testing is also sometimes called **acceptance testing**.

System testing is the second step of testing in the large. Although the first step of testing in the large, integration testing, is carried out by the developers, system testing is carried out by the customers. Using their understanding of the requirements, which may be different from the developers' understanding, the customers test the system to verify that the system they requested is the system that has been implemented.

System testing can be done in the actual environment in which the system is to be used. Often, however, the system test is executed in a special testing facility. In either case, the end users of the system perform a series of tests that mimic the type of real work that will be accomplished with the final system. In some of the system tests, the users should purposely enter incorrect data to ensure that the system responds and recovers in a manner that makes sense to the users.

Testing Steps

Now that these terms have been defined, we can examine the steps involved in the testing process. Regardless of whether we are unit testing, integration testing, or system testing, the basic steps are the same. Summary Points box 8.2 shows these steps, each of which is described in the following list [73]:

1. Determine what the test is supposed to measure. Before designing the test plan, the tester must understand what is being tested and why. Among the things that can be tested and measured are the completeness of the requirements specification, the cohesion of the modules in the system design, and the reliability of the implemented code.
2. Decide how to test the thing being tested. Once the tester understands what is to be tested, he or she must decide how to test that quality. There are many test approaches available, some of which are discussed later in this chapter. The tester must decide what kind of test is appropriate to measure the chosen quality and what kinds of test items should be used.
3. Develop test cases. Once the type of test has been established, the tester must create the actual test cases. The qualities embodied by a good set of test cases are discussed later in this chapter.

4. Determine what the expected result of the test is, and create the test oracle. The tester must understand what the correct results of a given test are before the test occurs. Creating the test oracle beforehand demonstrates that the tester understands the goals of the system and prevents the interpretation of incorrect results as correct results.

5. Execute the test cases. To carry out the tests, the tester may need to write some software that executes just the portion of the system that is to be tested. These throwaway pieces of software may be drivers or stubs, depending on whether the implementation, and therefore the testing, is proceeding in a bottom-up or top-down manner.

6. Compare the actual results of the test with the expected results represented in the test oracle. The comparison must be done very carefully so that incorrect results are not erroneously interpreted as correct results. If the actual results differ from the expected results, there is an error of some sort. Usually, the source of the error is in the system being tested, but it is possible that the error has arisen from the testing process itself or that the test oracle is in error.

8.5.1 Analysis of Test Results

Once a test has been performed, the results must be analyzed to determine whether the system behaved according to the requirements specification. For each test performed, a **test analysis report** must be created. In this report, the results of the test are documented. If a failure has occurred, the report provides information that allows the failure to be duplicated, found, and fixed. Through careful documentation of the results of the tests, the developers, testers, and users of the system gain confidence in the reliability of the developed system.

The test analysis report references other documents that describe the purpose and goal of the test. In particular, the test analysis report mentions the sections of the requirements specification, the implementation plan, and the test-plan documents that describe the various aspects of the system related to this particular test. The test analysis report then describes what was actually being demonstrated with this test. Finally, the test analysis report describes the results of the test. This results section presents information about how the test was carried out, any data measures that might have been gathered, and notations about whether the test requirements have been met. If the test requirements have not been met, the results section of the test analysis report may evaluate the severity of the fault and its impact on the system. When a fault occurs, the test analysis report must also include a **problem report form**.

In a problem report form, data concerning the problem that arose during testing is given. These forms include information about the location of the problem, when the problem occurred, the symptoms of the problem that could be observed during the test, the consequences of the problem, and the steps that caused it.

Special Issues for Testing Object-Oriented Systems

The techniques we have described can be used to test systems of all types. Testing object-oriented systems requires some special techniques that are not required in systems developed with other paradigms. On the one hand, because classes tend to be small, unit testing is often easier in object-oriented systems than in systems developed with other paradigms. On the other hand, the complexity of object-oriented systems is typically in the interaction between objects, so that integration testing is critical and must be more extensive.

The differences between traditional and object-oriented testing have been examined by a number of researchers [43, 46, 85]. Some of the features of object-oriented systems that make development somewhat easier also make testing more difficult. In particular, inheritance, which formalizes and encourages code reuse, makes testing more difficult in many systems. Similarly, many issues related to inheritance, such as polymorphism and dynamic binding, also make testing more difficult. Inherited methods cannot simply be tested in the context of the parent class in which they are originally defined. In a child class, the method may be redefined and must, therefore, be retested when the child is implemented. Even when the method is not redefined but is inherited as is from the parent, the method must be retested to ensure that it works properly and consistently with other methods in the child class [43]. In addition, if there is code that deals with objects whose type is the parent class, this code must be retested if there is a chance that an object of the child class might be used as though it were an object of the parent class. This situation arises whenever there is code that takes advantage of the fact that an object of the child class is also an object of the parent class and, therefore, can be substituted for the parent class object.

```
public void checkoutResource(Patron patron, Resource resource)
{   .
    .
    .                                              Path 1 Path 2 Path 3 Path 4
  if(patron.getTotalResourcesChecked( ) <= 15)        |      |      |        |
  { //patron may check out at most 15 items           |      |      |        |
    if(patron.getStatus( ) != HAS_OVER_DUE)           |      |      |
    {                                                 |      |      |
      if(resource.getStatus( ) == AVAILABLE)          |      |
      {                                               |      |
        resource.checkout(patron);                    |
      }                                               |
      else                                                          |
      {                                                             |
        new ErrorDialog("Resource is NOT available");               |
      }                                                             |
    }
    else                                                                   |
    {                                                                      |
      newErrorDialog("Patron has Overdue Resources out");                  |
    }                                                                      |
  {
  else                                                                           |
  {                                                                              |
    newErrorDialog("Patron already has 15 items checked");                       |
  }                                                                              |
    .
    .
    .
}
```

FIGURE 8.3 Exercising Paths through Code without Inheritance

To illustrate the complexities of testing code within one or more inheritance hierarchies, Figure 8.3 shows a partial method in the *LibrarySystem* class called *checkoutResource(Patron, Resource)*, which shows paths of execution to be tested without regard to inheritance. In the figure four paths are each represented by a vertical column in which a solid line indicates that the instructions residing next to the line are being executed, while the absence of a line shows that the neighboring code is not executed. Thus, if one's testing objective is to ensure that all paths through the code are exercised, only four paths are required for the illustrated nested if statement.

Considering the same nested if statement with the added complexity of inheritance hierarchies, to thoroughly test each path every line of code being exercised must be tested with all possible subclasses. Figure 8.4 adds the possible subclasses that must be added to fully exercise the code. Paths 1 and 2 must utilize all *Resource*

```
                    public void checkoutResource(Patron patron, Resource resource)
                    {  .
                                                            Path 1 Path 2 Path 3 Path 4
                       .
                       if(patron.getTotalResourcesChecked( ) <= 15)
                       { //patron may check out at most 15 items
                         if(patron.getStatus( ) != HAS_OVER_DUE)
                         {
                           if(resource.getStatus( ) == AVAILABLE)
                           {
                               resource.checkout(patron);
                           }
                           else
                           {
                               new ErrorDialog("Resource is NOT available");
                           }
                         }
                         else
                         {
                           newErrorDialog("Patron has Overdue Resources out");
                         }
                       {
                       else
                       {
                         newErrorDialog("Patron already has 15 items checked");
                       }
                       .
                       .
                       .
                    }
```

Possible Patron Subclasses
Faculty
Student
Library staff
Local resident

Possible Resource Subclasses
Book
Software
Reserve material
Music CD
Reference resource
Video
On-line research resources

FIGURE 8.4 Exercising Paths through Code with Inheritance

and *Patron* subclasses because the lines of code associated with these paths involve both classes. Thus, instead of the original two paths, we now have 2×4 (*Patron* subclasses) $\times 7$(*Resource* subclasses) or 56 paths to test. A similar argument holds for paths 3 and 4, but these paths do not involve the *Resource* subclasses and thus move from two paths to 2×4 or 8 paths, giving us a total of $56 + 8$ or 64 paths to test.

 ## *Case Study:* Testing the LMS

It is impractical to show here the entire test plan, set of test cases, and test oracle for the Library Management System. Instead, we will show representative examples of each piece of the testing process.

8.7.1 Test Plan

Because testing, especially unit testing, follows the sequence of implementation very closely, the test plan resembles the implementation plan. Deliverable 7.2 shows the implementation of the LMS in terms of use cases. Deliverable 7.3 shows how implementation, unit testing, and integration testing are related from a scheduling standpoint. The test plan specifies the testing of each use case in more detail by imposing an order on the testing of each class. It further specifies the order, within a class, for testing the methods of the class. A test plan very closely mirrors the implementation sequence for the system. The implementation sequence specifies a series of use cases to be implemented. Within each use case, a series of classes comprising that use case is listed, and within each class, the methods that support the use case are listed. Associated with each method is a **test specification**, which describes the general objectives of the tests. When possible, the test specification is worded without reference to specific characteristics of a particular class.

Deliverable 8.2 shows the entire test plan for the *CheckOutResource* use case of the LMS. To complete the test plan, we simply supply information pertaining to the remaining use cases. After the test plan is complete, unit testing begins. Of particular interest in the test plan for the LMS is the test specification information. Recall that the test specification should be worded without reference to specific characteristics of a particular class. For example, in Deliverable 8.2, test specification 2 requires the enforcement of correct ranges of values for each attribute. This test specification means that a cross-reference to the class definitions and their associated attributes with their correct value ranges must be created. The test specification does not itself specify the correct ranges for class attributes. Formulating the tests in as general a manner as possible reduces redundant documentation of such information.

DELIVERABLE 8.2

A Partial Test Plan for the LMS Case Study

Use cases	Classes	Methods	Purpose of Test
CheckOut Resource	LMSDatabase	addPatron(Patron)	1. Populate database, ensure only one instance per key (ID), end range of ID values 000000, 999999.
	Patron	create(. . .)	2. Ensure data are in correct form (i.e., no possible data exceptions). Enforce correct range of values.

	getnextPatronID( )	3. Ensure correct calculation of key.
LMSDatabase	addResource(Resource)	Same as 1
Resource	create(. . .)	Same as 2
LMSDatabase	addLibraryStaff(LibraryStaff)	Same as 1
Librarian	create(. . .)	Same as 2
	getPatron(PatronID)	4. Ensure no data corruption between add and get instance. Retrieve first/last element (0–highest ID).
	getResource(ResourceID)	Same as 4
	getLibraryStaff(LibStaffID)	Same as 4
Patron	validatePatron(Date)	5. Test before, after, on expiration date.
	checkout(Resource)	6. Test null, resource not in database, valid parameter. First, last, over limit, resources checked out.
	checkin(Resource)	7. Test resource not in Patron list, null pointer, resource not in database.
Resource	checkout(Patron)	8. Test null/not in database parameter, valid parameter.
	checkin( )	9. Check resource status: not out.
	checkStatus( )	10. Return only correct values.

Integration Test

Browse Resource	LMSDatabase	getResourceList(. . .)
. . .		
Request Resource	. . .	
. . .		

8.7.2 Unit Testing Phase I

Because the first use case implemented in the LMS is *CheckOutResource*, our unit testing will begin here as well. Before functional aspects of this use case are addressed, the creation of instances of each class involved in the use case is necessary. Typically, the first use case tested carries additional overhead because in order to test the use case, the instances comprising it must exist. Use cases that are tested later will probably require the use of instances that have been created in an earlier test. The creation of instances provides a good opportunity to test the system's persistence mechanism, as well. The LMS system is using a relational database management system with a front-end class, called *LMSDatabase*, that translates the contents of objects into relational table entries.

Within the *CheckOutResource* use case, the first class selected for testing is the *LMSDatabase* class. The first class to be tested for creation and persistence is the *Patron* class, of which the *LMSDatabase* class contains several instances (maybe thousands). Extracting a *Patron* instance from the *LMSDatabase* must be done in order to validate a patron before the patron is allowed to check out a resource. If a person attempting to check out a resource is not part of the database, librarians are instructed to offer them a library membership. Thus, the process of creating *Patron* instances and extracting them from the LMS database comprises part of the *CheckOutResource* use case.

At this point, the user interface for adding and validating patrons must be written if it has not already been implemented. Figure 8.5 shows a sample window that can be used for this purpose. The window is called the *PatronAddFrame*. The advantage of testing the creation of *Patron* instances through a GUI is that the data integrity enforced by the components comprising the GUI reduces the number of test cases necessary to test the system. For example, the specification of the *Patron* state of residence is done through a choice box that permits only valid two-letter state designations. This choice box reduces the need to test for invalid values. Likewise, text fields are used to enter the zip code and phone number. The text fields can be designed to permit the entry of only numeric data, thereby ensuring that the value entered is correct in form. Finally, the values of certain text fields can be determined by the system rather than requiring the data to be entered by a human user. For example, the system can calculate the membership expiration date based on a predetermined period of time after the start of the membership.

EXERCISE 8.2   Lay out the set of test cases necessary to test the entry of new patrons into the LMS system through the *PatronAddFrame*.

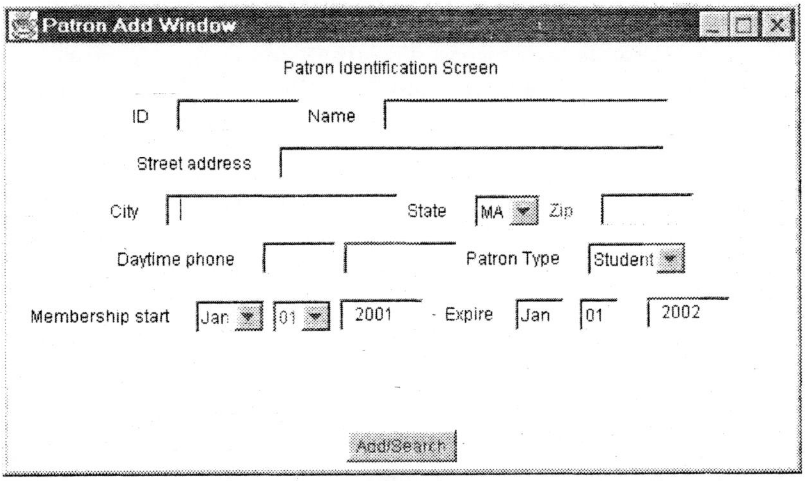

FIGURE 8.5   Sample Patron Add Window for LMS Case Study

After the creation and extraction of instances of *Patron*, *Resource*, and *Library Staff* classes are successfully completed, classes and methods that more directly address the semantics of the *CheckOutResource* use case are tested. For example, now that we have created instances of the *Patron* and *Resource* classes, the methods to allow a *Patron* to check a *Resource* out of the library can be tested. To implement this phase of the project, the system developers must write a method for the *Library Staff* class that allows the librarians to enter a user name and password to gain access to the check-out-resources screen. In addition, a method called *CheckOut( )* must be written for the *Patron* class. Finally, a method called *CheckOut( )* must also be written for the *Resource* class. These methods are called from the code that implements the check-out-resources screen. Each of these methods and the methods that call them must be unit tested as they are implemented.

The detailed process of unit testing requires the tester to carry out the objectives described in the test specifications of the test plan. Because these test specifications are frequently worded in general terms, the tester must refer to the class definition to determine the necessary detailed criteria for formulating test cases. This process is described in the following subsection.

8.7.3 Formulating Test Cases

Because exhaustive testing is impractical, the formulation of test cases is of particular importance. The nature of the test cases depends on the particular type of testing that one is engaging in. Stress testing frequently requires large volumes of data, while black box and white box testing require data with specific values. We will discuss formulating test cases based on black box testing. In black box testing, we derive test values from the inputs and outputs we expect from method invocations.

Deliverable 8.3 shows a subset of test cases formulated for the *CheckOutResource* use case. Each test case specifies one or more parameter values that must be tested. For example, to test the *addPatron( )* method in the *LMSDatabase* class, we first have two test cases, both of which are expected to cause the method to return a *false* boolean value. In the first of those test cases, the *Patron* object in the method's parameter list is *null*. In the second test case, the *Patron* object is not *null* but the *PatronID* attribute for the object already exists somewhere else in the *LMSDatabase* class. The third test case for the *addPatron( )* method returns a *true* boolean value and involves a *nonnull Patron* object with a *PatronID* attribute that does not already exist in the *LMSDatabase* class. Understanding the testing of the *addPatron( )* method tells us a fair amount about *Patron* objects stored in the *LMSDatabase* class. For example, we can tell that the *PatronID* attribute is the key for the *Patron* relational table, since no duplicates of that attribute are allowed.

DELIVERABLE 8.3

Partial Set of Test Cases for the *CheckOutResource* Use Case

Class:method	Return Value	Test Cases
LMSDatabase: addPatron(Patron)	False	Patron = null; PatronID = redundant
	True	PatronID = unique/000000/99999
Patron:create(. . .)	Null	Name = null, phone number = neg/0 Member/expiration date invalid: day=0,32; month=0,13; year=0000,>02000 02/30,02/31 etc. address=null PatronID<=0
	Memory address	Above attributes in correct range
Patron: getnextPatronID( )	1	First invocation
	2	Second invocation
	3	Third invocation etc.
LMSDatabase: addResource(Resource)	False	Resource = null; ResourceID = redundant
	True	ResourceID = unique/000000/99999

Lay out the set of test cases necessary to stress test the *CheckOutResource* use case.   **EXERCISE 8.3**

 Testing the *Class Project*

Each member of the class project development team is responsible for unit testing the classes that he or she is implementing, and thus must formulate the test cases based either on a black box or white box test strategy. These testing strategies are described in detail in section 8.5. The creation of integration test cases should be divided among individuals of the development team. A system test should be done before the project is demonstrated during the last week of the semester. The test plan should be developed by consolidating the contributions of each development team member.

CLASS PROJECT

Attend closely to Figure 1.11, which specifies the time frame for testing. Approximately five or six of the fifteen weeks for project development are devoted to testing. This time allotment reflects how difficult testing software is. Project managers frequently are too optimistic regarding testing. Seasoned programmers are aware that a few persistent, hard-to-find programming errors can steal significant time from the project, so it is advisable to plan for difficult errors. In anything but trivial programs, one expects to expend a significant amount of time resolving programming errors. To minimize the possibility of errors in conceptualizing the objective of the software, adequate analysis and design must be undertaken. There is no guarantee, however, that such errors will not occur. Such errors can be extremely difficult, time-consuming, and expensive to fix.

 Testing in the Face of Change: Configuration Management

That software changes frequently is a fact of life that few software engineers would dispute. Functionally related software systems are called **versions** or **releases**. These systems share common source code modules. For example, the Library Management System may be written to run on two or more operating systems because the libraries that use the software may vary in their hardware resources. To reduce redundancy, the Linux-based version of LMS shares all platform-independent modules with the Mac OS–based version as well as with versions written for other operating systems. Because the object-oriented paradigm is particularly suited to an evolutionary software development approach, we can expect object-oriented software systems to change even more quickly. Because we create a series of versions of the software during development, we need a technique for keeping track of what each version is about.

Configuration management is the process of controlling software development that produces multiple software systems that are related in functionality but differ in one or more of the following ways:

- The different versions may execute on a number of platforms, such as Unix, Solaris, Linux, Mac OS, and Windows NT.
- Various versions of the software may be written to interact with different database management systems. For example, one system may support Oracle, while another supports MySQL, and a third supports an object-oriented database management system.
- Certain versions may have additional functionality. For example, we may create a steamlined version of our software system that customers may purchase at reduced cost, while other customers may elect to pay for additional functionality.
- Several functionally modified versions of the software may exist for specific categories of users. For example, we may create tax calculation software with one version for domestic use and a second version for international use.
- As software is developed in an object-oriented system, it is frequently evolved over a series of phases, in which each phase is a functionally stable subset of the overall system.
- A new version of the software may correct errors in older versions.

Some software systems allow a user to select one of several mutually exclusive options that alter the functionality of the software in some way. For example, the Library Management System may be designed to support a variety of database management systems for object persistence. In order to accommodate multiple DBMSs, a class hierarchy is created to translate between a number of relational and object-oriented DBMSs and the internal object-oriented representation of the data. Such a situation is shown in Figure 8.6. The internal object-orientated representation of the data is shown by the classes labeled *Modules using DB Translator*. The Library Management System is shown to support classes that represent three DBMSs, Oracle, MySQL, and O2. Between the actual DBMSs and the internal object-oriented representation of the data are several additional classes. The object-oriented representation of the data uses an instance of the general *DBTranslator* class, which in turn determines whether the user has decided to use a relational or object-oriented DBMS. By using polymorphism and by propagating the specific instantiation of the

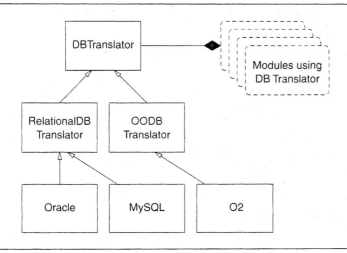

FIGURE 8.6 A User-Configurable System with a Hierarchy of Translation Classes

DBTranslator class, relatively little code needs to address the specifics of reading from and writing to the database other than the code in the *DBTranslator* class hierarchy. This user-configurable Library Management System scenario assumes that the interfaces to all classes in the class hierarchy are uniform.

Organizations may have numerous reasons for maintaining different versions and releases of software systems. During object-oriented development, it is sometimes necessary to retain previous phases of the system in addition to the developing version, because the subsets of functionality embodied in the various phases of development are sometimes released to users or sold to customers. When preliminary versions of the system are not retained, these phases of development are called **throwaway** versions.

Figure 8.7 shows an example of a system that has three versions of the software coexisting. Version 1 embodies a subset of the overall functionality of the system. Additional versions add functionality to the system by introducing new classes, by adding functionality to existing classes through inheritance, and by replacing certain classes with new classes.

Regression testing is extremely important when evolving or maintaining a software system or configuring a multiversion system. Regression testing is the process of retesting elements of the system that were tested for previous versions or phases of the system. In the face of new functionality, one may not assume that previously stable elements of the system are unaffected by the changes. Thus, previously existing elements of the system must be tested to determine that they

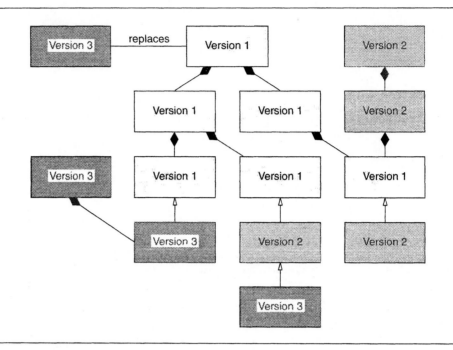

FIGURE 8.7   A System Consisting of Three Versions

are compatible with the new elements of the system. For example, Version 1 of the software, shown in Figure 8.7 is developed and tested. Additional functionality is added to produce Version 2 of the software by inheriting existing functionality from certain classes and using other unaltered Version 1 classes. The previously tested classes must be tested again to ensure that they continue to work properly with the added and modified classes of Version 2 of the software.

Ideally, the modularity produced through good software engineering practices will isolate the consequences of making changes to existing code to methods that are part of the changed classes and classes that use any modified methods. We cannot, however, make this assumption. There may be other classes that use objects of classes that are parents of the modified classes. Making changes to the child classes may affect these using classes, especially if the using class accepts an object of the child class in place of an object of the parent class. The modularity of object-oriented systems encourages computer professionals to neglect regression testing. We must remember, however, that when we make changes to the developing system, we must prove that those changes do not affect other aspects of the system.

Questions for Review

1. Explain the differences between error, fault, and failure.
2. How do failures of a software system help to identify faults in the software system?
3. Complete testing of a software system requires that every possible system state is tested at least once. Is such testing possible in a moderately large software system? Why or why not?
4. If complete testing is possible in a moderately large software system, is it cost-effective? Why or why not?
5. If complete testing is not possible in a moderately large software system, how do you know when you have tested enough situations?
6. Examine a program that you have written, and find a piece of code that has some sort of test expression (a loop or an if statement, for example). Develop a set of test cases for this piece of code that embodies every possible situation that might occur in the code. Develop the test oracle for these test cases.
7. If you were to undertake the exercise described in question 6 for an entire software system, would you be engaged in white box or black box testing? Explain the difference between the two.
8. Explain the difference between unit testing and integration testing. Can you think of a situation in which you would not need to undertake integration testing?
9. Describe a situation in which maintaining multiple versions of a software system is useful.
10. What is regression testing? Why is one tempted to ignore regression testing in object-oriented systems more so than in traditional systems?

Project Management

9.1 Key Concepts

- Project management
- Software metrics
- Size-oriented metrics
- Function-oriented metrics
- Object-oriented metrics
- Project estimation
- Quality control metrics
- Staff-month
- Configuration management
- Project scheduling
- Project plan

- Task network
- Gantt chart
- Critical path method (CPM)
- Program evaluation and review technique (PERT)
- Project deliverables
- Project teams
- Risk management
- Technical risk
- Human risk
- Consequences of risk

9.2 Introduction

The first chapter of this text motivated the topic of software engineering by discussing the air traffic control system as an example of a failed software project. The fact that software failure is not rare suggests that large software development efforts need to be carefully orchestrated. Careful orchestration of a project implies two things: the project must be structured well, and the project must be overseen effectively.

A well-structured project has a series of finite, effective, and well-defined tasks. One goal of a software engineering methodology is to define the tasks into which a software development project should be divided. These tasks are the phases of the software development life cycle. Additionally, all software engineering methodologies share the strategy of divide and conquer in that they attempt to break the project into modular building blocks that are individually developed and reassembled into the original project. Each individual building block is then the target of the tasks defined by the development methodology, thus multiplying the total number of tasks to be carried out.

For example, if five modules are defined during the analysis phase, and if the development methodology consists of the phases in the following list, then the project consists of a minimum of 23 tasks:

- Analysis—applied to the entire project, therefore one task.
- Product design—applied to the project as a whole, therefore one task.
- Class design—applied to individual modules, therefore five tasks.
- Method design—applied to individual modules, therefore five tasks.
- Implementation—applied to individual modules, therefore five tasks.
- Unit testing—applied to individual modules, therefore five tasks.
- Integration testing—applied to the project as a whole, therefore one task.

Of course, the preceding example presents a simplified version of the UCCD methodology presented in this text. Each phase of development can be further divided into smaller subphases, so that the number of individual tasks required to complete a project is larger than that shown in the preceding list.

Managing a project does not occur separately from the other tasks required to complete the project. Instead, how a project is managed depends upon other factors related to the project, such as how risky the project is to undertake. Risk plays an important role in determining how accurate time and cost estimates are. When we undertake steps to help manage risk, we openly acknowledge that large-scale software development projects are inherently risky and thus prone to failure. With risk management, we seek to identify sources of potential failure or delay, then determine procedures to minimize these risks. To manage a project successfully, the project manager must also manage risk in an attempt to create a realistic project schedule. The topic of risk management is discussed in detail later in this chapter.

EXERCISE 9.1   Contemplate the process of planting a garden with several kinds of vegetables and flowers. List the tasks necessary for planting a garden. Can any of these tasks be divided into subtasks?

Project Manager Responsibilities

The objective of effective project management is to guide the development of a software project within reasonable time and cost parameters, ensuring that the resulting software is of high quality. These three factors—time, cost, and result—are the major constraints on the project and must be managed by the project manager. If the resulting product does not perform its required functions, for example, the project is likely to be considered a failure. Similarly, negative consequences typically arise when projects are not completed on schedule and on budget. If all three of these constraints are met, the project is considered a success, and if any of the three are not met, the project is typically considered to have been a failure.

Project managers have several areas of potential responsibility as a result of taking the primary leadership role in the software development initiative. Project managers must do the following:

- Establish the project schedule: the manager is required to make time estimates.
- Establish the project budget: the manager must make cost estimates.
- Structure the project into units of work: the manager must identify iterations of the system development.
- Assemble a project team: the manager has to recognize any special skills or expertise needed to complete the project.
- Assign units of work to individuals on the software development team: the manager must understand each individual's productivity levels and technical strengths and weaknesses.
- Determine resources required for carrying out the project development: the manager must have knowledge of the development tools and facilities currently available.
- Carry out risk assessment: this procedure helps to minimize disruptions to the project schedule once it is created.
- Monitor the progress of the development project: the manager is required to request deliverables from the development team to demonstrate the completion of objectives constituting an iteration of the project development.
- Ensure that the resulting system meets its requirements: the manager has to monitor the quality of the software system as it is being developed to ensure that the functionality of the actual system matches the functionality laid out in the requirements specification.

The project manager must be adept at defining projects and then controlling the development of the project [97]. The first three items in the preceding list pertain to tasks related to project definition. In defining the project, the manager must first clarify the purpose of the project. Second, the manager must understand how the larger project can be broken down into smaller tasks that can be completed at regular time intervals. Finally, the project manager must define a schedule and a budget for the project. The schedule and budget relate directly to one another. Will additional resources need to be acquired? If so, what will they cost, and can they be obtained within an appropriate time frame? Note that these resources may include human resources in the context of specific skills required to complete the project.

The rest of the items in the list pertain to tasks related to project control. A successful project manager must be able to assemble an effective project team and assign the team members tasks that exploit their strengths as much as possible. The project manager must also be able to coordinate the efforts of the teams and monitor the team's adherence to the project's budget and time schedule as well as to the functional requirements of the project. If problems arise, the team manager must be able to intervene before the problems spiral out of control. And, of course, the project manager must ensure that the project is actually completed, delivered in final form.

As we have shown, one of the major tasks facing the project manager is the development of the project schedule. The main idea of project scheduling is that an estimate of the time necessary to develop the proposed project must be developed. As common sense suggests, given similar levels of complexity, larger projects require more time to develop than smaller projects. As common sense also suggests, given similar size, more complex projects require more time than less complex projects. These rather intuitive statements hide a fundamental challenge: how does one measure the size and complexity of a software project? An area of much research in the software engineering community attempts to answer this question. Through the use of **software metrics**, a project manager attempts to get a handle on the size and complexity of a project. If the size and complexity of the project can be accurately predicted, the time schedule and budget for the project can also be accurately predicted.

9.3.1 Software Metrics

A software metric measures software. There are several reasons to measure software:

- To facilitate the estimation of development time and costs for software projects.
- To assess the productivity of software developers.
- To assess the quality of the software project.

In this section we will focus on software metrics that will help us develop a project schedule and budget. How to measure a software project effectively and accurately is a topic that ignites much controversy. Various schools of thought accuse each other of inadequacy. The real problem is that each camp is correct in its criticism of the other camps. None of the methods for measuring software that have thus far been proposed is adequate for predicting future cost and time to develop new software systems.

We cannot simply throw up our hands in despair, however. In order to manage software development projects successfully, we must attempt to predict the size and complexity of the future software as accurately as possible. The measures of size and complexity are closely related to the amount of time that should be allotted to the development of a new project. Therefore, if we hope to give an accurate estimate of development time for a project, we have to use the software metrics that are currently available to us. All of the basic techniques for measuring software in order to estimate time and cost of a project involve examination of past software development initiatives. Metrics from past projects are used as the basis for time and cost estimates on the current project. As the project proceeds, actual time and expenses expended are compared to the estimates, and the project manager can monitor and control the project progress.

The current schools of thought on software metrics used for estimation may be categorized into the three general camps:

- Size oriented
- Function oriented
- Object oriented

Size-Oriented Metrics

Size-oriented metrics attempt to quantify software projects by using the "size" of the project to normalize other quality measurements of the software. For example, we may collect data for a series of projects that have been completed by our company in the past. The data that we collect might include the number of lines of code that make up the project, the number of person-months required to complete the project, the cost of the project, the number of pages of documentation created, the number of errors corrected before the software was released, the number of bugs found in the first year after release, and the number of people involved in the development of the project. We could then compare the projects by normalizing using the number of lines of code. Such normalization then allows us to compare the number of errors corrected before release per one thousand lines of code as well as the cost per line of code and the number of pages of documentation per one thousand lines of code.

Because lines of code are easy to count, size-oriented metrics have many proponents, but these metrics are not universally accepted as the best way to measure the process of software development. Using lines of code as a software metric suggests that a count of the lines of code contained in a project gives an accurate estimate of the size and complexity of the project. Unfortunately, the number of lines of code required to accomplish a particular task can be language dependent. In addition, well-designed systems with few lines of code are penalized. Anyone who has done any amount of programming can probably recall a particularly clever piece of code that accomplishes a fairly complex task in a small amount of code. The creation of such code usually requires thinking about the task for a while to discover a way to do a lot of work with very little code. Such systems may actually be more complex than the size-oriented metric implies.

Another problem that arises from the use of a size-oriented software metric is that in a project where a line count is used as a measurement of productivity, developers have little incentive to write good code. Redundant, inefficient code may contain a large number of lines, but it is also difficult to maintain and is likely to be slow. Developers also have little incentive to ensure that all lines of code are required to accomplish the task at hand. An excellent example of irrelevant lines of code making it to production can be found in Microsoft's Excel 97. This spreadsheet program has a flight simulator, complete with fairly complex graphics, built into it. If the user presses a certain combination of keys, the flight simulator starts to execute. A flight simulator is clearly not part of the average spreadsheet user's needs. So in the world of programming, more code is not always better code, and to measure a software project by the quantity of its code sends the wrong message to the developers. The lesson here is that the number of lines of code comprising a software project may not accurately portray the complexity or the appropriate size of a piece of software. Similarly, the number of lines of code may not accurately reflect the amount of work necessary to implement such a project.

The lure of using lines of code as a measure is that the metric is easy to apply to projects that have been completed, but how does one apply this measure to estimate future projects? Clearly, the number of lines of code that must be coded in a project is not immediately apparent. If one has a history of completed projects characterized in terms of lines of code, one wishes to take the new project and lay it beside the set of completed projects and determine the new project's **closest fit**. If we can find the closest fit, we can use the number of lines of code of the previously developed close fit as the estimate for the new project.

To use lines of code as a means to estimate future projects, we must develop a method to determine a closest fit from a list of previously developed software projects. If we can develop such a method, we have a new means for measuring software, since we can use this method to compare the size and complexity of two software projects, one of which has not yet been developed. In fact, the function-oriented metric allows just such a comparison of software projects.

EXERCISE 9.2

Assume you are a building contractor. All of your projects are billed and estimated based on square footage alone. No other consideration, such as type and quality of materials, is taken into account during estimation or billing. What problems do you foresee? What advantages are there?

Function-Oriented Metrics

Metrics that are **function-oriented** attempt to measure the functionality of a software system [1]. The units of measure for this approach are called **function points**. A function point is a generic type of system functionality whose complexity can be given a value. Such a measure may be more readily used as a predictor of the requested system than lines of code [2] because the functionality of the software system is assessed during analysis of the system rather than after implementation. After the analysis phase of development, sufficient information should exist to make a reasonable estimate of how much effort the project will require.

The biggest challenges in using a function-oriented measurement are determining which function points to use and then assessing the development project in terms of the selected function points. Figure 9.1 presents an example of a simple set of function points developed by Boeing, called **3D function points** [100].

Although these function points were developed with procedural systems in mind, they can be applied to object-oriented systems as well. The individual function points are as follows:

1. **Internal data structures**: data structures such as records, structures, classes, lists, arrays, and stacks.
2. **External data structures**: persistent data elements, such as files, database tables, and streamed objects.
3. **User inputs**: individual data items input by users through choice boxes and text fields. Note that an entire graphical user interface can be counted as a single user input by adjusting the complexity factor associated with the function point.
4. **User outputs**: system outputs such as monthly reports that are not counted as user inquiries.
5. **User inquiries**: the number of queries that will be used by end users.
6. **Transformations**: the number of algorithms required to transform information residing in the system from one representation to another. For example, the users may require a summary report at the end of the year. The algorithm that transforms individual data points into the summary would count as a single transformation.

7. **Transitions**: the number of state changes contained in the system. The notion of state change is very abstract, although state transitions can be characterized at various levels of abstraction. State transitions are modeled through state machines, which we introduced as part of the product design phase of development.

Of course, this list is just one set of possible function points that may be used to measure software. Various researchers have developed other sets of function points [2, 4, 44].

The use of function points is an attempt to quantify software that has been developed in the past. When we encounter new software development initiatives, we create a function point index for the new software and compare that index to past development efforts. By using this historical view of software, we hope to be able to accurately estimate the development effort required to complete the new software development. To use the function point metric, we must count the number of elements in each category that will comprise our software project. While counting these elements, we must also categorize the relative complexity of the element. We then multiply the number of elements in a particular category by the complexity factor for that category. For example, the complexity factor for user

| | Complexity Rating | | | | | |
| | Low | | Average | | High | |
Measurement Elements	Count	Factor	Count	Factor	Count	Factor
Internal data structures		7		10		15
External data structures		5		7		10
User inputs		3		4		6
User outputs		4		5		7
User inquiries		3		4		6
Transformations		7		10		15
Transitions		n/a		n/a		n/a
3D function point index					Total	

FIGURE 9.1 3D Function Points

inputs of average complexity is 4 in the function points shown in Figure 9.1. If our new software development initiative has 12 internal data structures of low complexity, 10 of average complexity, and 8 of high complexity, we then calculate the function point index for internal data structures as $12 \times 7 + 10 \times 10 + 8 \times 15 = 304$. We then calculate the function point index for the other elements and come up with a total function point index for the entire software development initiative. In other words, the function point metric characterizes the entire software system by a single number called the function point index.

The function point index is then used as a normalization factor, similar to the manner in which lines of code was used in the size-oriented metric. We can then calculate such values as the number of pages of documentation per function point, the number of function points per person-month, and the cost per function point. When faced with a new software development initiative, we count the various function point components that make up the new system and estimate the complexity of each component. We then find the historical system whose function point numbers compare most closely to the new system. We can then use the historical system as our estimate in terms of time, cost, and quality for the new system.

Usage of function points to create an accurate workload estimate requires that the analysis of the system and the product design be completed. User interfaces, external data structures, user outputs, user inquiries, and possibly transitions should all be produced during the product design phase of development. A reasonable estimate of the classes (internal data structures) required by the system should be produced during the analysis phase of development.

One of the problems with function-oriented metrics is that the validity of the workload estimation is limited to the accuracy of the analysis and product design of the project at the time of the estimation. Recall that as a software system progresses through its phases of development, one expects revision of earlier phases because the knowledge of the target system becomes more detailed through the phases of development. The workload estimation should allow function points to be added as they become known. This required flexibility in the estimation can be accommodated by weighting the function points. This weighting factor varies from organization to organization but is based on a set of criteria that is used to determine whether the particular function point has low, average, or high levels of complexity. This complexity determination is, of course, somewhat subjective.

Contemplate the house construction project. Assume you have been asked to estimate the amount of time a new construction project should take. What function points would you use to measure the project in order to make your estimate?

EXERCISE 9.3

Like the size-oriented metrics, function-oriented metrics are somewhat controversial. Proponents claim that function points are programming language independent. In addition, function points are based on data that are more likely to be known earlier in the evolution of the project. Critics, however, claim that function points are based entirely on subjective data. In addition, function points do not correspond to any direct physical part of the software because although there is an attempt to count things such as user inputs and user outputs, these values are then multiplied by a complexity factor to create a single number that represents the project as a whole.

Object-Oriented Metrics

Although the function-oriented metrics discussed in the previous subsection can be easily adapted to object-oriented projects, metrics developed specifically for object-oriented project estimation have been developed. The following have been suggested [65]:

- **Number of scenario scripts**: This metric assumes the existence of a relationship between the number of scenarios and the number of classes, methods, attributes, and collaborations. The number of scenario scripts can then serve as an indicator of program size.
- **Number of key classes**: A key class is a class that is developed specifically for a particular application [65]. Key classes are similar to primary classes, and, typically, key classes cannot be implemented by reusing a class from a different application. For example, a button is not a key class for an application, since many applications have buttons in their user interfaces. Although different buttons perform different operations, all buttons work in the same general way. A button class can therefore be reused across applications. It is estimated that between 20 and 40 percent of the classes required for implementation of new systems are key classes [65]. The remaining classes are called **infrastructure** classes, a concept similar to secondary classes. Infrastructure classes facilitate the creation of GUIs, data communications, and databases. This metric uses the number of key classes as an indicator of program size and complexity.
- **Number of subsystems**: A subsystem is an independently executing process that collaborates with other such processes to create an application system. This metric uses the assumption that the larger the number of these subsystems, the more complex the interprocess coordination and communication required for implementation of the overall system. This metric uses the number of subsystems as an indicator of the size and complexity of the project at hand.

The disadvantage of using a strictly object-oriented metric for project estimation is that any non-object-oriented projects will be excluded from the history base used for comparison. The advantage of function-oriented metrics is that they may

Project Name	LOC	User Inputs	User Outputs	Files and DB Tables	Classes	Algorithms	Staff-Months	People
Payroll System	17K	54	24	12	29	5	24	2.5
Inventory System	20K	65	33	17	36	10	32	3
Purchasing System	10K	30	15	8	19	3	15	2
Investment Expert System	6K rules	N/A	N/A	Rule base	N/A	N/A	36	2

FIGURE 9.2   A History of Previous Development Efforts

be adapted for object-oriented projects and thus allow a history base that includes both object-oriented and non-object-oriented projects.

9.3.2 *Case Study:* Project Estimation

A project manager is responsible for estimating the time and cost necessary for developing a software system. As discussed earlier, a simple approach to making such an estimate is to base the estimation on past experience. In this approach, previous software development efforts are cataloged, and the new project is compared to previous efforts. The historical project most similar to the new project is used for comparison. The time and cost for developing the historical project is extrapolated to encompass the new project.

CASE STUDY

   Figure 9.2 shows an example of a history of software development projects. This history was created for the development of function point estimates of new software development initiatives. Four sample projects are shown with their function point values. The function points used in this example are defined as follows:

- LOC: lines of source code.
- User inputs: the number of pieces of information the system accepts from a user, including both GUI elements and text-based prompts.
- User outputs: the number of reports and predefined queries supported by the system.
- Files and DB tables: the number of files and database tables defined in the system.
- Classes and other internal data structures: the number of classes and other internal data structures (if the system was not object oriented) defined in the system.
- Algorithms: the number of complex algorithms constituting the system.
- Staff-months: the total number of months that each member of the development team individually worked to complete the project. For example, if three people worked for one year on a project, 36 staff-months of effort went into the project.

- People: the number of people assigned to work on a project. The actual number of months required to complete the project can be determined by dividing the number of staff-months by the people assigned to the project, assuming that everyone worked concurrently.

Many of the function points in this example have a complexity factor associated with them. The complexity weighting strategy used in Figure 9.2 assigns the weight 1 to outputs, files, tables, classes, and internal data structures of average complexity; 0.75 to items of somewhat less than average complexity; 0.5 to simple items; 1.5 to reasonably complex items; and 2 to highly complex items. Note that in reality organizations will spend significant amounts of analysis time coming up with reasonable values for these complexity factors. Any weighting strategy that reasonably reflects distinctions of workload will work.

To use the information in Figure 9.2 for estimation, we first must characterize the new project in terms of user inputs, user outputs, files, classes, and algorithms. We count the number of each of these items and categorize the items in terms of their complexity. We then multiply the number of simple items by the complexity factor for simple items, the number of items of slightly less than average complexity by the appropriate factor, and so on. When we add up these values, we will get a series of function point values that we then compare to the numbers we get with the historical projects. It is unlikely that an exact match will occur, so we may need to extrapolate to find the appropriate values for staff-months and people.

For example, assume our new system has 20 user inputs of average complexity, 20 user inputs of very simple complexity, and 5 highly complex user inputs. To find the function point value for user inputs, we use $20 \times 1 = 20$ to get a value for the average complexity inputs (where 1 is the complexity factor), $20 \times 0.5 = 10$ to get a value for the simple inputs (where 0.5 is the complexity factor), and $5 \times 2 = 10$ to get a value for the highly complex inputs (where 2 is the complexity factor). If we add these numbers together, we find that the user inputs for our new system have a function point value of 40. We then use the product design results for the other components of our system to determine function point values for the overall project. Assume we find the following function point values for our new system:

- User inputs: 40
- User outputs: 25
- Files: 4
- Classes: 20
- Algorithms: 12

The new project does not perfectly match any of the previous projects. The values for user inputs in the new project falls approximately halfway between the value for user inputs in the Purchasing System and the Payroll System. Although we are using approximations in this simple example, most project management soft-ware applications will determine an exact placement of the new project between two other projects and then give an exact estimate for number of staff-months of development time. Using our approximations, however, based just on user inputs, we may expect the new project to require about 20 staff-months of development time. If we look at user outputs, however, we see that the new project is nearly identical to the Payroll System, suggesting that the new project will require about 24 staff-months of development time. If we look at the algorithms necessary for the new project, there are more than in any of the previously developed systems, suggesting that the project should take longer than 32 staff-months. The number of classes and files, however, matches the Purchasing System very closely, suggesting only 15 months of development time.

How does one make a reasonable extrapolation given a poor match? One thing to remember is that the quality of the estimate is limited to the quality of our development history. If we do not have a project that fits well with the project we are attempting to estimate, we may have low confidence in the accuracy of our estimate. One way we may formulate a final estimate is to average the estimates on the individual function points. Using this scheme, the hypothetical project is estimated to take 21.2 staff-months. However, we may determine that classes and internal data structures give a more accurate picture of the complexity of a project (and, therefore, of the required development effort). In such a situation, we might devise a weighting scheme so that the elements of the estimate vary in significance.

One of the major responsibilities of a project manager is to determine a rea-sonable estimate for the amount of development time. The project manager must also ensure that the quality of the developed project is high. Several metrics exist for project quality, and these are discussed in the next section.

9.3.3 Quality Control Metrics

The metrics discussed thus far have been for assessing project size and complexity in an effort to estimate the amount of work and money needed to develop new projects. Quality control metrics, however, measure the quality of the resulting software. By monitoring the number of errors that occur in the course of the development effort, we can find ways to improve the development process and ultimately cut down on development time. The following measures have been suggested for software quality [41]:

- **Correctness**: the degree to which a software system performs its intended task. The usual measure for this is **defects per thousand lines of code**. A defect is defined as a verifiable failure to implement a requirement. Because requirements span a wide spectrum of abstractness, this measure is difficult to assess. For example, suppose our system has the requirement that the last name of a patron can contain no more than 25 characters. If this requirement is not implemented properly, there is little impact on the success of the project. However, suppose our project has the requirement "subtract benefits from total pay." If this requirement is not implemented properly, the consequences are probably very serious.

- **Maintainability**: the ease with which the system can be changed. Because the amount of human effort devoted to maintaining systems is so great, an important objective of developing software systems is to minimize this effort as much as possible. A simple metric related to maintainability is **mean time to change**, which is the average amount of time necessary after receiving a request to modify a system until the change has been successfully tested and implemented in the production system.
- **Integrity**: the likelihood of thwarting an attack on the system. Integrity is difficult to measure because it requires an estimation of the likelihood of an attack on the system and a quantification of the likelihood the attack will be thwarted.
- **Usability**: the ease with which the system can be used. Usability is also a difficult measure to calculate. It requires quantification of the following:

  - Physical and/or intellectual skill required of users.
  - Time required for a user to become moderately proficient.
  - Net increase in productivity through use of the system.
  - Users' attitude toward the system.

EXERCISE 9.4   What kind of quality control metrics would you introduce to ensure that houses of increasingly higher quality are built by your firm?

9.3.4 The Mythical Staff-Month

The notion of a staff-month requires additional scrutiny. During project estimation, a staff-month represents the amount of work that is expected of a member of the development team in a month. For example, if five people work for one month on a project, presumably five staff-months worth of work is accomplished. Applying common sense to this scenario, one realizes that individuals vary in their productivity. In fact, an order of magnitude difference has been measured in the productivity of programmers [9].

The idea that a staff-month is mythical comes from Brooks' suggestion that there is a limit to how much a project time frame can be shortened by adding additional staff [19]. For example, consider a project that currently has ten people assigned to it and is scheduled to take two years to develop. Doubling the number of people working on it will not halve the amount of time it takes to develop the system. As more staff are added to a development effort, additional communication and coordination among the staff members are necessary. As we have seen with software, this additional communication and coordination significantly increase the complexity of the project. The increased complexity adds time to the development effort.

The question of how to incorporate the potentially wide spectrum of productivity levels in individual staff members and the overhead of large numbers of people working together is discussed in the next section.

 Configuration Management

Another important factor in successful project management is controlling change. A software system is typically developed in phases, with each phase making changes to the system so that some new functionality is implemented. In addition, a software system may have different versions that run on different platforms. Ensuring that the changes due to development phases and platform dependencies actually produce quality software is part of a task called **configuration management**. We briefly discussed configuration management in the context of regression testing in the last chapter. But the task of configuration management arises throughout the life cycle of a software system, not just during the testing phase. A **configuration** of the software system is a combination of different versions of the components of the software system.

As a simple example, assume that the development of the Library Management System is complete. Customers have the choice to implement the system on a Windows platform or on a Unix platform. Many of the classes developed in the system do not change as a result of differences in the platforms. Other classes, however, do change because of the differences in the various platforms. One configuration of the system includes all classes that do not change as well as all Windows versions of the classes that do change. A second configuration of the system includes all classes that do not change along with all Unix versions of the classes that do change. If we make a change in the software, we must ensure that all configurations of the software will still perform as expected.

Without adequate oversight, changes to a developing software system can quickly rage out of control. Software out of control has little chance of succeeding. Configuration management is an umbrella activity that contains several important subtasks. Summary Points box 9.1 shows these subtasks, which are described in more detail in the following subsections.

Tasks Involved in Configuration Management

1. Version control
2. Change control
3. Configuration audit
4. Configuration status reporting

9.4.1 Version Control

In an object-oriented software system, the software comprises a combination of class definitions. When we develop software evolutionarily, we may have several versions of a class, each of which represents the completed class for a particular phase. A successive version of the class embodies the functionality of the previous versions but also includes the functionality added to the system in this particular evolution of development. We must have a technique for keeping track of these various versions.

In addition, we may have different versions of the classes for different platforms or situations in which the software will be used. For example, one version of a class may allow our system to be implemented on a Unix-based machine, while another version of the class may be necessary for implementation on a Windows-based machine. Once again, we must have a technique for keeping track of these various versions.

Finally, as the software is used and tested, faults are discovered and corrected, and minor enhancements are made to the software. New versions of the software, with faults corrected and enhancements added, must then be developed and released. Once again, we must have a technique for keeping track of these various versions.

The simplest mechanism for tracking versions is to attach a version number to each component of the software as it is developed. A configuration of the software is then made up of a particular combination of software components. The configuration can be identified by its own version number or by a set of version numbers that comes from the individual version numbers of the components that constitute the configuration. As a very simple example, refer to Figure 9.3. In this example we have three classes, each of which has multiple versions. The figure also shows two configurations of the software. The first configuration comprises *Class 1, version 1, Class 2, version 1*, and *Class 3, version 1*. This particular configuration most likely represents the software in an early phase of its development evolution. The second configuration comprises *Class 1, version 3, Class 2, version 2*, and *Class 3, version 1*. This configuration most likely represents the software in its latest phase of development.

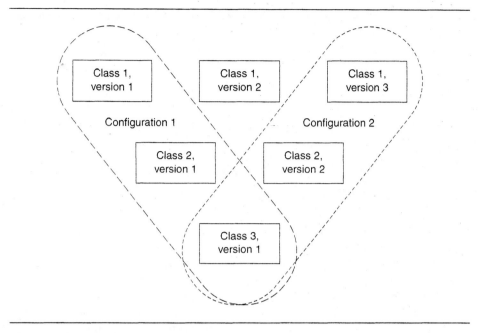

FIGURE 9.3 Two Configurations of a Software System

A number of different automated approaches to version control exist. The primary differences in the approaches are in the mechanism for constructing the specific versions and in the sophistication of the attributes used to specify how the versions differ from each other.

9.4.2 Change Control

If a large, developing system is allowed to change in an uncontrolled manner, chaos is the most likely result. Change control is a set of procedures for ensuring that change to the software system occurs in a controlled, predictable manner. The techniques for controlling change involve both human procedures and automated tools.

In a typical scenario, the need for a particular change is recognized and a **change request** is produced. The change request is evaluated on its technical merit, potential side effects, overall system impact, and cost. The results of this evaluation are placed in a **change report**. The change report is reviewed by the **change control authority**, a person or team of people charged with making decisions about whether to approve the change. If the change is not approved, the requester of the change is notified of the denial. If the change is approved, the change control authority generates a **change order**, which describes the change to be made along with any constraints that must be respected. The software module that is to be changed is **checked out** of the project database. While this module is checked out, no one else can make changes to it. This procedure prevents parallel changes from overwriting each other. This procedure can also be used as a security measure, ensuring that only certain individuals have access to certain modules in order to make changes to them. Once the change is made and appropriate testing (including, of course, regression testing) has been undertaken, the module is **checked in** to the project database so that others can make changes to the module. Appropriate version control procedures are then undertaken so that these changes are included in a new version of the software, and the new version is released.

9.4.3 Configuration Audit

The control mechanisms described in the last two subsections can only track a change until a change order is created. Once the change order has been generated, we must ensure that the change is properly implemented.

To ensure proper implementation of all but the most trivial changes, a formal technical review must be undertaken to ensure the technical correctness of the software module after the change. The reviewers must assess the changed module in the context of other modules to ensure consistency and make certain that no side effects have been created.

In addition to the formal technical review, a **configuration audit** should be undertaken after a change. During the audit the following questions should be answered:

• Has the change specified in the change order been made?
• Have any changes not specified in the change order been made?
• Has the formal review to assess technical correctness been undertaken?
• Has the change been properly documented within the source code? Proper documentation requires that the author of the change and the date of the change be placed in comments in the source code.
• Have all related software modules been updated and tested?

9.4.4 Configuration Status Reporting

Configuration status reporting is a configuration management task that ensures that everyone on the development team has access to information regarding modifications to the system. The status report should document the change that was made, who made the change, when the change was made, and what other parts of the system might be affected. This report can be placed in a database so that developers can access the information.

A configuration status report must be generated whenever a change order is generated. In addition, whenever a configuration audit is undertaken, a configuration status report must be generated. These reports become increasingly important as the size of the development team increases. The reports improve communication among team members, making it more likely that adverse effects will not result from changes to the system. Those with a need to know about a particular change are more likely to find out about it if the information is placed in a public repository to which everyone has access. Of course, it must be a part of each person's daily activities to check the database to see what changes are planned.

9.5 Project Planning and Monitoring

Software projects are notoriously late. Project managers must make reasonable development time estimates and keep the project within the projected time frame. If the project runs past schedule, the project manager must assess this situation far enough in advance so that the organization sponsoring the software development can accommodate the delay.

Project scheduling is one of the most challenging tasks of a project manager because it requires the reconciliation of numerous constraints in the software development process. The constraints include variation in productivity of development team members, interdependence of development tasks, and delay due to such external factors as

- Constraints on CPU utilization
- Need for quality production data for use in testing
- Need for additional software or development tools
- Lack of access to hardware because of downtime

For example, assume that the Game2D case study is being developed by three individuals, and the project has been simplified into four modules that can be independently developed but are mutually dependent on each other for completion. Figure 9.4 shows the dependencies among these four modules. The project manager must estimate the time frame for development for each project team member and understand the interdependencies of each development task so that minimal time is wasted as a result of the task interdependence.

The situation described in this example typically arises when the individual modules can be developed independently but must be tested in conjunction with each other. The testing phase is when the interdependencies often arise. As we discussed in Chapter 8, this interdependency can be overcome through the creation of stubs and drivers for testing. Some of the additional effort required to develop stubs and drivers can be avoided if each of the modules is completed in a timely

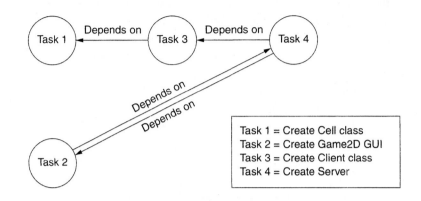

FIGURE 9.4 An Example of Development Task Interdependence

manner. For example, if Task 1 from the example is completed before Task 3, we must create a stub or driver to test Task 1, but once Task 1 is completed, we do not need to create a stub or driver to test those parts of Task 3 that interact with Task 1. Of course, not all tasks lend themselves to concurrency. For example, the design of a particular module cannot be done at the same time as the analysis of that same module.

9.5.1 Evolving the Project

Another responsibility of a project manager is to define the iterations or phases of development of the software project. Sometimes these iterations come directly from the requirements specification because the users have specified that certain functions must be completed first, whereas others are less important and can be completed later. Recall that one of the strengths of the object-oriented paradigm is that it is particularly suitable to an evolutionary software development process. Rather than analyzing, designing, coding, and testing the system as a whole, smaller functional partitions of the system are created and evolved to their complete functionality. The primary benefit of this approach is that it increases the likelihood that the system will be successfully implemented. Thus this approach can often reduce the risk of failure.

The specification of various functional partitions or iterations of the project has a significant influence on the planning and scheduling of the development effort, and is usually carried out during the analysis phase. The functional partitions must be defined before scheduling subtasks because these partitions indicate which subtasks must be developed together to form a functional subset of the system. The process of partitioning the project into functional subsets can be a challenge, especially if the system does not have clear functional boundaries. Partitioning such systems into effective phases of development requires a great deal of analytical skill and experience.

If dividing a project into subprojects increases the chance of the success of a project, then you might think that the project should be divided into as many subprojects as possible. This assumption, of course, is not true. Overhead is incurred when pulling together the subprojects into a final, cohesive project. We want to minimize that overhead, striking a balance between not enough and too many development iterations. The optimal number of subprojects is dependent on the size and nature of the finished software project. We will explore the process of functional partitioning in the following case study.

How would you structure the building of a house in discrete phases that are well defined and offer some distinct level of functionality?   **EXERCISE 9.5**

9.5.2 *Case Study:* Evolving Game2D

Game2D has a single, clearly defined objective that cannot be easily partitioned into autonomous subfunctions. In particular, partitioning the system into client and server iterations may seem plausible, but these functionally well-defined pieces are extremely dependent on each other. The client software does nothing by itself and requires the server software in order to do something meaningful. By slightly redefining the game's objective, however, we can create a client that is not dependent upon a server to work properly. If we characterize the game as a single-user game, the client can work properly independent of the server's communication of the opponent's moves. This slightly modified version of Game2D might make a successful, autonomous initial iteration of the system.

CASE STUDY

Modifying of the system's functionality in order to define completely independent iterations in the development should be done with extreme care. The overhead incurred by implementing a set of classes with a certain functionality and then changing the classes to capture the functionality specified in the requirements may be significantly larger than the overhead incurred by partitioning and delivering a system whose modules are interdependent. Typically, once a class has been implemented, we do not want to modify existing code to capture additional functionality. Instead, we would like to simply add new code, extra attributes and methods, to the class to capture this functionality.

If we decide not to change the functionality of Game2D in order to partition the project, we may instead divide the functionality of the system into essential functions and nonessential functions. For example, essential functions may be the following:

- Production of the GUI representation of the game board
- Communication from the server for the setting of dots
- Removal of dots in response to a mouse click
- Termination of the game when two neighboring dots are set

The following functions may be classified as nonessential:

- Tracking of player points
- Ability to change the time interval for dot setting
- Limitation of the time in which an opponent may join the game
- Communication from the server to the opponent concerning the state of the game board of the other player, in particular, the unsetting of dots and the setting of two neighboring dots (which indicates victory)

With just the essential functions of Game2D implemented, the software is not in a state that can be delivered to the users. This version of the software may, however, be internally evaluated by the development team. The advantage to this approach is that to move from the first phase of development to the second, we do not modify the code developed in the first phase. Instead, this code is simply added to, and existing methods and attributes remain unchanged, minimizing the possibility of introducing errors into the already-tested software.

9.5.3 The Project Plan

While orchestrating the development of software, a project manager must also verify the progress of the development effort. These tasks include the following:

- Defining phases or iterations of the project
- Specifying subtasks of the project
- Determining the project schedule and allocating time for each subtask
- Associating deliverables with each subtask to verify progress
- Dividing the subtasks among the development team members
- Scheduling any interdependent tasks to minimize delay

Scheduling interdependent tasks to minimize development delay is a difficult task for a project manager. To assist in this scheduling, the project manager may use a **task network** [88], in which each task is represented by a node and the interdependencies among the tasks are represented by edges. Figure 9.5 shows a task network for an application-independent development effort through a single

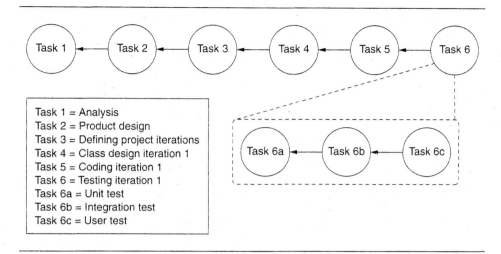

FIGURE 9.5 An Application-Independent Task Network

iteration of the project. This particular task network shows only the tasks that are common to all applications.

Task networks, like other modeling techniques, allow different levels of abstraction to be shown. For example, Figure 9.5 portrays each phase of software development as a task, with Task 6 shown with three subtasks. For project management this representation is too abstract to be useful, because it shows a strictly linear progression of tasks, prohibiting tasks to be developed in parallel. This linearity is not a true constraint on the project. Developing tasks in parallel, however, requires knowledge of application-specific tasks within each of the generic tasks shown in Figure 9.5. We will discuss and model these application-specific tasks in the next subsection.

9.5.4 *Case Study:* Project Plan for Game2D

The preceding discussion illustrates that although the object-oriented paradigm lends itself to an evolutionary software development process, the fundamental software engineering phases are linear in nature. One phase of development must be completed before another can begin, and one iteration of the project also must be completed before the next iteration may proceed. The opportunity for concurrent development in order to engage multiple development team members simultaneously arises when we decompose the project into modules, which are then assigned to individual development team members as work units. Because we are following the object-oriented paradigm, the work units will consist of classes.

CASE STUDY

In order to create a realistic and stable project plan, some analysis must have already taken place. Otherwise, the resulting plan is certain to fail or require substantial modification. Therefore, before the project plan is developed, a relatively stable set of classes must be identified. In reviewing the software development process for Game2D, as illustrated in Chapter 6, the majority of the classes necessary for Game2D were identified during analysis and product design. We will use the class diagram in Deliverable 6.19 as input to project planning.

A task network may be developed to portray class interdependencies that arise primarily from the need to compile and test classes. In theory, each class may be coded and tested in parallel, with sufficient stubs and drivers created. By laying out the development of classes carefully, a great deal of time and effort may be saved by avoiding the need to create certain stubs and drivers that might be necessary to ensure proper compilation of the classes.

Figure 9.6 shows a partial task network for Game2D with the *Game2DCoding* task expanded, showing the individual classes that must be coded and their interdependencies. The primary interdependencies arise through containment relationships. The *Cell* and *Timer* classes do not depend on any other class because neither of them contains another class. Both classes do, however, provide services to other classes. In contrast, the *Game2DClient* and *Game2DServer* classes both contain instances of the *Cell* class, and therefore they are both shown in Figure 9.6 as dependent upon the *Cell* class. The *Game2DServer* class also contains an instance of the *Timer* class and is, therefore, also dependent upon the *Timer* class.

Other class interdependencies are determined by a great deal of interaction. What constitutes a great deal of interaction is, of course, a subjective call. For example, the classes *Game2DClient* and *Game2DServer* share a socket connection and are thus seemingly interdependent. We may determine, however, that the information sent over the socket can be easily simulated, and thus no dependency is reflected in the project plan.

Based on Figure 9.6 it appears that Game2D can be readily implemented by two people, since there are two autonomous sets of classes to be coded with only the *Cell* class shared between them. Therefore, one may assume that the project time will be approximately cut in half if two people work on it as opposed to one. But will there be a similar time improvement if a third person is scheduled? The answer is probably no. Introducing a third person is awkward to schedule, because the project does not have three clearly delineated sets of classes. The third staff member will need to work on classes from the two independent sets of classes. The third person will have a greater need to communicate with the other two staff members than those two staff members have to communicate with each other. This additional communication requires additional time, and so adding a third person will not have the same effect as adding a second person.

Although a task network shows an efficient sequencing of tasks, it does not indicate how much time should be allocated for each task. The next subsection

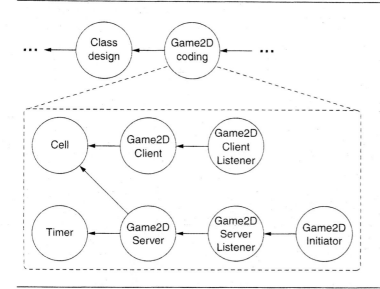

FIGURE 9.6 A Partial Task Network for Game2D

addresses tools for modeling a project plan in the context of a time frame for completion.

9.5.5 Scheduling

The scheduling of software development tasks is no different from scheduling any other complex undertaking, like the building of a bridge. Techniques used for scheduling in other domains can be easily adapted to software development needs. Two such well-known techniques are the **critical path method (CPM)** and **program evaluation and review technique (PERT)**, both of which were created in the late 1950s. Both techniques use information developed during project planning [88], such as

- Estimates of effort
- Decomposition of product function
- Selection of task sets

Both PERT and CPM include quantitative methods that have been automated in a variety of readily available software packages. These quantitative methods allow the project manager to perform the tasks in the following list [88].

- Determine the **critical path**, or sequence of tasks that determine the maximum time for completion of the project.
- Establish likely time estimates for individual tasks by applying statistical models.
- Calculate **boundary times**, which determine the earliest time that a task may start and the latest time it may end without disrupting the project schedule.

Recall that in Figure 1.11 we showed a graphical representation of a project schedule for the class project. This graphical representation is called a **Gantt** chart [37]. A Gantt chart shows, in the form of a bar chart, the time frame for completion of the tasks comprising a project (see Figure 9.7). Along the *y*-axis of the bar chart, the list of tasks derived from the task network is shown. Along the *x*-axis, time, measured in weeks, is shown. A bar associated horizontally with a task shows the time frame for that task. The date vertically associated with the bar's left-hand side represents the task's beginning date, while the date associated with the bar's right-hand side represents the task's ending date.

The disadvantage of a Gantt chart representation of a project schedule is that task interdependencies are not represented, so if one or more tasks are delayed, the effect on the project as a whole is not determinable. An ideal representation for a project time frame combines the illustration of a task's beginning and ending dates with the task interdependencies.

This combination of information is embedded in **PERT/CPM schedule networks** [37], an example of which appears in Figure 9.8. The PERT/CPM schedule network represents each task as a node, shown in Figure 9.8 as a rectangle containing both the task name and an integer that represents the amount of time each task is estimated to take. In Figure 9.8 the task time is expressed in days, although the

Week Number	1	2	3	4	5	6	7	8
Activity								
Code Cell class								
Code Game2DClient class								
Code Game2DClientListener class								
Code Timer class								
Code Game2DServer class								
Code Game2DServerListener class								
Code Game2DInitiator class								

FIGURE 9.7 A Partial Gantt Chart for Game2D

Key:

──────── Critical path

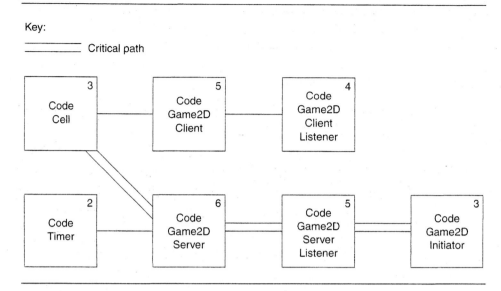

FIGURE 9.8 A Partial PERT/CPM Schedule Network for Game2D

time measurement may be weeks or even months. Tasks that are chronologically dependent on one another are connected with either a single or double line. Tasks that are not connected in the network can be developed in parallel. Chronological dependence means that it is optimal to complete the task on the left of the connecting edge before initiating the task to the right of such a connection.

If two tasks in the PERT/CPM schedule network are connected by a double line, these tasks are both on the project's critical path, which is determined by the linear progression of tasks requiring the most time to develop. In Figure 9.8, the critical path is determined by evaluating all tasks that are potentially being developed at a particular time and adding the task requiring the most time to the critical path. For example, *Code Cell* and *Code Timer* can be developed in parallel because there is no connection between them in Figure 9.8. *Code Cell* is added to the critical path rather than *Code Timer* because the coding of the *Cell* class is estimated to take longer than coding the *Timer* class. The next element of the critical path is *Code Game2DServer* because coding of the *Game2DServer* class is estimated to take longer than coding of the *Game2DClient* class.

9.5.6 Monitoring Progress

The best means to ensure that adequate progress is being made on project development is to define development milestones with associated deliverables. A deliverable is typically a written document, but is not limited to that. For example, the result of the implementation phase may be a set of files containing compilable code. Formal deliverables are a necessary means to confirm progress, since informal status reports can be misleading. Programmers usually spend 80 percent of their time almost done with a piece of code.

Milestones should be created so that the project manager receives sufficient feedback at regular intervals. If the milestones are not accomplished in a timely manner, the project manager can make the necessary adjustments to the project plan. Feedback should take the form of a natural artifact of the development process so that the development team is not spending its time creating output that is not useful to the development process. For example, a report about the progress of the development effort is not a good milestone deliverable. However, the class diagram for a specific phase of the project is an excellent milestone deliverable.

The phases of the UCCD software development methodology have associated deliverables as listed in Figure 9.9. These deliverables make excellent tools for checking the progress of the development effort.

Development Phase	Deliverable
Analysis	1. Refined requirements specification 2. Scenarios 3. Primary class list 4. Class diagrams 5. Use case diagrams 6. Structured walk-through
Product Design	1. Object diagrams 2. Refined class diagrams 3. User interface mock-ups 4. State machines
Class Design	1. Refined class diagrams 2. Collaboration diagrams 3. Sequence diagrams 4. Object diagrams 5. Class skeletons 6. Informal walk-through
Implementation	1. Implementation plan 2. Source code
Testing	1. Test plan 2. Test analysis report 3. System integration report 4. System delivery with demonstration

FIGURE 9.9   Deliverables for the UCCD Methodology

Project Teams

A team may be defined as a group of people working together toward a common goal [22]. A team should work together so that individual effectiveness is increased without the loss of individual creativity and strengths. A good project manager will facilitate such increased effectiveness while also nurturing the individuals that make up the team. A study published by the IEEE suggests that the most important factor in successful software projects is the development of successful teams [27].

Project teams are important in software development initiatives for a number of reasons:

- Many projects are too large to be developed on schedule by a single individual.
- Most individuals do not possess all the skills, talents, and responsibilities required to implement a large software project successfully. The strengths of one individual can often make up for the weaknesses of another.
- In solving problems, two heads are often better than one. By combining sub-solutions from individuals, teams often come up with better solutions to large problems than any individual could.
- Testing the validity of the software project is easier when there are multiple people working on it. Assumptions can be checked more easily, and mistakes are more likely to be caught. Note that this statement does not imply that all testing and verification should be done by members of the team.

9.6.1 Building a Project Team

One of the first tasks facing the project manager is the building of the project team. We use the word "building" rather than "choosing" because a project manager does not always have the luxury of picking the members of the project team but is always responsible for "building" a team out of the individuals working on a particular project.

One of the major reasons that teams fail to produce quality software on time and on budget is that at the beginning of the project, the emphasis was placed on the number of team members required rather than on the skills those team members possess. Such a situation often arises when the project team is imposed upon the project rather than chosen for the project. The ideal situation arises when the project manager is given the ability to pick the right people rather than just the right number. Often, however, the project team is imposed upon the project manager without regard to the specific needs of the project.

When faced with an imposed team, the successful project manager will attempt to deal with the situation using the following strategies. The project manager can suggest a different approach to team selection. Complaints often go unheeded, so the wise project manager will offer an alternative approach to the creating of teams in which project managers are allowed some say in the selection of their teams. The project manager may not have total control over the project team but may be allowed to at least participate in the team selection. In addition, if there are people in the organization who have performed well on past projects, the project manager may state preferences for those people as members of the team. Such requests might be taken into account when the team is selected.

EXERCISE 9.6   Think again about building a house. What kinds of problems might you encounter if you are allowed only to choose a certain number of people to assist you rather than being able to choose people who possess the skills needed to build the house successfully?

Even after suggesting this alternate approach, the project manager may end up with an imposed team. In this situation, the project manager will have to do the best that he or she can with what has been given. The successful project manager will give team members the chance to succeed. A team that is imposed may still contain members who can perform well. The project manager should attempt to assign tasks that most closely match each team member's skills and talents. With the imposed team, there may be some skills and talents that are required for successful completion of the project but are not possessed by any of the team members. In such a situation, the project manager will document the deficit and then do the best that can be done with the resources that have been made available.

Whether the team has been imposed or selected by the project manager, much work is required to get the individual team members to actually work as a team. The team must strike a balance between the needs of the each individual team member and the needs of the team as a whole. Each team member should feel empowered to apply his or her talents in coming up with solutions to problems, but the larger goals of the project must rule. The individuals on a successful team are committed to a common set of goals and agree on what is expected of the team. The individuals are also able to communicate with each other openly and honestly and are willing to share information with all other members of the team.

The project manager can help to build the team by providing an environment of trust. Each team member should feel included in the team. Differences of opinion should be encouraged and freely expressed. Mistakes made by members of the team should be treated as sources of learning rather than as threats to a team member's position. The project manager should recognize each member of the team as important to the success of the project and encourage mutual respect among the team members. There should be interdependence among the team members and a general feeling that each team member can influence what happens on the project. The project manager should ensure that there is efficient use of each member's time. Accordingly, meetings should be kept to a minimum and should be called only when the meeting is the most effective way to accomplish a particular task. For example, if there is information regarding external influences on the project schedule that must be disseminated, the project manager should draft and distribute a memorandum rather than call a meeting. The project manager should support and respect decisions made by the group rather than dictating all decisions. There should be a focus on group procedures and process as well as on results. For example, if a decision regarding choice of programming language must be made, the process for coming to the decision is as important as the actual decision. Finally, the project manager should encourage and reward effective work methods and procedures.

The idea that the project manager should encourage the development of a work environment that is based on trust implies that the successful project manager possesses certain attributes. These attributes include the following [84]:

- Recognizing that the whole is greater than the sum of its parts
- Understanding that sharing power increases the manager's own power
- Not being threatened by sharing power
- Continually placing emphasis on the team-building process

9.6.2 The Four Stages of Team Development

Summary Points box 9.2 shows the four stages of development that every successful team goes through [84]. The time required for each stage will vary from team to team. Since the project manager guides the team through these stages, the success of the team will often depend on the manager's actions and behaviors in each stage.

The first stage of team development is the **forming** stage. At this stage the team members generally have positive expectations and are eager to get to work. Very few tasks are completed during this stage because there is a fair amount of individual anxiety. Members are concerned about the purpose, goals, and priorities

SUMMARY POINTS 9.2

Four Stages of Team Development

1. Forming	3. Norming
2. Storming	4. Performing

of the team. They are also concerned about who the other team members are, what they are like, and whether they will fit in with everyone else. Individual team members are also concerned about whether their needs will be taken into account in the face of the goals of the team. At this stage it is very important that the project manager have a clear vision of the purpose, goals, and priorities of the team and be able to communicate that vision with the rest of the team. The project manager should be able to clearly communicate his or her philosophy of management, and should spend much energy on the tasks to be accomplished and little energy on management of the team interrelationships. To ensure the eventual success of the team, the project manager should direct the group, get the various members immediately involved in the project, and clarify the skills and talents of the team and its individual members.

During the second stage of team development, the team is somewhat unstable and is trying to find its way. For this reason, the second stage is called the **storming** stage. During this stage the goals and structure of the team should become clear, and the rate at which tasks are accomplished should steadily increase. The motivation of individual team members can drop because of mismatches between members' expectations and reality and because of negative reactions to the style of the project manager. The team members are concerned about their roles and responsibilities as well as the procedures that must be followed. Team members are also negotiating their sense of control of the project with other members of the team. During this stage, the project manager must begin to pay more attention to managing the relationships among the team members. The project manager should involve the team in defining roles, responsibilities, and procedures, in solving problems, and in developing strategies that will help the team meet its goals. If dissatisfaction on the part of team members arises, the project manager must not become defensive but should instead acknowledge the dissatisfaction and help to find ways to mitigate it. Most importantly, the project manager should continue to be a strong, supportive leader and develop strategies so that other team members can acquire the skills to begin to share in the leadership of the project.

During the third stage of team development, the team is stabilizing and the relationships among team members are normalizing. For this reason, we call the third stage the **norming** stage. During this stage, the productivity of the team should continue to increase, and the expectations of the team members should begin to more accurately reflect reality so that any dissatisfaction begins to disappear. The structure of the team and the progress it is making are clear to everyone on the team. Relationships among team members stabilize, and the team begins to act as a cohesive whole. The project manager will become less focused on tasks, since every team member knows what is expected. The manager is instead focused on ensuring positive relationships among the team members by involving them in key decisions. The manager finds ways to support the group as individuals begin to share leadership and to acknowledge the progress the team is making.

During the fourth and final stage of team development, the successful team is very productive and is performing at a very high level. We call this stage the **performing** stage. During this stage, the team is positive, eager, productive, confident, and proud of its work. The individual members are able to work autonomously, and the project manager becomes just one of the members of the group without special status. The project manager is able to communicate openly and freely with all members of the group and focuses his or her energy on producing results. At this stage, the only special functions the project manager should perform are those that support the autonomous functioning of the team. For example, the project manager should help the team to periodically review its progress toward meeting its goals and help the team tie up loose ends so that the final project can be delivered on time.

9.6.3 Conflict

Even the most successful teams will have instances of conflict. One of the responsibilities of the project manager is to help team members resolve conflicts before they spiral out of control. To begin to resolve conflict, the project manager must first understand something about work environments and the causes of conflict in those environments [22]. We are all affected by our work environments. For example, noise tends to impair performance on complicated tasks, so open-plan offices without floor-to-ceiling barriers are likely to increase frustration when team members are working on complex projects. It is the responsibility of the project manager to influence the environment to match the working preferences of the team members. By addressing the needs of the individuals on the team, the project manager is setting up an environment in which conflict is less likely to arise. Conflict may, however, arise anyway.

The successful project manager must be able to recognize the symptoms of conflict so that problem areas can be identified and corrected. The project manager should recognize these symptoms early, before they spiral out of control. Some of the symptoms of conflict are the following:

- Poor communication among team members and with upper management causes decisions to be made with incomplete information. Often the left hand doesn't know what the right hand is doing. Various parts of the company are working at different, conflicting solutions to the same problem.
- Hostility between groups is often expressed with such phrases as "They never tell us anything."

- Problems seem to be focused on individual personalities rather than issues concerning the project. Individuals communicate with each other in a cold, formal manner or only through arguments.
- Senior management steps in frequently to arbitrate arguments.
- Productivity is inhibited because of increased numbers of rules and regulations.
- Low morale is expressed as frustration and inefficiency.

9.6.4 Conflict Resolution

When the symptoms of conflict are discovered and the conflict cannot be resolved by rearranging the work environment, there are a number of other strategies that can be considered. Some of these strategies are shown in Summary Points box 9.3 and discussed in detail in the following list:

- **Arbitration**: In arbitration, a neutral arbitrator hears both sides of the conflict and recommends a solution. Both parties agree to abide by the decisions of the arbitrator. Arbitration is most useful when the conflict is specific and obvious. If the conflict is ongoing and vague, arbitration is not likely to be effective. The arbitrator must be agreed upon by all parties at the outset of the project, before any conflict arises.
- **Rules and regulations**: The development of new rules, regulations, and procedures may mitigate the conflict. Rules and regulations should, whenever possible, be developed through negotiation rather than imposed upon the parties. This strategy is useful when the conflict is recurring but should not be regarded as a permanent solution to the problem.
- **Confrontation**: In a confrontation, the parties meet to share their points of view openly and honestly. This approach will be effective if the issue of conflict can be clearly defined and is not simply a symptom of larger, underlying differences. Confrontation can be very useful in getting each side to understand more about the view of the other side.
- **Negotiation**: A variation of the confrontation approach is the negotiation approach in which each party negotiates and trades items of behavior. For example, one party may say, "I will stop doing X if you will stop doing Y." This approach may not actually resolve the conflict but may make life livable for both parties.
- **Separation**: If the conflicting parties conflict more as they interact more, separating them may relieve some of the conflicting pressures. This solution will work best when the true cause of the conflict is incompatible personalities. Allowing the two parties some say in the mechanism of separation (i.e., who will work on what) will help to make both at least somewhat happy with the resulting situation.

- **Neglect**: If the conflict is trivial and is not affecting overall productivity, an appropriate approach may be to ignore the conflict.
- **Coordination device**: If the conflict is exacerbated by contact, a position may be created between the conflicting parties. All communication between the parties is then channeled through the new, intermediate position. By eliminating the contact, this approach makes the conflict disappear. Of course, it increases administrative costs but may be the only solution for conflicts that are continuous.

Dealing with conflicting team members is one of the most trying aspects of the project manager's role. Developing effective conflict identification and resolution skills should be of utmost priority for the successful project manager. Conflict is a great diverter of energies. By better managing differences among team members, the project manager can help to increase the productivity of the team significantly as well as to make the project more pleasant to work on.

SUMMARY POINTS 9.3

Conflict Resolution Strategies

1. Arbitration
2. Rules and regulations
3. Confrontation
4. Negotiation
5. Separation
6. Neglect
7. Coordination device

Risk Management

As we discussed earlier in this chapter, risk management is a critical element in the success of large-scale development efforts. The results of project management are of little use if a series of disrupting events causes the project development time frame to shift continually. Risk management provides a structured evaluation of a development project to draw attention to sources of risk. In certain situations, steps may be taken to minimize risk. In other situations, additional time is built into the development schedule to accommodate some level of disruption.

Risk management should be undertaken for the testing phase of software development. In our experience, most project managers allocate far too little time for testing. Anyone who has programmed solutions to nontrivial problems understands that hard-to-find bugs are more of a rule than an exception. When bugs are found during testing, the project can fall behind schedule if time to fix the problems was not built into the schedule. A project manager who understands risk assessment knows that testing is highly risk prone, and so adequate time must be allocated for testing to avoid time overruns.

Risk management is a common topic in business planning. Because the development of software is a form of business practice, risk management is an appropriate topic for a software engineering text. The business world and software development also share a high failure rate. New businesses fail at an alarming rate, as do large software development initiatives. In 1997, 83,384 businesses failed owing creditors money [98]. Unlike businesses, software development initiatives are not formally registered anywhere, and so similar counts for failed software development projects are unavailable. Long-term observers of the software industry, however, have concluded that software development is risky business [9].

9.7.1 Sources of Technical Risk

What constitutes risk in a software development initiative? Recall that project management seeks to lay out the process of software development as a series of finite tasks. The project manager assigns tasks to members of a software development team, estimating how long each task should take. A risk is any unanticipated condition or event that causes a task, or more than one task, to be delayed, be lengthened, or fail. Risks can potentially delay or even prevent the completion of a task or project as a whole.

A project manager must take steps to prevent or reduce risks. Common sources of risk must be identified. Typical sources of risk fall into two categories: the first type of risk is related to technical aspects of the project, the second type to human factors.

Technical risk takes many forms and depends on the specific nature of the project. Figure 9.10 shows project objectives that work in opposition to each other. We wish a software system to respond in a reasonable amount of time to human users or to other software modules. If the system must acquire large amounts of information over a network or from large databases through time-consuming queries, that response time may be compromised. Similarly, if the system must await the results of time-consuming algorithms, the response time may be compromised. For example, an interactive system that must simultaneously execute CPU-intensive queries on a large database and be responsive to users is inherently risky. The risk is that real-time queries do not typically provide reasonable response times, and so if the functionality requires both reasonable response times and real-time queries, we are unlikely to be able to provide a system that provides them. The following are examples of technical risk.

Project Complexity

There are many problems in computer science that are intractable. In practice, solutions to these problems emphasize heuristics to find a near-optimal solution.

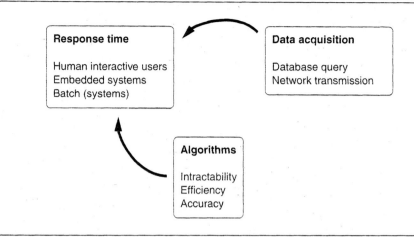

FIGURE 9.10   Risk Tradeoffs

If the system to be developed requires a heuristic approach to an algorithmically intractable problem, the resulting system embodies a large amount of risk. For example, we may need to determine the next move for an automated player in a game of strategy, like chess, checkers, or Othello. The risk lies in formulating an effective heuristic approach to finding the next move within a reasonable amount of time. Complexity in this context refers to solutions that are not algorithmically simple.

Project Size

The risk inherent in an extremely large project is that upon embarking on its development, the project is typically not understood in sufficient detail. Numerous unanticipated obstacles and added tasks are likely to be encountered after the project has begun. Risks may be mitigated by engaging in thorough analysis of the project to help identify as many hidden complexities as possible.

Project Software Change or Innovation

The need to utilize state-of-the-art technology in a software system may introduce another risk, because of the rate at which advances are made in the computer industry. A simple example involves a software development team using Java to develop a project over a one-year period. When the team begins the project, version 1.0 of the Java Development Kit is the state of the art. By the time the project is half finished, however, Sun Microsystems releases version 1.1 of the Java Development Kit, with radical changes in many aspects of the language. The development team incurs significant delay while they convert their existing code to the more up-to-date version of Java. The risk arises from the need to adopt leading-edge technologies that might develop during the course of project development.

Another example of technical innovation introducing risk into the system is the decision to use a framework as a basis for the new system. A framework is a set of code, typically classes, that has been developed for reuse by others. Perhaps no one on the development team has experience with a particular framework, but the project manager decides to use it anyway. The team finds that the framework is very difficult to learn and full of bugs; as a result, more time than anticipated is required for development. Often, however, the investment of time to learn to use the framework pays off during subsequent projects.

Security: Network Vulnerability

Many software systems consist of networked nodes cooperatively interacting. Other software systems are run on computers that have network connections. In either case, a security vulnerability exists, and potentially malicious intruders must be prevented from destroying or viewing the data or programs upon which the system is built. If such safeguards are not built in, the system embodies a huge amount of security risk and may in fact prevent other, more sensitive applications from being run on the same machines.

Security: Disgruntled Employees

The system must take measures to minimize the damage carried out by malicious insiders, whether they are prospective end users or development team members. Such risk is inherent in any software system, although the potential damage varies substantially with the application.

Security: White-Collar Crime

The system must be designed with sufficient checks and balances to discourage or prevent white-collar crime, such as theft of money from accounts and theft of information about individuals.

Data Attainability

In order to work properly, some systems require information that is difficult or impossible to attain. For example, we may want to create an expert system for a particular topic. If the experts that we know are hostile to the project, it will be difficult, if not impossible, for us to gather the domain expertise necessary to create the expert system.

An additional risk is that production-quality data may not be available for use in testing the system. A system that is not adequately tested should never be delivered. A classic example of this problem is the Strategic Defense Initiative (SDI), which had the goal of intercepting nuclear missiles. The problem raised by critics of the

SUMMARY POINTS 9.4

Sources of Technical Risk

Project	*Security/Reliability*	*Data*
Complexity	Network vulnerability	Attainability
Size	Disgruntled employees	Accuracy of data source
Software change	White-collar crime	Quality of graphics

system was that the system is difficult to test without firing missiles that could be shot down by the system. If the system is tested with missiles, what happens if the system fails to perform as expected? If the system is not tested with missiles, how can we rely on the system to perform as expected in a real situation? No solution for this problem was ever devised.

Accuracy of Data Source

A scientific system may require precision of measurements that are impossible to obtain within budgetary constraints. The risk is that the system will fail without such precision.

Quality of Graphics

Because many software systems require high-quality graphic artwork to be effective, the ability to produce the necessary artwork is a potential risk. The risk is that substandard graphic artwork may compromise the effectiveness of the system.

Summary Points box 9.4 lists the major categories for technical risk that were discussed in the preceding paragraphs.

Review the set of tasks that you devised for planting a garden in the previous **EXERCISE 9.7** chapter. What sorts of technical risks might compromise the success of your garden? Discuss these with your classmates, and create a composite list of potential risks. What measures can you take to combat these risks?

9.7.2 Sources of Human Risk

Sources of risk that are related to human involvement in software development can be introduced from three groups:

1. The development team
2. The end users
3. The administration

Humans are notoriously difficult to categorize and predict and are, therefore, a significant source of risk. Summary Points box 9.5 lists the types of risk introduced into the development process by these three groups of people. The members of the software development team introduce risk because project planning necessitates estimating how much work each team member will accomplish during project development. This estimate is complicated by large variations in productivity, experience, dedication, and competence between individuals on the development team.

End users add risk to the software development process in a number of ways. End users may feel that their livelihood is threatened by the new system being developed, and may therefore be hostile to the development process. This hostility may cause the end users to withhold vital information concerning their work procedures from the systems analysts. For example, let us imagine that a health maintenance organization (HMO), in its fervor to cut costs, wishes to put in place a nursing expert system to alleviate the necessity of hiring qualified nurses. The nurses can instead be replaced with minimally experienced and trained employees who consult with the nursing expert system for advice. In order for such a system to succeed, much information concerning nursing expertise must be gathered. If the nurses currently employed by the HMO are not willing to provide such information, it may have to hire other nurses, if they can be found, to provide the expertise.

End users may not be very technologically savvy and may therefore not have a good idea of the type of system that will actually meet their needs. The system developers then give the end users the system they asked for, despite the fact that the system does not actually provide the functionality required by the end users. When the system fails, the system developers blame the failure on the end users and move on with their professional lives. This situation results in wasted time, energy, and money, and it is not expedient to engage in an effort that is doomed to failure

---

SUMMARY POINTS 9.5

Sources of Human Risk

Development Team	End Users	Administration
Productivity	Technical knowledge	Budgetary constraints
Experience	Support for project	Project priority
Knowledge	Agreement on system	Realistic expectations
Dedication		

because the end users are not technically savvy. This immense element of risk must be attacked head-on if the project is to succeed.

Some end users may have enough technical knowledge to conceive of an effective system. Individual end users, however, may conceive of a system that is in conflict with the system envisioned by their colleagues. Such differences of opinion complicate the successful development of a useful system.

The administration of the organization sponsoring the software development may play a significant role in the success of the project. Administrators are responsible for imposing budgetary restrictions that may have dire consequences for the success of the project. If the administration is not well versed in the software development process, they may unintentionally sabotage the project by adjusting the schedule to save time and money without also adjusting the expectations of the resultant system. In addition, administrators tend to be unrealistic concerning the time frames for software development phases such as analysis, design, and testing, allotting very little time to each. Finally, priorities can shift within an organization because of a variety of factors, such as stockholders, earnings, or simply a whim of leadership. These new priorities, which the administration is charged with carrying out, may affect the project.

A project manager may take steps to reduce some of the risks due to the administration. The primary weapon against unrealistic expectations or an unreasonable project time frame is education. Through research, the project manager can make a solid business case for allocating sufficient resources to the analysis and design phases, since many software failures have been documented that are due to the high cost of correcting errors introduced during these phases [9]. Presenting these findings to administrators may encourage them to provide adequate resources for the analysis, design, and testing phases of the development process.

EXERCISE 9.8

Consider the process of building a house. You are the primary builder and have been asked to construct a house with your employees who do electrical, plumbing, carpentry, and masonry work. What human risks factors may compromise the quality of the house? What can you do to minimize these?

9.7.3 Consequences of Risk

The potential risk factors affecting a software development initiative have a variety of possible consequences if they come to fruition. For example, a member of the development team whose productivity has been overestimated will simply delay the delivery of the project, while the lack of cooperation of domain experts in the creation of an expert system will cause the project to fail completely. The following list presents the range of possible consequences of the risk factors:

- Delay the project
- Compromise the quality of the project
- Cause the project to fail
- Cause the project to be too expensive to implement or run

EXERCISE 9.9   Reconsider either the technical risk factors developed for the garden problem or the human risk factors formulated around the house construction problem, and determine the potential consequence of each risk factor.

 Reducing Risk

The single most important step that an organization may take to reduce the risk of failure for a software initiative is to utilize the object-oriented paradigm to its full extent. Full utilization implies that the project is conceptualized in an object-oriented manner and implemented in an object-oriented programming language. In addition, the project is evolved during the course of development with periodic delivery dates, as opposed to a single delivery date. Delivering a project in a series of incremental steps is a strategy with the highest success rate for delivering object-oriented software systems that meet user requirements. There are several advantages to incremental delivery of the project. These are discussed in the following subsections.

9.8.1 Early Product Evaluation

When software systems are delivered incrementally, users of the system have an opportunity to evaluate the product early. The adage that users do not know what they want in a software system until it is delivered rings all too true in the experience of the authors. No amount of explanation will allow all users to understand what the final system is going to look like. When the system is delivered incrementally, users can experience pieces of the system and request changes if necessary. For example, after a piece of the system is delivered, the users might request certain changes. If a major change is required in the look and feel of the user interface of a system, then this change can be applied before all the interfaces have been completed.

9.8.2 Early Implementation of Risky System Aspects

By planning to deliver the system incrementally, the developers can focus on technically risky aspects of the system so they can be resolved or fail early. In this chapter we outlined a number of technical objectives that can increase the risk in a system. For example, concurrent online access to large databases introduces much risk because such systems typically have poor response time. If the system development targets technically risky aspects of the system in early iterations of the system, these aspects will either be resolved or fail with less time investment in the system.

9.8.3 Early Use of New Technology

When a system is delivered incrementally, system developers can learn to use new technology, such as new programming languages or libraries, early in the development process. This early placement of potentially steep learning curves allows any negative effects the learning curves might have on the project's delivery time to occur at the beginning of the development effort, and adjustments can be made early.

9.8.4 Early Resolution of Class Interaction Problems

Important classes in a typical software system interact with each other in a substantial manner. Usually these interactions arise in early increments of the system. These potential interaction difficulties can thus be identified and eliminated early in the development effort. The inherent modularity of object-oriented systems also reduces risk by lending itself to well-structured code and enforceable interclass interfaces. Such modularity localizes the role and effect of any given class on the system and minimizes unintended side effects. These factors make the resolution of bugs much easier.

 Further Readings on Risk Management

A complete treatment of the topic of risk management is beyond the scope of this text. A complete examination of the risks of a semester-long project is also impossible to carry out over the course of a single semester. The point of this discussion is to alert students to the importance of risk management. Students interested in a more in-depth discussion of the topic are encouraged to consult the following sources:

- *Assessment and Control of Software Risks* by Capers Jones (Upper Saddle River, NJ: Prentice Hall, 1994).

- *Practical Risk Assessment for Project Management* by Stephen Grey (New York: Wiley, 1995).
- *Software Engineering Risk Management* by Dale Walter Karolak and N. Karolak (Piscataway, NJ: IEEE Computer Society Press, 1996).

9.10   *Case Study:* Risk Analysis in the LMS

We will consider the sources of risk in relationship to the Library Management System (LMS) to illustrate a simple version of risk assessment. The case study carried out here shows a cursory risk assessment that can be easily applied to projects that are not otherwise being formally assessed for risk. For more formal risk assessment, refer to the works listed in the previous section.

9.10.1 Risk Trade-Offs in the LMS

The Library Management System supports a number of concurrent users, such as library patrons searching for library resources or research entries and librarians carrying out their work functions. These users must access information from potentially large databases. As we have seen in this chapter, the need for real-time access to large amounts of information can often result in compromised response times for users. To assess the amount of risk in the LMS resulting from these competing needs, we must stress test the system. How does one stress test a system that does not yet exist? It is possible to simulate large database queries by populating the database with test data and attempting time-consuming queries, but how does one emulate multiple concurrent users making these database queries?

To determine whether the LMS has sufficient capacity to handle the estimated demand for information from concurrent users, we must write some software that emulates a number of concurrent users. Such software is easily created in Java with its easy-to-use Thread abstraction. We must write a driver program that spawns a number of threads, each of which makes a series of database requests. System time before and after each request gives an approximate idea of the response time that a similar number of users can anticipate.

No complex or time-consuming algorithms are anticipated in the LMS.

9.10.2 Technical Risks in the LMS

The LMS conforms to a typical organizational data-processing model in which a centralized set of databases contains information that is accessed through interactive transactions by a finite set of user types. Because many other systems also match this model, many developers have experience designing and implementing such systems. The project complexity and size of the LMS are not great enough to cause the system to be considered a special technical risk.

If the LMS is developed using a currently evolving programming language like Java, additional time should be factored in to accommodate changes in the Java Development Kit during system development. If, however, the LMS is being developed in a stable, unchanging language, no technical risk is assumed by the use of such a language.

The LMS does not handle data with significant financial implications. In addition, people's lives do not depend on the data stored in the LMS. Therefore, there is little security risk in the LMS. In contrast, banking systems typically attribute much monetary significance to their data, and so the security of data in such systems must be ensured. Similarly, many lives depend on systems like the air traffic control system, and much risk is associated with inaccurate, insecure data. We do not mean to suggest that security is of no concern in the LMS. The accurate representation of the status of the library's holdings is essential to its existence, and private information concerning library patrons' history of book selection must be guarded.

The final category of technical risk concerns data. The gathering of the data that constitute the LMS is not likely to be a major problem. The manner in which the information pertaining to the library's holdings is to be encoded, however, is a question that must be answered. Realistically, it is likely that the library holdings were already encoded electronically in a previous system, but if they were not, the issue of data entry to populate the initial database would be a serious consideration, adding significant cost to the overall project. Ensuring that the data are accurately entered is a second related consideration. The need for graphic artwork is not a likely obstacle to the success of the project.

9.11   Questions for Review

1. There are numerous schools of thought on the topic of software metrics. Research recent articles on the subject. List the advantages and disadvantages of the metrics proposed.
2. Formulate your own set of software metrics. Will your metrics outperform others? How will you establish the effectiveness of your metrics?
3. Contemplate other object-oriented metrics that may allow for more accurate estimates of project development time.

4. Create a project plan for the development of a single-player checkers game in which the computer is the other player. Recall that before you can create a project plan, you must have a stable list of primary classes. Assume two people will be working on this project. How much time savings would you anticipate if a third person worked on this project?

5. Create a project plan for a two-player ticktacktoe game. Recall that before you can create a project plan, you must have a stable list of primary classes. Assume you have two people on your development team. How much time savings would you anticipate if a third person worked on this project?

6. Create a Gantt chart for the complete Game2D project.

7. Create a Gantt chart for either the checkers program in question 4 or the tictacktoe program in question 5.

8. Create a PERT/CPM network for the complete Game2D project.

9. Create a PERT/CPM network for either the checkers program in question 4 or the ticktacktoe program in question 5.

10. What are the objectives of risk management? What characteristics of projects may make them risky?

11. Assume you are project manager for a large development initiative. Your manager suggests that two weeks may be saved by omitting the formal risk assessment and simply building extra time into the scedule to compensate for possible pitfalls. How would you respond? Defend your position.

12. Name sources of technical risk for Game2D.

13. Name sources of technical risk for a checkers-playing program.

14. Name sources of technical risk for an automated teller program.

15. Name sources of human risk for Game2D.

16. Name sources of human risk for a checkers-playing program.

17. Name sources of human risk for an automated teller program.

Design Patterns

10.1 Key Concepts

- Design patterns
- Creational patterns
- Structural patterns
- Behavioral patterns

- Decorator design pattern
- Iterator design pattern
- State design pattern
- Singleton design pattern

10.2 Motivation for Design Patterns

The process of building an object-oriented system typically requires the combination of classes in both new and familiar ways. Some aspects of the class definitions that make up the new system are likely to be unique to that system. If there are no new unique class definitions, off-the-shelf solutions might exist. Despite the unique aspects of the new system, the system is likely to include common solutions that have been incorporated in many other object-oriented systems.

The purpose of design patterns is to capture these classic solutions to common problems in an easy-to-understand manner, so that they may be readily applied to the development of new software systems. For example, if an efficient solution for iterating over the elements of some sort of aggregate class already exists, why should system developers need to develop a new solution each time such a situation arises? The answer is that to develop new solutions to familiar problems is a waste of time and effort, and, instead, developers should have access to the previously developed solution.

Thus, design patterns are a mechanism for naming and communicating these classic solutions. Various formats exist for communicating this information [38, 60].

We will present design pattern information through class diagrams and code segments.

Design patterns contribute to reusability because they specify a set of reusable design solutions. Another contribution to reuse provided by design patterns results from the fact that design patterns encourage the creation of more reusable classes. Reuse is enhanced by producing designs that decouple interobject interaction through intermediary classes, as will be demonstrated in the subsequent sections.

10.3   What Are Design Patterns?

Design patterns address common programming problems. To understand design patterns, one must have a sense of what these common problems are. The seminal book on design patterns by Erich Gamma et al. [38] defines three categories of design patterns. The categories, as shown in Figure 10.1, are **creational patterns**, **structural patterns**, and **behavioral patterns**.

Figure 10.2 summarizes the purpose of the various creational design patterns. Creational patterns address common methods for constructing objects. For example, consider a generic maze program that can display its maze three-dimensionally to give the illusion that the user is actually walking through the maze, two-dimensionally on the screen, or two-dimensionally in postscript to create a printed copy. The maze system includes an internal representation that is independent of any of its output forms. The translation from the internal form to any of the three external forms is delegated to the **Builder** class, which embodies the information necessary to convert the internal representation to any of the three external formats.

Creational Patterns	Structural Patterns	Behavioral Patterns
Abstract factory	Adapter	Chain of responsibility
Builder	Bridge	Command
Factory method	Composite	Interpreter
Prototype	Decorator	Iterator
Singleton	Facade	Mediator
	Flyweight	Memento
	Proxy	Observer
		State
		Strategy
		Template method
		Visitor

FIGURE 10.1   Design Patterns Introduced by Gamma et al.

Creational Pattern	Description
Abstract factory	Facilitates the creation of related objects without a concrete class reference.
Builder	If a class supports a number of different data representations, the builder encapsulates the details of the necessary data conversions.
Factory method	Defers the determination of which specific class to create to subclasses.
Prototype	Embodies information comprising prototypical instances, which serve as the basis of new instances.
Singleton	Ensures that the class has at most one instance and other classes have global access to it.

FIGURE 10.2   Brief Descriptions of Creational Design Patterns

Structural Patterns	Description
Adapter	Translates between interacting objects for which the method signatures are incompatible.
Bridge	Creates a more flexible mechanism for multiple implementations of an abstract class than inheritance.
Composite	Facilitates a generic hierarchical grouping of objects where the class and number of objects may change.
Decorator	Allows dynamic addition of new behavior to objects by acting as an outer wrapper containing the added features of the original core class.
Facade	Provides a front end for a series of classes so that users of these classes only need to know of and use the standard set of methods implemented by the facade to interact with these classes.
Flyweight	Describes a strategy for using an otherwise prohibitive number of very small-scale objects with minimal overhead.
Proxy	A means by which the instantiation of certain classes may be delayed until the proxied object is needed. This speeds up the instantiation of the class that contains the proxied class.

FIGURE 10.3   Brief Descriptions of Structural Design Patterns

Figure 10.3 summarizes the purposes of the various structural design patterns. Structural patterns resolve common problems of interobject relationships. Common problems include situations in which objects with incompatible interfaces must communicate with each other. For example, an **adapter** class may be used to translate between the method calls of otherwise incompatible classes, allowing them to exchange messages through the adapter class.

Finally, behavioral patterns, whose descriptions are shown in Figure 10.4, attempt to encapsulate variations in object behavior, such as behavior that varies depending on the context of the object. For example, the system may recognize a variety of states, such as *user-login*, *game initialization*, or *game-in-play*, and an object may react differently depending on the state. Another kind of behavioral encapsulation separates interobject communication from the rest of the system by introducing an intermediary object that isolates this behavior. This allows the two communicating classes to be written without the class-specific details of their intercommunication, thus producing more reusable code.

Behavioral Patterns	Description
Chain of responsibility	A strategy that sets up a series of objects that may respond to a message depending on the context of the request.
Command	Allows methods to be encapsulated in objects and invoked by a standard means as determined by the interface of the abstract command class.
Interpreter	If a set of problems is conducive to being represented as a simple grammar, a class may be defined for each rule in the grammar.
Iterator	Separates the class elements necessary for access and traversal from the aggregating class and encapsulates in the iterator.
Mediator	Helps to avoid highly coupled class definitions by moving explicit object references to an intermediary object.
Memento	A means to store the otherwise encapsulated internal state of an object for the purpose of creating a checkpoint or undoing transactions.
Observer	Allows multiple dependent instances of a class to be notified of relevant changes to the observed class.
State	A class hierarchy is defined around a set of states for an object, allowing the behavior of an object to vary depending on state by substituting the state-specific subclass in its composition.
Strategy	Selects a set of related algorithms and encapsulates them in such a way that they may be interchangeable for solving certain problems.
Template method	Structures a method in such a way that elements of the algorithm are deferred to subclasses.
Visitor	Allows the introduction of new operations on objects that comprise the visited object.

FIGURE 10.4   Brief Descriptions of Behavioral Design Patterns

10.4 Exploring Design Patterns

10.4.1 *Case Study:* Decorator Design Pattern

The **decorator** design pattern is used when a developer would like to add functionality to a predefined class. The decorator creates an easy-to-use interface for one or more classes by building functionality on top of the existing interface of these classes. An instance of the decorator class is created by sending an instance of the class to be enhanced as a parameter of the decorator's constructor; thus the decorator class serves as a wrapper around the original class. The class using this decorator-enhanced class interacts with the instance of the decorator, which in turn sends messages to the instance of the original object. In the following example, a decorator class provides an easy-to-use interface for Java's socket class.

The Java programming language allows easy creation of socket connections between processes. The manner in which data are written over a socket connection, however, is not very user-friendly. By creating a decorator object, a developer can treat a socket connection as though it were a simple output stream or input stream in order to write and read information sent over the socket connection easily. Figure 10.5 illustrates the series of encapsulations that allow clients to access a Java socket *InputStream*. The *InputStream* is sent to the constructor of an *InputStreamReader*, which in turn is sent to the constructor of a *BufferedReader*.

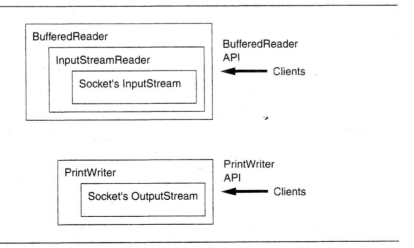

FIGURE 10.5 Decorating Socket Input and Output Streams in Java (API = Application Programmer Interface)

The resulting socket connection may then be used by clients as though it were a *BufferedReader* object. Reading information from a *BufferedReader* is much simpler than reading information from a socket. Writing information to a socket can be done easily by accessing the socket's *OutputStream* and sending the *OutputStream* to the constructor of a *PrintWriter* object. Clients of the socket class can then use the more convenient *PrintWriter* interface to send information to another process over a socket connection.

The decorator pattern specifies the creation of a decorator class that translates more functional method calls into method calls compatible with the decorated class. The use of the decorator class allows the decorated class to remain unchanged, while the class using the decorated class may utilize the simpler, more functional interface.

10.4.2 *Case Study:* Iterator Design Pattern

Iterating over a series of homogeneous elements in some sort of aggregating class is one of the most common activities undertaken in programs. The details of these iteration situations differ slightly depending on the details of the class that contains the elements and the details of the elements themselves. We might attempt to solve this problem time after time, varying the details of the iterative loop only slightly each time. Such a strategy is shortsighted. Instead, we can specify a strategy for solving this problem and reuse the approach over and over.

In the Library Management System, there are a number of elements that are aggregated. For example, a library patron can check out a number of library resources, and thus the *Patron* class contains a list of these checked-out items. Each resource may also retain a history of its being borrowed, and thus the *Resource* class contains a list of *Patron* objects, each associated with a date. In both of these situations, we can imagine wanting to print out the contents of the entire list. The details of how to print out the patron's checked-out-resource list may differ slightly from the details of how to print out the checkout history of a particular resource, but the overall process can be captured in a general iterator design pattern.

For the patron's checked-out-resource list, we choose a linked list implementation because resources can be removed from the list in any order, depending on when the patron returns that resource. For the resource's checkout history, we choose a vector implementation because historical entries are never removed. Thus, we have two very different implementation strategies for these lists. The linked list and the vector are **container** classes. Rather than embedding the attributes and methods necessary for item traversal in each of these container classes, we will implement the details once in an *Iterator* class that will communicate with the container classes.

Figure 10.6 is a class diagram for the *Iterator* class. The constructor of the *Iterator* class is overloaded to accommodate a variety of container classes. A reference to the container is maintained in an instance variable of the iterator. The constructor also initializes the *nextElement* instance variable with the first element in the container object, unless the container is empty. If the container is empty, the constructor sets the *containerEmpty* and *nomoreElements* variables to *true*.

The details of traversing the elements of the container are embedded in the *getnextElement( )* method. The user of the *Iterator* class calls the parameterless *getnextElement( )* method, which then extracts the class of the container object to call the overloaded *getnextElement(Container)* method, overloaded to contain the traversal details appropriate to the container class. The iterator keeps track of its position in the traversal and uses the *nextElement* variable in conjunction with the container-specific logic to return the next element when the client requests it.

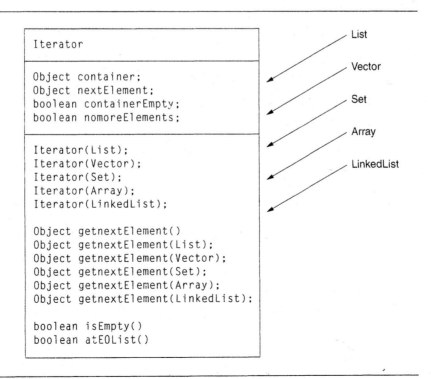

```
Iterator

Object container;
Object nextElement;
boolean containerEmpty;
boolean nomoreElements;

Iterator(List);
Iterator(Vector);
Iterator(Set);
Iterator(Array);
Iterator(LinkedList);

Object getnextElement()
Object getnextElement(List);
Object getnextElement(Vector);
Object getnextElement(Set);
Object getnextElement(Array);
Object getnextElement(LinkedList);

boolean isEmpty()
boolean atEOList()
```

List

Vector

Set

Array

LinkedList

FIGURE 10.6   The Elements Constituting an Iterator Class

EXERCISE 10.1   Examine a program that you wrote for another class. Can you identify any places where the iterator design pattern might be useful? Rewrite the code to use the iterator design pattern.

10.4.3 *Case Study:* State Design Pattern

The **state design pattern** is useful for situations in which various states of the system must be represented. This design pattern specifies the creation of an inheritance hierarchy. Each class in the inheritance hierarchy represents one state and contains the methods necessary for the system behavior associated with that particular state.

The state design pattern is useful for the design of the Galaxy Sleuth game. The game progresses through a series of states. Recall the previous discussion concerning the states of Galaxy Sleuth, as described in Chapter 4. Figure 10.7 shows a partial inheritance hierarchy with various classes that embody the state-dependent behaviors of Galaxy Sleuth. The thicker lines of the rectangle representing the *Game State* class indicate that this class is an abstract base class. Several other classes are derived from the abstract base class. Each of these classes may also have one or more child classes.

A large portion of the logic that makes up Galaxy Sleuth is devoted to carrying out state-dependent communication between the server and client. The server class interprets messages from clients differently depending on the state of the game. For example, a player may identify specific game elements for the purpose of either formulating a hypothesis or attempting to solve the crime. The server handles each request differently depending on the current state of the game. In addition, the partitioning of the possible game states is a way to break the larger system-development task into subtasks.

The state design pattern specifies that a variable representing the current state of the system be created. The type for this variable will be the abstract base class so that instances of any of the subclasses can be put into the variable. As the system starts, the current-state variable will contain an instance of the first system-state class. When the state changes, the current-state variable gets an instance of the class for the next state of the system. For example, in Galaxy Sleuth, we will create a variable called *currentState* whose type is *GameState*. The first value put into this variable will be an object of type *GetPlayerName*, which is a subclass of *PlayerJoinGame*, which in turn is a subclass of *InitiateGame*, the first state of the system. Note that every *GetPlayerName* object is also a *PlayerJoinGame* object,

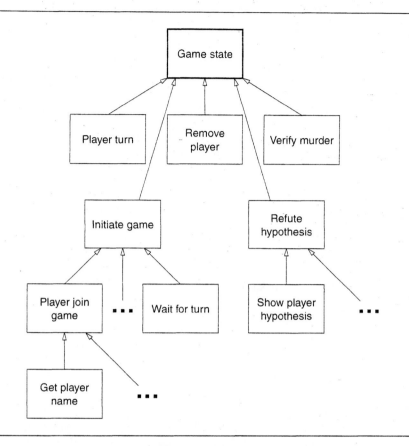

FIGURE 10.7 A Partial Inheritance Hierarchy Modeling the States Constituting Galaxy Sleuth

every *PlayerJoinGame* object is an *InitiateGame* object, and every *InitiateGame* object is a *GameState* object. The state design pattern makes extensive use of this aspect of the inheritance relationship among objects. Eventually, the *currentState* variable will contain an object of the next state, which is also a *GameState* object.

The server class for Galaxy Sleuth can listen over the socket connection for client messages. These messages can then be forwarded directly to the state object referred to by the *currentState* variable. The decision of whether to remain at the current state or advance to a new state can be embedded in each respective state object. Each state object must then embody both its state-specific behavior and the logic concerning which possible states the game may advance to and under what circumstances.

Figure 10.8 shows the basic elements of state transition in the *GalaxySleuth-Server* class. The server class contains the *currentState* instance variable, which

```
:GalaxySleuthServer

GameState currentState;
// other instance variables

String getclientMessage();

void advanceGame();
{ while(currentState != done)
  { String s = getclientMessage();
    currentState =
    currentState.handleMessage(s);
  }
}
```

```
:SpecificGameState extends GameState

// various state variables

GameState handleMessage(String m)
{ if (m.equals(Action1))
  { updateState(Action1)
    return new NextState();
  }
  else
    if (m.equals(Action2))
    { updateState(Action2)
      return this;
    }
  ...
}
```

FIGURE 10.8 Basic Elements of State Transition in Galaxy Sleuth

refers to a specific *GameState* subclass object, represented by the *SpecificGameState* object on the right side of the figure. The *GalaxySleuthServer* class also contains a method called *getClientMessage()*, which blocks until a message is received over the socket connection to the client. Once a message is read over the socket, the message is sent to the current *GameState* object through the *handleMessage()* method. The *handleMessage()* method contains the logic to modify the current state to reflect the content of the message and to then determine whether the transition to a new game state should occur. The transition to a new state is handled through the return value of the *handleMessage()* method. The *GalaxySleuthServer* class then uses this returned *GameState* object either to advance the game to the next state or to continue in the current state.

EXERCISE 10.2 Find a game program written by you or one of your classmates. Is the state design pattern useful for this program? Describe the states of the game. Design the classes that you would require in order to take advantage of the state design pattern.

10.4.4 *Case Study:* Singleton Design Pattern

The purpose of the singleton design pattern is to ensure that only a single instance of a class is created. There can be a number of reasons why only a single instance of certain classes is desirable in an application. For example, multiple instances of an object may affect data integrity, or the ability to exchange information effectively, or they may cause performance degradation.

In the Library Management System, for example, multiple *LMSDatabase* objects are unneeded because a single database object is all that is required to convert objects into relational form and back into object-oriented form. To take advantage of the singleton design pattern, the *LMSDatabase* class will be modified to contain a static variable, shared by all instances of the class. This static variable, called *LMSDB*, contains the reference to this singleton instance. In addition, a method called *getInstance()* that returns the static variable is created in the class. These details are shown in Figure 10.9. Designing the *LMSDatabase* class in this manner ensures that all instantiations of the class have access to a single *LMSDatabase* object.

Come up with another situation in which a single instance of a particular class should be ensured. How would you incorporate the singleton design pattern into this situation?

EXERCISE 10.3

```
LMSDatabase

static LMSDatabase LMSDB;

static getInstance()
{  if (LMSDB == null)
   {  LMSDB = new LMSDatabase();
   }
   return LMSDB;
}
```

FIGURE 10.9 Illustration of a Singleton Database Object

10.5   Questions for Review

Consider the following case study and answer the questions that follow it.

> You are creating a web-based polling facility, which provides for a number of types of responses that are entered through various graphical user interface (GUI) components like choice boxes, radio buttons, text fields, and text areas. You decide on a design strategy in which each GUI component is directly connected to a field in a relational database. As soon as the user of the polling system makes an entry, the component makes an update to the database immediately. This strategy distributes the responsibility for updating the database, leading to a modular and robust solution.

1. After considering your design approach, you realize that you have two basic options for pursuing your solution. You can follow an approach using inheritance alone, or you can use a design pattern.
2. Provide a class definiton including attributes and method signatures that produces a "self-updating" text field using inheritance alone.
3. Pick one or more design patterns that would meet the needs for creating a "self-updating" text field.
4. Provide a class definiton including attributes and method signatures that produces a "self-updating" text field using a design pattern selected in question 3.
5. Compare your inheritance-based solution to your design pattern–based solution. Which do you find easier to understand? Which requires less code?
6. Select another GUI component and apply both inheritance-based and design pattern–based solutions.
7. Evaluate the solutions of the GUI component from question 6. Which is better and why?

Software Development Horror Stories

Key Concepts

- Safety engineering
- Life-critical systems

- Professional ethics

11.2 Introduction

Software problems can take many forms and have a wide spectrum of consequences. The following is a sampling of such problems:

- Faye Starman receives an electric bill for $6.3 million instead of $63. The problem is traced to a data input error made by an operator who was unfamiliar with a new computer system [75].
- One of the coauthors of this text is denied a new credit card. A check of the credit report shows that her credit history was merged with that of her mother, who has the same name. As a result, the coauthor appears to have much more debt than her salary could support. The credit report, although easy to correct (in this case), was created by matching on the individual's name alone. Since many individuals have the same name, this approach is particularly error prone.
- Six people die or are injured by excessive radiation from a therapeutic linear accelerator. The software managing the machine is found to contain a series of programming errors that are difficult to reproduce because the software is so poorly structured. The difficulty of reproducing the errors contributes to the manufacturer's reluctance to recall the machine [5].

- The Mars Climate Orbiter spacecraft crashes into the surface of Mars. An investigation determines that inadequate testing did not catch a simple unit-of-measure conversion error in the software.
- Several Blackhawk helicopters crash, killing several people. Testing after the crashes shows that radio signals interfered with the on-board computer systems [76]. Thorough risk analysis should have made this vulnerability apparent and would have prevented this scenario.
- A travel reservation system called CONFIRM is canceled after an investment of $125 million [81]. Proper project management and accurate project reporting should have determined that the project was hopelessly off track, and rather than continuing to invest in it, the sponsors of the project could have abandoned it before losses climbed so high.
- Software initiatives are frequently abandoned because the end users find that the software does not meet their needs. In fact, one survey reports that 75 percent of large-scale development efforts result in systems that are never used or not completed [42]. Adequate requirements analysis engages the software developers in a well-structured dialogue with the users, better informing the developers of the users' needs and resulting in a more useful product.

While the consequences of these software failures range from death to inconvenience, each shares the possibility that the consequences of the failure could have been greatly reduced through rigorous software engineering. At first glance, the apparent exception to this generalization is the data-entry error causing the excessive electric bill. However, even this situation could have been avoided if the vulnerabilities of the resulting system had been examined during the design phase of development. For example, this system could have included a confirmation process enforced by the software to check for outlier values entered into the system. If a value was excessively high, the confirmation of a supervisor would be required before the bill was sent to the customer.

11.2.1 Causes of Failure

A key premise of this chapter is that software fails primarily because organizations do not engage in good software engineering practice. Given the potentially dire consequences of poorly developed software, we must ask ourselves why software engineering is not universally embraced by all organizations that engage in software development. We briefly discussed this topic in section 1.6, concluding that management and development staff are insufficiently informed about the importance of the early stages of software engineering. Too frequently, the production of lines of source code is the sole measure of progress on the project. Anything that does not result in lines of code is therefore not progress and does not merit the expenditure of time and resources.

In trying to assess what causes software to fail, Sara Baase cites the following [5]:

- The complexity of software
- Nonlinear (multithreaded) software
- Failing to plan for unexpected inputs or conditions
- Interfaces with external devices that behave unexpectedly
- Incompatibility between hardware or operating systems and software
- Poor management
- Insufficient testing
- Carelessness
- Pressure to cut corners
- Not communicating problems to management
- Inadequate risk analysis
- Data-entry errors
- Erroneous output interpretation
- Overconfidence in software
- Lack of market or legal pressure to produce better quality software

These causes of software failure are useful to us as a list of items to be vigilant about. The more we address potential causes of software failure, the less likely a system is to fail. For example, if we masterfully follow a software engineering methodology but do not ensure that users are adequately trained, data integrity errors may result, or the system may be deemed to be not useful.

We will now discuss the details of several actual software development horror stories. The purpose of this discussion is to provide you, as a new or current computer professional, with a set of case studies that will confirm the importance of developing software in a well-orchestrated manner These stories will also help you to argue in favor of using good software engineering practices at your workplace, if such practices are not already in use there.

Therac-25

The Therac-25 was a therapeutic linear accelerator which, depending on the type of therapy being administered, could produce beams of X rays or electrons. Because it was controlled by software running on a minicomputer, the machine was touted as being particularly "user-friendly" [86]. This control software consisted of approximately 20,000 lines of source code and had been written by a single person over a number of years. Each release of the software incorporated source code from previous models of the linear accelerator.

At the time the first problem was documented, 11 Therac-25 machines were being used in the United States and Canada. The chronology of events is as follows [86]:

- In June 1985 a female patient, after receiving follow-up treatment after the removal of a breast tumor, complained of a burning sensation. After several months, it was clear that she had been overradiated. She required a mastectomy as a result.

- In July 1985 an X-ray technician encountered an error with the Therac-25 while administering treatment to a patient's hip area. The machine indicated that no dose had been administered, so the technician repeated this same sequence of events five times until the machine shut itself down. The patient died of cancer in November of the same year, and an autopsy showed severe radiation damage to her hip.

- In December 1985, after receiving X-ray treatment, a women developed skin discoloration in a pattern matching the Therac-25 beam-emitting slots. This patient survived her injuries.

- In March 1986 a patient at a Texas clinic received treatment for a tumor in his upper back. The patient experienced a sharp pain in conjunction with this treatment. Since this experience was unlike his previous treatment experience, the patient became alarmed. Examination showed that he had suffered a radiation overdose. The Therac-25 console, however, showed an error message, called malfunction 54, indicating that an underdose of radiation had been administered. The patient died in September.

- In the same Texas clinic in April of the same year, a malfunction 54 message was once again observed during treatment of a patient for skin cancer on his face. The patient died three weeks later. The autopsy revealed radiation damage to his brain and brain stem.

- The final radiation overdose before the Therac-25 was taken out of circulation occurred in January 1987. The patient in this case, because a software error that appeared to be unrelated to the previous errors, was exposed to an intense electron beam. The patient died in April as a result.

The six cases of overradiation resulted from at least four different fatal software errors. The Therac-25 has been under much scrutiny to determine how one piece of software could do so much damage, in order to avoid similar mistakes in the future. In particular, Nancy G. Leveson, a pioneer in software safety, has extensively researched this case. According to Leveson, the source code comprising the Therac-25 reflected extremely poor coding styles that were common during the early 1970s, before software engineering techniques began to be adopted by industry [62]. This poorly structured code made it impossible to make a credible case that all bugs had been tracked down. Finally, this product was removed from market.

How this product remained on the market so long after the first overradiation incident occurred is an important question. One factor was the fact that the manufacturer refused to believe that its product was irreparably flawed and attempted to apply error-specific fixes to the software, while the device continued to endanger human life. The second factor was that each error was extremely hard to re-create, thus making it easier for the manufacturer to doubt the existence of these bugs. For example, the malfunction 54 error does not occur unless a complex sequence of events takes place. Specifically, the Therac-25 operator needs to input a treatment specification consisting of several values. One of these values is the type of beam, electron or X ray. Changing the beam type has mechanical ramifications, because magnets must change position. If the data input is complete before the magnets have completed their position change, they will remain out of position as the treatment is administered, producing a high dose of radiation. This sequence of events rarely occurred because the beam specification occurs early in the treatment specification screen. Only when a skilled technician entered all the data and then changed only the beam type did such a result occur. Because of the difficulty of reproducing this error, it went undetected for a long time.

The important question is, Could following proper software engineering techniques have prevented these errors? The manufacturer of the Therac-25 could not reliably indicate that the control software was free of bugs. This situation reflects the poor code structure of the software, which proper software engineering practice certainly would have improved. But could software engineering have prevented malfunction 54, which requires understanding timing constraints introduced by physical devices controlled by the software? A thorough risk analysis might or might not have scrutinized the timing dependencies that existed between the positioning of the magnets and the beginning of the radiation treatment. As Leveson suggests in her work on software safety, given the complexity of current software, it is unrealistic to expect the production of perfect software. We can simply reduce the number of software errors through software engineering.

To address this state of affairs, Leveson proposes that life-critical systems, systems that potentially endanger human life in the event they malfunction, be engineered to prevent the loss of human life. For example, the predecessor to the Therac-25, the Therac-20, had the same software flaw that lead to malfunction 54, but instead of overradiating patients, the earlier model blew a fuse [86]. The earlier model did not rely solely on software for its safety. The earlier model had hardware safeguards built in as well.

EXERCISE 11.1   Carefully consider the events associated with the Therac-25 disaster in conjunction with the list of causes of software failure in section 11.2.1. Determine which of these causes are relevant to the disaster. Also consider whether Therac-25 inspires additional items for this list.

11.4   CONFIRM

CONFIRM was an ambitious software development initiative that sought to integrate airline reservations, car rentals, and hotel reservations, along with their respective decision support mechanisms, into a single system. The project development firm was AMR Information Services, Inc. (AMRIS), a subsidiary of American Airlines. The project lasted three and a half years, spending $125 million and producing an unusable system [81].

Although no human life was at stake as a result of the CONFIRM fiasco, the loss of such a large sum of money translates into higher consumer costs. Through these higher consumer costs, society feels the effects of such a disastrous software development undertaking. In order to better evaluate what might have been done to prevent such a large loss of money, a brief chronology of events related to the development of this system follows [81]:

- In October 1987, Marriott, Hilton, Budget Rent-a-Car, and AMRIS form a consortium to develop and run CONFIRM, with AMRIS managing the development. The project is to be developed in two phases and be completed by June 1992.
- On May 24, 1988, AMRIS announces the beginning of the CONFIRM design phase through a press release.
- On December 30, 1988, AMRIS presents the base design of the system to the members of the consortium. Marriott objects that the functional specifications are not sufficiently detailed to convey user needs to the developers.
- In March 1989, AMRIS presents a development plan that is found to be unacceptable by the consortium members.
- In August 1989, AMRIS releases project financial estimates to consortium members. Based on these estimates, the other consortium members decide to remain involved in the project. The statements regarding the financial estimates are later found to severely underestimate personnel and operating costs.
- In September 1989, AMRIS finally completes the design phase to the consortium members' satisfaction. The cost estimate for the project increases to $72.6 million.
- In January 1990, AMRIS misses its first contractual deadline for completion of the terminal-screen design.

- In February 1990 a second project milestone concerning analysis of the business area for the system is missed. AMRIS admits to being 13 weeks behind schedule but claims that the original deadline can still be achieved.
- In February 1991, AMRIS presents the consortium members with a revised development plan that would provide Marriott with its full functionality by March 1993. Marriott later claims that AMRIS knew it could not meet the new deadline and forced employees to artificially inflate their timetables or face firing or reassignment. In the revised development plan, AMRIS also raises the price of the project to $92 million.
- In October 1991 the president of AMRIS and about 20 additional employees resign.
- On May 1, 1992, the new president of AMRIS acknowledges that the "system interfaces and databases are insufficient to providing the necessary performance and reliability." He also attributes the situation to AMRIS's misrepresentation of the status of the project.
- Finally, in July 1992 after spending $125 million on the effort, the consortium disbands.

A broad range of issues, from inept management to technical naïveté, plagued the CONFIRM project. Our primary interest is how proper software engineering practice might have prevented this disaster from occurring, but this case study also brings up an important issue of professional ethics. First, we will seek out the root causes of this software development failure.

Clearly, it is problematic that AMRIS's management lied about the status of the project. How did the project's problems evolve into something that management felt compelled to cover up? There were warning signs early in the project indicating that AMRIS could not deliver a viable product. The first sign was that, after seven months of effort, AMRIS produced a design document that was technically unsatisfactory. Such a poor design suggests that AMRIS was not technically competent to properly assess the quality of its own design work. In addition, the actions of AMRIS indicated that the projected time frame was more important in determining the completion of the initial design than the quality of the deliverable. A second deliverable was rejected by consortium members when AMRIS released its first development plan. Again, AMRIS seemed to be too inept to produce an adequate plan.

The chronology seems to repeatedly underscore AMRIS's inability to produce quality software engineering deliverables, suggesting that the effectiveness of these essential software development phases is questionable. Additionally, some basic risk analysis should have guided the consortium members to identifying at least two highly risky objectives. These risky objectives should have suggested that the consortium members engage in some pilot projects to determine the feasibility of these objectives. One high-risk objective for the CONFIRM system was the need to interface with the existing systems of the partners of the consortium. Such interfacing required the CONFIRM system to interoperate with heterogeneous hardware and software. The next high-risk objective was the need to integrate the reservation system with decision support systems for each business area. Some initial exploration exposing the complexity of such an undertaking might have created a more reasonable time frame for development.

EXERCISE 11.2 Carefully consider the events associated with the CONFIRM disaster in conjunction with the list of causes of software failure in section 11.2.1. Determine which of these causes are relevant to the disaster. Also consider whether CONFIRM inspires additional items for this list.

11.5 Telephones and Communications

In today's world, one would be hard-pressed to find a better example of technology well used than long-distance telephone networks. Covering much of the world with fiber optics that can reliably and instantaneously connect people from distant lands is one of the technological miracles of our culture. AT&T owns more than 115 switching stations that connect local phone companies around the world, carrying more than 115 million calls within the United States and 1.5 million overseas calls every day. Each switching station is capable of handling nearly 750,000 calls per hour.

A switching station, known as a 4ESS, is really a big, special-purpose computer that runs a piece of software containing 4 million lines of code. The software takes care of connecting the two telephones at either end of a call, billing for the call, and a number of other telephone-related services. More than 150 people are needed to keep the software up-to-date. Several incidents have disrupted telephone services in recent years, and all have involved this complex piece of software.

Early in the afternoon of January 15, 1990, managers of AT&T's worldwide network observed an increasing number of red warning signals on the video screens that display the network status. The warning signals indicated that the network was having trouble completing calls. Through the next nine hours, about 65 million calls were not routed through to their destination, costing the company approximately $60 million. The managers of the system had managed to fix the problem in only nine hours, but it would take several additional days to determine the cause.

About a month prior to the breakdown of the system, the software had been upgraded to allow certain types of messages to pass through the system more quickly. The upgraded software contained a bug in a couple of lines of poorly written code that had been made unnecessarily complicated. The bug had passed unnoticed through rigorous testing and a month of production use because the particular lines of code were invoked only when a particular combination of events occurred while the network was extremely busy. Each individual switching station worked properly, but the rapid pace of message passing between switching stations caused the stations to reboot themselves repeatedly. The only thing that allowed any calls at all to be completed during this time was that only about 80 of the 115 switching stations had the upgraded software installed. The rest of the switching stations were running the old software and handled as many calls as possible during the breakdown [61].

These types of "network bugs," which arise as result of communication of multiple machines across a network, are particularly difficult to find and plan for. It is difficult to accurately mimic and anticipate real-world network communications on a test system. AT&T had indeed tested the software on its test network, but such testing had failed to find the bug [86].

Carefully consider the events associated with the AT&T network breakdown in conjunction with the list of causes of software failure in section 11.2.1. Determine which of these causes are relevant to the breakdown. Also consider whether this breakdown inspires additional items for the list.

EXERCISE 11.3

Six months after the first breakdown, AT&T experienced another failure of the software controlling its switching stations. Over the course of three weeks in June and July 1991, eight incidents involving telephone outages were experienced by approximately 20 million phone customers. The cause of the outages was elusive, and the various local phone companies did not readily share information with each other concerning how to fix the problems. A six-month investigation by Bellcore Bell Communications Research, Inc., determined that the switching software was again the cause of these problems.

This set of incidents resulted from a software modification made by DSC Communications Corporation, the company that manufactures the machines, along with the software, that operate as switching stations. In April 1991, DSC Communications had released a new version of the software for its machines. Soon after, customers in Washington, Pennsylvania, California, and North Carolina began to experience problems. Each of the breakdowns began with a minor problem at one of the switching stations, in a piece of equipment called a signal transfer point (STP). This minor problem then would trigger a massive number of error messages, which would then shut down the STP and spread the failure to neighboring systems [66].

Bellcore finally tracked the problem to a three-bit error in the new version of the software. What should have been a binary D (1101) was a binary 6 (0110). This three-bit difference in the switching algorithm allowed the error message saturation of a single switch to start cascading through the network, causing other systems to shut down. Ordinarily, with the appropriate three bits in place, the saturated switch would simply alert the other systems to the congested conditions [90]. DSC Communications soon released a software patch that took care of the problem. The original program had been extensively tested. A programmer had made a change to three lines of code, one of which contained the typo, and the revised code had not been tested before release.

EXERCISE 11.4   Carefully consider the events associated with the switching software breakdown in conjunction with the list of causes of software failure in section 11.2.1. Determine which of these causes are relevant to the breakdown. Also consider whether this breakdown inspires additional items for the list.

We may be lulled into thinking that communications problems are a thing of the past, because the two examples cited occurred in the early 1990s. There are, however, numerous examples of such failures in the recent past. In 1998, for example, a technician from US West installing software for a new area code in Colorado inadvertantly shut down the 911 system for that area. A Longmont man, Thomas Carlock, died of a heart attack as his wife attempted, without success, to get through to emergency services using 911. She tried at least three times to get through to 911, and each time there was no answer, no telephone ring, no busy signal. Finally, after looking up the number, she called a hospital emergency room directly, and an ambulance was dispatched to her residence.

While this incident was unfolding, the technician was unaware that there was a problem with 911. Longmont emergency personnel were also unaware until an hour after the incident that there was a problem. According to a US West report, the company "has promised to establish additional steps to make sure software installation does not affect 911 service" [52].

EXERCISE 11.5   Again, consider the events associated with the 911 emergency system breakdown in conjunction with the list of causes of software failure in section 11.2.1. Determine which of these causes are relevant to the breakdown. Also consider whether this breakdown inspires additional items for the list.

CHAPTER

Completing and Presenting the *Class Project*

12.1 Succeeding with the Class Project

CLASS PROJECT

The objective of this text is to introduce students to fundamental software engineering techniques of the object-oriented paradigm and to guide the students in employing these techniques while developing a semester-long group project. At this stage in the course the project should be in the final phase of testing. Some development teams will be right on target, while others will have fallen behind for a variety of reasons, such as the following:

- A classmate quit the course, and his or her piece must be divided among the remaining team members.
- Insufficient analysis took place initially, and now unanticipated methods or classes are necessary with insufficient time to complete them.
- Development team members are new to a technology required by the class project, and thus additional time is necessary to accommodate a learning curve.
- A class or method is presenting itself to be more difficult or complex to implement than anticipated.
- A technology does not behave as anticipated.

At this point only a few more weeks remain for the project to be completed, so some revision may be necessary. The goal is to deliver a robust, well-designed piece of software, even if not all the functionality is delivered.

So that development teams who are at risk of not completing the entire project deliver as much functionality as possible, each development team member must assess the elements comprising his or her portion of the project to rank them for **risk** of not being completed and **importance** to the project. The factors that can be applied to rating the difficulty of completing an element of the project, and therefore its risk, are as follows:

- **Unfamiliarity** with the necessary technology or class of algorithms
- **Abstractness** of design in a method or interclass relationship
- **Incompleteness** of remaining code to implement a method or other aspect of a class definition
- **Complexity** of an algorithm or interclass relationship
- **Error** in the original design or analysis of an algorithm
- **Poorly structured solution** of an algorithm or interclass relationship that may cause testing to be particularly risky

The importance of a module to the overall project implementation is determined by assessing the functionality that depends on that particular element. The greater the dependent functionality, the more important the element is. Another consideration is how many other development team members are dependent upon this element for the successful operation of their solution. In order to prioritize elements of the project to facilitate the success of as many team members as possible, the interdependence of other team members should have precedence over the overall functionality of the project element.

The steps to assessing the importance of an element to the overall project and to other team members are as follows:

1. Identify risky elements of the solution based on the previous criteria for risk.
2. Associate each risky element with class and interaction diagrams.
3. From the diagrams in which each risky element plays a part, determine the functionality that would be sacrificed if the element were not completed.
4. Determine who else on your project team requires this functionality.
5. Prioritize the functionality at risk.
6. Create an ordered list of at-risk elements based on their importance to the project, prioritizing the needs of your development teammates.
7. Review this list and complete the software elements necessary to produce a coherent project with a subset of functionality.
8. As time permits, include additional functionality in the project.

Once the ordered list of at-risk items has been created, complete the functionality of the subproject not at risk. As time permits, implement as many of the at-risk items in order of priority as possible.

12.2   Reflecting on the Project

If you need to eliminate functional elements of your project, it is important to reflect on whether methodological issues could have eliminated this need. Even for those who are completing their systems, it is possible that things may have gone more smoothly. So the following questions should be considered:

1. Did lack of appreciation of the true complexity of certain aspects of the functionality of the system cause problems for you?
2. Were new areas of functionality needed after analysis or design had been completed?
3. Were additional human-computer interfaces required after product design was complete?
4. Was the flow of control between human-computer interfaces problematic or awkward?
5. Was object persistence more problematic than anticipated?
6. Was interprocess communication insufficient to support the full functionality of the system?
7. Was the process architecture inefficient?
8. Did your system require a significant number of methods and/or classes beyond what was provided for during design?
9. Were methods more complex than the algorithms specified during design?
10. Did classes require a significant number of additional attributes from the original design?
11. Did originally designated container classes need to be modified during implementation?
12. Did elements of the system require restructuring after the design phase?
13. Did unit testing take additional time because the design had to be altered?
14. Did integration testing require additional time because the interclass interfaces were inconsistent or inadequate?
15. Did integration testing require additional time because unit testing was not sufficiently thorough?
16. Did system testing reveal errors not caught during integration or unit testing?

The following subsection connects the preceding questions with methodological aspects, suggesting how similar problems might be avoided in future development efforts.

12.2.1 Analyzing What Went Wrong

If you answered yes to item 1 or 2, insufficient analysis took place. In the future, additional care needs to be taken. The scenarios produced should be scrutinized to determine whether they addressed adequate detail and sufficient complexity. It is not uncommon that the scenarios formulated during analysis address the basic functionality only, and that more complex scenarios that require additional software functionality are simply omitted. Unfortunately, the true complexity of a system is frequently made apparent during user testing in the event that scenarios are not adequately verified. Determining the need for significant functionality at such a late stage of development can result in the failure of a software project.

If you responded yes to one or more of questions 3 through 7, then product design is inadequate. Depending on which aspect of product design is problematic, verification should have identified inadequacies. In the case of problematic human-computer interface, prototyping the flow of control between interfaces with prospective users should have resolved these issues. In the case where interprocess communication or process architecture is at issue, using state machines to model the interprocess interaction should have identified problematic areas.

If you replied yes to one or more of questions 8 through 14, then class design or analysis is inadequate. The ultimate culprit is analysis if the scenarios that drove the process of class design did not address the full range of functionality, and therefore resulted in classes that did not support the complete functionality of the system. However, if the scenarios are deemed to be adequate and classes do not contain elements necessary to support full functionality, class design is at fault. In order to ensure that class design is adequate, it may be verified by ensuring that each scenario has a collaboration diagram that embodies its functionality. Also, a verification step may compare all diagrams resulting from class design and ensure that the resulting class skeleton contains all necessary methods and attributes.

If you answered yes to the last two questions, then testing was inadequate. The test cases did not address certain types of error, or unanticipated combinations of values were introduced into the system. The set of test cases should be verified by someone external to the software project to ensure adequate test case generation.

Finally, after the project has been refined and the development process has been reviewed for methodological weaknesses, the project is ready to be presented. The following section presents a general guideline for project presentation that may be used to present your term project.

12.3　Presenting the Project

There are essentially two types of audiences to distinguish when planning your project presentation: the nontechnical and technical audiences. The assumption made here is that the nontechnical audience consists of future or potential users of the system who are interested in its functionality and usability at a variety of levels. For example, management is likely to be interested in whether the system is easy to navigate for their data-entry staff, but may require detail concerning decision-support elements the system may provide. So the presentation should provide reasonable detail to the affected audience members without boring those who are not directly affected.

A presentation to a technical audience would include highlighting the usability of the system also, but in less detail than would be presented to the nontechnical community. The technical community would be more interested in how you determined that the system was usable than in the specifics of how data-entry operators maneuver the system. For example, a description of field tests or prototyping sessions with prospective users would be appropriate to such an audience.

Additional detail will be explored for each category of presentation in the following subsections.

12.3.1 Categories of Nontechnical Users

Let us assume that the nontechnical audience consists of a wide range of individuals —from front-line users to corporate executives. It is important to define the categories of users that may be present at a project presentation before we narrow our discussion to what is relevant for this semester's class project. The following list presents some important categories of users:

- **Front-line users**: Front-line users are typically service personnel who deal directly with the public, customers, or other sources of data. They may be data-entry operators who enter data from printed material, clerks who get input from the public, members of a sales force who enter their sales, or public servants who track their dealings with the public. Another characteristic of front-line users is that they are one of many user categories. The information entered into the system resulting from their activities is utilized by other user types. For example, supervisors may analyze these data when assessing their work performance, and managers may further assess the aggregate information to make corporate decisions.

- **Sole users**: The total functionality of the system is geared to a single user, such as the user of the class project. Although sole users may be distinguished in terms of proficiency of use, the essential functionality remains the same for this category.
- **Professional users**: The professional user is primarily interested in analyzing the information entered by the front-line users. Professional users can be supervisory, managerial, or scientific personnel, or have some other professional need for the information entered into the system. These users are interested in how the system provides decision support or integrates into other decision-support mechanisms, like spreadsheets.

12.3.2 Elements of the Nontechnical Presentation

A system presentation for nontechnical users should do the following:

- Walk the users through a clear and well-structured tour of the system's functionality
- Address each category of user as a unit
- Clearly portray user navigation through the system
- Highlight software features that emphasize ease of use

A well-structured walk-through of functionality can be brought about by returning to the set of use cases around which the system was originally developed. The walk-through should be clear as to what functionality is being demonstrated, and it should be systematic to be certain that all important functionality is addressed. Under most circumstances, different categories of user needs are embodied in separate use cases, so use cases will segregate this functionality. To address each category of user as a unit, the use cases pertaining to one category of user should be presented together.

The nontechnical user is particularly interested in the ease with which various elements of the system can be reached, so system navigation is of particular interest. The navigation should not be confusing, so a clear navigation model like a hierarchy is desirable. Also, users are interested in any features that may reduce their workload.

12.3.3 Elements of the Technical Presentation

A technical audience is interested in knowing that the system is effective from the user perspective and that the functionality specified in the functional requirements specification has been implemented. This audience has an additional set of interests pertaining to the internal structure of the software. A technical audience is interested in the composition of classes that make up the system and their interrelationships, which are conveyed in class and collaboration diagrams. Particularly complex algorithms, mechanisms of interprocess communication, and opportunities for code reuse are also of interest.

For a technical audience, a presenter wishes to concurrently walk through the essential functionality of the system and through the classes that support this functionality. To accomplish this purpose, one presenter demonstrates aspects of the system while another presenter is pointing out the underlying mechanism that supports this functionality.

12.3.4 The Project Presentation

The class project presentation should have the following characteristics:

- It should be a technical presentation.
- It should address a sole user.
- It should be structured around use cases.
- It should illustrate the underlying class structure that supports each area of functionality.
- It should highlight challenging algorithms, code reuse, and interprocess communication mechanisms.

References

[1]   Albrecht, A. J. Measuring application development productivity. In *Proceedings of IBM Application Development Symposium*, pages 83–92, Monterey, CA, October 1979.

[2]   Albrecht, A. J., and Gaffney, J. E. Software function, source lines of code and development effort prediction: A software science validation. *IEEE Transactions on Software Engineering*, November; 1983, pp. 639–648.

[3]   Anthes, G. Air traffic takes another turn. *ComputerWorld*, 28(17):79–80, April 25, 1994.

[4]   Arthur, L. J. *Measuring Programmer Productivity and Software Quality*. New York: Wiley-Interscience, 1985.

[5]   Baase, S. *A Gift of Fire, Social, Legal, and Ethical Issues in Computing*. Upper Saddle River, NJ: Prentice Hall, 1997.

[6]   Bancilhon, F., Delobel, C., and Kanellakis, P. C. *Building an Object-Oriented Database System, The Story of O2*. Los Altos, CA: Morgan Kaufmann, 1992.

[7]   Betts, M. Loral to buy IBM federal unit. *ComputerWorld*, 27(51):32, December 20, 1993.

[8]   Boehm, B. Software engineering. *IEEE Transactions on Computers*, 2:391–400, 1976.

[9]   Boehm, B. *Software Engineering Economics*. Englewood Cliffs, NJ: Prentice Hall, 1981.

[10]   Boehm, B. Software life cycle factors. In C. R. Vick and C. V. Ramamoorthy, eds. *Handbook of Software Engineering*, pages 494–518. New York: Van Nostrand Reinhold, 1984.

[11]   Boehm, B. A spiral model for software development and enhancement. *Computer*, 21(5):61–72, 1988.

[12]   Boehm, B., and Egyed, A. *Improving the Life-cycle Process in Software Engineering Education*. Internet site, http://sunset.usc.edu/ TechRpts/Papers/usccse98-509/usccse98-509.pdf, 1998.

[13]   Boehm, B., Egyed, A., Kwan, J., Port, D., and Shah, A. Using the winwin spiral model: A case study. *IEEE Software*, 31:33–44, 1998.

[14]   Booch, G. *Object-oriented Analysis and Design with Applications*. Redwood City, CA: Benjamin Cummings, 1994.

[15]   Booch, G., Jacobson, I., and Rumbaugh, J. *Unified Modeling Language for Object-oriented Development, Documentation Set Version 1.0*. Santa Clara, CA: Rational Software Corporation, 1997.

[16]   Booch, G., Rumbaugh, J., and Jacobson, I. *Unified Modeling Language User Guide*. Reading, MA: Addison-Wesley, 1998.

[17]   Brelis, M. In computer outage, 2 jets almost hit. *Boston Globe*, December 8, 1998.

[18]   Brooks, F. P. *The Mythical Man-Month: Essays on Software Engineering*. Reading, MA: Addison-Wesley, 1975.

[19]   Brooks, F. P. No silver bullet: Essence and accidents of software engineering. *IEEE Computer*, pp. 10-19, 1987.

[20]   Buhr, R. J. A., and Casselman, R. S. *Use Case Maps for Object-Oriented Systems*. Upper Saddle River, NJ: Prentice Hall, 1996.

[21]   Burgess, L. No easy way to reform the FAA. *Journal of Commerce*, p. 14, October 30, 1995.

[22]   Burke, R. *Project Management: Planning and Control*. Chichester, England: John C. Wiley and Sons, 1993.

[23]   Carano, F. *Data Abstraction and Problem Solving with C++: Walls and Mirrors*. Redwood City, CA: Benjamin Cummings, 1995.

[24]   Chen, P. The entity-relationship model—Toward a unified view of data. *ACM Transactions on Database Systems*, 1:9-36, 1976.

[25]   Coad, P., and Yourdon, E. *Object-Oriented Analysis*. Englewood Cliffs, NJ: Prentice Hall, 1990.

[26]   Collins, A. M., and Quillian, M. R. Facilitating retrieval from semantic memory: The effect of repeating part of an inference. In A. F. Sanders, ed., *Acta Psychologica 33, Attention and Performance III*, pages 304-314. Amsterdam: North-Holland, 1970.

[27]   Curtis, B. A field study of the software design process for large systems. *IEEE Transactions on Software Engineering*, 31(11):1268-1287, 1988 (November).

[28]   Davis, A., and Sitaram, P. A concurrent process model for software development. *Software Engineering Notes*, 19(2):38-51, 1994.

[29] Davis, A. M. *201 Principles of Software Development*. New York: McGraw-Hill, 1995.

[30] Debelack, A. S., Dehn, J. D., Muchinshy, L. L., and Smith, D. M. Next generation air traffic control automation. *IBM Systems Journal*, 34(1):63–77, 1995.

[31] DeMarco, T. *Structured Analysis and System Specification*. New York: Yourdon Press, 1978.

[32] Dijkstra, E. W. Goto statement considered harmful. *Communications of the ACM*, 11(3), 1968.

[33] Ellis, C. J. Help for the FAA is on the way. *Business for Central New Jersey*, November 15, 1995.

[34] Engler, N. Profiles. *ComputerWorld*, November 16, 1998, p. 107.

[35] Fagan, M. E. Design and code inspections to reduce errors in program development. *IBM Systems Journal*, 15(3):182–211, 1976.

[36] Fowler, M., and Scott, K. *UML Distilled: Applying the Standard Object Modeling Language*. Reading, MA: Addison-Wesley, 1997.

[37] Frame, J. D. *Managing Projects in Organizations*. San Francisco: Jossey-Bass, 1987.

[38] Gamma, E., Helm, R., Johnson, R., and Vlissides, J. *Design Patterns, Elements of Reusable Object-Oriented Software*. Reading, MA: Addison-Wesley, 1995.

[39] Gane, C., and Sarson, T. *Structured Systems Analysis: Tools and Techniques*. Englewood Cliffs, NJ: Prentice Hall, 1979.

[40] Gardner, A. C. *Practical LCP*. New York: McGraw-Hill, 1981.

[41] Gilb, T. *Principles of Software Project Management*. Reading, MA: Addison-Wesley, 1988.

[42] Gladden, G. R. Stop the life cycle, I want to get off. *Software Engineering Notes*, 7(2):35–39, 1982.

[43] Graham, D. R. Testing object-oriented systems. In *Ovum Evaluates: Software Testing Tools*. London: Ovum, Ltd., 1996.

[44] Group, International Function Point Users. *Function Point Counting Practices Manual, Release 4.0*. IFPUG, 1994.

[45] Guttag, J. Abstract data types and the development of data structures. *Communications of the ACM*, 20:396–404, 1977.

[46] Harrold, M. J., and McGregor, J. D. *Incremental Testing of Object Oriented Class Structures*. Technical Report. Clemson University, Clemson, SC, 1989.

[47] Horstmann, C. S., and Cornell, G. *Core Java Volume I—Fundamentals*. Mountain View, CA: Sun Microsystems Press, 1997.

[48] Horstmann, C. S., and Cornell, G. *Core Java Volume II—Advanced Features*. Mountain View, CA: Sun Microsystems Press, 1998.

[49] Hurley, R. B. *Decision Tables in Software Engineering*. New York: Van Nostrand Reinhold, 1983.

[50] IEEE. *IEEE Standard Glossary of Software Engineering Terms, IEEE Standard 729-1983*. New York: IEEE Society Press, 1983.

[51] IEEE. *IEEE Software Engineering Standards*. New York: IEEE Society Press, 1987.

[52] Illescas, C. US West retooling after 911 failure area-code work shut down system. *The Denver (CO) Post*, August 1, 1998, p. B-03.

[53] Jackson, M. *Principles of Program Design*. New York: Academic Press, 1975.

[54] Jalote, P. *An Integrated Approach to Software Engineering*. New York: Springer Verlag, 1997.

[55] Jarke, M., Turner, J., Stohr, E., Vassiliou, Y., White, N., and Michielse, K. A field evaluation of natural language for data retrieval. *IEEE Transactions on Software Engineering*, SE-11, 1:97–113, 1985.

[56] Joyce, E. Is error-free software achievable? *Datamation*, February 15, 1989.

[57] Kim, Y., and March, S. Comparing data modeling formalisms. *Communications of the ACM*, 38(6):103–115, 1995.

[58] Kjaer, A., and Madsen, K. H. Participatory analysis of flexibility. *Communications of the ACM*, 38:53–61, 1995.

[59] Kovacevic, S. A compositional model of human-computer dialogues. In Meera Blattner and Roger Dannenberg, eds. *Multimedia Interface Design*, chap. 21, pp. 373–404. New York: ACM Press, 1992.

[60] Larman, C. *Applying UML and Patterns, An Introduction to Object-Oriented Analysis and Design*. Upper Saddle River, NJ: Prentice Hall, 1998.

[61] Lefton, T. AT&T details cause, effects of long-haul network failure; switching shortcut backfires. *Electronic News*, 36(1793):23, 1990 (January 22).

[62] Leveson, N. G. Software safety in embedded computer systems. *Communications of the ACM*, 34(2):34–46, 1991.

[63] Lopez, R. Software solutions (advanced automation system for air traffic control). *Flight International*, 145(4425):30, June 15, 1994.

[64] Lorenz, M. *Object-Oriented Software Development: A Practical Approach*. Englewood Cliffs, NJ: PTR Prentice Hall, 1993.

[65] Lorenz, M., and Kidd, J. *Object-Oriented Software Metrics*. Upper Saddle River, NJ: Prentice Hall: 1994.

[66] Mallin, J. As bug eludes officials, phones could crash again. *Washington* (DC) *Times*, July 3, 1991, C1.

[67] McCabe, T. J. A complexity measure. *IEEE Transactions on Software Engineering*, December 1976, pp. 308–320.

[68] Mills, H. *Chief Programmer Teams, Priciples, and Procedures*. IBM Federal Systems Division Report FSC 71-5108, Gaithersburg, MD, 1971.

[69] Minskey, M. A framework for representing knowledge. In R. J. Brachman and H. J. Levesque, eds. *Readings in Knowledge Representation*, chap. 12, pp. 245–262. Los Altos, CA: Morgan Kaufman, 1975.

[70] Moganson, P., and Trigg, R. Artifacts as triggers for participatory analysis. In S. Kuhn, M. Muller, and J. Meskill, eds. *Proceedings of the Participatory Design Conference*, Palo Alto, CA, 1992. Computer Professionals for Social Responsibility.

[71] Moylan, M. J. Lockheed to buy Loral. *Saint Paul Pioneer Press*, January 9, 1996.

[72] Muller, J. Raytheon team wins air traffic control job. *Boston Globe*, September 17, 1996.

[73] Mynatt, B. *Software Engineering with Student Project Guidance*. Englewood Cliffs, NJ: Prentice Hall, 1990.

[74] Nassi, I., and Shneiderman, B. Flowchart techniques for structured programming. *ACM SIGPLAN Notices*, 8(8):12–26, August 1973.

[75] Neumann, P. Inside risks: Aggrevation by computer: Life, death, and taxes. *Communications of the ACM*, 35(7):122, 1992.

[76] Neumann, Peter. *Computer-Related Risks*. Reading, MA: Addison-Wesley, 1995.

[77] Nierstrasz, O., Gibbs, S., Tsichritzis, D. Component-oriented software development. *Communications of the ACM*, 35(9):160–165, 1992.

[78] Nordwall, B. Hinson to make decision on ATC upgrade in May. *Aviation Week and Space Technology*, 140(16):32, April 18, 1994.

[79] Ogden, W., and Boyle, J. Evaluating human-computer dialog styles: Command versus form/fill-in for report modification. *Proceedings of the Human Factors Society, Twenty-Sixth Annual Meeting*, pages 542–545, 1982.

[80] Orr, K. T. *Structured Systems Development*. New York: Yourdon Press, 1977.

[81] Oz, E. When professional standards are lax: The CONFIRM failure and its lessons. *Communications of the ACM*, 37(10):29–36, 1994.

[82] Ozsu, T. M., Peters, R. J., Szafron, D., Irani, B., Lipka, A., and Munoz, A. Tigukat: A uniform behavioral objectbase management system. *VLDB Journal*, 4(3):445–492, 1995.

[83] Parnas, D. *Information Distribution Aspects of Design Methodology*. Carnegie-Mellon University Technical Report, Pittsburgh, PA, 1971.

[84] Penner, D. *The Project Manager's Survival Guide*. Columbus, OH: Battelle Press, 1994.

[85] Perry, D. E., and Kaiser, G. E. Adequate testing and object-oriented programming. *Journal of Object-Oriented Programming*, 2:12–19, (January/February) 1990.

[86] Peterson, I. *Fatal Defect: Chasing Killer Computer Bugs*. New York: Random House, 1995.

[87] Pfleeger, S. *Software Engineering Theory and Practice*. Englewood Cliffs, NJ: Prentice Hall, 1998.

[88] Pressman, R. *Software Engineering: A Practioner's Approach*, 4th ed. New York: McGraw-Hill, 1997.

[89] Quillian, M. R. Word concepts: A theory and simulation of some basic semantic capabilities. *Behavioral Science*, 12(5):410–430, 1967.

[90] Robertson, J. Bellcore sets industry task force to study switch snag. *Chilton's Electronic News*, 37(1869):6, 1991 (July 15).

[91] Sackman, H., Erikson, W. J., and Grant, E. E. Exploratory experimental studies comparing online programming performance. *Communications of the ACM*, 11(1):3–11, January 1968.

[92] Schneiderman, B. *Designing the User Interface: Strategies for Effective Human-Computer Interaction*. Reading, MA: Addison-Wesley, 1987.

[93] Shneiderman, B. Control flow and data structure documentation. *Communications of the ACM*, 25(1):55–63, January 1982.

[94] Small, D., and Weldon, L. An experimental comparison of natural and structured query languages. *Human Factors*, 25:253–263, 1983.

[95] Software, Rational. Rational Rose CASE tool. Internet site, *http://www.rational.com/*, 1998.

[96] Steinmetz, R., and Nahrstedt, K. *Multimedia: Computing, Communications and Applications*. Upper Saddle River, NJ: Prentice Hall, 1995.

[97] Thomsett, M. C. *The Little Black Book of Project Management*. New York: American Management Association, 1990.

[98] Useem, J. Failure: The secret to my success. *Inc. Magazine*, May 1998, pp. 67–69.

[99] Warnier, J. D. *Logical Construction of Programs*. New York: Van Nostrand Reinhold, 1974.

[100] Whitmire, S. A. An introduction to 3d function points. *Software Development*, April 1995, pp. 43-53.

[101] Yourdon, E., and Constantine, L. *Structured Design*. Englewood Cliffs, NJ: Prentice Hall, 1979.

Index

JEROME KERN
COLLECTION

WRITTEN BY
HUGH FORDIN
AUTHOR OF "GETTING TO KNOW HIM:
A BIOGRAPHY OF OSCAR HAMMERSTEIN II"
PUBLISHED BY CROSSROADS UNGER

PHOTOGRAPHS, EXCERPTS AND QUOTATIONS
TAKEN FROM "JEROME KERN: THE MAN AND HIS MUSIC
IN STORY, PICTURE AND SONG"
COPYRIGHT © 1974 T.B. HARMS COMPANY
NEW EDITORIAL CONTENT BY DEAN KAY & SHARON HIGGINS

JEROME KERN COMMEMORATIVE STAMP
DESIGNED BY JIM SHARP
COPYRIGHT © 1984 U.S. POSTAL SERVICE.   USED BY PERMISSION.

COVER COURTESY OF BETTY KERN MILLER

TABLE OF CONTENTS
JEROME KERN COLLECTION